LEARNING AND COMPREHENSION OF TEXT

LEARNING AND COMPREHENSION OF TEXT

Edited by

Heinz Mandl

Deutsches Institut für Fernstudien
An der Universität Tubingen

Nancy L. Stein

Tom Trabasso

The University of Chicago

LEA LAWRENCE ERLBAUM ASSOCIATES, PUBLISHERS
1984   Hillsdale, New Jersey   London

Lawrence Erlbaum Associates, Inc., Publishers
365 Broadway
Hillsdale, New Jersey 07642

Library of Congress Cataloging in Publication Data

Main entry under title:

Learning and comprehension of text.

Includes index.
1. Discourse analysis—Psychological aspects.
2. Learning, Psychology of. I. Mandl, Heinz. II. Stein,
Nancy (Nancy L.) III. Trabasso, Tom.
P302.L42   1984   808'.00141   83-14050
ISBN 0-89859-258-5

Printed in the United States of America
10 9 8 7 6 5 4 3 2 1

Contents

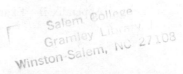

III

Preface

This book is the outcome of a conference on text comprehension and learning, held in Tübingen, West Germany, during the first week of July, 1981. The conference was made possible by funds from the Volkswagen Foundation to the Deutsches Institut für Fernstudien at the Universität of Tübingen. The first editor of this volume, Heinz Mandl, directs the research department of the Institute and oversaw the conference proceedings. A main goal of the conference was to promote scientific exchange between educators, cognitive scientists, linguists, and psychologists who are investigating the acquisition of information from written forms of discourse. A second goal was to promote communication about such work between German and American investigators.

The three editors of this book planned and organized the conference. The topics of text comprehension and learning from text attracted us for several reasons. In Germany, there has been a growing interest in discourse processing, stimulated by advances in text linguistics, experimental psychology, and educational practice. Meanwhile, in the United States, since the early part of the 1970s, several different approaches to the study of discourse have been initiated, stimulated by structural analyses as well as computer simulation and process models for interpreting and representing text, and by a growing empirical tradition on memory and comprehension of text. We believed that these different advances in both countries should be made known to the respective parties by a direct exchange. With these ideas in mind, we invited investigators who represented a variety of approaches to text understanding and text learning and who were active in research programs related to the central focus of the conference.

Our coverage was, as a result, broad and varied. We were fortunate that all of the American and German researchers who were invited accepted their invita-

tions. The other participants at the conference were 18 German-speaking psychologists from Austria, Germany, and Switzerland. The collection of papers
directly reflects the work presented by the participants at the conference, with no
additions or omissions.

We have arranged the chapters within the book into three main sections. The
first section (Part I) includes those chapters that examine some aspect of text
structure or knowledge, which has been acquired about the text. Here, studies are
reported on how different organizations of a text affect how and what people read
and remember (Meyer, Chap. 1; Schnotz, Chap. 2). Also, an analysis is proposed to illustrate how a listener or reader might construct a coherent representation of a text (Trabasso, Secco, and van den Broek, Chap. 3) and what types of
knowledge a reader or a listener acquires and uses to define a particular genre of
discourse (Stein and Policastro, Chap. 4).

In the second section (Part II), the collection of chapters deals directly with
the topic of learning from text. Learning is variously interpreted as change that
occurs as a result of a system of processes (de Beaugrande, Chap. 5), as a result
of using one's prior knowledge about a specific domain (Voss, Chap. 6), and as a
result of using one's metacognitive knowledge about oneself as a learner of
strategic skills (Fischer and Mandl, Chap. 7). Chapter 8 by Brown and her
colleagues and Chapter 9 by Campione and Armbruster both discuss learning in
the context of acquiring knowledge through training procedures for comprehending a text and include evaluative criteria for whether training is effective, especially where the learner is less skilled as a reader.

Strategic skills and their effects on the processing of text constitute the general
themes for the third section (Part III). Various measures of such skills are
explored via the use of eye-movement analysis (Just and Carpenter, Chap. 10),
via inferences made during reading per se (Ballstaedt and Mandl, Chap. 11), or
during active processing of connected discourse (Scardamalia and Bereiter,
Chap. 13), as a result of questioning following the reading of text (Lehnert,
Robertson, and Black, Chap. 12) or by the limitations imposed by one's information processing capacity (Bereiter and Scardamalia, Chap. 14).

Certain questions and recurring issues gave unity to the conference, despite
the variation in approaches. To comprehend and to learn from a text encom-
passes many different kinds of activity. In general, comprehension of a text
means that the reader makes use of prior knowledge to interpret the information
contained in a text. The process of understanding results in a fairly stable representation of what is interpreted. Learning from a text also involves comprehension but results in both the construction of a representation of the text and in a
change in the knowledge base used to understand the text in the first place.

These distinctions may not be satisfactory because all comprehension may
result in changes in knowledge. The differences may be in the amount of change
that occurs, as well as the methods used to assess the comprehension or learning.
Learning from a text usually involves a paradigm where an intervention is made

after an initial assessment of understanding. This intervention may be in the form of giving the reader additional information, teaching the reader a strategy to obtain information, or to structure and organize the information in the text. The chapters that pertain to learning, in this sense, are those by Brown, Palincsar, and Armbruster, and Campione and Armbruster. Fischer and Mandl examine two major views on metacognitive knowledge on the one hand, and the strategic use of executive regulation on the other hand. A proposal is made with regard to a further unification of the two approaches. Lehnert, Robertson, and Black also examine change—change brought about in constructing a representation by the nature of the question used to probe understanding.

Certain types of knowledge enable a reader to acquire new information from texts. Knowing how and when to monitor one's current understanding of a text may entail knowing how to ask oneself questions and how to answer these self-imposed queries, and knowing how to generate expectations and to instantiate these expectations by content contained in the text. These kinds of comprehension activities may be fostered by modeling instruction. Brown, Palincsar, and Armbruster demonstrate, in a series of training studies, how such instruction, when carried out in a reciprocal fashion, allowing the student as well as the teacher to perform these normally covert acts overtly, leads to an incorporation of the procedures and transfers to novel reading tasks. However, such transfer has to be assessed and Campione and Armbruster describe designs that allow determination of specific or general transfer.

The remainder of the contributions are more concerned with issues of comprehension without drawing upon theories about change in knowledge. These articles are characterized by the diversity of issues and problems that are encountered in attempting to construct theories of comprehension for different kinds of texts, knowledge, and readers.

One issue that characterizes several chapters pertains to the prior knowledge that readers are assumed to use in order to guide, identify, and interpret the written discourse. The knowledge previously acquired about different discourse structures is most frequently conceptualized as an organized set of elements and the relationships among these elements. In nearly all such descriptions of discourse types, the knowledge is believed to be generic and organized into a set of highly predictable structures. The major differences in the structures studied by various investigators contributing to this volume is between those texts that are expository and those that are narrative in nature. The latter, called stories, are of central concern to Stein and Policastro and to Trabasso, Secco, and van den Broek. Expository texts occupy the attention of de Beaugrande, Meyer, Schnotz, Scardamalia and Bereiter. Voss discusses both stories and exposition.

In expository texts, the organization of text material is a significant factor in predicting how much and what types of material will be understood. Meyer and Schnotz each demonstrate this phenomenon. Schnotz also presents an intriguing finding that the type and amount of prior knowledge a subject brings to a task interacts with how well certain types of texts will be remembered. Sophisticated readers can benefit from compare and contrast structures better than less knowledgeable ones, whereas both types of readers retain about the same information from text that is largely devoted to attribute descriptions of concepts.

Although texts are structured by writers according to certain purposes and criteria, it remains for the reader to interpret and arrive at his or her own construction of a representation of the text. Several investigators at the conference addressed this issue by focusing on the relationships among the propositions of a text and how they might be discovered by the reader. Voss illustrates how structured knowledge about a domain guides the construction of relations. For Voss, readers who are high in baseball knowledge organize new information about baseball into existing goal-hierarchy structures. Trabasso, Secco, and van den Broek look at how knowledge of physical and psychological causation is used to make connecting inferences between events in a story. To the extent that such inferences are made, the reader achieves a coherent interpretation of the text, demonstrates better recall, can more accurately report what is important and also can more appropriately answer questions about the text. Ballstaedt and Mandl's examination of elaborative inferences show these constructive interpretations to be related to better understanding and immediate recall of a text. Elaboration may or may not always lead to more successful long term retention of a text. Scardamalia and Bereiter monitor topic and propositional inferences by having young, elementary school readers talk aloud as they are reading and trying to understand a text. In all of these chapters, successful learning and comprehension of a text depends upon the discovery of certain relations among ideas in the text.

Voss and Stein and Policastro focus more on the meaning of the material presented to subjects rather than the structure of the text. For them, the knowledge base that the reader has about a domain is crucial for successful interpretation and generation of the text. Each strives to provide a structured description of what this knowledge is, how it may be general across instances within the domain, and how it is used to comprehend or produce text. These contributions begin to bridge the gap between reading and writing of text. Voss demonstrates that baseball experts acquire more relevant detail knowledge than do non-experts, providing support to the general conference theme of the importance of prior knowledge in comprehension and learning. Stein and Policastro analyzed stories generated by children, and then asked both children and adults to judge whether or not these texts belonged to the story category. Stein and Policastro showed that existing definitions of stories do not capture the way in which conceptual knowledge is organized. Both children and adults develop a "prototype" that represents the most frequent occurence of the story category. This prototype corresponds to the most complex definition of a story. As features are deleted from a text, subjects still include instances in the story category. The ratings of goodness in terms of the prototype significantly decrease until subjects no longer accept the text as an example of a story.

Individual differences in procedural as well as content knowledge occur in reading. There are few attempts to address individual differences theoretically and fewer still that characterize reading in terms of a process theory. Just and Carpenter's study of skilled reading does both. Skilled readers make more efficient eye movements and are much faster at several component skills in word recognition. One finding of interest is that processing strategies are dependent upon the acquisition of word knowledge from the reading task itself. Their approach, like that of de Beaugrande, focuses on processing of text in reading rather than on text structure or knowledge about text or procedural skills.

Bereiter and Scardamalia also discuss research on individual differences in information processing and its relationship to writing or composition. In their review, a number of tasks that normally would interfere with information processing actually fail to disrupt writing by children. However, if one takes gist as the level and unit of analysis, then deeper levels of inferencing are, in fact, disrupted by these secondary tasks.

Lauren Resnick served as a commentator at the conference. In her discussion, she brings out the instructional implications of the contributions more emphatically than did the presenters. The fact that she was able to interpret the conference papers in the light of educational needs is an important contribution. If Resnick's perceptiveness is prophetic, then we may come to feel that we have collectively made a useful contribution not only to cross-Atlantic scholarship and communication but also to the teaching of reading and writing.

We wish to thank all the people and institutions who contributed to the completion of the book. The conference in Tübingen was made possible by a grant from the Stiftung Volkswagenwerk, for which we would like to express our gratitude. We are also indebted to the Deutsches Institüt für Fernstudien and to the Universität Tübingen for their support and hospitality.

In addition to the above support, the second two editors were supported by grants from the National Institute of Education (NIE-G-79-0125), the Spencer Foundation, and the Benton Foundation. Finally, their year as Fellows at the Center for Advanced Study in the Behavioral Sciences enabled them to complete all aspects of their editorial chores under the most pleasant of circumstances.

Heinz Mandl
Nancy L. Stein
Tom Trabasso

LEARNING AND COMPREHENSION OF TEXT

1 Text Dimensions and Cognitive Processing

Bonnie J. F. Meyer
Arizona State University

A crucial question in the study of reading centers around how the reader constructs a mental representation of the text similar to that intended by the writer. My colleagues and I have been attempting to determine which dimensions of text affect the building of these cognitive representations by readers.

The communication between writer and reader involves a dual problem-solving task. On one side, a writer uses knowledge about topics, audiences, and writing plans in order to best satisfy the goal for a particular writing task (Flower & Hayes, 1977). The resultant text is a subset of the cognitive representation in the mind of the writer; the readers are expected to apply their world knowledge and knowledge of writing plans to build a similar cognitive representation. Thus, at the other side of this communication process between writer and reader (Grice, 1975), the reader also faces a problem-solving task. I am particularly interested in how prior knowledge about writing plans is utilized by readers as they attempt to resolve this problem-solving task.

A text is not just a series of sentences or paragraphs precisely because it follows a *hierarchy* of content, so that some facts or statements are superordinate or subordinate to others. It seems plain that the process of creating such a hierarchy must be governed by writing plans. But it is not at all plain how writers and readers form and implement plans, and whether in dealing with the same text they are following the same plans.

TEXT DIMENSIONS

This notion of hierarchy is central to the text factors to be investigated in this chapter. These text dimensions include *emphasis plans, organizational plans* (types of superordinate relationships), and characteristics of subordinate details.

3

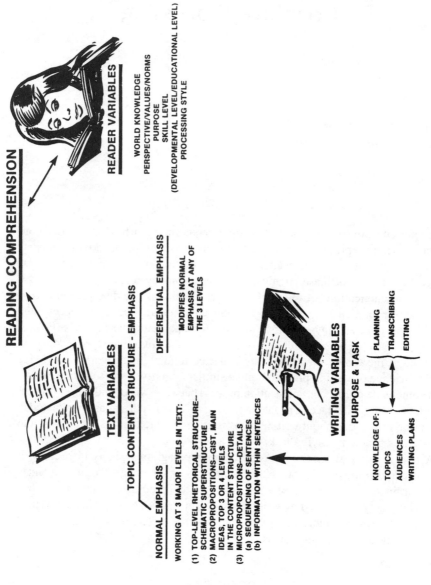

FIG. 1.1. Scheme of the writer, text, and reader variables that influence reading comprehension (from Meyer, 1981).

4

Examine the text variables listed in Fig. 1.1 (Meyer, 1981). Two types of emphasis plans are shown: normal emphasis and differential emphasis. A normal emphasis plan in text reflects a correspondence between the writing plans that organize or structure the topic and those that highlight aspects of the topic. That is, the emphasis plans particularly focus on the information high in the hierarchical structure. In contrast, a differential emphasis plan brings into the foreground from the background information that is located lower in the content structure or equally weighted at one level in this hierarchical structure.

Normal and differential emphasis plans can operate at each of the three levels in the text depicted in Fig. 1.1 (Meyer, 1981; van Dijk, 1979). These levels include the microproposition or sentence level, which is concerned with the way ideas are organized within sentences and the way sentences cohere and are organized within a text. The subordinate micropropositions are identified by $\bigwedge$ in Fig. 1.2, but are diagrammed in a full analysis of the content structure (Meyer, 1975, in press a). The second level is the macropropositional or paragraph level, which pertains to logical organization and argumentation. The final level is that of the top-level structure or overall organization of the text as a whole (see Fig. 1.2). The relationships that form the content structure can be divided into five major categories: description, collection (grouping), causation, response (e.g., problem/solution, question/answer), and comparison. Figure 1.2 exemplifies these relationships with a passage on supertankers.

The emphasis plans investigated in this chapter are two of the four types of signaling that were outlined in Meyer (1975). Signaling was described as information in text that does not add new content on a topic, but points out aspects of the structure of the text or gives emphasis to certain aspects of the topic content. One emphasis plan investigated followed a normal emphasis plan; the superordinate relationships of the organizational plan were explicitly cued or signaled for readers with such words as ''in contrast'' for comparison relationships and ''as a result'' for causative relations. The other emphasis plan followed a differential plan and emphasized low-level details in the text by the use of pointer devices, such as ''in the notable year of 1829.''

Different types of organizational plans were thought to affect expectations differentially during reading, as well as affect search plans during retrieval. The major organizational plans to be investigated were the response: problem/solution top-level structure, the comparison top-level structure, and the collection: time/order top-level structure. These organizational plans are patterns, frameworks, or ways of thinking about topic content and in the mind of the writer or reader can be viewed as a type of schema.

INFORMATIONAL PROCESSING MODELS

The level of subordination of propositions in the content structure of a text relates to its recall; high-level propositions are recalled better than low-level proposi-

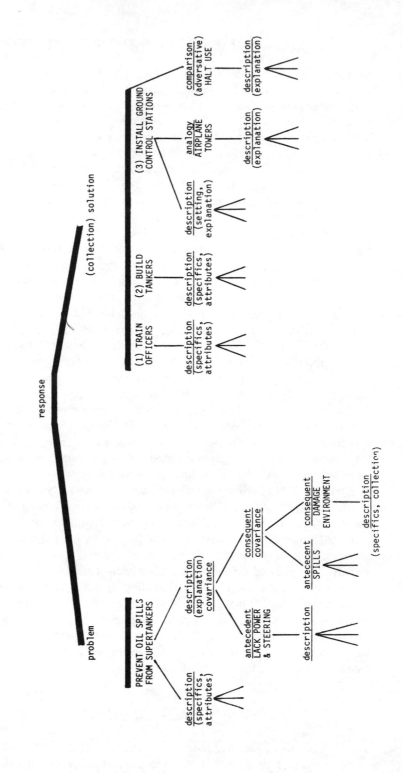

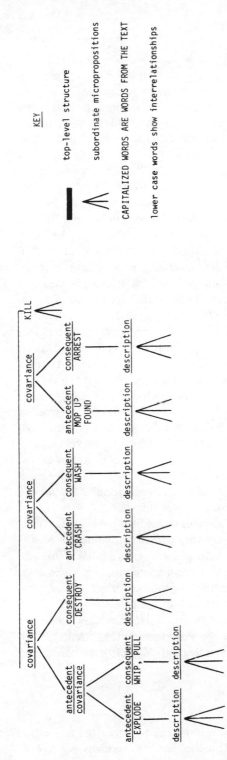

FIG. 1.2. Superordinate structure of relationships of a magazine article on supertankers.

7

tions (e.g., Kintsch & Keenan, 1973; Meyer & McConkie, 1973; Meyer, 1975). However, the levels effect has not been reported on recognition tests (Yekovich & Thorndyke, 1981). An information processing model suggests at least three aspects of processing that could lead to the levels effect. These processes are selective encoding, differential frequency of encoding, and differential retrieval. Models have been proposed by investigators that differ in their focus on these processes.

A selection model (Cirilo & Foss, 1980; Meyer, 1975) attributes the levels effect to a greater number of high-level propositions actually encoded and stored in long-term memory than low-level propositions. Results of studies that appeared incompatible with this model found no differences in reading time of high- and low-level paragraphs (Britton, Meyer, Simpson, Holdredge, & Curry, 1979) and no levels effect on recognition tests (Yekovich & Thorndyke, 1981). However, differences between high- and low-level propositions have been reported for reading times per sentence (Cirilo & Foss, 1980) and per idea unit (Just & Carpenter, 1980) and for cued recall tasks (answers to questions, or passage content for recall cues) (Meyer, 1975, 1977; Meyer & Rice, 1981a,b).

Kintsch and van Dijk (1978) have attributed the levels effect to multiple processing of high-level information in the short-term memory buffer. That is, more practice is allotted to high-level propositions. This model is compatible with studies showing no difference in reading times for high- and low-level propositions and the differential levels effects for recall and recognition tasks.

Thorndyke and Yekovich (1980) propose a retrieval model; text information is stored hierarchically with unbiased encoding of all of the text propositions. The retrieval process is a top–down search of this hierarchy. High-level propositions are recalled, but not recognized better than low-level information due to access to retrieval starting with the high-level information. Although this model explains the recognition data, it doesn't explain the cued recall data nor the different reading times for high- and low-level propositions.

It is plausible that all three processes play roles in producing the levels effect. The relative contribution of each process may vary with the properties of the text materials and the nature of the task. Emphasis plans, organizational plans, and degree of subordination and characteristics of subordinate propositions in texts are properties of text that appear to relate to the contribution of each of these processes and the types of schemata guiding each of the processes.

Figure 1.3 depicts a general approach for trying to understand how the reader constructs a representation in memory of the text. In Fig. 1.3, three types of reading strategies are labeled: the structure strategy, the default/list strategy, and other strategies.

The Structure Strategy

The structure strategy is the dominant reading strategy hypothesized for skilled comprehenders in a prose learning task. Thus, in the first two diamonds in Fig.

1.3, skilled readers participating in a prose learning experiment say "YES." Skilled readers appear to approach text with knowledge about how texts are conventionally organized and a strategy to seek and use the top-level structure in a particular text as an organizational framework to guide encoding and retrieval (Bartlett, 1978; Meyer, 1981, in press a, in press b; Meyer, Brandt, & Bluth, 1980; Meyer & Freedle, in press).

Processing activities for the structure strategy focus on a search for major text-based relationships among propositions. That is, there is a search for organizational plans that can subsume all or large chunks of this information and tie it into a summarized comprehensible whole. Readers employing the structure strategy are hypothesized to approach text looking for patterns that will tie all the propositions together and the author's primary thesis, which will provide the content to be bound by these schemata. Then, they search for relationships among this primary thesis and supporting details. For example, when reading the super-tanker text, they recognize in the title or first sentence that the propositions may fit their problem schema. Each new proposition is related back to the problem, making the problem of oil spills from supertankers continually selected for retention in the short-term memory buffer for interpreting the new propositions. Previous knowledge about problems keeps the readers searching for causal relationships among descriptive information about the problem, such as why it is a problem and what caused it. In a long text with a large number of hierarchical levels, the reader selects this information for encoding over tangentially related details. Also, prior experience with problems leads readers to anticipate and search for solutions, solutions that must satisfy most of the previously stated causes of the problem. Thus, the problem and its causes are retrieved continually from long-term storage and placed into the short-term memory buffer for relating to the subsequent propositions in the passage. This additional processing of these superordinate propositions increases the ease with which they can be retrieved.

Readers process text line by line in a linear fashion; they do not wait until after they have read the entire text to find the top-level structure and other superordinate relations, which subsume large chunks of text. Words in the text, such as "problem," "need to prevent," "in contrast," "others disagree," "others believe," "as a result," and, other signaling words and content words, help readers to make educated guesses about which organizational plan or schemata to assign to the text. If later sentences are not compatible with an initial assignment, then reassignment can be made.

The top-level structure and major interrelationships are also employed to guide retrieval and production of the recall protocol; it is hypothesized to be a top–down retrieval search, guided by the structure of relationships. Readers are assumed to construct memory representations of the text propositions that are similar in terms of both hierarchical relationships and content to the content structure depicted in Fig. 1.2. When recalling the text, they begin their retrieval search with the top-level structure and systematically work from the superordinate relationships and content downward.

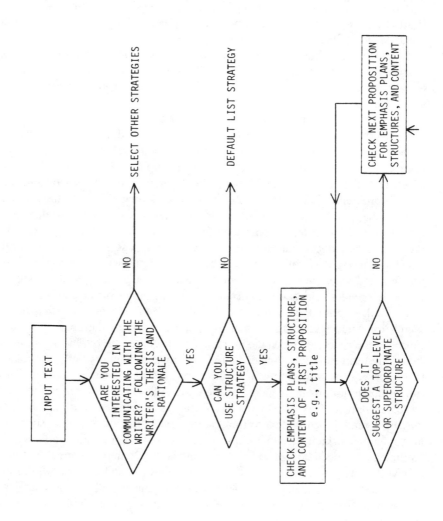

INPUT TEXT

ARE YOU INTERESTED IN COMMUNICATING WITH THE WRITER? FOLLOWING THE WRITER'S THESIS AND RATIONALE

NO → SELECT OTHER STRATEGIES

YES

CAN YOU USE STRUCTURE STRATEGY

NO → DEFAULT LIST STRATEGY

YES

CHECK EMPHASIS PLANS, STRUCTURE, AND CONTENT OF FIRST PROPOSITION e.g., title

DOES IT SUGGEST A TOP-LEVEL OR SUPERORDINATE STRUCTURE

NO

CHECK NEXT PROPOSITION FOR EMPHASIS PLANS, STRUCTURES, AND CONTENT

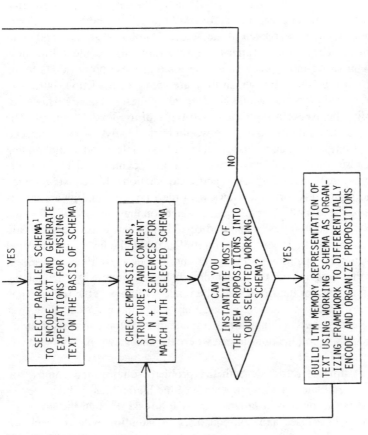

YES

SELECT PARALLEL SCHEMA[1] TO ENCODE TEXT AND GENERATE EXPECTATIONS FOR ENSUING TEXT ON THE BASIS OF SCHEMA

CHECK EMPHASIS PLANS, STRUCTURE, AND CONTENT OF N + 1 SENTENCES FOR MATCH WITH SELECTED SCHEMA

CAN YOU INSTANTIATE MOST CF THE NEW PROPOSITIONS INTO YOUR SELECTED WORKING SCHEMA?

NO

YES

BUILD LTM MEMORY REPRESENTATION OF TEXT USING WORKING SCHEMA AS ORGAN-IZING FRAMEWORK TO DIFFERENTIALLY ENCODE AND ORGANIZE PROPOSITIONS

FIG. 1.3. Model for getting text information into organized schemata in memory.

[1]Type of schema selected here influences processes of selection and buffer rehearsal.

Different emphasis plans and organizational plans in texts should influence selection, buffer rehearsal, and retrieval components of processing. For example, for this investigation titles for versions of texts with normal emphasis plans signaling superordinate relationships were "Some Solutions for the Supertanker Problem" and "Disagreement Over Early American Railroad Development." Thus, the first proposition (see Fig. 1.3) strongly cues a problem/solution schema for the supertanker passage and a comparison for the railroad passage. The next phase in the model applied to these texts involves checking the match between the schemata selected and the first sentence in the texts, "A problem is prevention of oil spills from supertankers," and "When railroads were first developing in America, not everyone approved of them." For both texts, readers would generate expectations related to the selected problem/solution and comparison schemata. They would search out propositions that could fulfill these expectations and spend more processing time relating these propositions to the organized mental representation, which they are creating. Selection, buffer rehearsal, and retrieval processes would be affected by these schemata. However, differences might be expected from these two types of top-level structures. The cueing of the problem/solution in the title would immediately set up an expectation for description, causes, and consequences of the problem and a solution that matches the causes of the problem. However, at the beginning of the text, the comparison structure would set up less specific expectations. If the text presented two views and arguments for these views with the first view and its arguments presented before the second, then differential selection may not occur in the first part of the text, but only in the second portion. That is, few expectations would occur when reading the first view on an unfamiliar topic; the levels effect would result from argument repetition in the buffer and top–down retrieval processes. However, for the second view, the reader already has a structure by knowing the points made in defense of the first view. The reader will expect the second view to present corresponding counterpoints and may select these for encoding over tangentially related details. (Contrast this organization of the comparison structure and its processing implications to one where the two views are not presented separately but interleaved.)

However, at time of retrieval, both the problem/solution and comparison schemata would facilitate a systematic search of the hierarchical memory representation. That is, an organized progression is followed through the hierarchy from problem to its causes and consequences, to solution with a check for matches with the causes of the problem or from one view with its rationale of crucial points, to another view with its rationale on these same points.

A text organized as a collection of descriptions (without a time sequence) about an unfamiliar topic (e.g., lasers) may generate few expectations other than generally knowing that more is to come; selection processes may be minimally responsible for a levels effect with responsibility primarily on argument repetition in the STM buffer. Retrieval over time may not be as effective as with problem/solution and comparison structures. If portions in the hierarchical representation of the text are forgotten, knowing that a number of unrelated descriptions were stated will not give the subject as much of a retrieval cue as knowing that a solution that matches a remembered cause of the problem must be recalled. With descriptive text on more familiar topics (e.g., descriptions of Jennifer's pet dog) prior knowledge schemata about the appearance and behavior of dogs could facilitate or interfere with retrieval of the text.

The model in Fig. 1.3 depicts the early search behavior employed by readers utilizing the structure strategy to identify the text's top-level structure. Cirilo and Foss (1980) found longer reading times for sentences early in text as compared to late in the text. The titles of the supertanker and railroad texts under the condition of differential emphasis (without signaling the superordinate relationships) are "The Supertanker is in the News" and "Early Development of Railroads in America." With little prior knowledge of supertankers, this title may suggest a descriptive text. With some prior knowledge, it may suggest "oh, no, more news reports of oil spills," a problem. The railroad title suggests an historical sequence. The first sentences of these texts are "Prevention is needed of oil spills from supertankers" and "When the railroads were first starting in America, businessmen wanted to see them develop." For the supertanker text, the description schema would be dropped, and a problem schema with embedded explanatory causal schemata and possible solutions would be selected. For the railroad text, the historical sequence (narrative, Brewer, 1980) can be maintained with an expectation for time-ordered events and causal relations. Thus, normal and differential emphasis plans for these texts set up different expectations on the basis of the schemata suggested by their titles and first sentences; these expectations are more dissimilar for the railroad text than for the supertanker text. The final section of this chapter will present some data from recall of these texts related to these different predictions from the model in Fig. 1.3.

Default List Strategy.   Figure 1.3 shows a group of subjects who would like to communicate with the writer, but cannot utilize the structure strategy. Although the structure strategy is a systematic plan for processing text, the default strategy is not. The reader has no plan and simply tries to remember something from the text. About 50% of a sample of ninth graders exhibited this reading behavior (Meyer, Brandt, & Bluth, 1980).

Other Strategies.   As seen in Fig. 1.3, readers can choose not to follow the text from the writer's perspective. In this case, readers (e.g., experts in a field) could have well-organized schemata for selection, differential processing, and retrieval that are different from those suggested by the texts (Meyer & Freedle, in press).

In a recent study (Meyer & Rice, 1981a), we thought we had identified an alternative strategy from the structure strategy for middle and old adult readers for a passage without explicit signaling of its logical structure (Parakeets: Ideal Pets, Meyer, 1975). In this study, college-educated young (18–32), middle (40–54), and old (65+) adults read, recalled, and answered questions about the parakeet text which contains 343 idea units at 17 discrete levels. No age differences were found in overall quantity of recall, nor recall of the writer's thesis, "Parakeets are ideal pets for people with limited time, space, and money" (levels 1–5). However, an age by hierarchical level interaction was significant ($p < .01$) for the question data and approach significance ($p = .053$) for the recall data. Middle and old adults were found to remember more specific details (e.g., dates, names at levels 9–17) than the young adults, while the two older groups remembered less of the major details (levels 6 and 7) that directly supported the logic of the author than did the young adults. Thus, although all adults tended to remember more high-level information than low-level information, this levels effect diminished for the middle and old adults.

A biological deficit model with age did not seem appropriate for explaining these data because the age groups showed equivalent total recall, and the pattern for the middle aged group matched the old. Instead, we considered cultural generational factors related to reading strategies adopted in school. The young adults were all college undergraduates or graduate students, whereas the older groups were not. We thought that schooling may cause students to adopt the structure strategy. Another possibility was that current schooling placed less emphasis on learning details than schooling for the middle and old adults. We labeled the strategy of middle and old adults the *detail strategy*, where emphasis at encoding and retrieval was placed on details (such as names, dates, numbers) at the expense of logical structure and rationale supporting the writer's thesis.

Some support for this explanation concerning different reading strategies comes from data from a pilot study (Meyer, 1980) with old adults on the effect of signaling the superordinate logical structure. With signaling, the pattern of recall of high- and low-level information for the retired adults looked like that of the young subjects. However, without signaling, the number of high-level propositions recalled decreased although the number of low-level propositions increased; the pattern of recall looked similar to the older age groups' recall of the parakeet text. These data suggest that older adults can alter their reading strategies and are capable of greater sensitivity to the hierarchical prose structure if it is clearly signaled.

Recently, a study has been conducted (Theobald, 1981) to test one of the schooling hypotheses. Middle-aged registered nurses in their third or fourth year of a bachelor's degree program in nursing were compared to a similar group of registered nurses who had been away from a university program for at least 10 years. The nurses in school were expected to perform like the young adults in the Meyer and Rice (1981a) study, whereas the nurses out of school were expected to perform like the middle-aged and old-aged adults in that study. However, unexpectedly, both groups of nurses performed like the middle and old age group of the prior study. The results did not support the schooling hypothesis, but do support the generality of the recall pattern exhibited by middle-aged and old adults in the earlier study.

Differential emphasis on details for the three generations is still a possible explanation for the findings. Alternatively (or in addition), experiences as an older adult may encourage adding more details (e.g., experiences with recipes, instruction manuals) or simply a focusing on ideas of relevance to self rather than the text author.

In summary, the strategy envisioned for older adults is a modified structure strategy. They appear to follow the model depicted in Fig. 1.3 to determine the author's primary thesis or main idea. However, instead of following the logical relations that relate this thesis to supporting details, specific details are preferred for extra processing during reading. This detail strategy was posited to result from a preference for details, rather than a deficit in identifying or using organization.

PROCESSING AND PERFORMANCE PREDICTIONS OF VARIATIONS IN TEXT DIMENSIONS

The experiment to be presented in this chapter examines the text dimensions of emphasis and organizational plans and how they may influence the selection of reading strategies by older adults. These reading strategies are thought to guide the cognitive processes involved in building the reader's own semantic representation of a text. The effects of these text dimensions are examined with a group of expert readers of age 65 and over and a group of nonexpert readers of the same age. In this section, the text dimensions will be specified, and their predicted effects on recall will be outlined.

Emphasis Plans and Characteristics of Subordinate Details

Normal emphasis plans highlight the logical structure and superordinate text propositions. One way to accomplish this normal emphasis plan is to signal the top-level structure and superordinate logical relationships (see the paraphrase of high-level information with signaling in italics for the supertanker and railroad texts in the Appendix).

Differential emphasis occurs when this logical structure is left implicit (not emphasized) and emphasis occurs at low levels in the content structure. One way to emphasize this low-level information is to use pointer words, like "it is notable that . . ." Another way is to place highly salient information at this level. We (Meyer & McConkie, 1973) have found that numbers and familiar proper names are particularly well recalled immediately after reading texts containing few numbers and names. We attributed this finding to the von Restorff effect, distinct items in a homogeneous group will be better remembered due to increased attention given to these items. Thus, numbers and familiar proper names at the subordinate levels of the content structure should give greater emphasis to this level in the text and boost its importance and frequency of encoding than general terms (e.g., 1975 versus several years ago, the Empire State Building versus a skyscraper). This type of differential emphasis plan was particularly appropriate for the current investigation because older adults with their hypothesized detail strategy were thought to consider dates, numbers, and names of great importance. In addition to writing versions of the supertanker and railroad texts with specific detail versus general detail, a version of the text was written with numbers, dates, names, and pointer words emphasizing this low-level information, such as "in the notable year of 1829."

For this investigation five versions of each topic were written. Two followed a normal emphasis plan: with-signaling logical structure and general details, and with-signaling logical structure and specific details. Two followed a differential emphasis plan: without-signaling logical structure and specific details, and without-signaling logical structure and emphasized specific details. One version, without-signaling logical structure and general details, did not contain signaling of the logical relations as in the other normal emphasis plans, nor did it contain signaling of low-level information. No explicit emphasis plan was used, but it implicitly followed the normal plan.

Types of Organizational Plans

The detail strategy overlaps with the structure strategy in that it is used to identify the writer's main thesis; however, the reader's remaining capacity for selection and practice of propositions is focused on details rather than propositions directly tied to the writer's thesis by supporting logical relationships. Therefore, the model in Fig. 1.3 applies to older adults as they match their prior knowledge schemata about how texts are organized with top-level structures suggested by the text.

The text used in the Meyer and Rice (1981a) study had 17 levels, a descriptive: evidence top-level structure, and a time line emphasized with specific dates. For the current study, texts with different top-level structures were used in an attempt to extend the generality of the findings; structures for the texts are depicted in Fig. 1.2 and 1.4. The passages originally came from a ninth-grade magazine (Meyer, Brandt, & Bluth, 1980) and a history text (Bartlett, 1978); however, they were modified to match the crucial dimensions for this study that are listed in Table 1.1. The dates, names, and numbers occur at about the same order of presentation in all versions on both topics. For the experiment the passages were double spaced; the third paragraph of each version (containing new structure relevant to selection of schemata in the without-signaling versions) began on the second page.

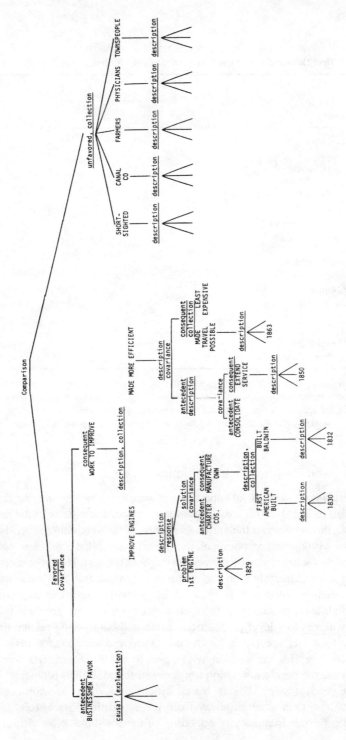

FIG. 1.4. Superordinate logical structure of railroad text.

17

TABLE 1.1
Text Dimensions of the Supertanker and Railroad Passages

Text Dimensions[a]	Text Topic	
	Supertanker	Railroad
Number of Words	388	388
Scorable Idea Units	244	244
Levels in Content Structure	9	9
High Level	1–5	1–5
Number Idea Units at High Level	114	114
Low Level	6–9	6–9
Number Idea Units at Low Level	130	130
Number of High Level Logical Relationships	14	14
Number of Low Level Names, Dates, Numbers	22	22
Familiar Names	8	8
Unfamiliar Names	4	4
Dates	4	4
Numbers	6	6
Type of Top-Level Structure	Problem/Solution	Comparison
Historical Sequence (Time Line)	NO	YES

[a]Text dimensions held for five versions on each topic. With-signaling versions made the 14 logical relations explicit (implicit and inferable in Without-signaling versions). The 22 names, dates, and numbers were specified in the Specific Detail versions; general terms were substituted in the General Detail versions. These 22 specific details were emphasized in the Emphasized Specific Detail version.

Processing and Performance Predictions

The five versions on the topic of supertankers were examined by moving through the flow chart in Fig. 1.3. Figure 1.5 points out important aspects of the interaction between this model and the various versions of the supertanker text. For the two versions with normal emphasis plans, the title suggested a problem/solution schema, and this schema was confirmed throughout the text. Expert readers were expected to show extremely high use of the problem/solution top-level structure to organize their recall protocols. Also, a large levels effect was expected because the high-level propositions fulfilled expectations of the problem/solution schemata, whereas low-level propositions presented tangentially related details. The same effects were predicted for the nonexpert readers on the general detail version. However, for the version with specific details nonexperts were still expected to use the problem/solution top-level structure in their protocols, but to revert to the detail strategy. That is, the specific names, dates, and numbers were expected to draw their attention away from the supporting logical relationships and toward a greater frequency of encoding of the low-level propositions.

With both groups of old adults for the without-signaling versions, most recall protocols were expected to utilize the problem/solution top-level structure, but to a lesser extent than in the versions with normal emphasis plans due the delay in identifying a problem/solution top-level structure until the second page of reading (see Fig. 1.5). Both groups of readers were expected to use the detail strategy on the two without-signaling versions with specific details regardless of the use of additional emphasis with pointer words. Thus, a small levels effect was expected. However, for the version with general details, the lure to use the detail strategy would be diminished, and the structure strategy would be employed. Some deficit in the ability to generate logical inferences in this without-signaling condition was expected for the nonexpert readers (Meyer & Rice, 1983).

Figure 1.6 depicts steps in processing versions of the railroad text. With-signaling the logical structure and general details, both groups of readers were expected to encode the text from the title onward with a comparison schema. The high-level propositions were to be instantiated readily into this schema and facilitate its frequency of encoding and position at the top of the cognitive structure at the time of retrieval. Thus, recall protocols with large levels effects and comparison top-level structures were expected from high use of the structure strategy. A subordinate level time line was expected, but its recall was predicted to be low. However, for the specific detail variation, the expert readers were expected to stick with the explicitly cued structure strategy, but the nonexperts were expected to get side-tracked by the specific details and employ their preferred detail strategy.

In contrast in the without-signaling logical structure and specific detail versions of the railroad text, both groups of readers were expected to favor a time order schema throughout their processing of the text. This schema is suggested by the titles and confirmed with the specific dates; this schema emphasizes the historically related events about railroad development (levels 6–9) as do the names, numbers, and pointer words. The last paragraph tags on a group of opposition to this narrative. The differential emphasis plans with the time line, lacking in the supertanker text, actually modify the hierarchy or content structure and push the time related events from the bottom of the logical structure to the top of the time lines as shown in Fig. 1.7. This content structure is flatter than the original structure (see Fig. 1.4); it contains six levels instead of nine. The time order information is now in the top half, and the causal relationships concerning the businessmen's efforts are found at the bottom half. Thus, recall protocols can be expected with a strongly emphasized time order schema and a reversed levels effect as measured on the original content structure of the texts following a normal emphasis plan. The recall protocols may mention that businessmen helped the railroads, give the history, and say others opposed them; this is all high-level information in Fig. 1.7. However, the logical relationships relating the businessmen's intentions and actions were expected to be poorly encoded and recalled.

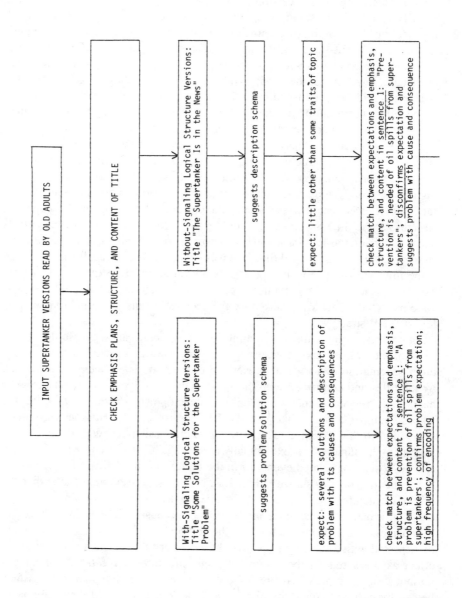

INPUT SUPERTANKER VERSIONS READ BY OLD ADULTS

CHECK EMPHASIS PLANS, STRUCTURE, AND CONTENT OF TITLE

With-Signaling Logical Structure Versions: Title "Some Solutions for the Supertanker Problem"

suggests problem/solution schema

expect: several solutions and description of problem with its causes and consequences

check match between expectations and emphasis, structure, and content in sentence 1: "A problem is prevention of oil spills from supertankers"; confirms problem expectation; high frequency of encoding

Without-Signaling Logical Structure Versions: Title "The Supertanker Is in the News"

suggests description schema

expect: little other than some traits of topic

check match between expectations and emphasis, structure, and content in sentence 1: "Prevention is needed of oil spills from supertankers"; disconfirms expectation and suggests problem with cause and consequence

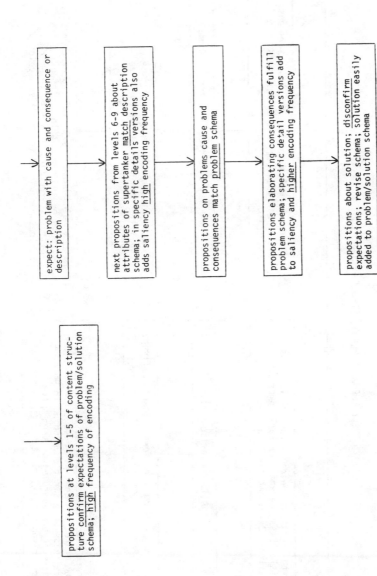

FIG. 1.5. Interaction of supertanker texts that vary in emphasis plans with structure strategy model for identification of memory schemata to organize text propositions.

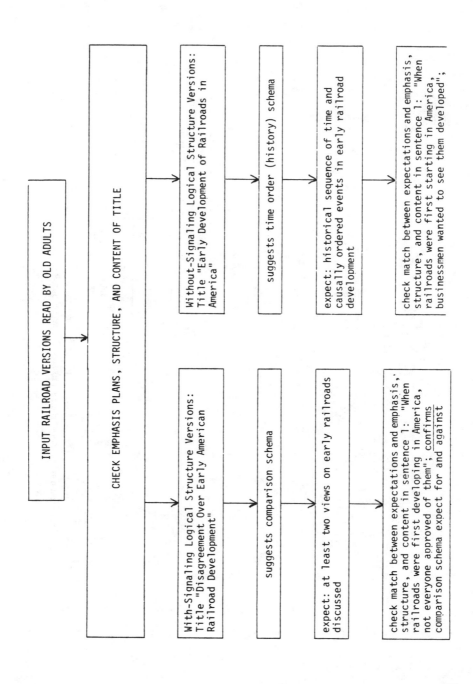

INPUT RAILROAD VERSIONS READ BY OLD ADULTS

CHECK EMPHASIS PLANS, STRUCTURE, AND CONTENT OF TITLE

Without-Signaling Logical Structure Versions: Title "Early Development of Railroads in America"

suggests time order (history) schema

expect: historical sequence of time and causally ordered events in early railroad development

check match between expectations and emphasis, structure, and content in sentence 1: "When railroads were first starting in America, businessmen wanted to see them developed";

With-Signaling Logical Structure Versions: Title "Disagreement Over Early American Railroad Development"

suggests comparison schema

expect: at least two views on early railroads discussed

check match between expectations and emphasis, structure, and content in sentence 1: "When railroads were first developing in America, not everyone approved of them"; confirms comparison schema expect for and against

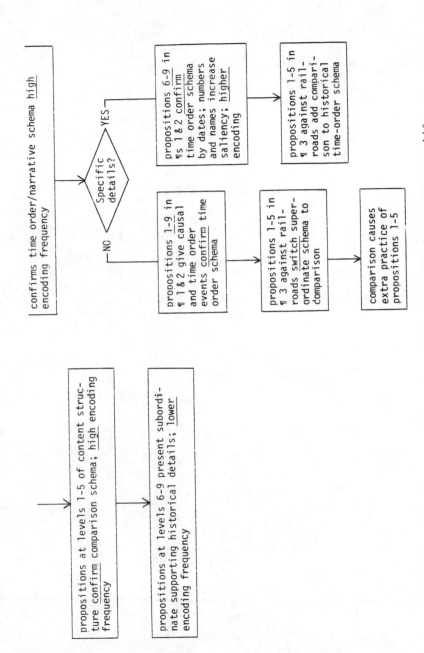

FIG. 1.6. Interaction of railroad texts that vary in emphasis plans with structure strategy model for identification of memory schemata to organize text propositions.

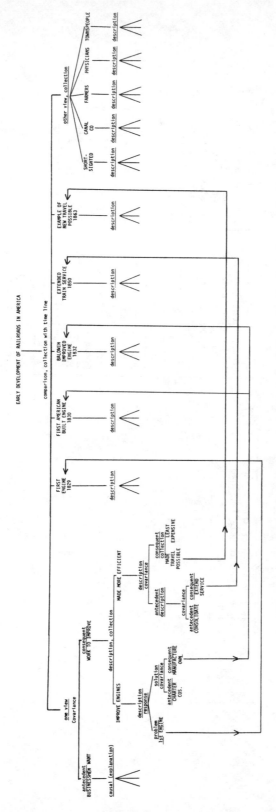

FIG. 1.7. Expectations for cognitive structure built for without-signaling logical superordinate structure + specific (± emphasized) details versions of the railroad text.

24

For the without-signaling logical superordinate structure and general details version both groups were expected to organize their recall protocols with a comparison top-level structure (see Fig. 1.6). The structure strategy was expected; some deficit in making logical inferences was again expected for the non-expert readers.

For all versions of the supertanker text, the readers' recall protocols were expected to show a high frequency of use of the problem/solution top-level structure. However, for the railroad text, two structures were possible, time order and comparison; both were expected from all versions, but predominance of one structure over another was expected to occur differentially in the different versions. Also, confusion over these structures might lead to a greater proportion of list-like structures (collections of nonrelated descriptions) than from the super-tanker text. The time order structure was expected to dominate for the without-signaling logical structure and specific detail version due to confirmation of this structure through the five time-ordered dates depicted in Fig. 1.8a. However, the comparison was expected to dominate for the general detail versions (see the diminished time line for these versions in Fig. 1.8b), and also for the expert readers on the with-signaling logical structure and specific detail version.

Retrieval from the time order and comparison structures was expected to produce recall of different types of propositions due to the different hierarchies of the resulting structures. However, immediate total recall was expected to be equivalent. In contrast, over time the comparison structure was considered a better mnemonic (Meyer & Freedle, in press), and total recall from readers who constructed a comparison structure was expected to be superior.

These manipulations were expected to influence the cognitive processes of selective encoding, frequency of encoding, and the subsequent organization of the reader's cognitive structure for use during the retrieval of text propositions. The levels effect was the primary measure used to assess changes in the way readers built cognitive representations of the text. With a large levels effect the difference in recall of high-level information and low-level information is large, and the reader is assumed to have built a cognitive structure very similar to the content structure. In contrast, a small levels effect indicates differences between the cognitive structure built by the reader and the content structure built following the text's logic and a normal emphasis plan.

The problem is that there are no norms for the levels effect, the finding that Miller and Kintsch (1980) cite as the most salient finding from research on prose memory. In research with college students (Meyer & McConkie, 1973; Meyer, 1975; Meyer & Rice, 1981a) the top third of the propositions in the content structure has been recalled better than the bottom third; the middle third usually doesn't differ significantly from either the top third or the bottom third. With college students in a number of studies the top third differed from the bottom by 15–22%.

In the current study the propositions in the content structure were divided into

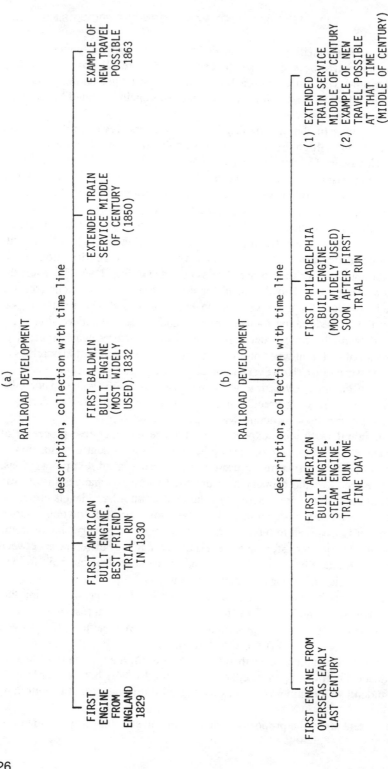

(a)

RAILROAD DEVELOPMENT

description, collection with time line

FIRST
ENGINE
FROM
ENGLAND
1829

FIRST AMERICAN
BUILT ENGINE,
BEST FRIEND,
TRIAL RUN
IN 1830

FIRST BALDWIN
BUILT WIDELY
(MOST WIDELY
USED) 1832

EXTENDED TRAIN
SERVICE MIDDLE
OF CENTURY
(1850)

EXAMPLE OF
NEW TRAVEL
POSSIBLE
1863

(b)

RAILROAD DEVELOPMENT

description, collection with time line

FIRST ENGINE FROM
OVERSEAS EARLY
LAST CENTURY

FIRST AMERICAN
BUILT ENGINE,
STEAM ENGINE,
TRIAL RUN ONE
FINE DAY

FIRST PHILADELPHIA
BUILT ENGINE
(MOST WIDELY USED)
SOON AFTER FIRST
TRIAL RUN

(1) EXTENDED
TRAIN SERVICE
MIDDLE OF CENTURY
(2) EXAMPLE OF NEW
TRAVEL POSSIBLE
AT THAT TIME
(MIDDLE OF CENTURY)

FIG. 1.8. Comparison between historical sequence presented in the specific detail (a) versus the general detail (b) versions of the railroad passage.

halves (see Table 1.1), levels 1–5 versus levels 6–9. In the appendix, information from each of these two levels is paraphrased independently. Levels 1–5 capture the author's thesis and logical relations and propositions that support it, the emphasis of the structure strategy. In contrast, levels 6–9 contained the subordinate details. Because the levels effect to be examined in this study divides the middle third of the content structure between the top and bottom halves, a smaller levels effect would be expected than in the previous studies. High verbal young adults read and recalled all of the passages used in this study to give an index of the levels effect for readers employing the structure strategy. The mean difference in recall by the young adults was 12.4% between levels 1–5 and 6–9 in the content structures for all versions on both topics.

Figures 1.9 and 1.10 summarize the overall predictions made concerning the levels effect for the five versions of the supertanker and railroad texts. The manipulations of the text dimensions of emphasis were expected to have similar effects for both topics. However, the different types of top-level structures for the two topics and particularly the presence or absence of a historical time order schema were expected to interact with the emphasis manipulations. Greater effects were expected for the railroad text.

In summary, with the emphasis plans of the text focused on the text's superordinate structure of logical relations, older adults were expected to employ the structure strategy. Their recall protocols were predicted to be organized with the same type of organization as that used by the writer, and large levels effects were expected (see Fig. 1.9). This prediction, although compatible with past studies (Meyer & Rice, 1983), is contrary to the findings of Cohen (1979) who found age-related deficits with high verbal adults on recall of main ideas, total recall, and recall of modifiers, a category that included logical relations.

However, when the emphasis plans were not focused on this logical structure, older adults were expected to revert to their preferred detail strategy, find out the writer's thesis, de-emphasize most of the writer's rationale with its logical relations, and focus on those *important facts* of interest, particularly propositions highlighted with dates, numbers, and names. Removal of dates, numbers, and names was expected to free up processing capacity for logical relations and major details and, thus, increase their likelihood of employing the structure strategy (see Fig. 1.10).

SUBJECTS AND PROCEDURES FOLLOWED IN CONDUCTING THE EXPERIMENT

Subjects

The subjects came from a larger sample of 166 old adults who participated in a series of related studies (Meyer & Rice, 1983). For this study a comparison was made of the 50 older adults who scored highest on the Quick Word Test (Borgatta & Corsini, 1964) and the 50 who scored lowest on it. The older adults in the

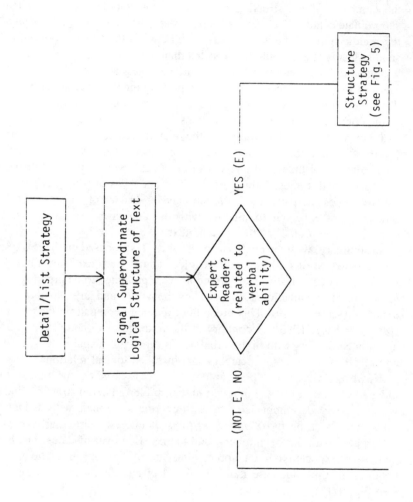

Detail/List Strategy

Signal Superordinate Logical Structure of Text

Expert Reader? (related to verbal ability)

YES (E)

(NOT E) NO

Structure Strategy (see Fig. 5)

28

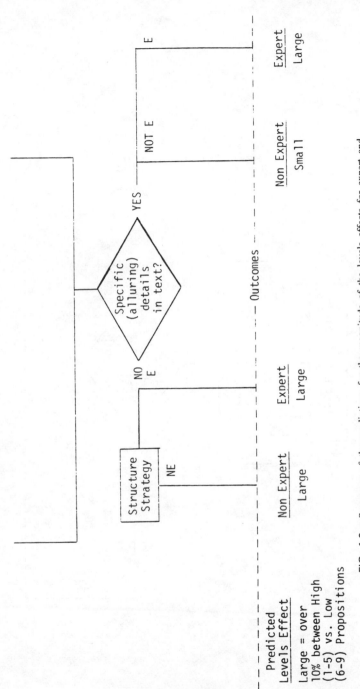

FIG. 1.9. Summary of the predictions for the magnitude of the levels effects for expert and nonexpert readers who read the with-signaling versions of the supertanker and railroad texts.

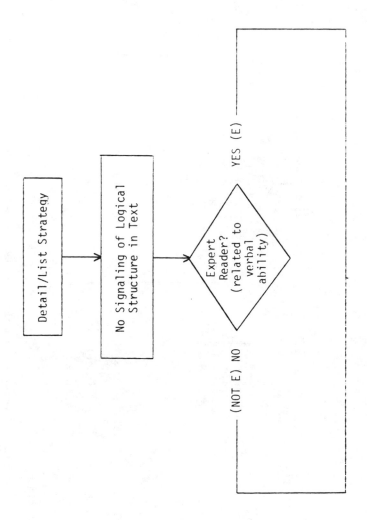

Detail/List Strategy

No Signaling of Logical Structure in Text

Expert Reader? (related to verbal ability)

YES (E)

(NOT E) NO

30

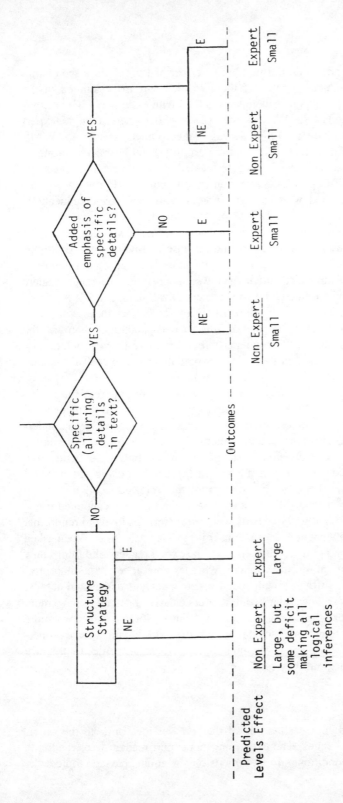

FIG. 1.10. Summary of the predictions for the magnitude of the levels effects for expert and nonexpert readers who read the without-signaling versions of the supertanker and railroad texts.

prior studies that found the diminished levels effect had vocabulary scores that fell between the vocabulary scores of the two older groups examined in the present study. Thus, the expert readers were adults with extremely high vocabulary skills (Quick mean = 82, WAIS scaled score = 16) whereas the nonexpert readers fell within the average to high average range (Quick mean = 45, WAIS scaled score = 12). The average age for each group was 69 years. The group of expert readers consisted largely of college-educated professionals (mean years of education = 16.18, 70% professionals) whereas the nonexpert group was composed largely of blue and white collar workers with high school educations (mean years of education = 12.22, 24% professionals).

An assessment through questionnaires and interviews showed that the expert readers did more reading, read more for the purpose of finding out something, enjoyed reading more, and read better than the nonexpert group. In addition, evidence from the questionnaires and interviews indicated that the expert readers tended to be more sophisticated with respect to organization in text. For instance, the expert group was significantly more likely to report that they wrote their recall protocols by organizing information into related paragraphs than was the nonexpert group. In contrast, the nonexperts reported more frequently that they wrote "the hard things first" in their recall protocols and repeated information over and over when they wanted to remember it.

When asked to underline items they considered important from the supertanker passage, 50% of underlining from the expert readers could be mapped on the top levels (1–4) of the content structure, whereas the nonexpert group underlined ideas from all levels in the content structure equally (four levels examined: 1–4, 5, 6, and 7–9; these divisions were based on dividing the structure into fourths in number of idea units). When asked to explain their choices, the expert group was much more likely to use explanations that referred to organizational properties of the text, such as "If you analyzed it, the theme is contained in the first sentence." Additionally, the experts were three times as likely to report that they "argue back" to what they are reading if they disagree with it. When asked what is the hardest thing to remember, most of the expert readers said things they considered "unimportant or irrelevant," whereas the nonexperts more frequently complained of difficulty with specific items, such as names and details.

In summary, the high vocabulary adult readers clearly appeared to have more expertise in reading than the average vocabulary adults. Not only were they more practiced readers, but they tended to be more familiar with organizational properties of text (main ideas, top-level structures) and use these properties to organize their own recall of material they read.

Procedures

All 100 subjects read and recalled one of the five versions on both the supertanker and railroad passages. The expert and nonexpert readers were randomly assigned to the five conditions of text dimension variations; passage topic order (supertankers or railroads first) was counterbalanced across all text dimension conditions and reading groups.

Half of the subjects from the text dimension, order, and expertise cells participated in one experimental session. They read the passages and recalled them; next, they answered questions about the passages in the order read. The questions were comprised of 14 questions tapping superordinate logical relations from each text and 14 questions asking for the 14 names and numbers that were given in specific or general terms in the texts. For example from the supertanker text, a relationship question was ''According to the text what is not a reasonable solution to the supertanker problem?,'' whereas a detail question was ''How many seabirds died?''

The other half of the subjects did not answer the questions after the recall test, but instead returned to the university one week later to again recall the texts and then to answer the questions on the logical relationships and details.

The subjects were instructed to read the passages at their normal reading speed for a magazine article of interest to them. They were instructed in the use of digital timers to record their reading and writing times. They were told that we wanted to see how many ideas they could remember and if they could remember how the ideas were interrelated; they were instructed to write in sentences and paragraphs rather than listing ideas and use the words in the passage or their own words. Before beginning to work on the texts, a practice passage and recall test were used to familiarize them with the procedures.

The recall protocols were scored for presence or absence of the 244 idea units in the content structure of each passage (Meyer, 1975). In addition the number of idea units from levels 1–5, high in content structure, and levels 6–9, low in the structure, were tallied. Also tallied were the number of the 14 major logical relationships recalled and the number of the 14 names, dates, and numbers recalled. Reliability in scoring between independent scorers was over .95.

In addition, the numbers of questions correctly answered for the logical relations and details were scored. The answers counted as correct for the detail questions were the details (specific or general) that appeared in the version read by a subject.

Also, the recall protocols were scored for top-level structure. A record was made concerning whether or not the subjects used the same top-level structure in their recall protocol as used in the text (Meyer, Brandt, & Bluth, 1980). In addition, the railroad texts were scored for existence and strength of a historical time line.

FINDINGS AND DISCUSSION

Levels Effects and Recall Organization

The text dimensions examined were predicted to affect the type of information remembered from text by older adults, but not the amount of information remem-

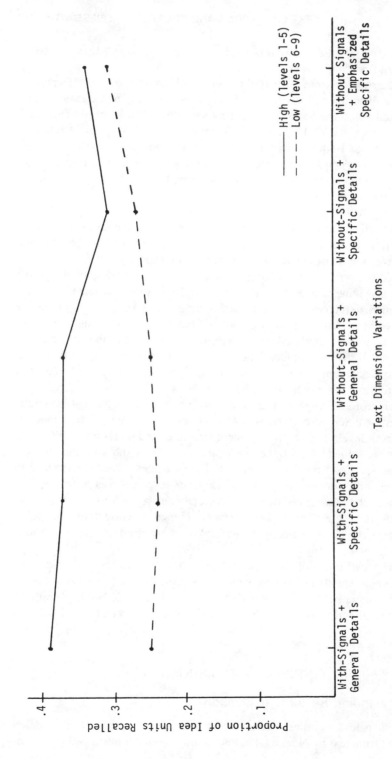

FIG. 1.11. Proportion of idea units recalled from high and low in the content structure for the five text dimension variations on the immediate free recall task for the 96 older adults.

bered. Differences in type of information remembered were assessed by examining the high-level propositions (levels 1–5) versus low-level propositions (levels 6–9) in the content structure.

A four-factor analysis of variance (reader expertise × text dimension variations × levels × passage topic-repeated measures on levels and topic) on the immediate free recall data of the 96[1] subjects yielded statistically significant main effects on reader expertise (37% recall for experts versus 24% nonexperts, $F_{1, 86} = 43.98, p = .0000$) and levels (37% high versus 25% low, $F_{1, 86} = 122.34, p = .0000$). As expected, text dimension variations did not affect total recall ($F_{4, 86} = .71$); these variations also had no affect on total number of ideas recalled per time spent reading. There was no difference in total recall between the supertanker and railroad topics; on the immediate free recall task 31% of the ideas were recalled from each topic. (A week later 19% were recalled from each topic.)

As predicted, there was a statistically significant text dimension variation × levels interaction ($F_{4, 86} = 8.68, p = .0000$). Figure 1.11 displays this interaction; the magnitude of the levels effects supports the predictions summarized in Figs. 1.9 and Fig. 1.10. Thus, the text dimensions had the predicted effects in varying the type, but not the amount of information recalled. This same pattern was maintained by the 48 subjects who returned one week later to again recall the text (text dimension variation × level interaction: $F_{4, 37} = 10.11, p = .0000$).

Also, the predicted reader expertise × text dimension variation × levels interaction was supported by the data ($F_{4, 86} = 3.47, p = .0112$). Based on reading expertise the subject groups were predicted to function with parallel reading strategies on all text dimension variations, except the one emphasizing both logical relations and details, with-signaling superordinate logical relations and specific details. As seen in Fig. 1.9, expert readers were expected to use the structure strategy and manifest a resultant large levels effects, whereas nonexperts were expected to follow the detail strategy and show a small levels effect. Table 1.2 depicts the prediction for the various text dimension variations and a summarization of the data. The data support the predictions.

The only other statistically significant interaction for this analysis was a passage topic × levels interaction ($F_{1, 86} = 22.38, p = .0000$). The levels effect is stronger for the supertanker topic across all versions (37% high versus 25% low) than across all versions on the railroad topic (34% high versus 28% low).

In summary, the data supported the predictions specified in Fig. 1.9 and Fig. 1.10. The text dimensions of emphasis had similar effects for both topics. The next section examines the logical structure used by readers to organize what they remembered from the various versions of texts about supertankers and railroads.

The detail strategy was expected for both groups of readers for the two

---

[1]Incomplete data on four subjects across various conditions resulted in deletion from the original 100 subjects.

TABLE 1.2
Predicted Levels Effects Compared with Data on Levels Effects for 96 Old Adults on the Immediate Free Recall Task

Magnitude of Levels Effects	With-Signaling Logical Structure				Without-Signaling Logical Structure					
	General Details		Specific Details		General Details		Specific Details		Emphasized Specific Details	
	Nonexpert	Expert	Nonexpert	Expert	Nonexpert	Expert	Nonexpert	Expert	Nonexpert	Expert
Predicted Data	Large	Large	Small	Large	Large	Large	Small	Small	Small	Small
High > Low (1–5) (6–9)	.28 > .15[a]	.51 > .32	.27 > .20	.46 > .29	.31 > .19	.43 > .31	.25 > .19	.36 > .34	.29 > .23	.38 > .38

[a]Mean difference for a group of high verbal young adults = .12; difference .12 or above are underlined.

versions on each topic with differential emphasis. In contrast, the structure strategy was predicted for the other three versions with one exception, a detail strategy or default strategy for the nonexperts on the with-signaling logical structure and specific detail version.

As expected for the supertanker topic (see Fig. 1.5), use of the problem/solution structure to organize what the readers remembered was high. As expected it was slightly lower (79%) for the versions with differential emphasis than for the other versions (82%). The levels effect was diminished in the passages with differential emphasis (10% difference) in comparison to the other versions (18% difference). In summary, the predictions generated from the model in Fig. 1.5 were supported.

The time order structure for the railroad texts was expected to magnify these expected effects (see Fig. 1.6). The differential emphasis plan was expected to emphasize the historical time order structure that would result in its greater use to organize recall protocols (see Fig. 1.7) and a minimal or reversed levels effects, as gauged by the content structure seen in Fig. 1.4.

In the two versions of the railroad texts with differential emphasis, the historical time order structure (87%) occurred more frequently in recall protocols than did the comparison structure (64%). Also, the levels effect was minimal and slightly reversed for these versions (high = .28, low = .31). In contrast, for the three versions where use of the structure strategy was posited, the time order structure (63%) was used less frequently than the comparison structure (70%). In addition, the levels effect was robust (high = .37, low = .25). Thus, support was seen for the model in Fig. 1.6. As expected from the models in Fig. 1.5 and Fig. 1.6, the comparison schema (68%) suggested by the railroad text was less frequently employed than the problem/solution schema (81%) from the supertanker text.

For both topics different predictions were made for expert and nonexpert readers on the version labeled with-signaling logical structure and specific detail. Overall this prediction was supported as previously discussed and shown in Table 1.2, but when the topics were examined separately the findings only held for the railroad topic. For this condition, experts were expected to override their preferred detail strategy and follow the text's logic by employing the structure strategy. However, nonexperts were expected to use the detail strategy or due to confusion use a default/list strategy. For the supertanker text, the experts and nonexperts follow the same pattern: high use of the problem/solution structure (experts = 90%, nonexperts = 70%) and large levels effects (experts = .48 > .29; nonexperts = .29 > .16); both groups appear to be following the structure strategy. For the railroad text, the experts follow this pattern (levels effect = .44 > .29), but the nonexperts do not (.24 > .23). Half of the nonexperts in this condition use the default strategy, simply listing ideas with no attempt to interrelate them. Even though the logical relations ($N = 14$) were explicitly stated in this version, nonexperts remember few of them (2.9), and questions as

TABLE 1.3
Mean Number of Questions Correctly Answered on the Immediate Test About the 14 Logical Relations and 14 Details from the Five Versions of the Texts Varying on Emphasis Plans

	With–Signaling Logical Structure		Without–Signaling Logical Structure		
	General Details	Specific Details	General Details	Specific Details	Emphasized Specific Details
Logical Relations					
Nonexpert	3.70	4.00	6.00	3.70	5.38
Expert	7.70	7.60	8.20	7.40	7.87
Names & Numbers					
Nonexpert	1.50	3.40	4.00	3.60	4.00
Expert	2.50	5.80	4.70	6.70	6.50
Predictions					
Nonexpert	structure strategy	detail strategy	structure strategy	detail strategy	detail strategy
Expert	structure strategy	structure strategy	structure strategy	detail strategy	detail strategy

cues provide no assistance. They remember many more logical relations from this version of the supertanker text (6.2), but again cues do not increase their recall of these relations. In contrast, experts on the cued recall task recalled an average of 10.6 of the logical relationships from the supertanker text and 9.2 from the railroad text. The logical structure appears to be more difficult to follow and remember in the railroad text; on this text most nonexpert readers cannot perform adequately. Thus, it appears that for this condition, nonexperts will use the structure strategy if they can figure out the structure; reduction in the levels effect does not result from application of the detail strategy by nonexperts in this condition, but from being unable to perform the task, the default strategy.

Other predictions that were not supported also deal with the free and cued recall of these 14 major logical relationships in each version of the texts. First, as can be seen in Fig. 1.10, a deficit in recall of logical relations by nonexperts was expected on the without-signaling logical structure version with general details in comparison with the corresponding with-signaling version. That is, signaling was expected to help nonexperts identify and remember the logical relationships. However, as shown in Table 1.3, this prediction was not supported.

In fact, there was an expertise × signaling interaction for the immediate free recall data ($F_{1, 96} = 6.96$, $p = .01$). Explicitly signaling the logical relations assisted the experts in their free recall of them (8 versus 5.2), but had no facilitative effect for nonexperts (4 versus 4.7). Thus, nonexperts performed poorly on logical relations (31%), and explicit signaling did not assist them nor did explicit retrieval cues (questions).

In contrast, retrieval cues for the logical relations were particularly helpful to the expert readers in the conditions with differential emphasis plans (no signaling of these relations) (free recall = 5.2, cued recall = 7.7). As seen in Table 1.3, logical relations were stored almost equivalently for all versions of the texts, but differential selection for encoding occurred for details (type × cued interaction, $F_{1, 38} = 7.06$, $p = .0115$). Thus, for expert readers, the text dimensions influenced the type of protocol produced and the number of details stored, but not the number of logical relations processed. The older expert's recall of logical relations was equivalent to that of high verbal young adults (Meyer, in press a; Meyer & Rice, 1983). However, the recall of logical relations by old nonexpert readers was significantly worse than that of young adults with equivalent or lower vocabulary test scores (Meyer & Rice, 1981b).

Relationships Between Findings and a Model for Building Cognitive Representations of Text

Figure 1.12 depicts a model that points to the interaction between the text dimensions examined in this chapter and the reading strategies that were discusssed; these text dimensions and strategies interact, and their interaction affects the processes identified, which are the mechanisms for building a reader's cognitive representation of a text.

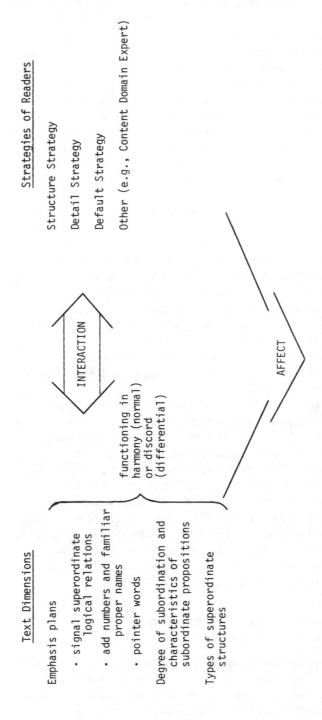

Text Dimensions

Emphasis plans

- signal superordinate logical relations
- add numbers and familiar proper names
- pointer words

Degree of subordination and characteristics of subordinate propositions

Types of superordinate structures

functioning in harmony (normal) or discord (differential)

INTERACTION

Strategies of Readers

Structure Strategy

Detail Strategy

Default Strategy

Other (e.g., Content Domain Expert)

AFFECT

Processes for Building Cognitive Representation of the Text

- Selection for encoding into long-term memory
- Differential practice or frequency of encoding
- Differential retrieval

FIG. 1.12. Dimensions of text that affect the building of a cognitive representation by a reader.

The findings from this study tell something about the interaction among the identified text dimensions. First, emphasis plans that focus on the top-level and superordinate structures of problem/solution and comparison texts appear to have parallel effects on older expert readers; they increase the levels effect and use of the text's top-level structure as an organizational schema. However, differential emphasis plans that emphasize details through the use of numbers, names, and pointer words appear to interact with characteristics of the subordinate information that is emphasized. For the supertanker text the subordinate information was unrelated examples of oil spills without an underlying historical time order structure; however, for the railroad text the subordinate information, examples of businessmen's interventions with railroads, was interrelated on a historical time order structure. Emphasis of the details from the railroad text made the time order structure a potential superordinate schema for organizing the text propositions. It provided a viable alternate framework for encoding the text (see Fig. 1.7); this alternative framework was more like a narrative text than like the logical thrust of expository text (Brewer, 1980). This alternative structure was flatter, more horizontal, than hierarchical with three less hierarchical levels. Smaller levels effects would be expected from such structures. We plan to further investigate retrieval and retention differences between cognitive representations that better match Fig. 1.4 or Fig. 1.7 for the railroad text. No differences were expected nor found between the conditions promoting these two structures on the immediate free recall task. However, the comparison structure was thought to be a better mnemonic over the retention interval than the time order structure. For the delayed test, expert readers remembered less from the versions with differential emphasis plans (.175) than from the normal plans (.23), but the biggest effects are on types of information remembered rather than amounts remembered.

The differential emphasis plans for both topics that emphasized details appeared to be particularly effective in highlighting information for older adults. The altered structure of the railroad text (Fig. 1.7) ideally fits the preferences of the detail strategy, hypothesized to be a frequently used strategy by expert readers in the older age range.

The findings do not give support for the idea that older adults with expert reading skills employ the detail strategy due to deficits in finding logical relations in text. However, this explanation is plausible for nonexpert readers. Old adults who are expert readers are quite good at recalling the logical relations (45% compared with 48% for a group of expert readers at the graduate school level, Meyer & Rice, 1983). Table 1.3 shows that older expert readers can correctly answer more than half of the questions pertaining to logical relations. These expert readers shifted from the detail strategy to the structure strategy depending on the emphasis plans of the text. They are quite good at picking up the text's logical structure and employing the structure strategy when they are cued to do so by the writer through normal emphasis plans.

The expert readers shifted their reading strategies to match the text variations more than the nonexpert readers (examine Table 1.2). Experts show a bigger levels effect on the with-signaling logical structure and specific details version than the nonexperts and a smaller levels effect on the text with the differential emphasis plans focused on details (expertise × levels × text dimension interaction, $p = .0112$).

When compared with the expert readers, the nonexperts show a deficit in recall of logical relations (31% versus 45%). Table 1.3 displays the immediate question data for the reading groups across the five variations of text dimensions. There was a statistically significant levels × expertise interaction for these data ($F_{1, 38} = 7.21, p = .0107$); the experts performed better than the nonexperts on details, but particularly on logical relations.

Thus, the nonexperts show deficits on identification of logical relations, and this deficit is not remedied with explicit signaling of these relationships. In fact, as shown in Table 1.3, the nonexperts tended to do better on questions dealing with logical relations in two of the three conditions without explicit signaling. Therefore, simply signaling a writer's logical structure does not ensure its comprehension by older adults with high average or average vocabulary scores.

In summary, the findings have provided some important information about how expert adult readers interact with text dimensions to select and employ reading strategies. The models in Fig. 1.3, Fig. 1.5, Fig. 1.6, Fig. 1.9, and Fig. 1.10 work through some of the interactions that were supported by the data.

This interaction of text dimensions and reader strategies affects the building of the cognitive representation from the text in the mind of the reader. It was hypothesized that different cognitive representations could be built as a result of selective encoding of some propositions over others. The question data in Table 1.3 show that differences in cognitive representations exist between expert and nonexpert readers based on the magnitude of propositions that can be encoded into long-term memory and differences in the relative proportions of logical relations versus details that were encoded. However, it is possible that these cognitive representations differ primarily in quantity not quality; experts' superior cued recall on logical relations could result from inferences made at retrieval rather than selection and integration during encoding, but most propositional theories argue for integration at encoding rather than at retrieval (Kintsch, 1974, Chapter 8).

A comparison of the cued recall data from the two different topics shows that the different passages resulted in differential selection of logical relations versus details (passage topic × levels interaction, $F_{1, 38} = 90.29, p = .0000$; supertankers, 7.29 logical relations versus 3.07 details; railroads, 5.52 logical relations versus 4.78 details). Thus, there are qualitative differences in cognitive representations between the two topics.

The text dimension variations did not appear to result in differences in selective encoding of logical relations, as evidenced by the number of correctly answered questions about these relations (see Table 1.3). We need to further examine potential differences in the types of relations recalled from the different variations of the text. The more emphasis placed on these details (through giving specific names and numbers and highlighting them with other differential emphasis devices), the greater their selection for encoding into long-term memory. To clarify the selection issue eye movement data on the idea units would be helpful (Just & Carpenter, 1980).

Although the logical relations did not differ in recall with cues, there were differences on the text dimension variations on free recall tasks. It could be argued that these differences result from differential practice in the short-term memory buffer of the logical relations from the different text dimension variations. This differential practice for the superordinate logical structures was proposed for the text versions with- and without-signaling (see Fig. 1.5 and Fig. 1.6). All versions on each topic are approximately equal on repetition of arguments; they differ on explicitness of structure (e.g., "the problem is" versus "prevention is needed") and emphasis of details. However, the number of concepts and their order in the texts remained constant. A model is required that attributes an active influence on the frequency of encoding different text propositions to specific prior knowledge schemata about text organization that are set into action by text dimensions of the type identified in this study. This component is missing from the clarification given to the levels effect by the Kintsch and van Dijk (1978) model. It is apparent from this study that repetition of concepts alone does not explain all of the levels effect.

The more frequent processing from short-term to long-term memory of propositions most closely linked to the organizational schemata would place these propositions high in a top–down retrieval structure in a reader's memory. Greater practice of the high level propositions in a reader's cognition representation, as they are linked to incoming subordinate propositions, appears more plausible than equal practice with all propositions, but storage in a hierarchical structure accessed by top–down retrieval.

The construction of this retrieval hierarchy relates to retention of text propositions over time. Earlier, the unusual finding in Table 1.3 was noted concerning the higher immediate cued recall scores on logical relations from the without-signaling version than from the corresponding with-signaling version with general details. There was a significant text dimension variation $\times$ level $\times$ task interaction ($F_{4,\ 38} = 4.14$, $p = .0070$); the free and cued recall scores were equivalent on the with-signaling structure and general details version, logical cues assisted the recall from text with differential emphasis of details more than detail cues, and both types of cues improved recall substantially and equivalently for the other two versions. Thus, although immediate cued recall is lower for the with-signaling structure version and general details, immediate free recall was high, and the subjects practiced all of these relations when they wrote their free recall protocols. The cued recall task one week later (see Fig. 1.13) shows that

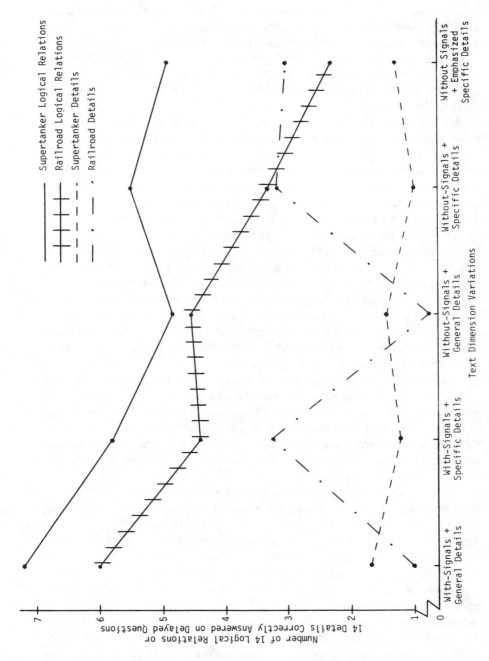

FIG. 1.13. Number of logical relations and details answered correctly on the delayed cued recall test for the five variations on text dimension for both passage topics.

cued recall of logical relations from this version is much higher than their recall in all other versions for both passages. Also, use of the problem/solution or comparison top-level structure is highest for this condition. Thus, this version, due to greater selection at encoding (see levels effect in Fig. 1.11 and cued details in Table 1.2) and consistent practice of its hierarchical structure, appears to yield a more fixed structure with clearer differentiation among storage of high- and low-level propositions. The suitability of the strategy employed for this text version would depend on the pragmatics of a particular learning situation.

More forgetting over time occurs for the details of the supertanker texts, whereas more forgetting over time occurs for logical relations of the railroad texts (passage topic $\times$ level $\times$ time, $F_{1,\ 76} = 7.03, p = .0098$; refer to Fig. 1.13 and Table 1.3). This finding coincides with the frequency of using the problem/solution and comparison top-level structures on the delayed free recall task. The details are at the bottom of a hierarchy organized with the problem/solution (Fig. 1.2) and comparison/adversative (Fig. 1.4) structure; however, the comparison/alternative and time line structure (Fig. 1.7) pushes the details to the top of this structure. Propositions at the bottom of these hierarchical structures are more likely over time to be subsumed (Ausubel, 1965), decay, or become inacessible even with cues. Greater forgetting over time of low-level propositions has been reported in other studies (Kintsch, 1977; Meyer, 1975).

In summary, text dimensions were examined. These dimensions of emphasis and types of organizational structures in text were shown to interact with reader expertise and reader strategies. Their interaction affects the mechanisms of cognitive processing that form a representation in the reader's mind of the text. Different cognitive representations can be stimulated by the use of different structures and emphasis plans in text. These cognitive representations determine what kinds of information from text can be remembered. Important implications from this work can be applied to the teaching of writing techniques and the teaching of reader expertise.

ACKNOWLEDGMENTS

This chapter was presented at a symposium on *Learning from Texts* held at the German Institute for Distance Studies at the University of Tübingen, Tübingen, West Germany, June 29–July 3, 1981. This research was supported in part by Grant MH 31520 from the National Institute of Mental Health.

REFERENCES

Ausubel, D. P. Cognitive structure and the facilitation of meaningful verbal learning. In R. C. Anderson, & D. P. Ausubel (Eds.), *Readings in the psychology of cognition*. New York: Holt, Rinehart, & Winston, 1965.

Bartlett, B. J. *Top-level structure as an organizational strategy for recall of classroom text*. Unpublished doctoral dissertation, Arizona State University, 1978.

Borgatta, E. F., & Corsini, R. J. *Manual for the Quick Word Test*. New York: Harcourt, Brace, & World, 1964.

Brewer, W. F. Literary theory, rhetoric, and stylistics: Implications for psychology. In R. J. Spiro, B. C. Bruce, & W. F. Brewer (Eds.), *Theoretical issues in reading comprehension*. Hillsdale, N.J.: Lawrence Erlbaum Associates, 1980.

Britton, B. K., Meyer, B. J. F., Simpson, R., Holdredge, T. S., & Curry, C. Effects of the organization in text on memory: Tests of two implications of a selective attention hypothesis. *Journal of Experimental Psychology: Human Learning and Memory*, 1979, *5*, 496–506.

Cirilo, R. K., & Foss, D. J. Text structure and reading time for sentences. *Journal of Verbal Learning and Verbal Behavior*, 1980, *19*, 96–109.

Cohen, G. Language comprehension in old age. *Cognitive Psychology*, 1979, *11*, 412–429.

Flower, L. S., & Hayes, J. R. Problem solving and the writing process. *College English*, 1977, *39*, 449–461.

Grice, H. Logic and conversation. In P. Cole, & J. Morgan (Eds.), *Syntax and semantics*, Vol. 3: *Speech acts*. New York: Academic Press, 1975.

Just, M. A., & Carpenter, P. A. A theory of reading: From eye fixations to comprehension. *Psychological Review*, 1980, *87*, 329–354.

Kintsch, W. *The representation of meaning in memory*. Hillsdale, N.J.: Lawrence Erlbaum Associates, 1974.

Kintsch, W. *Memory and cognition*. New York: Wiley, 1977.

Kintsch, W., & Keenan, J. M. Reading rate as a function of number of propositions in the base structure of sentences. *Cognitive Psychology*, 1973, *6*, 257–274.

Kintsch, W., & van Dijk, T. A. Toward a model of text comprehension and production. *Psychological Review*, 1978, *85*, 363–394.

Meyer, B. J. F. *The organization of prose and its effects on memory*. Amsterdam: North-Holland Publishing Company, 1975.

Meyer, B. J. F. The structure of prose: Effects on learning and memory and implications for educational practice. In R. C. Anderson, R. Spiro, & W. Montague (Eds.), *Schooling and the acquisition of knowledge*. Hillsdale, N.J.: Lawrence Erlbaum Associates, 1977.

Meyer, B. J. F. *Signaling in text and its interaction with reader strategies*. Paper presented at the annual meeting of the American Educational Research Association, Boston, April 1980.

Meyer, B. J. F. Basic research on prose comprehension: A critical review. In D. F. Fisher & C. W. Peters (Eds.), *Comprehension and the competent reader: Inter-specialty perspectives*. New York: Praeger, 1981.

Meyer, B. J. F. Prose analysis: Purposes, procedures, and problems. In B. K. Britton & J. Black (Eds.), *Analyzing and understanding expository text*. Hillsdale, N.J.: Lawrence Erlbaum Associates, in press.(a)

Meyer, B. J. F. Organizational aspects of text: Effects on reading comprehension and applications for the classroom. In J. Flood (Ed.), *Reading comprehension*. Newark, Del.: International Reading Association, in press.(b)

Meyer, B. J. F., Brandt, D. M., & Bluth, G. J. Use of the top-level structure in text: Key for reading comprehension of ninth-grade students. *Reading Research Quarterly*, 1980, *16*, 72–103.

Meyer, B. J. F., & Freedle, R. O. The effects of different discourse types on recall. *American Educational Research Journal*, in press.

Meyer, B. J. F., & McConkie, G. W. What is recalled after hearing a passage? *Journal of Educational Psychology*, 1973, *65*, 109–117.

Meyer, B. J. F., & Rice, G. E. Information recalled from prose by young, middle, and old adult readers. *Experimental Aging Research*, 1981, *7*, 253–268.((a)

Meyer, B. J. F., & Rice, G. E. Organizational strategies in prose comprehension across the adult life span. Paper presented as part of a symposium titled *Studies of semantic memory in aging* at the annual meeting of the American Psychological Association, Los Angeles, August 1981.(b)

Meyer, B. J. F., & Rice, G. E. Learning and memory from text across the adult life span. In J. Fine & R. O. Freedle (Eds.), *Developmental studies in discourse.* Norwood, N.J.: Ablex, 1983.

Miller, J. R., & Kintsch, W. Readability and recall of short prose passages: A theoretical analysis. *Journal of Experimental Psychology: Human Learning and Memory,* 1980, *6,* 335–354.

Theobald, C. *Effect of schooling on the type of information recalled by middle-aged women.* Unpublished manuscript, Arizona State University, 1981.

Thorndyke, P. W., & Yekovich, F. R. A critique of schema-based theories of human story memory. *Poetics,* 1980, *9,* 23–49.

van Dijk, T. A. Relevance assignment in discourse comprehension. *Discourse Processes,* 1979, *2,* 113–126.

Yekovich, F. R., & Thorndyke, P. W. An evaluation of alternative functional models of narrative schemata. *Journal of Verbal Learning and Verbal Behavior,* 1981, *20,* 454–469.

Appendix

HIGH AND LOW LEVEL INFORMATION IN THE SUPERTANKER TEXTS WITH IDENTIFICATION OF SIGNALED HIGH LEVEL LOGICAL RELATIONS

Paraphrase of High Level Information with Signaling of Logical Relations in Italics

A problem is prevention of oil spills from supertankers. *Attributes of a typical* supertanker deal with size and carrying capacity. *The trouble is that* a wrecked supertanker spills oil in the ocean. *As a result of this spillage,* the environment is damaged. *Four examples are given dealing with* resulting destruction, damage from crashes which result in washing ashore, mop ups and findings which led to arrests, and oil spill killings.

Oil spills result from the lack of power and steering equipment to handle emergency situations, such as storms. Supertankers have one boiler to provide power and one propeller to steer the ship.

The solution to this problem is not to halt the use of tankers on the ocean *since* the world's oil supply is carried by supertankers. *Instead, the solution lies in the following three tactics. First,* officers of the supertankers must get top training in how to run and maneuver their ships, *such as that* provided by the tanker simulator at the Maritime Research Center. *Second,* tankers should be built with several propellers for extra control and backup boilers for emergency power. *Third,* ground control stations should be installed at places where supertankers come close to shore *because they* would guide tankers along busy shipping lanes and through dangerous channels. The ground control stations *would act like* airplane control towers which guide airplanes.

Paraphrase of Low Level Information with Specific Details Italicized

(The passage said) a *half-million* tons of oil, *five* football fields, the *Empire State Building* easily fit in its cargo area. In *1970* near Spain an oil spill from a wrecked tanker exploded into fire. Winds of the force of a hurricane whipped the oil into mist. Several days later black rain from this oil spill (was on) crops and livestock in the neighboring villages. In *1967* the tanker, *Torrey Canyon,* (was) off the coast of *Cornwall;* ashore (there were) *200,000* dead seabirds. Nearer to home in *July 1975* the *United States Coast Guard* (saw) acres of oil from the beach at *Geiger Key,* Florida, north of *Key West.* Guardsmen (saw) chemical clues. On *November 7, 1975* a *Greek* Tanker captain, *Vasilious K. Psarroulis,* (had something happen). He failed to report the loss of an estimated *40,000* gallons of oil. Microscopic plant life provide food for sea life and produce *70* percent of the world's oxygen supply.

About *80* percent (was also stated).

HIGH AND LOW LEVEL INFORMATION IN THE RAILROAD TEXTS WITH IDENTIFICATION OF SIGNALED HIGH LEVEL LOGICAL RELATIONS

Paraphrase of High Level Information with Signaling of Logical Relations in Italics

When railroads were first developing in America, *not everyone approved of them.* Businessmen were *in favor* of developing the early railroad *because* they believed that the railroads had great economic potential. *As a result of this conviction,* businessmen worked to improve rail travel. *For example,* they made improvements in the locomotive engine. They experienced a number of *problems* with the first locomotive. *To solve these problems* businessmen chartered companies *for the purpose* of manufacturing their own locomotives. Two examples were given of manufacturing and building these locomotives.

Another improvement which businessmen instigated was to make railroad travel more efficient. *For instance,* they consolidated and *as a result* extended travel and made it possible for the transport of people and goods. *Another result of consolidation was that* railroads became the form of transportation in the United States for all but very bulky items.

As stated earlier, however, railroad development was not favored by everyone. Various groups of people *opposed* and had other ideas about railroad development. *Specifically*, short-sighted people refused to believe they would ever be (anything). Canal companies made efforts to prevent the railroads from building. Farmers complained of fright and fire. Physicians were afraid for survival. *In addition*, townspeople didn't want their quiet disturbed by steam engines and strangers.

Paraphrase of Low Level Information
with Specific Details Italicized

A locomotive was shipped from *England* in *1829*. The first *American-* built locomotive, *Best Friend*, made its trial run one in *1830*. This locomotive was designed by *Horatio Allen*, pulled *40* people in *four* cars, and it attained the speed of *21* miles an hour. The *American*-made locomotives which were built by *Mathias Baldwin* became most widely used. His first locomotive was built in *1832*.

   (There were) numerous short times and direct railroad service from the *Eastern seaboard* to the *Mississippi River* by the middle of the century (for going) hundreds of miles within a few days. Traveling by rail on one of *G. M. Pullman's* sleeping cars between *New York City* and *Detroit* took only *four* days in *1863*. Traveling by water the same trip required *10* days. (It was) least expensive.

   Many (thought) railroads were just a supplement for waterways. Lines compete with canals. Some (thought) noise (affects) livestock and that sparks which came from the engines (affect) their fields. A number (thought) human body (affected) by travel at speeds as high as *30* miles an hour. Many *New Englanders* (were affected).

2 Comparative Instructional Text Organization

Wolfgang Schnotz
Deutsches Institut für Fernstudien
an der Universität Tübingen

INTRODUCTION

In instructional texts the same content may often be organized in different ways. For the author this means that he will have to decide which type of organization will be the best with respect to the information he would like to see emphasized. Because the author usually has a specific learning objective in mind, he will choose the type of organization most likely to stress the information that is most important according to this objective. Specific types of organization also pose specific processing demands. The learner always meets the text with specific learning prerequisites (prior knowledge, cognitive skills, goals, interests, etc.), which influence the quality of processing and the result of learning (Anderson, 1977; McConkie, 1977). Hence, the author is also confronted with the question of how willing and how capable the learner is in meeting the specific processing demands of the text. It depends on the interaction between text organization and individual learning prerequisites, whether the learning process will actually involve the kind of processing intended by the author.

Although research on learning from texts has been increasingly concerned with the aspect of interaction between learner and text (Frederiksen, 1977; Kintsch & van Dijk, 1978; Lesgold & Perfetti, 1978), the studies conducted so far usually confined themselves to very short and simple narrative texts. Research on the effects of the organization types frequently used in lengthier and more complex instructional texts is still at its beginnings (cf. Meyer, 1979, 1980; van Dijk, 1980). Particularly, there is a lack of investigations concerning the interaction between specific types of text organization and individual learning prerequisites. However, the analysis of this interaction would be of great practical importance: Knowing more about the effect of various types of organization on the learning process of individuals with different prerequisites (prior knowledge, cognitive skills, etc.) would facilitate the decision concerning the type of organization most adequate for reaching specific objectives with a particular type of learner.

The aim of the following study was to identify the effects of different kinds of text organization on learning and to analyze this interaction. The study was concerned with two variants of text organization that are frequently used in instructional texts. The author of an instructional text is often confronted with the task of describing and contrasting two or more objects (events, facts, opinions, etc.). This usually amounts to describing the objects under several aspects. Let us take, for example, different modes of therapy for the treatment of neuroses. One can first describe the general theoretical foundation of each mode of therapy, then the principle of treatment, followed by assumptions concerning the nature of neurotic disorders, then the assumptions on the problem of symptoms, and, finally, the scientific position to which the therapy form is oriented. Any type of organization may be characterized by the fact that the propositions are ordered according to specific categories and dealt with in a specific sequence. Thus, if two kinds of therapies are to be presented, e.g., psychoanalysis and behavior therapy, basically this could be done in two ways; one possibility being the first one of the therapies (e.g., psychoanalysis) is described as a whole, i.e. with respect to all the aspects mentioned above, followed by an equivalent description of the other therapy. A text constructed in this way may be considered as being *organized by object* (cf. Fig. 2.1a). Another possibility is to pick out the aspects mentioned before, one by one, and to describe both therapies under each aspect. In this case, the statements on both kinds of therapy concerning a particular aspect of description follow upon each other more closely than in a text organized by object. A text structured in this way may be considered as being *organized by aspect* (cf. Fig. 2.1b).

The question about the advantages and disadvantages of these two variants is not a new one. In a number of earlier studies, the effects of these two types of organization on the learning process have already been analyzed (DiVesta, Schultz, & Dangel, 1973; Frase, 1969, 1973; Friedman & Greitzer, 1972; Myers, Pezdek, & Coulson, 1973; Perlmutter & Royer, 1973; Schultz & DiVesta, 1972). But for several reasons their findings may not generalize to normal learning situations. For one thing, the contents used in the tasks were extremely simple. Usually the task consisted in memorizing specific name–attribute associations. (Hence, the two text variants were labeled *organization by name* and *organization by attribute*.) These associations could be learned in a rather mechanical way as no deeper understanding of interrelations was required. When learning from texts, however, the material to be acquired is usually meaningful and comparatively complex.

In order to study the effects of both types of organization, researchers have tried to exclude preexperimental associations as far as possible by using mainly

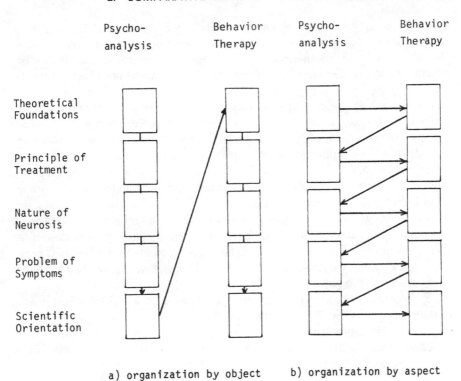

a) organization by object   b) organization by aspect

FIG. 2.1.   Example for a text organization by object and a text organization by aspect.

fictitious learning material. The normal goal in reading, however, is to enlarge, differentiate, and update prior knowledge on a specific topic. People usually read texts on topics they already know something about, and they make use of this knowledge to structure the information found in the text. Thus, one basic characteristic of learning from texts is to relate novel information to information already known and to integrate this novel information into the existing knowledge structure. The studies mentioned above, however, reduced this interaction to a minimum. Spiro (1977) has pointed out that most studies on prose learning are not valid from an ecological point of view, as the experimental situation is mainly considered as a memory task by the learners. In order to reproduce the learning material as correctly as possible, subjects may try to avoid any interaction between the learning material and their prior knowledge for fear of confusion or inaccuracies.

Because interaction of text content and prior knowledge is a basic characteristic of text processing under normal learning conditions, the process of comprehension will look different depending on the amount of an individual's prior knowledge. It is possible that specific differences in prior knowledge may have different effects depending on the organization of the text. In the studies mentioned previously such interaction effects between prior knowledge and text organization could not even appear from the outset, prior knowledge having been eliminated. In summary therefore, the findings of these studies may hardly be generalized to the learning of complex meaningful material under normal learning conditions.

For this reason, the present study was aimed at a learning situation in which a lengthier instructional text with relatively complex content was to be worked upon. To increase the ecological validity of the experimental setting and to insure interaction effects with prior knowledge, the content of the learning material should not be completely new to the learner. Therefore, a topic of rather popular interest was chosen on which one could expect the subjects to have already some prior knowledge. The topic chosen concerned the treatment of neuroses; in particular, (as was mentioned previously) a comparison was made between psychoanalysis and behavior therapy. The two types of therapy were described according to the aspects mentioned earlier. The contents were presented once with organization by object and once organized by aspect. The two text versions may be seen in the appendix.

For higher ecological validity an attempt was made to avoid any resemblance to pure memory tasks. Thus, the experimental setting was conceived in such a way as to induce problem-oriented learning aimed at understanding the overall structure of the contents of the text. Within this framework the following issues were to be investigated:

1. How do the two types of organization differ with respect to their processing demands, and what are the effects on processing and the resulting memory structure?

2. How do these different processing demands interact with differences in prior knowledge?

3. How may these effects be explained?

First, we look at the effects of both organization types on individual components of cognitive processing that are to be expected according to a theoretical analysis based on available research findings and at the role played by differences in prior knowledge. The next step will be to analyze which empirical hypotheses may be derived therefrom, i.e., what actual consequences follow from the interaction of these components for the learning process and learning results with each of the organization types.

THEORETICAL ANALYSIS

According to Grimes (1975, 1978), three dimensions may be identified in analyzing texts: the dimensions of content, cohesion, and staging. The content dimension refers to the statements contained in a text and to the semantic relations between these statements regardless of their sequencing in the text. The content dimension corresponds to the question: What does the text say? The cohesion dimension refers to the way each individual statement in the text is to be related to earlier statements. Thus, this dimension amounts to answering the question: How does what I am reading right now relate to what I have read earlier in the text? The staging dimension refers to the perspective under which the content is communicated, that is, the information and semantic relations which are emphasized according to this perspective. It answers the question: What is most important, and what is less important?

The interesting point now is to see what changes occur in a text along these three dimensions if the content is organized either by object or by aspect. With respect to the content dimension nothing changes, of course, because in both cases we have the same propositions only in a different order of presentation. As regards the dimension of cohesion, however, we should expect differences, because the organization of a text determines which propositions are presented together and which are presented separately. This will lead to different grades of difficulty for the reader trying to find the right referent for each proposition within the text read up to that point. The construction of a coherent knowledge structure may thus be either facilitated or hampered by the type of organization of the text. Changes may also be expected with respect to the dimension of staging as the structure of a text usually reflects a particular communicative goal. Staging signals to the reader what is important and what is less important, suggesting thus a specific reading perspective. This means that some of the information is particularly stressed. Hence, the two types of text organization accentuate different parts of information. These differences concerning the facility of constructing a coherent knowledge structure and concerning staging will now be analyzed more specifically. But first, the content structure of the text used in this study will be considered in more detail.

Content Structure

As everyone knows, texts are more than simple arrays of sentences. A number of semantic relations connect the various propositions to a coherent whole. Thus, the knowledge communicated by a text represents a network with closely interrelated propositions. Texts in which two objects are described and contrasted with each other show two major kinds of semantic relations: relations *within* the objects and relations *between* the objects described. Relations *within* the objects refer to the coherence existing between the single statements concerning one object only. They integrate the various statements to a coherent picture of that object. Relations *between* objects, on the other hand, concern the similarities and differences between the set of objects we are talking about. These are the relations that are stressed if two objects are compared with each other.

A closer analysis of the text on psychoanalysis and behavior therapy used in this study (see the appendix) reveals that within the description of each therapy, the propositions are closely interrelated semantically. The treatment principle always depends on the general theoretical foundation and on the assumptions concerning the nature of neurotic disorders. The statements concerning the symptom issue are considered as a specification of these assumptions. In contrast, direct semantic relations between the therapies (objects) are relatively scarce, because the two types of therapy represent completely different ways of thinking and operate with completely different concepts: Psychoanalysis is concerned with conflicts between id and superego, with repression into the unconscious, with libido. Behavior therapy is interested in stimulus–response connections, in classical and operant conditioning. If one disregards the fact that in both cases the theoretical foundations, treatment principles, and assumptions concerning the nature of neurosis serve to organize the content, the contents of the statements on each side appear to have comparatively little in common. There is one exception, however. The statements in the passages concerning the symptom issue and scientific orientation of the two therapies refer directly to each other. It is even relatively easy to infer the statements of the opposite position in each case, because it always says exactly the contrary. For example, in the passage on psychoanalysis, neurotic behavior is seen as a symptom of some deeper unconscious cause which can only disappear if this unconscious motive is recognized and eliminated. On the other hand, behavior therapy does not assume any unconscious reasons for neurotic behavior that it considers to be curable by simply treating the symptoms. The same is true of the comments on the scientific tradition of the therapies: Psychoanalysis is said to be hermeneutic and interpretative in its orientation, to ignore the standards of experimental procedures and thus, to avoid making predictions. Behavior therapy is said to be experimental in its orientation, to try to predict therapeutic effects, and to be rather sceptical with respect to hermeneutic or interpretative procedures. Thus we may characterize the content of the text as follows: Within the description of each kind of therapy there are a number of direct semantic relations between the propositions. The two kinds of therapy are hardly interrelated via direct semantic relations between corresponding propositions as far as statements about general theoretical background, principles of treatment and assumptions on the nature of neurotic disorders are concerned. In contrast, the statements concerning assumptions on the symptom issue and scientific orientation of both therapy forms are closely interrelated.

Coherence

One major aspect during the construction process of a coherent knowledge structure in the head of the reader is that the input of information or of the corresponding propositions, occurs in a linear sequence and must be integrated at the right place into the knowledge structure built up so far. This is what Frederiksen, Frederiksen, Humphrey, and Ottesen (1978) termed connective inferences. Connective inferences relate propositions that have just been processed to previously processed propositions represented in memory. Two propositions can only be related to each other if they have both been activated, i.e., if they are present in working memory. Due to limited processing capacity only few propositions may be processed at the same time. According to the model of comprehension developed by Kintsch and van Dijk (1978), processing becomes more difficult if the referent of the proposition being processed is not to be found in working memory or in the short-term memory buffer. In this case, a rather laborious and time-consuming search for the referent of the ongoing proposition will have to be started. In addition, it seems reasonable to assume that this search process will be harder the further away these referents are in time. Hence, we may conclude that when processing the second of two propositions that are semantically related, it will be easier for the reader to connect the two propositions, and the relation between the propositions will become an integrative part of the memory structure with greater probability, the smaller the temporal distance between these two propositions is in the text (cf. Walker & Meyer, 1980).

As change in text organization leads to changes in temporal distance between the propositions, the following assumptions concerning the influence of both types of organization on connective inferences may be deduced: In the text organized by object (O-organization), the semantic relations within the description of the two therapies show comparatively small temporal distances between related propositions as the statements concerning each therapy form immediately follow upon each other. In the version organized by aspect (A-organization), the distance between these propositions is greater on the average, as passages concerning one type of therapy are always intercalated between passages concerning the other therapy form. With A-organization the propositions relating to one therapy are presented with greater *gaps* in between. Thus, connective inferences—as far as they serve the connection of propositions within the description of one object—will be less easy to realize in a text organized by aspect.

For semantic relations between the two types of therapy, however, the reverse is true: Because A-organization means that the passages describing the same aspect of both therapies always follow upon each other immediately, the temporal distance between corresponding propositions is comparatively small. The O-organization, on the other hand, means that these propositions are rather far apart from each other: For one of the therapies is first described under all the aspects mentioned earlier before the other therapy is taken into consideration. Thus, in the experimental text the passages corresponding to each other for the two therapies were always separated by four passages on other aspects. Accordingly, connective inferences between the two objects will be harder to realize if the text is organized by object than if it were organized by aspect. As was said before, direct semantic relations between propositions concerning both therapy forms may be only found in the two passages on the issue of symptoms and on scientific orientation. Therefore, connective inferences resulting in a connection of propositions between the two kinds of therapy are only possible in these passages. In short, the facilitative effect organization by aspect generally has on connective inferences between the objects may only be found in these two passages on symptom interpretation and scientific orientation but not in the other passages.

Graesser (1978) refers to the number of semantic relations connecting one statement to other statements in the text as relational density. The degree of interrelatedness between propositions in memory structure after the learning process will depend on the amount of processing time invested in the effort, another factor being how difficult it is for the learner to make connective inferences interrelating the corresponding propositions. Our earlier considerations showed that with each type of text organization some of the connective inferences are facilitated and others made more difficult. The construction of a coherent knowledge structure may therefore be easier on the average with one type of organization or the other, but one should also bear in mind that facilitation of coherence through specific types of organization might well apply to only some points of the memory representation to be acquired whereas at other points the same organization might act as an impediment.

Staging

Authors usually communicate the content from one particular point of view. This is also reflected in the way a text is organized. This suggests a particular reading perspective to the learner, emphasizing some of the contents against the rest. One important aspect in determining what will be emphasized is the context in which information will be presented. Following the levels–of–processing approach (Cermak & Craik, 1979; Craik & Lockhart, 1972), we may assume that processing operations occurring during comprehension result in memory traces that may be used to reconstruct the information of the text during recall. The quality of these traces depends on the kind of processing. For Klein and Saltz (1976) as well as for Eysenck (1978), one major characteristic of such a memory trace is how well it is discriminated from other memory traces. The more it differs from other traces, the less likely confusion will occur during the process of reconstruction. The learned information will thus be recalled more precisely. The way information is processed depends on the other information it relates to or has to be differentiated from, i.e., the context in which it is presented. The degree of distinctiveness of memory traces thus is influenced by context (see Jacoby & Craik, 1979).

A change in organization produces contextual changes for the propositions in the text. Looking at the experimental text, it will appear that for O-organization, the propositions concerning one kind of therapy are always found within the context of other propositions concerning the same therapy. For A-organization things are different: Here one may say that the propositions concerning each type of therapy occur more frequently within the context of propositions relating to the other therapy, because for both objects the passages corresponding to each other (i.e., describing the same aspect) directly follow upon each other. Aspect organization thus focuses attention particularly onto the comparison between the two objects of description. In this case the emphasis lies on the similarities and differences between psychoanalysis and behavior therapy whereas with organization by object only the description of the therapy types is focused upon. Of course, the learner may also make comparisons between the objects with a text organized by object, but, on the whole, this will probably happen less often than with A-organization. The differences between the two types of organization as to staging may be summarized as follows: With a text organized by object the reader is in a way implicitly given the instruction to try and get a consistent overall picture of each of the objects. With aspect-organization, on the other hand, the learner is not only required to construct a coherent mental representation of the objects but also to work out the similarities and differences between them.

Individual Differences in Prior Knowledge

Basically, we may assume that it will always be the easier for the learner to process a text the more he/she already knows about the topic, i.e., the greater his/her prior knowledge is. It may be deduced that a learner with high prior knowledge on the topic will be able to perform a greater number of processing steps during a given time interval than a learner with low prior knowledge. The learner's processing rate and learning performance will thus be higher. This is rather trivial, of course. But the question of how much processing rate may be accelerated by a specific increase in prior knowledge is less trivial. The strength of the impact of prior knowledge on processing rate or learning performance is the topic of this question. Of course, prior knowledge may be expected to have a positive influence on processing rate with each type of text organization; however, the strength of this influence may differ according to organization type, meaning that one type of organization may be found to *react more sensitively* to differences in prior knowledge than the other.

A text organized by aspect contains several *thematic switches* where the topic is shifted from one object to the other, in this particular case, from psychoanalysis to behavior therapy and vice versa. At these points, the reader has to mentally shift focus and to concentrate on a new topic. If the object has already been referred to earlier in the text, the knowledge structure constructed so far has to be reactivated for the new propositions to be properly integrated into what has been learned up to that point. Thematic switches may thus be considered as a kind of obstacle in the flow of processing. Hence, it is to be expected that with A-organization processing will run less smoothly on the average than with O-organization. Processing rate of a learner will depend, among other things, on his/her flexibility in realizing these mental switches. It seems reasonable to assume that greater flexibility may be expected from someone who knows already something about the topic, i.e., from someone with higher prior knowledge. The problem of mental shifts is much more salient with A-organization than with O-organization, the latter requiring switching only once thus allowing for smoother processing. For this reason, processing rate will be affected more strongly by mental flexibility, and, thus, the influence of prior knowledge on processing rate will presumably be more powerful with A-organization than with O-organization.

EMPIRICAL HYPOTHESES

The analysis above shows that for both types of organization we must expect a comparatively complex interaction of influences on the individual components of cognitive processing. Now we will see which are the empirical hypotheses that may be derived from this, i.e., how, in fact, learning performance and learning results should be affected by the interaction of these components with both kinds of text organization.

Reading Time

We assumed before that due to the thematic switches a text organized by aspect would be processed less fluently than a text organized by object. Even if in both cases learners were doing the same amount of processing operations on the average, we should still expect longer reading time for A-organization for this reason. According to the analysis we made, O-organization merely requires from the learner that he/she construct a consistent overall picture of the individual objects presented. A-organization additionally requires the learner to work out the differences and similarities between these objects. Accordingly, A-organization will induce a greater amount of processing operations. This is another reason why A-organization should require more reading time than O-organization.

Recall Performance

If both types of organization lead to the construction of a coherent overall picture of the individual objects and if this is done with equal care, meaning that relational density of the resulting memory structure will be equally high in both cases, then no difference in recall performance is to be expected in this respect. But because A-organization additionally requires a comparison between the objects, which amounts to a greater number of processing operations on the average, we should expect better recall performance than in O-organization. For in order to make comparisons between various propositions processed earlier on, these propositions have to be reactivated in memory. Additional encoding therefore occurs, creating more favorable conditions for recall.

Learning Rate

If for A-organization we are to expect longer reading time on the one hand but better recall performance on the other hand, the question naturally arises which of these effects prevails. May learning be said to be more effective or less effective in this case, that is, is the amount of propositions recalled per unit of reading time greater or smaller than with O-organization? The number of propositions recalled per unit of reading time is called *learning rate*. Predicting learning rate is problematic, because a number of factors play a role and the influence of only some of them can be estimated. As regards the difficulty of connective inferences we may deduce from the earlier analysis that this will depend on the temporal distance between the corresponding propositions in the text. Accordingly, we may compute average distances for both types of organization. We made lists of propositions for the different text versions with the procedure of Kintsch (1974; Turner & Greene, 1977) and determined the temporal distance between directly connected propositions. The average distance amounted to 14.0 for O-organization and 14.6 for A-organization. Thus, on the average connective inferences should hardly be more difficult for A-organization than for O-organization, which means that for the total text we should not expect any important differences in average learning rate.

But for some passages in the text, the construction of a coherent knowledge structure is facilitated by A-organization whereas for other passages the reverse is true, owing to the different properties of both types of text organization concerning the facilitation of connective inferences. The extent to which connecting interrelated propositions to each other is facilitated by the structure of the text in a particular passage may be computed via the average distance between the propositions in the passage and any of remaining propositions in the text with which they are semantically related in a direct manner. Applied to the text in this study, this means that for A-organization the average distance and, hence, the difficulty in interconnecting the propositions is greater in the passages on theoretical foundations, principles of treatment, and assumptions on the nature of neurosis. Thus, we should expect a less favorable learning rate. As regards the passages concerning the issue of symptoms and scientific orientation, the reverse is true, and learning rate should be higher than with O-organization.

The facility of making connective inferences or of interrelating the propositions merely constitutes one of the factors influencing learning rate, however, According to the previously mentioned analysis, processing should also be expected to run less smoothly on the average because of the more numerous thematic switches. Fewer propositions may be read during the same time interval. For this reason a certain reduction of learning rate should be expected with organization by aspect as compared to organization by object.

Another assumption that was made earlier on referred to the greater amount of comparative processing expected to occur with A-organization. This means that the propositions that are to be compared have to be reactivated in memory, which amounts to new encoding. Hence, better recall performance is to be expected. But these comparative operations also need additional processing time. If this will increase or reduce learning rate, cannot be decided on the grounds of the above analysis. Thus, prediction of differences in average learning rate between the two types of organization is left with some degree of uncertainty.

In the previous analysis, it was assumed that processing rate would be affected by the amount of prior knowledge. This influence was supposed to be stronger with A-organization than with O-organization because of the frequent thematic switches. Accordingly, we should reckon with a stronger impact of prior knowledge on learning rate with A-organization: Specific differences in prior knowledge should affect learning rate to a greater extent in this case than with O-organization.

Distinctiveness of Knowledge Structure

Following the earlier analysis A-organization focuses attention in particular onto the comparison between the two objects, whereas O-organization merely stresses the description of the two types of therapy. Thus, A-organization will have a higher average of comparative processing operations than O-organization. It may reasonably be expected that processing induced by A-organization will produce a knowledge structure in which the two forms of therapy will be more distinct, i.e., better discriminated. The differences between them are worked out more thoroughly than with O-organization.

METHOD

Experimental Text

As was mentioned before, the text used in this study concerned psychoanalysis and behavior therapy. In the German (original) form, length of the text comprised 1079 words. The two types of therapy were each presented under the five content aspects described earlier on, resulting in one passage for each aspect and therapy type. The 10 passages were then sequenced once according to O-organization and once according to A-organization. Additionally, the order of the two therapy forms was alternated: In one of the variants, psychoanalysis came first, followed by behavior therapy, and in the other variant the sequence was reversed. This led to two variants organized by object and two variants organized by aspect. All text variants were completely identical except for the sequencing of individual passages. The variant organized by object and the variant organized by aspect beginning with psychoanalysis may be seen in the appendix.

Subjects

Subjects were undergraduate students of psychology, education, biology, and chemistry. There were 20 participants in all who were randomly assigned to the four text variants (five subjects per variant).

Experimental Procedure

Assessment of Prior Knowledge. To assess prior knowledge concerning the text content subjects were first presented with a number of concepts from the realms of psychoanalysis and behavior therapy with the instruction to explain these concepts as far as they were familiar with them.

Learning Phase. Prior knowledge having been assessed, subjects received the text in the organizational variant to which they had been assigned. They were instructed to read the text with the objective of subsequently communicating the content to another student in free recall. This other student should be able to answer questions on the basis of this communication. It was made clear that the questions would not concern simple facts where the emphasis would depend upon the recall of as many details as possible, but that they would concern comprehension aimed at understanding overall meaning. Problem-oriented learning was expected to be induced this way. Introducing a real person as an addressee for the reproduction phase was supposed to approximate the experimental setting to a real life situation. No time limit was given for reading. Reading time was recorded for each passage and for the text as a whole.

Recall Phase. Fifteen minutes after finishing reading, subjects had to communicate the content in free recall to another student.

Comparison Task. Having communicated the content, subjects were presented with a number of written statements in which psychoanalysis was compared to behavior therapy. The similarities and differences between the two therapies maintained in these statements were partly correct and partly false. Errors consisted in mixing up some elements of the two therapy types in a way as to make the statements seem plausible at first sight. For each statement subjects were to judge whether they were true or false with reference to the experimental text and to justify their answers. This task was to establish how well subjects had learned the similarities and differences between the two kinds of therapies.

Scoring

For prior knowledge assessment, subjects received *knowledge marks* according to a predetermined scoring schedule on the basis of their concept definitions. Recall protocols were scored with the help of the proposition list obtained by analyzing the content with the procedure of Kintsch (1974; Turner & Greene, 1977). Recall performance was measured by the number of correctly reproduced propositions. The number of recalled propositions for each subject was not only registered for the complete text but also for each of the content aspects (theoretical foundation, principle of treatment, etc.) under which the two therapies had been described. Furthermore, learning rate of each subject was determined once for the whole text and also for each of the content aspects. Learning rate was computed by the number of recalled propositions per minute of reading time for the whole text and for each content aspect, respectively. Comparison task performance was scored by analyzing the judgments made by the subjects on the comparative statements with respect to the number of detected errors. Thus, for each subject the following measures were available: degree of prior knowledge, reading time, total recall performance, aspect specific recall score(s), total learning rate, aspect specific learning rate(s), and performance in the comparison task.

RESULTS AND DISCUSSION

For prior knowledge, reading time needed, total recall performance, total learning rate, and performance in comparison task, the means and standard deviations are given in Table 2.1 for the two main experimental groups: subjects with text organized by object (object group) versus subjects with text organized by aspect (aspect group).

The first thing to be remarked is that the two groups hardly differ with respect to their average prior knowledge with $\bar{x} = 14.4$ versus $\bar{x} = 14.2$ points. Both groups may be considered as equivalent as far as their learning prerequisites go.

TABLE 2.1
Means (and Standard Deviations) in Both Groups

Dependent Measure	Group	
	Object	Aspect
Prior Knowledge Score	14.4 (7.99)	14.2 (5.87)
Reading Time (minutes)	17.4 (5.9)	18.7 (3.7)
Recall Performance	51.4 (17.4)	55.3 (15.2)
Learning Rate	3.16 (1.23)	3.03 (.92)
Comparison Task Performance	3.70 (2.31)	5.30 (1.06)

Reading Time

Reading time had been expected to be longer on the average in the aspect group than in the object group. As appears in Table 2.1, there was a difference in the expected direction, but it was fairly small; average reading time amounted to 18.7 minutes in the aspect group and 17.4 minutes in the object group. In view of the high variation of individual reading times, however, the difference was not significant ($t = .61$, df $= 18$). The relatively small difference may be due to the fact that the aspect group, while realizing a greater number of comparative operations, makes fewer connective inferences, and thus, does less *networking* than the object group. Accordingly, the aspect group could be said to do the additional comparative processing at the expense of merely description-oriented processing directed at interrelations within objects.

Recall Performance

Better recall performance had been predicted for the aspect group. As Table 2.1 shows, in spite of going into the predicted direction the difference in this case, too, was comparatively small; mean recall performance was 55.3 for the aspect group and 51.4 propositions for the object group. Considering the great variation between individuals, the difference proved not significant (t $= .53$, df $= 18$). Here also the reason may be that although the aspect group does more comparative processing, it might do so at the cost of less thorough processing of internal connections of both objects, resulting in lower relational density in memory representation as compared to the object group, thus reducing potential differences between the groups.

Learning Rate

Table 2.1 shows that in the object group, learning rate for total text amounted to an average of 3.16 propositions per minute of reading time, which was only slightly higher than for the aspect group, which averaged 3.03 propositions per minute. The difference was not significant (t $= .25$; df $= 18$). For individual content aspects or passages, however, there were some striking differences in learning rates. These results may be seen in the left columns of Table 2.2. The third column contains ratios from these learning rates; these values indicate how many times the learning rate of the aspect group exceeds the learning rate of the object group with respect to that particular content aspect. On the basis of the theoretical analysis, a prediction had been made that the interconnection of propositions in the passages on theoretical foundations, principle of treatment, and nature of neurosis would be more difficult with A-organization, whereas in the case of the passages concerning the question of symptoms and scientific orientation it would be facilitated as compared to O-organization. The reason was higher average temporal distance between related propositions in the former case and smaller distances in the latter case. For the various content aspects or passages, the fourth and fifth columns in Table 2.2 present average distances between the propositions of the passage and their related propositions in the rest of the text with each particular type of organization. In the right most column, the ratios from these mean distances are given. The values may be interpreted as the degree to which interconnection of related propositions should be easier with A-organization than with O-organization according to the temporal distances between propositions.

Figure 2.2 is a graphical representation of the curve showing where interconnection of propositions will be enhanced or inhibited across the five content aspects according to theoretical analysis and the corresponding curve showing increase or reduction of learning rate. The two curves correlate with r = .77 (the third and sixth columns in Table 2.2). Considering that interconnection of propositions merely refers to connective inferences and does not take into account other aspects of processing, this correlation is rather high.

From these findings it may be concluded that a specific type of text organization may increase learning rate for some content aspects whereas reducing it for others and that one important factor is the distance between semantically related propositions in the text.

A stronger influence of prior knowledge on learning rate was predicted for organization by aspect. Indeed, the correlation between prior knowledge and learning rate for the total text amounted only to r = .27 for the object group, whereas it reached r = .75 for the aspect group. Although the difference between the two correlations was not statistically significant owing to the few degrees of freedom, it nonetheless supports the assumption that processing rate depends more largely on prior knowledge with A-organization than with O-organization. If prior knowledge affects processing rate to different degrees in the two types of

TABLE 2.2

Average Learning Rates for Each Content Aspect and Average Distances
from the Proposition of Each Content Aspect to All Other Semantically
Related Propositions in the Rest of the Text for Both Groups

	Average Learning Rates			Average Distances Between Propositions		
	Object Group	Aspect Group	Ratio	Object- Organization	Aspect- Organization	Ratio
Theoretical foundations	5.06	3.65	.072	13.2	14.8	.89
Principle of treatment	3.26	3.79	1.16	12.6	17.3	.73
Nature of neurosis	1.85	1.86	1.01	24.1	25.2	.96
Problem of symptoms	1.76	3.01	1.71	12.7	7.7	1.65
Scientific orientation	2.60	2.52	.97	10.0	8.7	1.15

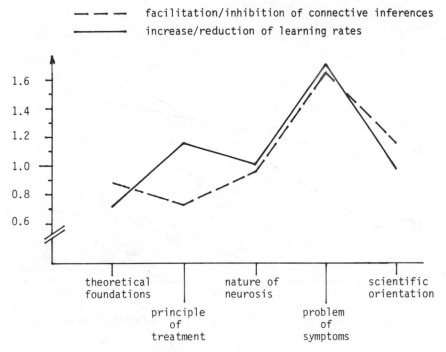

FIG. 2.2.   Predicted facilitation versus inhibition of connective inferences and increase versus reduction of learning rates with A-organization as compared to O-organization for each content aspect.

organization, the question may be asked how effectively learners with different prior knowledge may learn with these different text organizations.

Figure 2.3 shows the regression for the prediction of learning rates for total text from amount of prior knowledge in both groups. In accordance with the differential influence of prior knowledge on learning rate, the regression lines show an obvious interaction effect. With low prior knowledge, O-organization seemed to allow for more effective processing, whereas with high prior knowledge A-organization seemed to be of advantage. In line with our considerations so far, this finding could be interpreted as follows: With low prior knowledge the mental switches made necessary by A-organization require so much effort that the learner is severely hampered on the whole in working through the text. Thus, he/she will perform less processing operations during the same time than he/she would have done if his/her text had been organized by object, where processing would have been relatively smooth. To a learner with high prior knowledge, on the other hand, the repeated mental switches required by A-organization seem to create little difficulty, and the construction of a coherent mental representation of the two objects appears to be done as easily and as fast as with O-organization. In

Learning rates

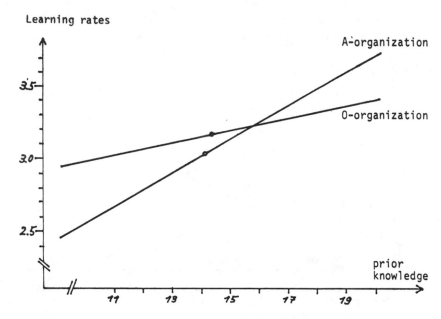

FIG. 2.3   Regression lines for the prediction of learning rates from prior knowledge in both groups.

addition, however, there is an advantage with respect to comparative processing, which is considerably facilitated due to the much smaller distances between the propositions that are to be compared in the text. The propositions to be compared having to be reactivated and, thus, encoded anew in memory—resulting in improved recall performance—the facilitation of comparative processing with A-organization should lead to an increase in learning rate compared to O-organization. For this reason, learners with high prior knowledge obtain higher learning rates with texts organized by aspect.

Distinctiveness of Knowledge Structures

It was assumed that the aspect group would make more comparisons between the two therapy types on the average and that it would therefore be better aware of the differences between them. The group was expected to construct a mental representation in which the two therapies would be more distinctive, i.e., better discriminated against each other than in the object group. This expectation was clearly supported. Using performance on the comparison task as an indicator of distinctiveness, the aspect group showed significantly higher means than the object group (see Table 2.1), averaging 5.30 correct while the latter scored 3.70 ($t = 1.99$; df = 18; $p < .05$). The result shows clearly that the process of concept-formation is affected by text organization. In sum, there is a difference between both types of organization not only in the way various propositions are stored and how well they are recalled; the propositions constructed in memory representation are also different in quality, namely different with respect to their distinctiveness.

SUMMARY

Taken altogether, the findings of this study suggest several things. As long as total reading time and total recall performance are considered alone, there seems to be little difference between the learning processes induced by the two types of text organization. Aspect organization has the tendency to improve recall performance on the average, at least a little, but it also takes somewhat longer reading time. A more detailed analysis showed that the two types of organization have processing demands that are distinctly different and influence learning processes accordingly. This results in different knowledge structures for both organization types, although the text content may be the same.

If a text is organized by object, attention is focused in particular upon the relations within the objects being described, i.e., emphasis lies on the way the information on one object interrelates. On the other hand, organization by aspect puts the emphasis on the relations between the objects, and, hence, their similarities and differences come into focus. On the average, organization by aspect induces more comparisons between the objects, leading to better conceptual differentiation (i.e., in the knowledge structure resulting from organization by aspect, the objects are better discriminated than with organization by object). The two types of organization also differ with respect to the effectiveness with which individual passages are learned. The construction of a coherent knowledge structure may be either hampered or facilitated for a specific part of the content depending on the type of organization that determines the distances between propositions that are semantically related. This results either in an increase or decrease of learning rate for specific paragraphs.

Another difference between the two types of organization resides in their *sensitivity* towards individual differences in learning prerequisites. With organization by aspect, processing rate is more strongly affected by the amount of prior knowledge than with organization by object, probably due to the frequencies with which *mental switches* from one object to the other have to occur. Learners with low prior knowledge seem to be favored by object-organization, which enables them to learn more effectively, the order of presentation allowing for smooth processing as the difficulty of repeated mental switches is avoided. For learners with high prior knowledge, however, learning appears to be more effective with organization by aspect as, for one thing, the frequent mental switches do not seem to bother them particularly and, furthermore, the fact that comparative processing is much easier than with object-organization comes to bear as an advantage.

Practical Implications

We may conclude from these findings that the question as to which of the two types of organization would have more positive effects on the learning process is put the wrong way. Neither the learning process nor the learning results may be said to be generally better or worse in one case or the other. They are merely *different*, i.e., better or worse from a particular point of view. Thus, one should ask for a particular content which type of organization would best be suited to reach a specific goal with a particular type of addressee. This is the only possible way to make well-founded decisions concerning the adequate type of organization for a particular purpose. It is not adequate, of course, to make definite suggestions concerning practical realization of texts on the basis of one study. To test these findings again and to gain more precise knowledge on the interplay of the various processing operations with both organization types, a number of further investigations with different contents, different groups of learners, and different learning prerequisites will be necessary. For example, it should be tested whether these findings would not only apply to free recall but also to cued recall. Another question worth studying is, whether the results significantly change after longer intervals between reading and recall. If, however, further studies should confirm the picture emerging from the present study, then the following practical suggestions would appear. If the objective is high readability and one merely wishes that the reader construct a coherent mental representation of the objects, organization by object should be recommended. If, however, similarities and differences between the objects should be analyzed in addition to their description, organization by aspect should be chosen, even though it requires more effort in processing and takes more time. From the viewpoint of economy of time and effectiveness, the interaction between text organization and individual learning prerequisites should be taken into account. With learners of high prior knowledge, aspect organization should be favored as it provides for relatively effective processing of both the description as well as the comparison between the objects presented in the text. If, on the other hand, learners' prior knowledge is rather poor, organization by object seems more adequate as more processing may be done during the same time interval, thus producing more effective learning, at least as far as pure description of objects is concerned. Another factor to keep in mind when deciding on a specific type of organization is that it will either facilitate or hamper processing of certain parts of the text content. Therefore, it will be necessary to analyze the interplay between type of organization and actual content in each case in order to find out which aspects benefit or are rendered more difficult by the organization type.

Research on the effects of various types of text organization on learning process is still at its beginnings. It appears from the present analysis that one should expect complex interactions between different processing demands and differential learning prerequisites leading to different consequences for the single components of processing and their interplay in the learning process. More detailed analysis of these interactions by research on learning from texts could provide a basis of orientation to the didactic problem of choosing the *right* text structure. In helping the practitioner to ask the right questions and in indicating which consequences may be expected when applying a specific type of organization to a specific group of learners, this research would prove useful in supporting practitioners' efforts to make better founded decisions concerning practical problems of text organization.

REFERENCES

Anderson, R. C. The notion of schemata and the educational enterprise. In R. C. Anderson, R. J. Spiro, & W. E. Montague (Eds.), *Schooling and the acquisition of knowledge*. Hillsdale, N.J.: Lawrence Erlbaum Associates, 1977.

Cermak, L. S., & Craik, F. I. M. (Eds.) *Levels of processing in human memory*. Hillsdale, N.J.: Lawrence Erlbaum Associates, 1979.

Craik, F. I. M., & Lockhart, R. S. Levels of processing. A framework for memory research. *Journal of Verbal Learning and Verbal Behavior*, 1972, *11*, 671–684.

DiVesta, F. J., Schultz, C. B., & Dangel, T. R. Passage organization and imposed learning strategies in comprehension and recall of connected discourse. *Memory and Cognition*, 1973, *1*, 471–476.

Eysenck, M. W. Levels of processing: A critique. *British Journal of Psychology*, 1978, *69*, 157–169.

Frase, L. T. Paragraph organization of written materials: The influence of conceptual clustering upon the level and organization of recall. *Journal of Educational Psychology*, 1969, *60*, 394–401.

Frase, L. T. Integration of written text. *Journal of Educational Psychology*, 1973, *65*, 252–261.

Frederiksen, C. H. Structure and process in discourse production and comprehension. In M. A. Just & P. A. Carpenter (Eds.), *Cognitive processes in comprehension*. Hillsdale, N.J.: Lawrence Erlbaum Associates, 1977.

Frederiksen, C. H., Frederiksen, J. D., Humphrey, F. M., & Ottesen, J. *Discourse inference: Adapting to the inferential demands of school texts*. Paper presented at the American Educational Research Association, Toronto, Canada, 1978.

Friedman, M. P., & Greitzer, F. L. Organization and study time in learning from reading. *Journal of Educational Psychology*, 1972, *63*, 609–616.

Graesser, A. C. How to catch a fish: The memory and representation of common procedures. *Discourse Processes*, 1978, *1*, 72–89.

Grimes, J. *The thread of discourse*. The Hague: Mouton, 1975.

Grimes, J. Narrative studies in oral texts. In W. U. Dressler (Ed.), *Current trends in textlinguistics*. Berlin, N.Y.: de Gruyter, 1978.

Jacoby, L. L., & Craik, F. I. M. Effects of elaboration of processing at encoding and retrieval: Trace distinctiveness and recovery of initial context. In L. S. Cermak & F. I. M. Craik (Eds.), *Levels of processing in human memory*. Hillsdale, N.J.: Lawrence Erlbaum Associates, 1979.

Kintsch, W. *The representation of meaning in memory.* Hillsdale, N.J.: Lawrence Erlbaum Associates, 1974.

Kintsch, W., & van Dijk, T. A. Toward a model of text comprehension and production. *Psychological Review,* 1978, *85,* 363–394.

Klein, K., & Saltz, E. Specifying the mechanism in a levels–of–processing approach to memory. *Journal of Experimental Psychology: Human Learning and Memory,* 1976, *2,* 671–679.

Lesgold, A. M., & Perfetti, C. A. Interactive processes in reading comprehension. *Discourse Processes,* 1978, *1,* 323–336.

McConkie, G. W. Learning from text. In L. S. Shulman (Eds.), *Review of research in education.* Itasca, Ill.: Peacock, 1977.

Meyer, B. J. F. *A selected review and discussion of basic research on prose comprehension.* Prose Learning Series, Research Report No. 4, Department of Educational Psychology, College of Education, Arizona State University, 1979.

Meyer, B. J. F. *Text structure and its use in the study of reading comprehension across the adult life span.* Paper presented at American Educational Research Association Convention in Boston, April 1980.

Myers, J. L., Pezdek, K., & Coulson, D. Effect of prose organization upon free recall. *Journal of Educational Psychology,* 1973, *65,* 313–320.

Perlmutter, J., & Royer, J. M. Organization of prose materials: Stimulus, storage, and retrieval. *Canadian Journal of Psychology,* 1973, *27,* 200–209.

Schultz, C. B., & DiVesta, F. J. Effects of passage organization and note taking on the selection of clustering strategies and on recall of textual materials. *Journal of Educational Psychology,* 1972, *63,* 244–252.

Spiro, R. J. Remembering information from text: The "state of schema" approach. In R. C. Anderson & R. J. Spiro (Eds.), *Schooling and the acquisition of knowledge.* Hillsdale, N.J.: Lawrence Erlbaum Associates, 1977.

Turner, A., & Greene, F. *Construction and use of a propositional text base.* Technical Report No. 63. Institute for the Study of Intellectual Behavior, University of Colorado, 1977.

van Dijk, T. A. *Macrostructures.* Hillsdale, N.J.: Lawrence Erlbaum Associates, 1980.

Walker, C. H., & Meyer, B. J. F. Integrating information from text: An evaluation of current theories. *Review of Educational Research,* 1980, 50, 421–437.

Appendix

EXPERIMENTAL TEXT VARIANTS

Text type: Organization by Aspect
Sequencing: (1) psychoanalysis and (2) behavior therapy

The general theoretical basis of psychoanalysis is Freud's personality theory. The model of personality assumed in this theory is based on conflict. Three personality instances are supposed to collide with each other: ID, EGO, and SUPER-EGO. ID represents the realm of impulses and needs, its energetic aspect supposedly consisting of an overall striving for pleasure called "libidinous energy". SUPER-EGO stands for the rules and prohibitions imposed by society. It aims at restricting the power of ID or, respectively, tries to direct the libidinous energy of ID into channels that are in keeping with social standards. EGO is responsible for the interaction with the external world and for conscious behavioral control. Its nature is determined—among other things—by the needs coming into consciousness from the ID and by the social standards emanating from SUPER-EGO. EGO tries to create a balance between the two opposing sides. If, in the course of psychological development very strong libidinous impulses are confronted with unrelenting prohibitions on the part of SUPER-EGO, EGO may fail to manage its mediating function. In this case, the needs threatening to overthrow the balance are repressed from consciousness. They may, however, continue to influence behavior by reappearing in the guise of other needs.

The general theoretical basis of behavior therapy is constituted by behavioristic learning theories. In these theories learning is considered as a process, by which the behavior of an organism (humans, animals) changes as a function of an environmental situation. They proceed on the assumption that behavior is determined by environmental cues: connections are supposed to exist between the stimuli of the environment (S) and the response of the organism (R). Learning occurs through changing these S-R connections. This change may be induced either by classical or operant conditioning. Classical conditioning presupposes the existence of some reflex-like S-R connections. Another stimulus S+ which so far has been "neutral" is presented together with stimulus S. After several repetitions S+, too, can elicit the response R. In other words, there has been created a new connection S+-R. In operant conditioning the organism finds itself in a new situation (i.e., stimulus condition S), which it does not consider optimal. The organism reacts to S by trying out several responses from its behavioral repertoire. If one response R has a successful outcome, this increases the probability that in the future the response R will occur under condition S.

The basic therapeutic principle in psychoanalysis consists in removing the psychological complex at the bottom of any neurosis. This is done via the therapist who helps to bring back into consciousness the original early experiences repressed into the unconscious and to relive them. Due to the importance attached to experiences of early childhood, psychoanalysis often concentrates on very remote events of the biography. The re-activation of suppressed experiences is supposed to offer a possibility of repeating the originally unsuccessful conflict of EGO with ID and with SUPER-EGO in a more constructive manner thus leading to the resolution of the psychological complex. Removal of the unconscious origins leads at the same time to the disappearance of the problematic neurotic behaviors.

The fundamental principle of treatment in behavior therapy is to resolve engrained inadequate S-R connections and to replace them by more adequate ones with the help of classical or operant conditioning. In the case of behaviors conflicting with the social standards of the culture in question, the therapist has the function of destroying the S-R connections at the basis of these behaviors and encouraging alternative behaviors that cause the extinction of the previous problem behavior. If a desirable behavior is merely lacking in specific situations he will have to develop corresponding ways of acting for this situation step-by-step. Treatment is confined to the behavioral habits exhibited by the patient in the present and dispenses with a far-reaching analysis of earlier experiences.

Neurotic behavior according to psychoanalysis is the result of repression. Its roots usually reach back into early childhood, during which "traumatic" (i.e., psychologically wounding) experiences occurred necessitating the repression of libidinous impulses and thus also increasing susceptibility for later traumatic experiences. The consequence of repression is the so-called psychological complex residing in the subconscious and being the actual cause of the neurotic disorder. This complex constitutes the pool of energy responsible for the symptomatic behavior and the persistence of the neurosis. For this reason, psychoanalysis aims at removing this psychological complex.

A neurotic disorder is considered by behavior therapy as a maladapted behavior that has its origins in a learning process. Behavior therapy proceeds on the

assumption that "neurotic" behavior is basically acquired along the same principles as "normal" behavior and that both kinds of behavior are amenable to
change via learning. Accordingly, the principles of learning theory may offer an
explanation for the conditions of origin as well as suggestions for the corresponding therapy methods. Therefore, behavior therapy may be considered as the
application of the principles of classical and operant conditioning from learning
theory to the realm of neurotic disorders.

Psychoanalysis considers neurotic problem behavior as a symptom of a deeper
unconscious psychological complex. For psychoanalysis symptoms represent the
visible discharges of some hidden unconscious causes. It is only by removing
these causes that the symptoms may be brought to extinction. According to
psychoanalysis, a therapy that merely attempts to remove the symptoms may be
quite successful for a limited period of time. But because the actual causes have
not been removed relapses occur after a while or it leads to "symptom shifts,"
that is, the appearance of new symptoms caused by the same psychological
complex.

According to behavior therapy, neurotic problem behavior does *not* represent
a symptom based on some deeper unconscious cause in the psyche of man. A
neurotic symptom is simply considered a maladapted behavioral habit resulting
from erroneous learning. Behavior therapy does not know of any neurosis "behind" the symptom, merely the neurotic symptom itself: if the symptom is
removed, the neurosis has disappeared, too. "Therapy of the symptom" of this
kind results in continuous improvement without danger of relapse or return of the
"same" neurosis in the guise of other symptoms, that is, of symptom shifts.

Psychoanalysis belongs in the main to a hermeneutic interpretative tradition of
science. It attempts to interpret the verbal statements of the patient on his/her
experiences and phantasies as a way of understanding the developmental history
of the neurotic disorder in retrospect. Psychoanalysis does not evaluate itself by a
concept of science based on experiment and prediction. Because its objective is
to therapy the overall personality (that means taking into account a greater
number of interacting factors) and because the psychoanalytical treatment usually lasts over several years, individual therapy goals can scarcely be determined
in advance. For this reason, too, it is difficult to objectively evaluate therapeutic
success.

Behavior therapy lies in the line of a scientific tradition based on experiment
and prediction and is rather sceptical towards hermeneutic interpretative approaches. On the basis of its fundamental learning theories, behavior therapy
may, by means of deduction, come to statements that are empirically testable.
Because behavior therapy confines itself to the extinction of problem behavior
and, hence, a well-defined objective, and because, furthermore, the therapy does
not take very long, the goals of the therapy are easy to determine beforehand.
This also creates the possibility of assessing successfulness with a fair degree of
objectivity.

Text type: Organization by Object
Sequencing: (1) psychoanalysis and (2) behavior therapy

The general theoretical basis of psychoanalysis is Freud's personality theory. The model of personality assumed in this theory is based on conflict. Three personality instances are supposed to collide with each other: ID, EGO, and SUPER-EGO. ID represents the realm of impulses and needs, its energetic aspect supposedly consisting of an overall striving for pleasure called ''libidinous energy''. SUPER-EGO stands for the rules and prohibitions imposed by society. It aims at restricting the power of ID or, respectively, tries to direct the libidinous energy of ID into channels that are in keeping with social standards. EGO is responsible for the interaction with the external world and for conscious behavioral control. Its nature is determined—among other things—by the needs coming into consciousness from the ID and by the social standards emanating from SUPER-EGO. EGO tries to create a balance between the two opposing sides. If, in the course of psychological development very strong libidinous impulses are confronted with unrelenting prohibitions on the part of SUPER-EGO, EGO may fail to manage its mediating function. In this case, the needs threatening to overthrow the balance are repressed from consciousness. They may, however, continue to influence behavior by reappearing in the guise of other needs.

The basic therapeutic principle in psychoanalysis consists in removing the psychological complex at the bottom of any neurosis. This is done via the therapist who helps to bring back into consciousness the original early experiences repressed into the unconscious and to relive them. Due to the importance attached to experiences of early childhood, psychoanalysis often concentrates on very remote events of the biography. The re-activation of suppressed experiences is supposed to offer a possibility of repeating the originally unsuccessful conflict of EGO with ID and with SUPER-EGO in a more constructive manner thus leading to the resolution of the psychological complex. Removal of the unconscious origins leads at the same time to the disappearance of the problematic neurotic behaviors.

Neurotic behavior according to psychoanalysis is the result of repression. Its roots usually reach back into early childhood, during which "traumatic" (i.e., psychologically wounding) experiences occurred necessitating the repression of libidinous impulses and thus also increasing susceptibility for later traumatic experiences. The consequence of repression is the so-called psychological complex residing in the subconscious and being the actual cause of the neurotic disorder. This complex constitutes the pool of energy responsible for the symptomatic behavior and the persistence of the neurosis. For this reason, psychoanalysis aims at removing this psychological complex.

Psychoanalysis considers neurotic problem behavior as a symptom of a deeper unconscious psychological complex. For psychoanalysis symptoms represent the visible discharges of some hidden unconscious causes. It is only by removing these causes that the symptoms may be brought to extinction. According to psychoanalysis, a therapy that merely attempts to remove the symptoms may be quite successful for a limited period of time. But because the actual causes have not been removed relapses occur after a while or it leads to "symptom shifts", that is, the appearance of new symptoms caused by the same psychological complex.

Psychoanalysis belongs in the main to a hermeneutic interpretative tradition of science. It attempts to interpret the verbal statements of the patient on his/her experiences and phantasies as a way of understanding the developmental history of the neurotic disorder in retrospect. Psychoanalysis does not evaluate itself by a concept of science based on experiment and prediction. Because its objective is to therapy the overall personality (that means taking into account a greater number of interacting factors) and because the psychoanalytical treatment usually lasts over several years, individual therapy goals can scarcely be determined in advance. For this reason, too, it is difficult to objectively evaluate therapeutic success.

The general theoretical basis of behavior therapy is constituted by behavioristic learning theories. In these theories learning is considered as a process, by which the behavior of an organism (humans, animals) changes as a function of an environmental situation. They proceed on the assumption that behavior is determined by environmental cues: connections are supposed to exist between the stimuli of the environment (S) and the response of the organism (R). Learning occurs through changing these S-R connections. This change may be induced either by classical or operant conditioning. Classical conditioning presupposes the existence of some reflex-like S-R connections. Another stimulus S+ which so far has been "neutral" is presented together with stimulus S. After several repetitions S+, too, can elicit the response R. In other words, there has been created a new connection S+-R. In operant conditioning the organism finds itself in a new situation (i.e., stimulus condition S), which it does not consider optimal. The organism reacts to S by trying out several responses from its behavioral repertory. If one response R has a successful outcome, this increases the probability that in the future the response R will occur under condition S.

The fundamental principle of treatment in behavior therapy is to resolve engrained inadequate S-R connections and to replace them by more adequate ones with the help of classical or operant conditioning. In the case of behaviors conflicting with the social standards of the culture in question, the therapist has the function of destroying the S-R connections at the basis of these behaviors and encouraging alternative behaviors that cause the extinction of the previous problem behavior. If a desirable behavior is merely lacking in specific situations he will have to develop corresponding ways of acting for this situation step-by-step. Treatment is confined to the behavioral habits exhibited by the patient in the present and dispenses with a far-reaching analysis of earlier experiences.

A neurotic disorder is considered by behavior therapy as a maladapted behavior that has its origins in a learning process. Behavior therapy proceeds on the assumption that "neurotic" behavior is basically acquired along the same principles as "normal" behavior and that both kinds of behavior are amenable to change via learning. Accordingly, the principles of learning theory may offer an explanation for the conditions of origin as well as suggestions for the corresponding therapy methods. Therefore, behavior therapy may be considered as the application of the principles of classical and operant conditioning from learning theory to the realm of neurotic disorders.

According to behavior therapy, neurotic problem behavior does not represent a symptom based on some deeper unconscious cause in the psyche of man. A neurotic symptom is simply considered as a maladapted behavioral habit resulting from erroneous learning. Behavior therapy does not know of any neurosis "behind" the symptom, merely the neurotic symptom itself: if the symptom is removed, the neurosis has disappeared, too. "Therapy of the symptom" of this kind results in continuous improvement without danger of relapse or return of the "same" neurosis in the guise of other symptoms, that is, of symptom shifts.

Behavior therapy lies in the line of a scientific tradition based on experiment and prediction and is rather sceptical towards hermeneutic interpretative approaches. On the basis of its fundamental learning theories, behavior therapy, may by means of deduction, come to statements that are empirically testable. Because behavior therapy confines itself to the extinction of problem behavior and, hence, a well-defined objective, and because, furthermore, the therapy does not take very long, the goals of the therapy are easy to determine beforehand. This also creates the possibility of assessing successfulness with a fair degree of objectivity.

3 Causal Cohesion and Story Coherence

Tom Trabasso
Tom Secco
Paul Van Den Broek
The University of Chicago

In reading or listening to narratives such as stories, what do children acquire? In terms of content, they may acquire knowledge about explanation, about human personal problem solving, about social interaction, about human intentionality, about feelings, about values, about morals, about myths, and about history. However, in order to acquire this knowledge, they must understand the individual events portrayed in the story, and they must organize and store these events in a memory representation. This representation allows them to retain the information and draw upon this knowledge for other purposes. The extent to which they find this prerequisite understanding and the construction of a representation easy to accomplish is directly dependent upon the coherence of the story in question. This coherence depends directly upon how potentially cohesive, logically and causally, the individual story events are to one another. The more cohesive the elements, the more easily the child will find *relationships between the events* and construct a coherent representation.

The attempt to understand an event is an attempt to discover the causes (the events producing it) and effects (the events resulting from it). Discovering the causes and tracing the consequences of events lead to an experience of a sequence rather than a disconnected series of events. This impression of connectivity extends to discourse where we interpret or generate a series of utterances about events that are related to one another in some manner.

Causal connections between events play a role in a variety of models for representing stories. Notably, the construction of causal event chains is central to Schank's (1975) (see also Lehnert, 1978) view of memory for narrative events and the kinds of causal connections identified by Schank were elaborated upon in taxonomies of inferences in discourse by Trabasso and his co-workers (Nicholas

83

& Trabasso, 1981; Trabasso, 1981; Trabasso & Nicholas, 1980; Warren, Nicholas, & Trabasso, 1979). In story grammars, the representation of the story was initially depicted by Rumelhart (1975) in terms of syntactic and semantic components. The syntax of the grammar involved categorization of events and a set of rewrite rules for combining and sequencing the events; the semantic component comprised the possible temporal, contiguous, and causal relations between categories. These components were synthesized in the models of Mandler and Johnson (1977), Stein and Glenn (1979), and Thorndyke (1977). Finally, the notion of causal chaining of events into sequences played a central role in two approaches to story representation, namely Black and Bower's (1980) model on state transition hierarchies and Omanson's (1982) decomposition of stories into goal–outcome sequences.

Although all of these approaches assume that causal relations existed, only Black and Bower (1980) and Omanson (1982) examined the implication for event memory of causal paths through the story. The problems with their approach lie mainly in the use of intuitive definitions of causation, the lack of explicit and logical criteria for deciding whether or not a causal relation exists between two events, and the absence of criteria for starting and ending the causal chain. Finally, the causal sequence of events in all of the aforementioned analyses is decidedly *linear* in time. However, an analysis of all possible causal relations is more likely to form networks rather than linear orders. Causes are frequently disjunctions of conjunctions of sufficient conditions rather than single causes (Mackie, 1980).

We shall, then, describe the process by which the comprehender uses causal reasoning to connect events, what memory representations result from this reasoning, and to test implications of these representations against data. To do this, we first define how causality and meaning are related. Then we sketch what features of a theory of causation seem to be needed in order to have formal criteria for judging the existence of a causal relation between two events. The definitions and criteria are drawn from writings on causation by legal theorists (Hart & Honore, 1959) and by philosophers (Mackie, 1980). Following our definition of causality, a general model for comprehension and inferences about event relations is sketched. The application of this analysis is then made to a set of stories used by Stein and Glenn (1979) in a study of children's comprehension and recall. Given a set of stories, first, the event relations for each story are found on judgmental and intuitive grounds. Then, they are tested using the logical criteria of necessity and sufficiency. Then, all the events are represented into a *causal network* with the conceptualizations of the events as nodes and the inferences are arcs. Given the causal network, a causal chain of the important events in the story is found, using criteria for opening, continuing, and closing the chain. Causal *cohesion* for a story is then quantified in terms of the percentage of events in the story that are contained in the causal chain. This measure of cohesion is then interpreted as a predictor of several sets of data obtained by

Stein and Glenn (1979), namely immediate and delayed recall of events, conditional probabilities of event recall, recall of events over stories that vary in causal cohesion, recall of story grammar categories, importance judgments on events, and answers to why questions.

COHESIVENESS, COHESION, AND COHERENCE

Causal cohesiveness of the events in a story is determined at the level of event meanings, where meaning includes both the underlying conceptualization of the event itself and the event's causal or logical relations to other events (Dewey, 1933/1963; Hospers, 1967). Events are states or actions, usually involving one predicate and its arguments. In the short term, linguistic cohesions such as anaphoric or catephoric reference and lexical co-reference (Halliday & Hasan, 1976; Kintsch & van Dijk, 1978) are assumed to be used by the comprehender to relate sentences, but their long-term connectivity is determined by whether or not an event can be causally inferred from another event, using world knowledge about the events. This inferential process leads to cohesion, namely the integration of the events into units. However, cohesion is local in that it deals with connectivity between subsets of events. Coherence, on the other hand, is a property of the whole in that the units or subsets themselves become interconnected.

CAUSALITY

Causal statements relating two events, A and B, are made in some context against a background that includes the construction by the comprehender of a *causal field* (Mackie, 1980). Cause and effect are seen as differences or changes within this field. Anything that is presupposed and often is unstated is a part of the circumstances. The causal field or a nexus of causal fields is generated by the comprehender mainly from setting statements that introduce protagonists, give background information, and provide information on location and time. However, any statement in the story can contribute information that results in changes in the causal field, for example, new information that tomorrow is someone's birthday. These possibly relevant factors of the causal field are referred to by the phrase, *in the circumstances*. The circumstances of the story form a possible world in the mind of the comprehender.

Once we determine a possible world, to say that A causes B means that A and B are changes that occurred such that A was necessary *in the circumstances* for B. When B occurs, A is necessary in the circumstances for B because if A did not occur, then B would not have occurred. This counter-factual reasoning constitutes a logical entailment of the comprehender's inferences that B is causally related to A and constitutes our formal criterion for judging that a relation between A and B is causal.

In Mackie's (1980) view, the distinguishing feature of a causal sequence is the combination of necessity-in-the-circumstances with causal priority. The core of the notion of causal priority is that the cause has prior existence to its potential effects. Causal priority is also associated with both necessity and sufficiency:

1. A is sufficient for B in the circumstances and causally prior to B provided that if A is put into the world in the circumstances and the world runs on from there, B will occur.

2. A is necessary in the circumstances for B and causally prior to B provided that if A were kept out of the world (in the circumstances referred to) and the world were allowed to run on from there, B would not occur.

MODEL FOR COMPREHENDING EVENTS AS CAUSAL RELATIONSHIPS

When the comprehender hears or reads a story, we suppose that he or she assumes one or more causal fields whose nexus serves as a possible world in which the story events can occur (similar views may be found in Collins, Brown, & Larkin, 1981; Wilensky, 1978). These causal fields, as indicated earlier, are mainly inferred from content contained in setting statements, although each event may alter the causal field by bringing in new relevant factors not previously anticipated (e.g., another protagonist does something to the main protagonist). When more than one causal field is established (e.g., birthday party, father, little girl), their intersection is found and establishes the background conditions or circumstances in which the story events (changes in states and actions) occur. The comprehender's task is now, like that of an historian (Fischer, 1970), to establish the facts and to order them into a causal chain. The comprehender sets up general expectations because he or she most often lacks knowledge about all the necessary and sufficient conditions to predict events; upon occasion, the necessary and sufficient conditions are known, and specific predictions are made. However, the comprehender is generally uncertain and waits for each event to be told before making causal inferences. Given a new, focal event, the comprehender instantiates an expectation by a backward inference from the focal event to those events that are causally prior to it. The processes of expectation, prediction, and instantiation are achieved by the comprehender's use of naive theories of psychological and physical causality (Wilks, 1977). This knowledge is sufficient to generate causal fields, that is, to specify the relevant factors and generate expectations. In the absence of such knowledge, the comprehender may use contiguity of events in space and time as a basis for making a causal inference (Mackie, 1980).

Once events are intersected as causal fields or have been instantiated by inferences, they become linked together into a causal network. This network serves as a representation of the story. Other representations can be derived from it, such as a causal chain (cf. Black & Bower's, 1980, critical path; Omanson's, 1982, causal–purposeful chain).

The comprehender determines which events enter into a causal chain by: (1) selecting statements that open the causal field; (2) tracing links between the causal field statements and subsequent events as long as links to other nodes exist (i.e., expectations continue and are instantiated); and (3) closing the field when there are no more new expectations, and prior expectations have been either instantiated or disconfirmed. At this point, the notion of story schema becomes useful. In the story grammars cited above, setting statements allow episodes to occur. This is analogous to our assumptions about how setting statements established causal fields and expectations. That is, they are used by the comprehender to establish the circumstances (assumed but unstated conditions) or possible world in which the story occurs.

The causal chain, then, is opened by setting statements that are causally linked to other statements. Then, once the nexus of these causal field statements is found, differences or changes in the causal field that occur can be explained causally in the circumstances. In the story grammars, there are usually initiating events such as actions on the part of others or nature towards the protagonist, changes in state or in perceptions by the protagonist. These events are more obviously *causal* than are setting statements and entail a cause versus condition contrast. Once events occur, however, they in turn establish expectations (or predictions) and are instantiated against other events. Goals express a desire to change one's state, are frequent in episodes where the protagonist's actions are under his control, and may often be the first event following causal field statements (Stein & Policastro, this volume). Because the pathways resulting from an event occur often in parallel through the network, some pathways may terminate while others continue. Those pathways that do not continue and that do not lead to goal satisfaction are regarded as "dead-end" (Schank, 1975) chains. Thus, we distinguish between events that are causal chain events and events that are dead-end. Causal chain events essentially focus on a series of explicit or overt goal-directed states, actions, and goal-attainment state changes; dead-end events are typically reasons for actions that are expressed as cognitions or goals, emotional reactions, or actions that have no further consequences. The identification of causal chain and dead-end events is a procedure by which the comprehender *edits* or revises the original causal network. This editing, though not necessarily conscious, deletes dead-end events and includes causal-chain events as a network representation for purposes of recall.

Once the episode is running, the question is: How does it end? Because the causal reasoning is driven by expectations, one answer is to stop when no further expectations occur. This does not suffice because some dead-end chains lead to no further expectations. Here, the basic episodic structure of the story grammars plays a role. The episode(s) (i.e., causal chain) ends when the desired state of change occurs or clearly fails. In most stories, goals are satisfied and when goal satisfaction occurs; the protagonist engages in no further action. Thus, consequences that entail goal satisfaction are identified for purposes of completing the chain. Goal failures usually result in further consequences, either to the protagonist or to others. These, however, establish further expectations that are not specified in the story. Here, we shall assume that the chain ends with the subsequent, overt consequences to others and to the protagonist, even though further expectations exist.

APPLICATION OF THE CAUSAL ANALYSIS

The above analysis was carried out on the four stories used by Stein and Glenn (1979). These stories are respectively summarized in Tables 3.1–3.4 and their respective causal inference networks are shown in Figs. 3.1–3.4.

The first step in the process is to identify causal field statements. These are,

TABLE 3.1
Text for Story 1: Epaminondas

	Stein-Glenn Category
1. Once there was a little boy	Major Setting
2. who lived in a hot country.	Minor Setting
3. One day his mother told him to take some cake to his grandmother.	Initiating Event
4. She warned him to hold it carefully	Initiating Event
5. so it wouldn't break into crumbs.	Initiating Event
6. The little boy put the cake in a leaf under his arm	Attempt
7. and carried it to his grandmother's.	Attempt
8. When he got there	Direct Consequence
9. the cake had crumbled into tiny pieces.	Direct Consequence
10. His grandmother told him he was a silly boy	Reaction
11. and that he should have carried the cake on top of his head	Reaction
12. so it wouldn't break.	Reaction
13. Then she gave him a pat of butter to take back to his mother's house.	Initiating Event
14. The little boy wanted to be very careful with the butter	Internal Response
15. so he put it on top of his head	Attempt
16. and carried it home.	Attempt
17. The sun was shining hard	Minor Setting
18. and when he got home	Direct Consequence
19. the butter had all melted.	Direct Consequence
20. His mother told him that he was a silly boy	Reaction
21. and that he whould have put the butter in a leaf	Reaction
22. so that it would have gotten home safe and sound.	Reaction

TABLE 3.2
Text for Story 2: The Tiger's Whisker

	Stein-Glenn Category
1. Once there was a woman	Major Setting
2. who needed a tiger's whisker.	Internal Response
3. She was afraid of tigers	Internal Response
4. but she needed a whisker	Internal Response
5. to make a medicine for her husband	Internal Response
6. who had gotten very sick.	Initiating Event
7. She thought and thought	Internal Response
8. about how to get a tiger's whisker.	Internal Response
9. She decided to use a trick.	Internal Plan
10. She knew that tigers loved food and music.	Internal Plan
11. She thought that if she brought food to a lonely tiger	Internal Plan
12. and played soft music	Internal Plan
13. the tiger would be nice to her	Internal Plan
14. and she could get the whisker.	Internal Plan
16. She went to a tiger's cave	Attempt
17. where a lonely tiger lived.	Minor Setting
18. She put a bowl of food in front of the opening to the cave.	Attempt
19. Then she sang soft music.	Attempt
20. The tiger came out	Attempt
21. and ate the food.	Direct Consequence
22. He then walked over to the lady	Attempt
23. and thanked her for the delicious food and lovely music.	Direct Consequence
24. The lady then cut off one of his whiskers	Direct Consequence
25. and ran down the hill very quickly.	Direct Consequence
26. The tiger felt lonely and sad again.	Reaction

as indicated previously, typically setting statements. In story 1, *Epaminondas*, the causal field is established by statements (1) and (2). The nexus of the causal field is given as an intersection (∩) between causal field statements, for example, (1) ∩ (2) in story 1 (see Fig. 3.1). In story 2, *The Tiger's Whisker*, statements (1), (3), (6), (10), and (17) are causal field statements that specify the protagonist, her state of fear of tigers, the state of her husband's health, and her knowledge about tigers' likes and needs. These establish conditions for much of the action in the story. In story 3, statement (16) provides a temporal information and intersects an event with a concurrent event. In story 4, the statements establish a birthday party (1) and the fact that the protagonist is a young girl (2).

We also have used the intersection (∩) symbol to link statements that were tautological to other statements or were continuations of concurrent events. In story 4, statement (7) is a continuation of (6), as is (18) a continuation of (17). In this sense, the relations *and* and *and then* are noted as noncausal.

Given the causal field statements that open the story, each of the subsequent statements is read in terms of whether it instantiates some expectation of the

TABLE 3.3
Text of Story 3: The Fox and Bear

	Stein-Glenn Category
1. There was a fox and a bear	Major Setting
2. who were friends.	Minor Setting
3. One day they decided to catch a chicken for supper.	Internal Response
4. They decided to go together	Internal Response
5. because neither one wanted to be left alone	Internal Response
6. and they both liked fried chicken.	Minor Setting
7. They waited until night time.	Attempt
8. Then they ran very quickly to a nearby farm	Attempt
9. where they knew chickens lived.	Internal Response
10. The bear, who felt very lazy	Internal Response
11. climbed up on the roof	Attempt
12. to watch.	Attempt
13. The fox then opened the door of the henhouse very carefully.	Attempt
14. He grabbed a chicken	Attempt
15. and killed it.	Direct Consequence
16. As he was carrying it out the henhouse	Initiating Event
17. the weight of the bear on the roof caused the roof to crack.	Initiating Event
18. The fox heard the noise	Initiating Event
19. and was frightened	Internal Response
20. but it was too late	Minor Setting
21. to run out.	Internal Response
22. The roof and the bear fell in	Direct Consequence
23. killing five of the chickens.	Direct Consequence
24. The fox and the bear were trapped in the broken henhouse.	Direct Consequence
25. Soon the farmer came out	Attempt
26. to see what was the matter.	Internal Response

previous statements. When an instantiation is found for a prior event, an arrow is drawn from the instantiating event back to the event that was causally prior to it. Thus, in story 1, the existence of the little boy sets up expectations such as that he has a mother. In (3), his mother tells him to do something. We are not given explicit reasons for her act, but we can infer them from (1), (3) → (1), because if the boy were not little, then his mother is not likely to tell him to do something. Likewise, if he didn't exist, then she couldn't tell him to do something. Little-ness seems to be a critical precondition. Statement (4) is inferred from (1) and (3) and (5), i.e., (4)↦(1), (4)↦(3) and (4)↦(5), because he is little, and may make a mistake, and she wants the cake to get there safely. If he wasn't little, wasn't capable of making mistakes, and if she didn't tell him to carry the cake to his grandmother's, she would not, in the circumstances, tell him to be careful with the cake. Statements (6) and (7) can be inferred from (3) because these are actions carrying out his mother's directive. Applying our criteria of necessity in circumstances and causal priority, we argue that (3) is necessary in the circumstances for (6) and (7), because if (3) did not occur then neither (6) or (7) would happen in the circumstances. That is, if the mother did not tell him to take the cake to the grandmother, then he would not have put it under his arm and carried it to the grandmother. Further, (3) is causally prior to (6) and (7) because the event of his mother telling him existed before the subsequent event of putting the cake under his arm and carrying it. Statement (6) established a specific set of expectations, one of which is (9), and (9) can be inferred from (6) because (9) would not have occurred if (6) did not happen. We have indicated in Fig. 3.1 the prediction as a double arrow relation, (6)↔(9). Statement (11) is inferred from (12) even though (12) occurs after (11) in the story because (12) contains the reasons for (11). If the reasons did not exist, (11) would not have happened in the circumstances. Given the full list of events and their relations, causal networks such as those depicted in Figs. 3.1–3.4 are then constructed.

The events in the causal chain are then identified by opening the causal field

TABLE 3.4
Text of Story 4: Judy's Birthday

	Stein-Glenn Category
1. Judy is going to have a birthday party.	Initiating Event
2. She is ten years old.	Major Setting
3. She wants a hammer and a saw for presents.	Internal Response
4. Then she could make a coat rack	Internal Response
5. and fix her doll house.	Internal Response
6. She asked her father	Attempt
7. to get them for her.	Internal Response
8. Her father did not want to get them for her.	Internal Response
9. He did not think that girls should play with a hammer and a saw.	Internal Response
10. But he wanted to get her something.	Internal Response
11. So he bought her a beautiful new dress.	Direct Consequence
12. Judy liked the dress	Internal Response
13. but she still wanted the hammer and the saw.	Internal Response
14. Later she told her grandmother about her wish.	Attempt
15. Her grandmother knew that Judy really wanted a hammer and a saw.	Internal Response
16. She decided to get them for her	Internal Response
17. because when Judy grows up	Internal Response
18. and becomes a woman	Internal Response
19. she will have to fix things	Internal Response
20. when they break.	Internal Response
21. Then her grandmother went out that very day	Attempt
22. and bought to tools for Judy.	Direct Consequence
23. She gave them to Judy that night.	Direct Consequence
24. Judy was very happy.	Reaction
25. Now she could build things with her hammer and saw.	Reaction

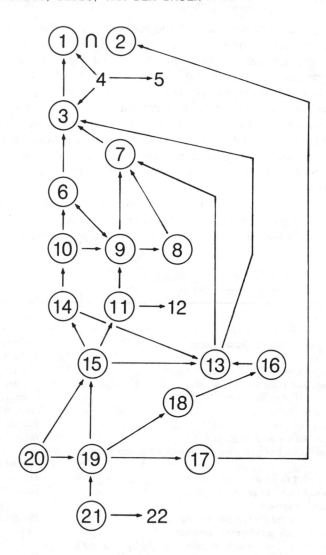

EPAMINONDAS

FIG. 3.1.   Causal inference network of story 1: Epaminondas

and tracing pathways to goal outcomes and their consequences to other protagonists or failed goal consequences. In story 1 both (1) and (2) are in the causal
field nexus and are in the chain because both lead to instantiated expectations that
continue until the field is closed. Statement (21) is a consequence of a failed
attempt and closes the field. From (1) and (2) through to (21), statement (4) is a

dead-end event, which has no instantiated expectations. Statements (5), (12), and (22) have no causes and are reasons for events on the chain.

It will be noted that dead-end events in the stories are: (1) unmotivated or uncaused reasons for events; (2) emotions; (3) cognitions; (4) minor settings such as temporal relations, which have no instantiated expectations, and consequences that are unrelated to the protagonist's goals. In order to get a sense of the causal chain as a story summary, read the circled events for each story.

In our analyses, two judges independently scored the event relations. For the four stories, 148 relationships were identified, and the two judges agreed on 92% of the judgments. Disagreements were resolved by discussion and application of logical necessity criteria.

IMPLICATIONS

Recall of Events

If the comprehender represents the story as a causal network of events and their relations and if events are separable into causal chains and dead-end paths, then

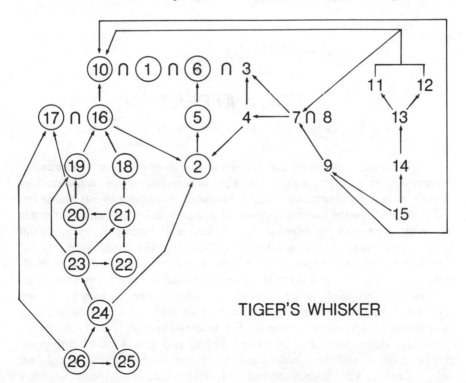

FIG. 3.2. Causal inference network of story 2: The Tiger's Whisker

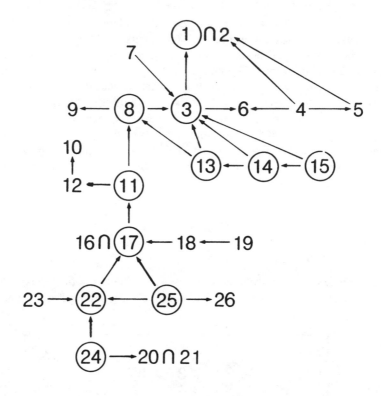

FOX AND BEAR

FIG. 3.3.   Causal inference network of story 3: The Fox and the Bear

one might expect events on the causal chain and/or those events with more causal connections, to be better recalled. These predictions follow from considerations of both encoding and retrieval. The likelihood of connecting events during encoding depends on the number of potential causal connections that an event has in the circumstances. In retrieval, the likelihood of finding an event should increase given more alternative pathways to the event. The causal chain expectations result from further operations upon the initial causal network. Here dead-end events are deleted and hence less likely to be entered into a new representation and are less likely to be recalled. In addition, causal chain events are expected to be better retained over time because they are consolidated into a more coherent representation than are the dead-end events.

In their study, Stein and Glenn (1979) had two groups of 12 fifth-grade children listen to and recall subsets of two different stories from the set of four analyzed above. The children recalled each story twice, once immediately after hearing the story and once one week later. We reanalyzed the recall for these

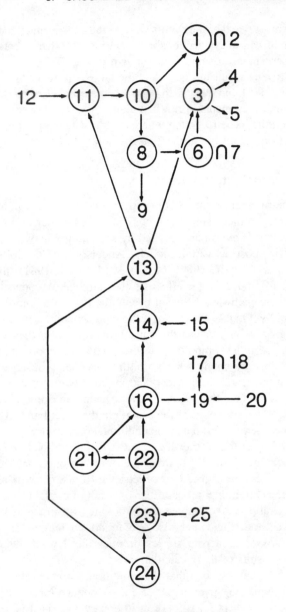

JUDY'S BIRTHDAY

FIG. 3.4. Causal inference network of story 4: Judy's Birthday

children in terms of whether the events were in the causal chain and as a function of the number of causal connections an event had to other events. These data, presented as percentages of recall, are shown in Fig. 3.5.

The most striking result in Fig. 3.5 is the large differences in recall between causal chain and dead-end events. In contrast, the number of causal connections lead only to small increments in recall. Finally, over the 1-week interval, dead-end events continue to be forgotten whereas almost no forgetting occurred over the 1-week period for events in the causal chain.

Conditional Probability Analyses

In Fig. 3.5, the number of causal connections that an event had to other events was a small factor in increasing recall compared to whether or not an event was in the causal chain. If events are recalled by searching a network through nodes as is assumed in most activation models (Anderson, 1976; Collins & Loftus, 1975; McKoon & Ratcliff, 1980; Ratcliff & McKoon, 1981), then we would have expected to find a larger effect of the number of connections between events. With more pathways between events, activation of more events should occur more rapidly. On the other hand, if the representation activated is primarily one containing only (or largely) the causal chain events, then the number of connections per se is less important. Rather, what is important is the fact that causal chain events are connected with both causes and consequences.

Suppose that the search is bi-directional in the network or in the causal chain representation. If so, then the likelihood of retrieving an event, given retrieval of its cause or consequence would be the same. On the other hand, if retrieval were from causes to consequences, then the conditional probability given retrieval of a cause would be higher than retrieval of a cause given retrieval of a consequence. Data from Black and Bern (1981) favor the bi-directional retrieval assumption.

In order to address these questions of retrieval from a network representation, we calculated the conditional probabilities of recall of causal chain and dead-end event pairs, as causes and consequences, for all the fifth-grade children across all stories and over both time intervals. We found no numerical differences of interest on these values across stories or over the 1-week delay. Table 3.5 summarizes the results of these calculations.

In Table 3.5, it can be seen that the conditional probabilities of recalling a cause (or a consequence) given recall of a consequence (or a cause) were independent in all cases except for pairs of dead-end events. That is, the conditional probabilities of recall were equal to the unconditional probabilities of recall for causes or consequences regardless of the pairs in the probability except when both events were dead-end. Here, the conditional probabilities were larger (the difference being about .22 on average). The latter result supports the assumption of retrieval from a network through causal paths; the former results do not.

One reason why there were no effects of single causal connections in Table 3.5 for the first three pairs of events is that there are multiple pathways by which

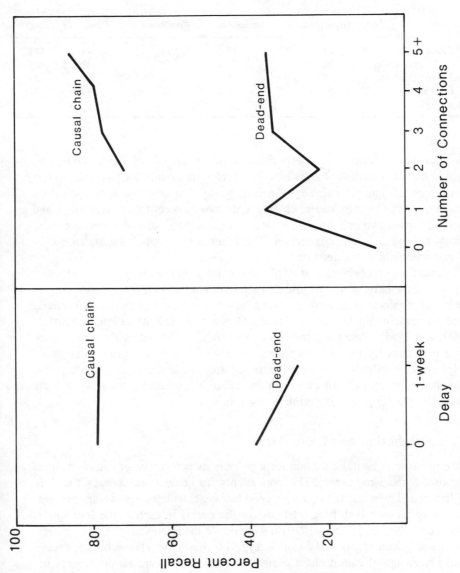

FIG. 3.5. Recall of causal chain and dead-end events over time and as a function of causal connections

TABLE 3.5
Probabilities of Recall

Event Pair	Consequence/ Given Cause	Consequence	Cause/Given Consequence	Cause	Number of Pairs
Both Causal Chain	.81	.79	.79	.78	144
Dead End-Causal Chain	.76	.74	.43	.42	24
Causal Chain-Dead End	.38	.41	.74	.79	25
Both Dead End	.59 — * — .36		.52 — * — .32		31

*p < .05

one can access most events, especially those on the causal chain. Thus, one would have to conditionalize events on all adjacent connections in order to test for effects of multiple pathways. In fact, to say that an event is on the causal chain does this because causal chain events have, except for some settings and consequences, two or more connections whereas the dead-end events are more likely to have only one connection. The latter is reflected in the higher conditional probabilities for dead-end events.

Conditional probabilities of single-link pairs would not seem to be sufficient to resolve the issue of the specific characteristics of the representation used in the retrieval of information. Rather, a more sensitive indicator of causal connectivity and retrieval might be retrieval time (McKoon & Ratcliff, 1980; Ratcliff & McKoon, 1981). Here the retrieval of an event is facilitated by the prior activation of a causally related event. Using the prior event as a prime, one could explore the facilitation effect on retrieval for causal chain events where the distance between pairs of events in the chain is a predictor variable. We are currently planning such experiments on this issue.

Causal Cohesion and Story Recall

One measure of causal cohesion for a story is its percentage of causal chain as opposed to dead-end events. The more events that lie on a causal chain, the more coherent and memorable the story should be. We calculated the average percentage of recall over both time intervals for the events in each of the four stories studied by Stein and Glenn (1979) and examined the relationships to the percentage causal chain events in the stories. Fig. 3.6 shows the relation between recall and percentage of causal chain events. Because there were no differences between the slopes for immediate and delayed recall, Fig. 3.6 reports the average of the two kinds of recall.

The data show a striking linear relation between recall and the percentage of causal chain events. Memorability of a story does depend on causal cohesion among its events.

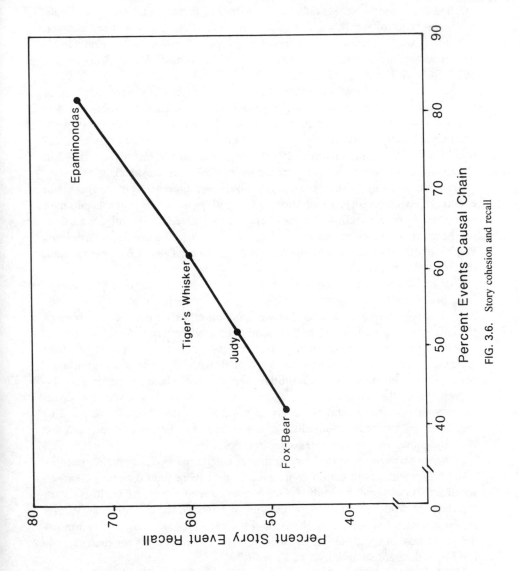

FIG. 3.6. Story cohesion and recall

99

Recall of Story Grammar Categories

One well-established fact is that certain story grammar categories are better recalled than others. Across cultures, variation in literacy and the ages of subjects, the order of recall, from high to low, is setting, consequence, attempt, initiating event, reaction, and internal response (Mandler & Johnson, 1977; Mandler, Scribner, Cole, & DeForest, 1980; Nezworski, Stein, & Trabasso, 1982; Stein & Glenn, 1979).

One possible explanation is that the categories contain different numbers of events that are in the causal chain, and therefore, those categories that are best recalled contain a greater proportion of causal chain events; those less well-recalled contain proportionately more dead-end events. We tested this explanation by using Stein and Glenn's (1979) categorization for each event (listed in Tables 3.1–3.4), identifying whether the event was in the causal chain or was on a dead-end pathway in the network and found the proportion of causal chain events for each category. In addition, we found the proportion of causal chain versus dead-end connections for the events in each category. Finally, we calculated the proportion of events recalled in each category. Figure 3.7 summarizes graphically the comparisons between these proportions; Table 3.6 shows the rank orders of the proportions for the categories.

Figure 3.7 shows strikingly similar patterns of recall and causal chain proportions over the set of categories. Table 3.6 shows near perfect rank–order correlations. An event being in the causal chain accounts equally well as the number of causal chain connections for the frequently reported pattern of category recall.

Although one might be tempted to view this account as critical of story grammar approaches, it should be noted that aspects of the story grammars correspond to elements of the definition of the causal chain. In particular, the beginnings of the sequence used to open the causal field and start the chain correspond to settings, and those events used to end the chain correspond to consequences and/or reactions. In addition, as noted earlier, causal relations are used by grammars to order categories into episodes.

If the patterns of recall for story grammar categories were solely the result of different percentages of causal chain events, then there should be no pattern of recall across categories when the events contained within them are exclusively on the chain or dead-end. In order to test this, we divided the fifth graders' recalls into immediate and delay conditions, and for each kind of recall, we examined the percentage of recall for causal chain versus dead-end events for each category. These data are summarized in Table 3.7.

Table 3.7 reveals several facts of interest. First, within each category for both types of recall delay, causal chain events are recalled far better than dead-end events. However, even though the events are equated on criteria of being in the causal chain, there appears to be a pattern of recall similar to that reported so frequently in the literature, namely: settings, direct consequences, initiating

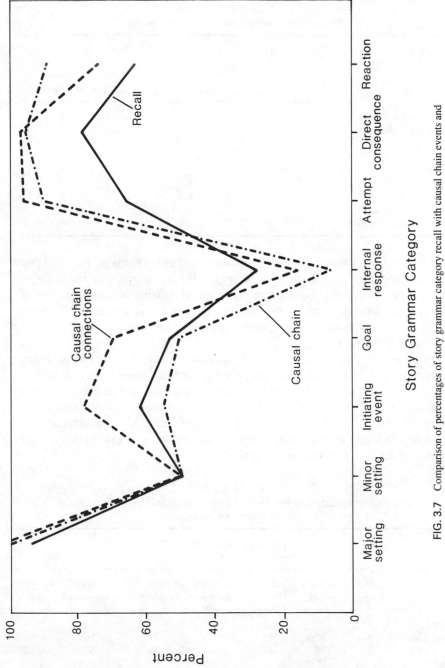

FIG. 3.7 Comparison of percentages of story grammar category recall with causal chain events and connections

TABLE 3.6
Rank Order Predictions of Category Recall

		Rank	
Category	Recall	Proportion Causal Chain	Proportion Causal Connections
Major Setting	1	1	1
Direct Consequence	2	2	2
Attempts	3	3.5	3
Initiating Event	4.5	5	4
Reactions	4.5	3.5	5
Goals	6	6.5	6
Minor Setting	7	6.5	7
Internal Response	8	8	8
Correlation with Recall		.98	.99

events, reactions, attempts, internal responses, and minor settings. For dead-end events, this pattern is not as striking except for direct consequences and settings. Thus, certain categories of events are better recalled than others, independent of their causal network status. Omanson (1982) has found category effects on recall, importance ratings, and summaries where he controlled for causal connectivity of events.

Those events that are well-recalled, however, share the property of being overt, complete, imaginable states and actions, whereas those events that are less well-recalled seem to be less complete, less imageable, internal states or enabling actions. Data is currently being collected on the imagery or concreteness of the statements in order to see if this factor contributes to their recallability. However, lacking such information, there are story category effects that are not accounted for by the causal model analysis.

TABLE 3.7
Story Grammar Category Recall for Causal Chain and Dead-End Events
(Fifth-Grade Children)

	Probability of Recall Story Grammar Category						
Recall-Type	Major Setting	Minor Setting	Initiating Event	Internal Response	Attempt	Direct Consequence	Reaction
Immediate							
Causal Chain	.94	.67	.83	.73	.74	.86	.81
Dead End	.67	.36	.42	.36	.21	.67	.28
Delay							
Causal Chain	.94	.75	.83	.68	.68	.84	.76
Dead End	.33	.25	.27	.27	.17	.58	.31

The data in Table 3.7 indicate that those events that define the causal field, open the chain, and close it are the most memorable. Hence, the important story grammar categories are included in the critical assumptions about causal chains.

Importance of Events

One goal of teaching comprehension is that children learn to identify "main ideas" (Baker & Stein, 1981). Stein and Glenn (1979) asked the children in a second experiment to tell them what was most important, then, what was next important, and then, what was next most important in the story. They report their data (their Table 7, p. 104) in terms of the proportion of children reporting events as categorized by their grammar. In order to predict these data, we calculated a weighted average of importance for each category by ranking the order of importance requests, 1, 2, and 3, and multiplying each rank by the proportion of children offering that category as important to the request. Then, the rank order of these weighted values was found for the categories. We then found the percentage of causal chain events in each category and ranked them. The two sets of ranks are shown in Table 3.8.

The rank order correlation between the ranks in Table 3.8 is .95. Thus, in judging the importance of an event in a story, children make use of their knowledge as to which events lie on the causal chain. The reason that major goals are most important is that they are always on the causal chain (hence the name *major*). They also tend to have more causal connections. Similarly, most consequences are on the causal chain. In contrast, many reactions and *minor* settings are dead-end events. The intuition that something is important must reflect the meaning of an event in terms of its causal connectivity with other events.

Answering Why Questions

The causal network may be used to provide a basis for determining answers to why questions. Why questions generally request an explanation for an event. In

TABLE 3.8
Predictions of Importance Ratings

Category	Rank	
	Importance	*Percent Causal Chain*
Major Goals	1	1
Direct Consequences	2	2
Attempts	3	3
Initiating Events	4	5
Reactions	5	4
Minor Settings	6	6

causal chain theories (Lehnert, 1978; Trabasso, 1981), they ask for an antecedent cause(s) for the event contained in the question.

Stein and Glenn (1979), in their second experiment, asked a number of why questions on statements contained in each story. The why questions were administered after the requests for important events. They reported their data as probability distributions of categories in response to questions on four types of categories: internal responses, attempts, direct consequences, and reactions. The original data in terms of particular events given as answers were unavailable (Stein, personal communication). Despite the absence of exact answers, we attempted to predict the categorized data using the causal network representations in Fig. 3.1–3.4.

With reference to story 1, *Epaminondas,* consider the question, "Why did the butter melt?" This question focusses on node (19) for the statement, "the butter had all melted." What the comprehender does, in our view, is first to access the conceptualization expressed in the question (e.g., node (19)). Then, he traces the causes via the inference arcs back to events that are causally prior to the queried conceptualization. In the example, nodes (15), (17), and (18) are found. The comprehender then examines the conceptualization stored at each node and decides whether or not the conceptualization is a cause or an enabling condition because the latter more properly answers how or when questions rather than why questions (see Lehnert, 1978; Nicholas & Trabasso, 1981). Thus, (18), "when he got home" is not given as an answer because this is an enablement. The conditions that are jointly necessary and sufficient in the circumstances are (15), "he put it on top of his head," and (17), "the sun was shining hard." These nodes contain, therefore, causal antecedents and are generated as answers. The general rule is to trace prior causes; if the immediate condition is an enablement, continue the trace. If it is a causally prior condition, generate it as a causal answer. In Stein and Glenn's (1979) terms, a why question on a direct consequence (19) is answered by a minor setting (17) and an attempt (15). We followed this procedure for each of the 48 why questions asked by Stein and Glenn. Two questions were on initiating events, whose data are not reported by Stein and Glenn, and two questions on internal responses could not be answered by content expressed in the story. For the remaining questions, we found the probability distributions of categorized answers for each of the four types queried. Table 3.9 shows the results of these calculations.

The *fit* of the predicted to the observed answer distributions is reasonable given the fact that we are not predicting exact but categorized answers. Further, Stein and Glenn included answers outside the stories (Stein, personal communication), and these were frequently "internal responses" or goals. Our main failure is to predict the higher proportion of internal responses, precisely those categorized responses that were often not in the original story. To the extent we achieved a fit here, the data indicate that these children agreed with our judgments as to causal antecedents. A more proper test of the analysis, however, awaits data on exact rather than categorized responses.

TABLE 3.9
Observed (and Predicted) Proportion Responses to Why Questions

	Category Probed			
Response Category	Internal Response	Attempt	Direct Consequence	Reaction
Setting	.07 (.07)	.01 (.00)	.13 (.00)	.00 (.00)
Initiating Event	.10 (.27)	.19 (.13)	.09 (.17)	.00 (.00)
Internal Response	.40 (.20)	.55 (.33)	.30 (.33)	.00 (.00)
Attempt	.00 (.07)	.00 (.07)	.00 (.08)	.04 (.25)
Direct Consequence	.00 (.00)	.10 (.13)	.13 (.25)	.52 (.50)
Reaction	.00 (.07)	.12 (.27)	.00 (.00)	.15 (.00)
IE + IR	.16 (.13)	.03 (.00)	.06 (.00)	.00 (.00)
IR + IR	.23 (.13)	.00 (.00)	.20 (.08)	.00 (.00)
DC + A	.00 (.00)	.00 (.00)	.03 (.00)	.29 (.25)
IR + Setting	.04 (.07)	.00 (.00)	.02 (.08)	.00 (.00)
A + Setting	.00 (.00)	.00 (.07)	.04 (.00)	.00 (.00)
Number	? (15)	? (15)	? (12)	? (4)

Developmental Comparisons

Stein and Glenn (1979) also collected data on first grade children (average age 6 years). We were able to obtain only the original delayed recall data on these children for purposes of comparison. For the most part, all of the previous findings were replicated on the first graders with some age-related differences of degree rather than kind.

First, we examined delayed recall for causal chain and dead-end events as a function of both grade levels. These data are depicted in Table 3.10.

The data in Table 3.10 replicate those in Fig. 3.5 with respect to type of event and causal connectivity. For both groups, causal chain events are recalled far more often than dead-end events, regardless of the number of connections. When events have two or more connections, recall increases with increases in the

TABLE 3.10
First- and Fifth-Grade Children's Recall: 1-Week Delay

	Probability of Recall					
	Number of Connections					
Type-Grade	0	1	2	3	4	5+
Causal Chain						
First	—	—	.53	.62	.66	.69
Fifth	—	—	.71	.75	.79	.82
Dead End						
First	.08	.31	.17	.19	—	.29
Fifth	.00	.30	.18	.32	—	.33

number of connections. The difference between causal chain and dead-end events does not seem to increase much with age. Such an increase might have been expected if one assumes that the older children were better able to use causal chain criteria. This does not seem to be the case. The difference is mainly that the older children recall more than do the younger ones, a well-known finding.

We compared the first and fifth graders in delayed recall across the four stories in terms of percentage of causal chain events and replicated the findings in Fig. 3.6. The age comparison data are reported in Table 3.11.

Of interest in Table 3.11 is that the first grade children showed a smaller effect of causal cohesion than did the fifth graders. These data, together with those in Table 3.10, suggest that both age groups were good at determining local cause/consequence relations (see also Trabasso, Stein, & Johnson, 1981), but that the fifth graders were more able to integrate more of these relations into a coherent representation. This could result from differences in working memory capacity or speed of processing independent of knowledge about psychological and physical causality.

We examined the first graders' delayed recall for story grammar categories and found that their pattern of recall correlated highly ($\rho = .97$) with their fifth grade counterparts. These recalls are reported in Table 3.12.

Likewise, with two interesting exceptions, the first grade children showed a similar pattern of recall to the fifth graders when the causal chain versus dead-end dichotomy was imposed. Table 3.13 gives the first grade data.

Comparing Tables 3.7 and 3.13, one can see that for causal chain events, both age groups show better recall for settings, consequences, and initiating events. However, the first graders do not show as good relative recall on internal states and reactions. For the fifth graders, the difference averages .15; for the first graders, it averages .31. These differences could result from differences in understanding and reporting of internal states and reactions, such as emotions (Gnepp, Klayman, & Trabasso, 1981; Schwartz & Trabasso, 1983). However, the present analyses do not allow us much further understanding as to why these

TABLE 3.11
Delayed Recall Across Stories

Story	Percent Causal Chain Events	Grade	
		First	Fifth
Fox-Bear	.42	.45	.43
Judy	.52	.44	.47
Tiger	.62	.46	.62
Epaminondas	.82	.52	.73

TABLE 3.12
Story Category Recall:
1-Week Delay

	Grade	
Category	First	Fifth
Major Setting	.72	.94
Minor Setting	.32	.50
Initiating Event	.50	.58
Goal	.35	.50
Internal Response	.26	.28
Attempt	.56	.63
Direct Consequence	.62	.71
Reaction	.39	.61

categories are omitted more often by the younger children. It is possible that the older children are able to connect more necessary and sufficient conditions with emotional responses than are the younger children because of more sophisticated knowledge about causal antecedents of emotions as well as knowledge of emotion terms. Evidence supporting this claim comes from Stein and Glenn (1979), who found that the younger children answered why questions on internal responses and reactions as well as the older children but that the older children gave more events as answers.

CONCLUDING REMARKS

In overview, we have shown that an analysis of the causal relations among narrative events provides a good account of a range of variables in story under-

TABLE 3.13
First Grade Category Recall for Causal Chain and Dead-End Events After 1-Week Delay

	Probability of Recall						
	Story Grammar Category						
	Major Setting	Minor Setting	Initiating Event	Internal Response	Attempt	Direct Consequence	Reaction
Event Type							
Causal Chain	.92	.36	.73	.43	.67	.68	.50
Dead End	.42	.28	.21	.24	.17	.75	.17

standing and recall. Using notions of causality from philosophy and the law, knowledge of physical and psychological causality, abstract knowledge of the concept of a story, and general process models of story understanding, we have shown how people might generate causal network and causal chain representations, which could be used in retelling stories, determining important events, and answering why questions. We found that events that were in a causal chain were recalled and retained over one week better than events that lacked causes or consequences. We found that the coherence of a story and its memorability were related directly when we defined coherence in terms of the percentage of events on the causal chain. We found that recall of events increased as the number of connections an event had increased, although this factor was of lesser value than being on the causal chain. When we examined conditional recall, the results showed that being on the causal chain overrode any single causal-link effects. Further patterns of story category recall were correlated with patterns of events being in the causal chain. However, these patterns remained to a lesser degree when we matched story categories for events in the causal chain. We noted, however, that those events that define the causal chain, open the field, and end the chain are best recalled. Goals, which have the most causal chain consequences, however, were most important in judgments. Finally, developmental comparisons between 6- and 10-year-old children indicated that all of the conclusions held for both age groups.

These analyses and data attest to the importance of constructing causal chains in understanding narratives, as was first anticipated most explicitly by Schank (1975). One is tempted to treat the causal episodic structure as a representational unit in memory. This structure arises from a general consideration of viewing story understanding in terms of an attempt by the comprehender to infer relations among events in terms of human goals and purposes. Given the similarity between children of different ages, these abilities develop early.

The issue of unique identifiability of our causal representation must be raised (Yekovich, 1982) lest we leave readers with the impression that we believe that the causal representation is uniquely identifiable. We do not. In the process of constructing a cohesive representation of events, the comprehender must make a number of bridging inferences that do not depend upon causal relations (see Nicholas & Trabasso, 1981, for a taxonomy of such inferences). Among these could be those identified as lexical coreference, which make up a large part of the propositional argument overlap or repetition measure of coherence in Kintsch and van Dijk's (1978) system of representation. These alternative representations may be contrasted in predictions on primed reaction times to verify the truth or falsity of statements taken from the stories after subjects have read them. That is, although cohesive devices, lexical coreference, and argument overlap may all contribute to comprehension, the enduring memory representation may be more closely akin to that identified in the present analysis.

In the teaching of comprehension of written discourse, teachers and basal readers (Baker & Stein, 1981; Johnson & Barrett, 1981; Pearson & Johnson, 1978) emphasize the identification of main or important ideas, the verification or recall of facts in the story, the temporal sequencing of events, and the discovery of cause-effect relations. Of these, the latter seems to be most critical because, as we have shown, all the others may be derived from the causal network and causal chain representations. There are two implications of this argument. Instruction or assessment of causal reasoning about events (why, how, what happened, when, etc.) either may promote or diagnose reading comprehension (and subsequent operations such as recall, judgments, and other evaluative or implicational reasoning). Hence teachers and basal readers should give more emphasis to and provide more systematic questioning of causal relations either during or after reading sections of text (cf. Trabasso, 1981). In addition, the explicit coherence of a story, especially for young readers, should be a primary goal of writers of stories. By this we mean clear, ordered statements of the events so that the events *per se* are readily understood, and their causal relations are easily inferred from the surface order of events. This also means that causal sequences should not be disrupted by introduction of new and irrelevant causal fields or chains or by descriptive detail that is unnecessary to the current chain. Such writing requires the writer to pose questions to him or herself on the logical necessity for events in relation of other events. Beck's and her colleagues' (Beck, McKeown, McCaslin, & Burkes, 1979) analyses of basal readers give examples from basal readers that fail to meet one or more of these strictures.

ACKNOWLEDGMENTS

The writing and research reported in this chapter was supported by funds from the Benton Foundation, by National Institute of Education Grant NIE-G-79-0125 and the Spencer Foundation to T. Trabasso. We wish to thank Karl Kilgore for his assistance in computer programming. We also wish to thank Reid Hastie, Robin Hogarth, and Nancy Stein for their constructive comments on an earlier draft of this chapter. In addition, we are indebted to Nancy Stein for providing us with the original recall protocols of the Stein and Glenn (1979) study and for her advice and suggestions throughout the course of the development of this chapter. A paper based on the research reported herein was read as a Division C Invited Address by the first author at the annual meetings of the American Educational Research Association, March, 1982, in New York City.

REFERENCES

Anderson, J. R. *Language, memory, and thought*. Hillsdale, N.J.: Lawrence Erlbaum Associates, 1976.

Baker, L., & Stein, N. L. The development of prose comprehension skills. In C. M. Santa & B. L. Hayes (Eds.), *Children's prose comprehension: Research and practice*. Newark, Del.: International Reading Association, 1981.

Beck, I. L., McKeown, M. G., McCaslin, E. S., & Burkes, A. M. Instructional dimensions that may affect reading comprehension: Examples from two commercial reading programs. Pittsburgh: University of Pittsburgh, Learning Research and Development Center, 1979 (LRDC Publication 1979/20).

Black, J. B., & Bower, G. H. Story understanding as problem solving. *Poetics*, 1980, *9*, 223–250.

Black, J. B., & Bern, H. Causal coherence and memory for events in narratives. *Journal of Verbal Learning and Verbal Behavior*, 1981, *20*, 267–275.

Collins, A. M., Brown, J. S., & Larkin, K. Inference in text understanding. In R. J. Spiro, B. C. Bruce, & W. F. Brewer (Eds.), *Theoretical issues in reading comprehension*. Hillsdale, N.J.: Lawrence Erlbaum Associates, 1981.

Collins, A. M., & Loftus, E. F. A spreading activation theory of semantic processing. *Psychological Review*, 1975, *82*, 407–428.

Dewey, J. How we think. In R. M. Hutchins & M. J. Adler (Eds.), *Gateway to the great books* (Vol. 10). Chicago, ILL.: Encyclopedia Britannica, 1963 (Originally published by Heath, 1933).

Fischer, D. H. *Historians' fallacies: Toward a logic of historical thought*. New York: Harper & Row, 1970.

Gnepp, J., Klayman, J., & Trabasso, T. The use of personal, normative, and situational information to infer emotional reactions. *Journal of Experimental Child Psychology*, 1981, *33*, 111–123.

Hart, H. L. A., & Honore, A. M. *Causation in the law*. Oxford: Clarendon Press, 1959.

Halliday, M. A. K., & Hasan, R. *Cohesion in English*. London: Longman, 1976.

Hospers, J. *Introduction to Philosophical analysis*. Englewood Cliffs, N.J.: Prentice-Hall, 1967.

Johnson, D. D., & Barrett, T. C. Prose comprehension: A descriptive analysis of instructional practices. In C. M. Santa & B. L. Hayes (Eds.), *Children's prose comprehension: Research and practice*. Newark, Del.: International Reading Association, 1981.

Kintsch, W., & van Dijk, T. A. Toward a model of text comprehension and production. *Psychological Review*, 1978, *85*, 363–394.

Lehnert, W. G. *The process of question answering*. Hillsdale, N.J.: Lawrence Erlbaum Associates, 1978.

Mackie, J. L. *The cement of the universe:* A study of causation. Oxford: Clarendon Press, 1980.

Mandler, J. M., & Johnson, N. S. Remembrance of things parsed: Story structure and recall. *Cognitive Psychology*, 1977, *9*, 111–151.

Mandler, J. M., Scribner, S., Cole, M., & DeForest, M. Cross-cultural invariance in story recall. *Child Development*, 1980, *51*, 19–26.

McKoon, G., & Ratcliff, R. Priming in item recognition: The organization of propositions in memory for text. *Journal of Verbal Learning and Verbal Behavior*, 1980, *19*, 369–386.

Nezworski, T., Stein, N. L., & Trabasso, T. Story structure versus content in children's recall. *Journal of Verbal Learning and Verbal Behavior*, 1982, *21*, 196–206.

Nicholas, D. W., & Trabasso, T. Towards a taxonomy of inference. In F. Wilkening, J. Becker, & T. Trabasso (Eds.), *Information integration by children*. Hillsdale, N.J.: Lawrence Erlbaum Associates, 1981.

Omanson, R. C. The relation between centrality and story category variation. *Journal of Verbal Learning and Verbal Behavior*, 1982, *21*, 326–337.

Pearson, P. D., & Johnson, D. D. *Teaching reading comprehension*. New York: Holt, Rinehart, & Winston, 1978.

Ratcliff, R., & McKoon, G. Does activation really spread? *Psychological Review*, 1981, *88*, 454–462.

Rumelhart, D. E. Notes on a schema for stories. In D. G. Bobrow & A. Collins (Eds.), *Representation and understanding: Studies in cognitive science*. New York: Academic Press, 1975.

Schwartz, R. M., & Trabasso, T. Children's understanding of emotions. In C. Izard, J. Kagan, & R. Zajonc (Eds.), *Emotions, cognition, and behavior*. Cambridge, England: Cambridge University Press, 1983.

Schank, R. C. The structure of episodes in memory. In D. G. Bobrow & A. Collins (Eds.), *Representation and understanding: Studies in cognitive science*. New York: Academic Press, 1975.

Stein, N. L., & Glenn, C. G. An analysis of story comprehension in elementary school children. In R. O. Freedle (Ed.), *New directions in discourse processing*. Hillsdale, N.J.: Lawrence Erlbaum Associates, 1979.

Thorndyke, P. W. Cognitive structures in comprehension and memory of narrative discourse. *Cognitive Psychology*, 1977, *9*, 77–110.

Trabasso, T. On the making of inferences during reading and their assessment. In J. T. Guthrie (Ed.), *Comprehension and teaching: Research reviews*. Newark, Del.: Internationational Reading Association, 1981.

Trabasso, T., & Nicholas, D. W. Memory and inferences in the comprehension of narratives. In F. Wilkening, J. Becker, & T. Trabasso (Eds.), *Information integration by children*. Hillsdale, N.J.: Lawrence Erlbaum Associates, 1981.

Trabasso, T., Stein, N. L., & Johnson, L. R. Children's knowledge of events: A causal analysis of story structure. In G. H. Bower (Ed.), *Learning and motivation*, Vol. 15. New York: Academic Press, 1981.

Warren, W. H., Nicholas, D. W., & Trabasso, T. Event chains and inferences in understanding narratives. In R. O. Freedle (Ed.), *New directions in discourse processing*. Hillsdale, N.J.: Lawrence Erlbaum Associates, 1979.

Wilensky, R. Why John married Mary: Understanding stories involving recurring goals. *Cognitive Science*, 1978, *2*, 235–266.

Wilks, Y. What sort of taxonomy of causation do we need for language understanding? *Cognitive Science*, 1977, *1*, 235–264.

Yekovich, F. R. Comments on Trabasso's causal chain and story coherence. Paper presented at the American Education Association Meetings, New York, March 1982.

4 The Concept of a Story: A Comparison Between Children's and Teachers' Viewpoints

Nancy L. Stein
The University of Chicago

Margaret Policastro
Roosevelt University

The major focus of this chapter is an investigation of the concept of a story both from a child's and from a teacher's point of view. The study was organized around the following two questions:

1. Do existing definitions of stories provide a mechanism for accurately describing the conceptual organization of story knowledge? If not, what are appropriate alternatives?
2. What types of changes occur in the representation of a story concept (i.e., How does the concept of a story evolve?), and what theories would account for these changes?

An important assumption underlying many current approaches to story understanding is that stories are perceived to be a unique form of discourse having a consistent identifiable structure. Indeed, Prince (1973) argues that:

Everyone may not know how to tell good stories, but everyone in every human society known to history and anthropology knows how to tell stories, and this at a very early age. Furthermore, everyone distinguishes stories from non-stories, that is everyone has certain intuitions—or has internalized certain rules—about what constitutes a story and what does not [p. 9].

Despite the popularity of this belief (Bremond, 1973; Leondar, 1977; Prince, 1973), no one has systematically examined whether or not a stable concept for a story exists. One reason is that the conceptual organization of complex linguistic information, like the story, is difficult to define. Although many theorists have provided a partial listing of some of the relevant features central to a story concept, an essential component often omitted is an adequate description of all features that must always be included in a text in order to label it a story. Another prerequisite of a story definition is that it be concrete enough to be tested for its descriptive adequacy. Several current definitions (Abrams & Sutton-Smith, 1977; Baker & Greene, 1977; Botvin & Sutton-Smith, 1977; Brewer & Lichtenstein, 1981; Labov & Waletsky, 1967) suffer, because the features described are so abstract that an operational definition cannot be constructed.

There are certain investigators, however, who have generated story definitions that can be tested for their descriptive adequacy. Some theorists have dealt directly with the concept of a story (Prince, 1973), whereas others describe stories in terms of the schemata used to comprehend and remember stories (Mandler & Johnson, 1977; Rumelhart, 1975, 1977; Stein & Glenn, 1979; Thorndyke, 1977). Although the latter efforts focus on how a story schema is used as a processing mechanism, the detailed description of a hypothetical story schema provides a starting point to begin an examination of the features used to define a story.

In addition to characterizing the conceptual structure of story knowledge, we have also investigated differences in story knowledge as a function of development and experience. From current models of language acquisition and concept development (Anglin, 1977; Bowerman, 1978; Gentner, 1979; Goldman, 1982; Huttenlocher, Smiley, & Charney, 1983; Mervis, 1981; Mervis & Pani, 1980), we know that children form initial representations of events and objects and then gradually change their representations with more experience. The story concept may not be any different. In this chapter, the types of changes that might occur as a function of development and experience are examined by comparing children's and elementary school teachers' concept of a story.

THE STORY CONCEPT

Functions of Stories

The reasons for telling stories are an integral part of understanding how people come to recognize stories versus other forms of discourse. Basically, two general functions predominate. Stories can be used to convey some form of social message, or stories can be used to solve real-world, personal social problems. For each function, there is a wide range of motivations that underlie the act of storytelling.

Historically, the story was used to preserve the culture of a given civilization. Often the only records of a society were the oral stories passed down from generation to generation. These tales were told with great care (Baker & Greene,

1977) as to the events thought to be influential in the evolution of a given society. As time passed, however, stories were also used as a means of instructing others. Stories were told to explain natural phenomena (e.g., the process by which a caterpillar becomes a butterfly) as well as to convey the predominant social and moral codes of a society. Indeed, organizations exist in the United States today for the sole purpose of using the story to instruct children in the lessons of life and to give them insight into the motives for and patterns of human behavior (National Association for the Preservation and Perpetuation of Storytelling, 1980).

The second primary function of storytelling concerns the role of the story in the reorganization of personal experience (Applebee, 1978; Goffman, 1974; Labov & Waletsky, 1967; Quasthoff & Nikolaus, 1981; Sutton-Smith, 1976). Labov and Waletsky most aptly describe the problem-solving functions of story-telling by showing that children and adults often tell stories to understand their own past experience, imposing a more elaborate structure on their personal knowledge of a social situation. In this way, the teller can often integrate uncon-nected segments of information into a more cohesive representation.

Hunt and Hunt (1977), in describing the divorce experience of many couples, contend that the construction of a story, involving reconstructions of past experi-ence, is essential for the emotional and psychological survival of each member of the divorced couple. This reconstruction involves substituting new explanations for past behavior as well as changing beliefs and expectations about the current behavior of the spouse. Rainer (1978) and Progoff (1977) provide similar argu-ments for diary writing or personal story writing, which they contend is neces-sary for self-growth. The story, they argue, is a medium for resolving current or recurrent conflicts so that a clear focus on one's priorities can be achieved. Thus, although stories can be used to transmit important social information, there is wide consensus and belief about the therapeutic value of the story as a medium for solving personal social problems.

In some current approaches to storytelling (Brewer & Lichtenstein, 1982; Kintsch, 1980), the multifaceted nature of the story and its functions are over-looked or ignored. Instead, what is being proposed is that the story is told primarily for purposes of entertainment. Indeed, Brewer and Lichtenstein (1981) even argue that current approaches to story comprehension fail to consider the functional role of storytelling, especially in relation to the importance of the entertainment value of a story.

In reviewing anthologies of stories from different cultures, almost all collec-tions have a definite subgroup of stories that are used to *entertain* or to create a *pleasurable* effect in the comprehender. However, this type of tale is not the primary group in most anthologies. The range of purposes for telling a story is as varied as the motives that underlie human behavior. Thus, stories can be used to cause pain as well as pleasure (e.g., to embarrass, to humiliate, to parody, to flatter, to console, to teach, to arouse guilt, etc.). A review of recent anthologies of stories (Ausubel, 1980; Calvino, 1980; Johnson, Sickels, Sayers, & Horovitz, 1977) substantiates this viewpoint.

Ausubel (1980), Bettelheim (1977), and Levi-Strauss (1955) claim that even when stories are used as entertainment devices, they often go far beyond the pleasurable, addressing issues of intense personal importance. For example, Ausubel (1980) shows that although humorous and droll tales exist in the Jewish culture, almost all of the narratives have a ''biting edge'' in the form of a profound satire or moral ending. Levi-Strauss (1955) expresses similar opinions, arguing that storytelling is a medium created primarily to transmit the socially prescribed values of a society. Bettelheim contends that stories allow children to deal with the most intense personal conflict by creating a context where children are not immediately threatened by the end results of their own conflicts and desires.

Thus, in contrast to Brewer and Lichtenstein's (1981) argument, we would content that the story serves a variety of functions, primarily because the story mirrors those events that occur in everyday social interchanges. In order to capture the diversity and richness of human interaction, stories span the gamut of human motivation and behavior, which occur in almost any social setting. The only constraints placed upon the content and function of stories originate in the teller.

The Concept of a Story

Definitions of stories can be found in almost every discipline of the social sciences. To date, we have found over 20 different definitions of a story. It should be noted, however, that only one investigator, Prince (1973), evolved a definition with the explicit intent of describing the minimal features of a story concept. Other definitions were constructed to examine the prototypical organization of story knowledge used during the comprehension process (Johnson & Mandler, 1980; Mandler & Johnson, 1977; Rumelhart, 1975, 1977; Stein, 1979; Stein & Glenn, 1979; Thorndyke, 1977), whereas still other descriptions were derived from attempts to capture the invariant features of stories generated by children (Botvin & Sutton-Smith, 1977; Stein & Glenn, 1982; Sutton-Smith, Botvin, & Mahoney, 1976). Despite the diversity of intentions underlying the development of each story description, we have used all of them for the purposes of contrast and comparison. The critical differences among the definitions provided an excellent starting point for an examination of the story concept.

The definitions to be compared in this study come from the fields of linguistics, anthropology, and psychology. Many of them overlap to such an extent that not all of them are presented here. We have grouped them into four categories: (1) those that describe the minimal components of stories in terms of *state–event–state change,* without including the dimension of goal-directed behavior in a story sequence; (2) those that describe stories as basically reflecting *goal-directed behavior* in relationship to the unfolding and resolution of personal social problems; (3) those that criticize existing goal-based descriptions and propose a more detailed model for the story concept; and (4) those that contend that there is not a unique set of features that defines a story. This last viewpoint is based upon a contextual approach to the story concept, where the specific events in a passage are thought to be critical determinants of the necessary set of features used to classify texts as stories and nonstories.

State–Event–State Change Definitions.   Of the definitions included in this class (Colby, 1973; Prince, 1973), Prince's definition is the most explicit. He defines a story as having a specific number of units, with those units being organized in a nonarbitrary fashion. A unit is any event that can be expressed as a simple sentence. The sentences are connected by conjunctive features, which are akin to causal and temporal connectors. A minimal story (e.g., a text containing all of the necessary features of a story) consists of three conjoined events, where the first and third events are stative, and the second is active. The first event must precede the second, and the second event must precede the third in time. However, the second event must also cause the third event to occur. An example of Prince's minimal story is the following:

John was sad.
Then John met a woman.
As a result, John was happy.

Although this example contains the inclusion of a specific animate protagonist, Prince does not explicitly state that this feature must be included. Furthermore, a physical action can be substituted for a personal action, such that the following sequence would also be classified as a story:

It was a quiet peaceful night in the forest.
Suddenly, a hurricane descended from the sky
and in a matter of minutes, chaos reigned.

In this text, there is a state–event–state change occurring in the physical environment, where no overt mention of a protagonist is made. Thus, although all of Prince's examples refer to internal state changes of a protagonist, this type of state change need not occur in a story. Changes in the physical environment, without the inclusion of an animate protagonist, are acceptable as instances of a minimal story in Prince's definition.

Goal-Based Definitions of Stories.   In this approach, stories are described as forms of discourse that reflect experiences in everyday social interaction. These experiences can be either real or fantasized, depending on the storyteller's preference. One of the main components of these definitions is the inclusion of a protagonist who is *motivated* to carry out some type of *goal-directed action*, with the intention of attaining a goal (Black, 1977; Black & Bower, 1980; Johnson & Mandler, 1980; Mandler & Johnson, 1977; Rumelhart, 1975, 1977; Stein, 1979; Stein & Glenn, 1979; Thorndyke, 1977). Although there are variations in these definitions, the basic structural properties of the story are described in highly similar terms. Because Stein and Glenn (1979; Stein, 1979) and Mandler and Johnson (1977; Johnson & Mandler, 1980) describe the minimal set of features that must be included in a story text, we will use their definitions to represent these goal-based approaches to stories.

In order to propose a definition of the story concept, Stein and Glenn (1979) first describe the prototypical structure of a story. A prototypical story for these investigators has six major constitutents: (1) the setting; (2) the initiating event; (3) the internal response; (4) the attempt; (5) the consequence; and (6) the reaction. The setting includes the introduction of a specific animate protagonist and normally contains information that refers to the physical, social, or temporal context in which the remainder of the story occurs. The setting, although not formally part of the episode, often contains information that constrains the subsequent events in the story sequence. The remaining five constituents occur in an invariant order and are integrated into a structure called an episode.

The *initiating event,* which begins the episode, contains information that marks some type of change in the protagonist's environment. Its major function is to evoke an emotional response in the protagonist as well as a desire to achieve some sort of goal (or change of state). This type of information is included in the second category, the *internal response.* The protagonist's thoughts and plans about how to attain a goal can also be included in the internal response category. The goal, however, is thought to be the most critical piece of information, for story knowledge is basically organized around the goal of the protagonist. The primary function of internal response information is to motivate the protagonist to carry out a set of overt actions in the service of the goal. These actions are classified as the protagonist's *attempt.* The attempt then results in the *consequence,* signifying whether or not the protagonist succeeded in attaining the goal. The final type of information found in an episode is classified in the *reaction* category. Three different types of information can be classified as reaction statements: (1) the protagonist's emotional and cognitive responses to the goal attainment; (2) future or long term consequences that occur as a direct result of goal attainment; or (3) a moral, summarizing what the character learned from achieving or pursuing a particular goal.

In addition to the particular types of information that are included in a story sequence, the logical relationships that connect the five episodic categories are also specified. Direct causal connections must link each of the episodic categories to one another. The one exception is the connection between the attempt and consequence category, where either a direct causal or an enablement relationship is hypothesized to connect the two categories.

In order for a text to be labeled a story, however, all of the five constituents of an episode need not be included. Stein and Glenn (1979; Stein, 1979, in press) as well as Mandler and Johnson (1977; Johnson & Mandler, 1980) argue quite clearly that the prototypical description of a story represents an idealized schema, existing in the head of the comprehender. The surface structure of a particular story text need not, and empirically often does not, contain all of the parts of a prototypical story. It is assumed that the comprehender will use available knowledge about the prototypical structure of a story to supply missing information, in order to construct a coherent representation of the event sequence. For the comprehender to be able to construct a meaningful representation of a story, however, certain features must always be present in the text structure.

Stein and Glenn (1979) claim that a story text must contain direct or indirect reference to:

(1) a specific protagonist capable of intentional behavior;
(2) the motivation and/or goals of a protagonist;
(3) overt actions carried out in the service of a goal; and
(4) information concerning the attainment or nonattainment of the goal.

With respect to the six constituents of an episode, a story text must contain: (1) a *setting* that includes or introduces an animate character; (2) either an *initiating event* or an *internal response* containing information from which the motives, goals, and emotional response of the protagonist can be inferred; (3) an overt *attempt* on the part of a protagonist or a *plan* outlining the overt attempt; and (4) a *consequence,* reflecting whether or not the goal has been attained. Table 4.1 contains the necessary features of this definition, as well as reference to the features of Prince's and Mandler and Johnson's definition.

Mandler and Johnson (1977; Johnson & Mandler, 1980) define a story in similar terms. However, there are two important differences between their definition and that of Stein and Glenn (1979). First, Mandler and Johnson (1977) propose two different definitions of a story, one which is goal-based and one which is not. Their definition of a goal-based story is similar to Stein and Glenn's (1979) definition with one difference. Mandler and Johnson (1977; Johnson & Mandler, 1980) argue that in addition to the four features included in Stein and Glenn's minimal story, an ending (Stein and Glenn's reaction category) must also be included in the text sequence, especially when the text consists of a single-episode story. Thus, Mandler and Johnson's goal-based definition would include the following categories:

(1) a setting;
(2) an initiating event or internal response;
(3) an attempt;
(4) a consequence; and
(5) a reaction.

TABLE 4.1
Three Definitions of a Minimal Story

I. Prince's Minimal Story (State-Event-State Change)

   (a) three conjoined events
   (b) the first and third events must be stative, the second must be active
   (c) the first event must precede the second, whereas the second must precede and also cause the third
   (d) the first event must be the inverse of the third

II. Stein and Glenn's Minimal Story (Goal-Based)

   (a) a setting that contains reference to a specific animate protagonist
   (b) either an initiating event or an internal response
   (c) an overt attempt to attain the goal
   (d) a consequence, signifying whether or not the goal has been attained

---

III. Mandler and Johnson's Minimal Story

Goal-Based	*Nongoal Based*
(a) setting	(a) setting
(b) either a beginning or a complex reaction	(b) a beginning
(c) an attempt	(c) a simple reaction
(d) an outcome	(1) an emotional response
(e) an ending	(2) an unplanned action
	(d) an ending

The description of Mandler and Johnson's nongoal-based story allows for the occurrence of unplanned, automatic actions to form part of the episode. This type of story includes the following components: (1) a setting, introducing the protagonist; (2) a beginning, similar to Stein and Glenn's initiating event; (3) the protagonist's emotional response to the initiating event; (4) an automatic unplanned action that results from feeling a particular emotion; and (5) an ending (similar to Stein and Glenn's reaction category). As an example of this nongoal-based episodic sequence, consider the following story:

Once there was a Czar (setting)
who had three lovely young daughters (setting).
One day, the three daughters went walking in the woods (initiating event).
They were enjoying themselves so much (emotional reaction)
that they forgot the time (cognition)
and stayed too long (unplanned actions).
They were then kidnapped by a dragon (ending).

Anyone who has been exposed to many fairytales or myths knows, however, that stories rarely end here without some type of overt attempt on the part of another protagonist to come to the aid of these three lovely, young maidens. Mandler and Johnson (1977) agree with this point, arguing that even though these simpler episodes do contain all of the necessary features of a minimal story. These types of nongoal-based sequences rarely occur by themselves. Rather, the simpler type of unplanned behavioral episodes occur as part of a more detailed, elaborate story, such as the following:

> There was once a Czar who had three lovely daughters.
> One day, the three daughters went walking in the woods.
> They were enjoying themselves so much that
> they forgot the time
> and stayed too long.
> A dragon came and kidnapped the three daughters.
> As they were being dragged off, they called for help.
> Three heroes heard the cries
> and set off to rescue the daughters.
> The heroes found and
> fought the dragon.
> They defeated the dragon and
> rescued the maidens.
> The heroes then returned the daughters safely to their palace.
> When the Czar heard of the rescue,
> he rewarded the heroes handsomely.

As we can see, the simpler episode unfolds first within a more complex multiple-episode story where there are not only daughters and dragons, but heroes rushing to the aid of young maidens. Thus, even though Mandler and Johnson argue for the existence of more than one definition of a minimal story, they also explicitly state that in traditional folk tales and fables, the nongoal-based episode rarely, if ever, occurs by itself.

Comparing Mandler and Johnson's (1977; Johnson & Mandler, 1980) non-goal-based definition to Prince's (1973) definition, certain similarities emerge. Prince assumes that the important component is a change of state, with an intervening event causing the state change. In Mandler and Johnson's nongoal-based definition, the episode begins with an initiating event marking some kind of change in the protagonist's environment. Here we can infer that the *environment* refers to either a physical or internal state change, where this change has some significance for the protagonist. In order to ensure protagonist involvement, however, Mandler and Johnson require an emotional response and unplanned action on the part of a protagonist, as well as an ending to the sequence.

Prince (1973) does not overtly require a protagonist's involvement, but relies more heavily on the comprehender making inferences about the significance of a state change for the welfare of the protagonist in his examples. Thus the major differences between Prince's (1973) and Mandler and Johnson's (1977) nongoal-based definition is that Mandler and Johnson explicitly include reference to the resultant emotional reaction and unplanned actions of a protagonist in response to changes in the environment. In Prince's definition, these are not stated.

Comparing Prince's (1973) definition to the goal-based definitions, there are two critical differences. First, mention of a specific animate protagonist is required in the goal-based definition. Second, although the goal-based definition incorporates the notion of changes of states, the focus is on changes of goal states, as suggested by Black (1977). Thus, an intentional action must occur between a goal state and the projected consequence or outcome. The consequence need not result in a change of goal state, however. Sometimes the attempt fails, because the protagonist has not considered all of the relevant preconditions necessary for goal attainment. Thus the story revolves around an attempt at changing the goal state of the protagonist, rather than an absolute change from one goal state to another.

More Complex Definitions.   Investigators adhering to more complex definitions of stories fall into two categories: (1) those who criticize goal-based definitions without formulating an alternative definition; (2) and those who actually propose an alternative, more detailed definition. Black and Wilensky (1979) are examples of the first group of investigators, whereas Brewer and Lichtenstein (1981), de Beaugrande and Colby (1979), Labov and Waletsky (1967), Morgan and Sellner (1981), and Wilensky (1980) are examples of investigators included in the second category. First, we review Black and Wilensky's (1979) criticisms of current story definitions, and then we discuss the more detailed definitions of a story.

Black and Wilensky (1979) and Black and Bower (1980) have argued that goal-based definitions, derived from a story "grammar" approach to comprehension, are lacking in critical detail because, using these definitions, one cannot discriminate adequately between the classes of stories and nonstories. To illustrate their point, Black and Wilensky (1979) argue that there are instances of texts that have all the necessary features of stories, as proposed in goal-based definitions, but that would not be classified as a story. Conversely, they argue that there are also instances of texts that do not contain all of the features of a story, but that would be classified as stories.

Black and Wilensky (1979) use the "procedural" exposition as an example to illustrate their point concerning texts that contain all of the features of a story but would not be included in the story category. Thorndyke's (1977) grammar is used to ensure that all requirements for a story have been met. The following is an example of a *procedure* that contains all of the features of a story:

> It is fishing season in Illinois and a friend asks you to go fishing, but you do not
> know how. Well, I am going to tell you how to catch a fish. First, you need to get

some fishing equipment. Therefore, you should go to a sporting goods store and buy a pole, some line, some hooks, some bait, and a lure. When you have this equipment, you need to find a good place to fish. The best strategy here is to consult either a friend or a guidebook. If you follow the guidelines I have set forth here, you cannot help but come home with a batch of fish.

Black and Wilensky (1979) argue that this passage contains a setting, theme (superordinate goal), plot, and resolution, according to Thorndyke's (1977) story grammar. The setting contains a time (fishing season), location (Illinois), and characters (you, a friend, and I). There is an initiating event (a friend asks you to go fishing, but you do not know how) and a goal (to catch a fish). The remainder of the story contains several episodes, which include subgoals, attempts, outcomes, and resolutions. Thus, Black and Wilensky argue that the grammars would accept these procedures as stories. These investigators contend, however, that most individuals would not include these procedures in their concept of a story. Because the grammars are inadequate in fully discriminating between the class of stories and nonstories, the definition needs change.

The problem with Black and Wilensky's (1979) example is that it *does not* include all of the parts and relationships contained in a prototypical story. First, there is no specific protagonist introduced. The text also does not include an overt attempt, a consequence, or a reaction. The procedure describes a plan of action that, if carried out, should lead to a successful outcome. However, we are not told whether the protagonist actually carried out the plan, whether the goal was achieved, and what happened as a result of achieving the goal. Thus, Black and Wilensky's (1979) procedure does not serve as an example of the class of texts that contains all of the components of stories, but one that is not included in the story category. As we will show in our present set of experiments, if there is a problem with the goal-based definitions, it is that they operate at a level of too much specificity. Thus, there will be texts that do *not* have all the necessary features of a goal-based definition. Yet, these texts will be included in the story category.

The second set of criticisms directed at the goal-based definitions contain suggestions for revisions of the story definition. Morgan and Sellner (1981) and subsequently Brewer and Lichtenstein (1981) argue that an affective response, such as curiosity, suspense, or surprise, must be experienced by the *comprehender* in order for a text to be labeled a story. Both sets of investigators contend that because the goal-based definitions don't include an affective dimension, as experienced by the comprehender, the definitions are lacking in sufficient detail to serve as an adequate definition of a story.

Both Stein and Glenn (1979) and Mandler and Johnson (1977) state that although the explicit emotional response of the protagonist does not have to be included in the surface structure of the text, the comprehender must be able to infer the specific emotional response of the protagonist. Moreover, the emotional response must be directly (causally) related to the prior initiating event as well as to the subsequent goal of the protagonist. If the protagonist's emotional response cannot be inferred and if there are not direct causal connections from the initiating event to the emotional response to the goal, etc., then the text is *not* considered to be a story. Thus, the goal-based definitions require an affective response from the protagonist whereas Brewer and Lichtenstein (1981) require the comprehender to experience an affective response.

The third and final set of definitions in this more complex category come from linguistic rather than psychological studies of the story. Labov and Waletsky (1967) and subsequently de Beaugrande and Colby (1979) argue that stories must include some type of unexpected event so that a complication arises when the protagonist cannot pursue the normal course of action. The additional component in these definitions is concerned with a novel method of solving the problem at hand or an obstacle to be placed in the path of the protagonist.

Comparing Labov and Waletsky's (1967) and de Beaugrande and Colby's (1979) definitions to the goal-based definitions, it is apparent that the necessity of carrying out a novel plan of action is *not* incorporated into the goal-based definitions. The goal-based definitions do include the element of an unexpected event, but there is no specification of the type of plan that must be used by a protagonist. The element of a novel plan on the part of the protagonist and/or the addition of an obstacle in the path of a protagonist are additional features of a story definition when compared to goal-based definitions.

An Alternative Viewpoint of the Story Concept.   From the previous review, it is evident that there are important differences when definitions of stories are compared. Most investigators would probably contend that their definition is the one that accurately portrays the set of features used in defining a story. The basic issue, however, may not revolve around which definition is the correct one, but rather around the issue of whether there is just one set of features used to define a story. In order to advance and formulate a theoretical perspective for the study of the story concept, we have drawn upon the work of Rosch (1975) and Mervis (1981; Mervis & Rosch, 1981; Rosch & Mervis, 1975) concerning the organization of natural object categories. The organization of story knowledge may be similar to that advanced for object classifications.

According to Rosch and Mervis (1975; Mervis & Rosch, 1981), people categorize objects that they encounter by comparing the external object to an "ideal" form, called a prototype. The prototype is a cognitive structure that is constructed through an inductive, inferential, and abstractive process, resulting from repeated exposure to particular objects. In Rosch and Mervis's view, all members of a category have some overlapping features with other members of the category. However, for a particular category, some features may be more important or salient than other features, and it is not necessary for each member of a category to have an attribute in common with all other members.

Category membership is contingent upon the degree of perceived similarity to the prototype. If an object has enough features in common with the prototype (or alternatively, enough of the most typical or salient features), then it will be classified as part of the category being considered. Two members may not have all of the same features in common, because the context in which the object occurs becomes a critical determinant of the features used to judge category membership.

Determining which features can be deleted from a member of a category is less clear. Rosch and Mervis (1975; Mervis & Rosch, 1981) argue that category boundaries, for the most part, are "fuzzy" and not well-defined. A person may not have a consistent basis for judging category membership when an object lacks certain critical features or when the object contains a combination of features from two or more categories. Thus, when a presented object is missing critical features, subjects may use inconsistent classification schemes, ranging from including the object as part of the specific category under consideration to creating a *new* category to account for the differences in perceived similarity between a particular prototype and the object under consideration.

For those objects within the boundaries of a category, however, some will be considered better examples of the category than others, because some instances occur with more frequency and represent the largest number of instances of a particular category (Rosch & Mervis, 1975; Mervis & Rosch, 1981). Support for this assertion can be seen when subjects are asked to list members of a category or are asked to identify whether or not an object is a member of a category. Certain instances are always listed first and/or more frequently in comparison to other instances, and these frequently occurring instances are always identified faster than those instances that are less representative of a category (Mervis & Rosch, 1981). These data have been used to support the assertion that within a category, there are instances that more closely approximate the prototype and, therefore, will be considered better examples than other members of the category. Instances ranked at the lower end of the goodness continuum would be those objects that are missing certain features but that still retain enough similarity to the prototype to be included in a particular category.

In considering the usefulness of Rosch and Mervis's approach to the concept of the story, there are important similarities. We have outlined these similarities in terms of hypotheses about the story concept. The first concerns the issue of whether there is one set of features consistently used to identify texts belonging to the story category. It may be that there is not a unique set of features that is used to judge whether or not a text is a story. The context in which a story occurs may predominate and guide the comprehender in considering the relevant features necessary for identification of the text as a story.

Especially sensitive to contextual constraints may be the necessity of including goal-based behavior in a story sequence. In real life, there are situations where a protagonist is simply overcome by the environment, without being able to exert any control over the circumstances that result as a function of a particular set of initial events. Examples of these situations are found when a protagonist is placed in a novel or threatening environment, where there is not enough time to

plan, or where the protagonist doesn't have the prerequisite knowledge to generate a plan of action. Thus, there should be instances where an approximation of
Prince's nongoal-based definition would be the most accurate in describing the
set of features that is used to identify a text as a story.

The critical question is whether a nongoal-based definition would suffice in
describing all texts that are considered to belong to the story category. Our
conclusion is that it would not. Although nongoal-based episodes occur in real
life, these are not the most frequently occurring types of social episodes. For the
most part, natural disasters don't occur on an everyday basis. More representative of everyday social interchange are those situations where man does have the
time or knowledge to formulate and carry out a set of intentionally conceived
activities. Therefore, goal-directed behavior would be the expected course of
action for a protagonist.

Only in those stories where there is absolutely no chance of initiating goal-
directed behavior would a nongoal-based definition suffice in describing the
minimal features of a story. In those texts where there is the possibility of
initiating goal-based behavior, the text would have to contain some type of
intentional action and outcome or some explanation for the lack of goal-directed
behavior in order for the passage to be included in the story category. If these
components were missing, then the text would not be classified as a story. What
we are proposing is that a critical factor influencing whether or not goal-based
behavior need be included in a sequence concerns the possibility and probability
that a protagonist *could formulate* a plan of action.

A second basis of similarity between natural object categories and the story
concept concerns the idea of best examples of a category and the ranking of
category instances according to a continuum of goodness of fit with respect to the
prototype. Although certain nongoal-based episodes should be considered part of
the story category, these instances don't occur very often. Goal-based episodes
are more typical, with different kinds of goal conflicts occurring as a function of
complex interactions among different characters. Therefore, there should be a
definite preference for goal-based stories in terms of a goodness ranking of fit to
a prototype. Nongoal-based stories should be ranked consistently lower than
goal-based stories.

Several questions remain unanswered, however, even with the consideration
of these hypotheses. The first concerns the issue of which type of goal-based
episode will be considered the best example of the story category. Although we
have proposed that goal-based stories will always be ranked higher than nongoal-
based stories, we have not discussed the possibility of ranking within the class of
goal-based stories. We don't know how stories corresponding to the more complex definitions of Labov and Waletsky (1967) or de Beaugrande and Colby
(1979) will be ranked. Whether or not stories with novel goal paths will be
ranked higher than stories without *complications* remains to be seen.

However, we would argue that stories that contain obstacles to be overcome
and require the generation of a new plan may be the most representative type of

story in both oral and written literature. For the most part, participation in social interchange requires overcoming obstacles, stemming from interaction with other people or with the environment. Evidence of this can be seen in the stories children and adults tell (Quasthoff & Nikolaus, 1981; Stein & Glenn, 1982). Although nongoal-based stories and simple goal-based episodes are told by elementary school children, the majority of their stories contain multiple episodes with obstacles in the path of the protagonist. Thus in ranking stories according to a goodness continuum, the most prototypical may be the one that contains an initial obstacle in the path of the protagonist's goal attainment or an episode with a novel goal-path.

A second unanswered question concerns the changes that occur in the story concept as a function of experience and development. From the analysis of stories children tell (Stein & Glenn, 1982; Stein, Glenn, & Jarcho, 1982), we know that as children develop they begin to add more features to their stories, in terms of the definitions reviewed in this chapter. Because younger children include fewer features in their own stories, they may accept a wider array of texts as belonging to the story category than older children or adults.

This hypothesis, however, would account for only part of the data collected on children's story comprehension and production skills. Although young children may accept nongoal-based texts as stories more readily than older children and adults, older children may accept violations of the expected sequence of a goal-based episode as stories more readily than younger children. When children's comprehension of stories is assessed, older children are able to comprehend more accurately texts that violate the temporal or causal sequence of the expected course of action in a story. In fact, as children develop they begin to understand and enjoy more fully stories that don't conform to the expected canonical sequence.

The development of the story concept could involve both a narrowing and broadening of features deemed necessary to define a story. The changes in the concept would be dependent upon the type of text under consideration. The present study was completed to examine these issues. Second-grade children and elementary school teachers were asked to judge whether different kinds of passages were included in their concept of a story. Furthermore, all participants in the study were asked to rank each passage on the basis of how good (representative) the passage was according to their definition of a story. By examining these data, we can better understand how the story concept changes as a function of age and experience.

METHOD

Subjects

The subject pool consisted of two different populations. The first group was composed of 42 second-grade children who attended an upper middle-class school in a suburb of Chicago. Appoximately half of the children were male, and half were female.

The second group was composed of 38 elementary school teachers from both the Chicago and suburban public school districts. Approximately half of the teachers came from Chicago and half from suburban schools. There were more female than male teachers participating in the study.

Stimulus Materials

The stimulus materials consisted of two different sets of 31 passages. Each set ranged in complexity from single words and sentences to complexly constructed narrative passages. The materials in one set were identical to those in the second set in terms of the structural complexity of the passages. The only factor that varied across sets was the specific semantic content of the passages. The passages within each set of materials could be categorized into four different clusters of items, corresponding to the basic questions underlying the rationale for the study.

The first cluster of items was devised to test Prince's (1973) concept of story. The second cluster was designed so that two comparisons could be made: one between nongoal-based and goal-based definitions; the other between goal-based and the more complex definitions. Cluster three was devised to investigate the goal-based definitions in a more detailed fashion. Cluster four was used to test certain hypotheses advocated by Black and Wilensky (1979). Because of the complexity underlying the construction of passages, the detailed description of the four clusters of materials is presented in the results section, immediately preceding the data presentation for that cluster.

Design

All children and teachers completed two tasks on both sets of stimulus materials:

1. A Yes–No judgment task required that each passage be rated as to whether it was or was not a story. Yes responses signified that a passage was identified as a story, whereas No responses signified that a passage was not identified as a story.

2. A seven-point rating scale task required subjects to rate each passage according to a continuum. At the lower end of the scale, one was assigned to those texts that could be classified as NOT a story; four represented the number assigned to those texts that could be classified as a story; seven represented the category of texts that were considered really good stories (see the following for details).

Each of the groups of children and teachers were divided further into two equal groups so that the order of tasks and stimulus sets could be counterbalanced within a group. Half of the subjects within each population completed the Yes–No task first, and half completed the rating scale task first. Within each group, the resulting sequence of tasks, sets, and items are given in Table 4.2.

Each subject received both sets of materials for each task with different item orders in each set of materials. All subjects completed one type of task first on both sets of materials. Then the second task was completed on the same sets of the materials. The set order, as well as the item order, was changed for second task.

Procedure

Children. Each of the two groups of children was tested together as a classroom. Before beginning the testing, the children were told that they were going to be given some reading material and that they were going to be asked whether passages in their booklets could be classified as stories. The children were asked to think about stories and what they knew about stories (e.g., what made something a story and what made it not a story). They were also told that in making these judgments there were no right or wrong answers. They were to use their knowledge about stories that they had read or heard. Children were then given two sets of materials. The instructions for each task were as follows:

Yes–No Judgment Task. Children were told that the experimenter would read each passage aloud and that they should follow along reading silently to themselves. When the experimenter finished reading each passage each child was to decide whether or not the passage was a story. If the child thought the passage was a story, the answer *Yes,* appearing underneath the passage, was to be circled. If the child thought that the passage was not a story, then *No* was to be circled. The experimenter told the children that some passages might be stories

TABLE 4.2
Design Used for the
Administration of Judgment
Tasks for Children and
Teachers

Group 1	Group 2
Task 1: Yes–No	*Task 2: Rating Scale*
A. Set order: A/B B. Item order: 1/2	A. Set order: A/B B. Item order: 3/4
Task 2: Rating Scale	*Task 1: Yes–No*
A. Set order: B/A B. Item order: 5/6	A. Set order: B/A B. Item order: 7/8

and some might not. The important thing was that the children use their knowledge about stories to make their decisions.

Rating Scale Task.   The instructions for this task were similar to those for the Yes–No judgment task. The experimenter read each passage in a set and asked the children to use their knowledge of stories to make judgments about each passage. The nature of the judgment, however, was somewhat different from the previous Yes–No judgment task. For the rating scale task, children were presented with a seven-point scale at the bottom of each passage and were asked to assign a number to each passage. The scale used for passage judgments was the following:

1	2	3	4	5	6	7
not a story at all	only part of a story	almost, but not quite a story	a story	a good story	a very good story	really good, best story

Children were told that a number 1 meant that the children did not consider the passage to be a story at all. A score of 4 would mean that the child considered the text to be a story, and a score of 7 meant that the text was considered to be a really good story, perhaps one of the best and most representative examples of stories that they had heard. The other points on the scale were then explained. The number 2 meant that the passage contained only part of a story, whereas the number 3 meant that the passage was almost a story, but still had something missing. By using gradation from 1 to 4, children could provide an indication of what factors influenced the ratings that were given to passages not included in the story category.

The gradations from 4 to 7 were explained in terms of different levels of the quality of a story. The children were told that although a lot of texts could be rated as stories, some might be better examples of stories than other texts. Thus, a rating of 4 would mean that the text was definitely a story, but not the best or most representative of a story. A rating of 5 would mean that the text was a good story. A rating of 5 would mean that the text was a good story, whereas 6 would mean that the text was considered a very good story, and 7 would indicate that the text was really good, probably the best and most representative type of example. Thus, if children decided that the text was a story, they had to rank the text according to how good an example of their prototype the text was.

In order to ensure that the scale would be used properly, a 10-minute training procedure was initiated before the beginning of the task. During the training procedure, none of the children had difficulty making distinctions among the various gradations.

Teachers.   The procedure used for the teachers was similar to that used for the children, with a few exceptions. Teachers read all passages silently, self-pacing their progress. Also, teachers were explicitly asked to rank all passages in terms of their *own* knowledge of stories. The teachers were told that they might choose to rate these passages from a child's viewpoint, but the experimenter explicitly stated that this information was not wanted. The teachers were asked to rate stories from *their* point of view as to what was and what was not a story.

RESULTS

Cluster 1

Description of Materials.   The passages in this cluster were designed to test the validity of Prince's (1973) concept of a story. Passages were constructed so that some of them contained all of the necessary features of Prince's definition, whereas others contained only a partial set of the necessary features. Texts ranged from the presentation of single words and single sentences to passages with two or three sentences. Although the inclusion of single words seems somewhat extreme, Hoover (1980), in a pilot study, found that some 5-year-old children did include single words in their concept of a story.

The features that varied across passages were: (1) an animate being; (2) an inanimate object; (3) a description of the physical state of an object; (4) a description of the physical state of an animate being; (5) a description of the internal state of an animate being; (6) a physical event; and (7) a personal action. Each passage was written so that it contained one or more of the seven features just listed.

The important constraint on passage construction was that all three-line passages conformed to Prince's definition of a story, with an animate protagonist included, and that the sequence of events conveyed a change from one internal state to another. An example of one three-line passage was:

Once there was a boy who was sad.
He found his toys.
Then he became happy.

Texts corresponding to Prince's minimal definition, in which only physical changes in the environment occur, were not included in this cluster, but appear in Cluster II. In Cluster I, the validity of Prince's definition of a story was tested only as it pertained to internal state changes in a protagonist.

Passages containing two-line sequences were written so that some but not all of Prince's necessary features would appear in the text. Especially central to our interest was whether children would judge a description of a simple state–state change sequence as being included in the story category. Examples of the couplets included in this cluster were:

(1) The boy was very sad.
    Then he became very happy.

(2) The girl wanted a dog.
    So she got it.

Results: Children's Data.   In order to determine whether each passage in the cluster was considered to be a story or nonstory, a proportion test was carried out on the data. Traditionally, this type of test allows one to determine whether the proportion of Yes and No responses reflect chance-level responding, normally set at the .50 level. On both of our tasks children were asked to use their knowledge of stories to make decisions about a passage, so we cannot say formally that children were incorrect in their judgments or were even uncertain about their decisions. What the proportion scores reflect is the degree of consensus concerning whether each passage should be considered a story. Therefore, the results of the analysis tell us whether the consensus concerning a passage is above or below a significant level of agreement among subjects.

In order to determine whether there were significant levels of agreements across passages, upper and lower confidence band limits were set. Proportion scores that were at .65 or above indicated that a particular text was judged to be a story by a significant majority of subjects at least 95% of the time. For proportion scores that were at .35 or below, texts were judged to be nonstories at least 95% of the time.

The results from the Yes–No task showed that all of the items in Cluster 1 were judged to belong to the category of a nonstory. The mean proportion of Yes responses for passages in Cluster 1 was .06, with proportion scores ranging from .00 to .19. The data from the seven-point scale task substantiated the results from the Yes–No task. Table 4.3 includes a summary and comparison of mean scores across the two tasks and across the two populations.

On the seven-point scale task, the mean score assigned to all passages in Cluster 1 was 1.19, falling between the categories of not a story at all and only part of a story. There were virtually no passages that were rated as a 3 or above. These data indicate that all children considered all of the items to fall outside the category boundaries of a story. For those items that directly corresponded to Prince's concept of a story, the mean scores were not significantly higher than those scores for other items. Thus, Prince's concept of a story, as it pertains to the simple description of changes in the internal state of an animate being, does not correspond to children's concept of a story.

TABLE 4.3
Cluster 1: Mean Proportion Scores and Mean Scale Scores

	Yes–No Task Mean Proportions		Seven-Point Scale Mean Scores	
	Children	Teachers	Children	Teachers
All items except those corresponding to Prince's definition	.05	.09	1.19	1.40
Items corresponding to only Prince's definition	.13	.62[a]	1.59	3.14[a]

[a]p < .01.

Results: Teachers' Data. The results from the Yes–No task, appearing in Table 4.3, showed that all items, with the exception of those conforming to Prince's definition of a story, were judged as definitely not a story. The mean proportion of Yes responses on these items was .09. Those items that corresponded to Prince's definition were judged to be a story 62% of the time. The significant difference between these two proportion scores (p < .01) suggests that the majority of teachers were rating the three-line passages as stories and were making clear distinctions between texts containing all of the necessary features of Prince's definition and those containing only a subset of the features.

It should be noted, however, that although texts corresponding to Prince's definition were clearly distinguished from the other category of texts, the proportion score of .62 for these more complex texts fell just below the upper confidence band limit of .65. This suggests that although texts corresponding to Prince's definition are differentiated from simpler texts, there is still significant disagreement among teachers as to whether Prince's definition is adequate in describing a story. The results from the seven-point scale task shed more light on the nature of this disagreement.

On the scale task, the mean rating for those texts containing only a subset of Prince's features was 1.4. For those texts corresponding to Prince's definition, the mean scale rating was 3.19, a significant increase in ranking compared to the ranking of simpler texts.

On the scale task, as opposed to the Yes–No task, however, texts corresponding to Prince's definition were rarely included in the story category. Only two teachers gave this type of text a 4 ranking. The other teachers ranked these texts as primarily a 3, indicating that they thought the texts to be representative of passages that were almost stories, but still had something missing. The variation in scale judgments was small, indicating a high agreement among teachers' ranking on these passages. The scale data for these texts corresponding to Prince's definition are helpful in understanding the disagreement resulting on the Yes–No task.

The scale data show that when teachers are given an opportunity to make finer discriminations among texts (e.g., the decision to rank a text as a story or almost a story versus the decision to call a text a story or nonstory), there is little disagreement among the rankings. All teachers agree that texts conforming to Prince's definition are quite similar to a story, but agree that the text is still missing something. The Yes–No task brings different criteria into consideration. Given that there are two nonoverlapping categories, stories and nonstories, how should a text be rated that is thought to be highly similar to a story?

For some teachers the fact that a text had almost all the necessary features makes it more closely associated with the category of story than nonstory. These teachers might use a decision rule that involves assessing whether any other discourse category name could be assigned to a passage. Because of the similarity of the passage to the story and because of the lack of another acceptable label, many teachers might choose to assign texts representing Prince's definition to the story category.

Other teachers, however, may use an absolute criterion in deciding what texts should be included in the story category. Although they might not be able to categorize these texts in terms of other available discourse structures; the decision rule used might be less flexible, not allowing for the inclusion of any text that omits critical features of their definition.

Cluster 2

Description of Materials.   The second cluster of materials was designed to evaluate the adequacy of nongoal-based versus goal-based definitions of stories. Also, a comparison was made between simple goal-based definitions and the more complex goal-based definitions, which include obstacles and novel goal paths. The questions underlying these comparisons focused on whether or not the following features had to be included in a story text:

(1) a specific animate protagonist;
(2) temporal and causal relations among events;
(3) the inclusion of an emotional response and unplanned actions in nongoal-based passages;
(4) the inclusion of goal-directed action;
(5) the inclusion of an obstacle in the path of a protagonist.

In order to test for the necessity of including these features in a story, seven different types of passages were constructed. Figure 4.1 contains a tree diagram illustrating how the inclusion of features was varied across the different types of passages.

The first text in this cluster contained none of the features outlined in any definition. The resulting passage, labeled a *physical descriptive sequence,* was

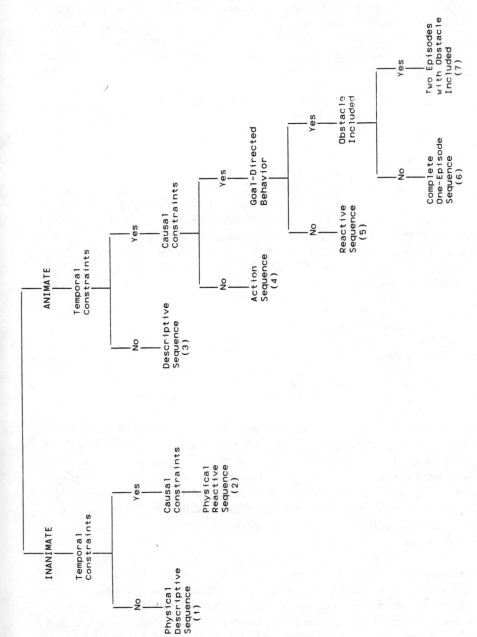

FIG. 4.1. Decision Tree used to construct the seven passages contained in cluster 2. (Numbers in parentheses refer to examples given in the text.)

given a number (1) in the decision tree. It contained a description of a physical object. There were no references to a specific animate protagonist, nor were there any temporal or causal connections among events. Therefore, there was no possibility for state changes to occur. The following is an example of a physical descriptive sequence:

(1) The ball was red and white.
    The ball was stored in the gym.
    The ball had a small hole in it.
    The ball was used for volley ball.
    The ball could fit into a person's hand.
    The ball was dirty on one side.
    The ball was three inches round.

The second passage included in this cluster, a *physical causal sequence,* also contained no reference to an animate protagonist. However, it did include a series of physical events that were temporally and causally related. Additionally, specific state changes occurred in the physical environment. The following is an example of a physical causal sequence:

(2) The ball rolled down the hill.
    It hit the window in the house.
    The window broke into pieces.
    Rain poured through the window
    and flooded the room.
    Soon the furniture floated out
    leaving the room barren.

In this passage, there is a possible *beginning* and *end,* simply because there are a series of state changes occurring in the environment. Because these events could have either a good or bad effect on some potential protagonist, Prince would consider this passage to belong to the story category. However, no mention of a specific animate protagonist is made, and no references to planful or automatic actions are included. By the criteria outlined in all other definitions, however, this sequence should not be considered a story.

The remaining five texts in Cluster 2 all contained reference to one or more specific animate protagonists and varied in the degree to which each text included the essential features of the nongoal and goal-based definitions. The first text containing an animate protagonist was labeled an *animate descriptive sequence.* It contained reference to a specific protagonist but contained few, if any, temporal or causal connections among the series of statements in the sequence. The following is an example of an animate descriptive sequence:

(3) The fox had a grey mane.
    He had a long silvery tail.

He was quite ferocious.
He lived in a cave near the woods.
He collected straw and rocks for his cave.
His favorite food was young rabbit.
He also liked to eat freshly picked berries.

Although this passage corresponds to the setting category in many stories, it lacks both temporal and/or causal connectors and, therefore, should not be rated as a story according to any definition.

The next passage, an *animate action sequence,* contained reference to a specific protagonist, but contained only temporal connections among a sequence of events. This type of passage corresponded closely to a scripted action sequence that describes the daily activities of a character. The following is an example of just such a sequence:

(4) Alice lived down by the ocean.
     Every day Alice went down by the beach.
     She hunted for sea shells.
     Then she built a sand castle.
     Then she took a sun bath.
     Then she went for a swim.
     Then she went home.

Although this passage contains actions that are intentionally based, there is no clear overriding goal connecting all of the events. Despite the inclusion of a temporal beginning and end, the sequence is not organized according to an episodic structure and would not be considered a story according to any current definition.

The remaining texts in this cluster all included events that were causally related. The critical features varied were the presence or absence of goal-directed action as well as the presence or absence of an unsuccessful goal attempt on the part of the protagonist. The first text in this group, labeled an *animate reactive sequence,* contained reference to a specific animate protagonist and included a change of state in the physical environment of the protagonist; however, it contained no reference to any activity on the part of the protagonist. The only reference made about the protagonist was how the physical events affected her or him, in terms of having a good or bad consequence on future activities. Thus, the element of a planful or even an automatic reaction was missing, as exemplified in the following passage:

(5) One day the fox was outside playing
     when it started to rain.
     Suddenly the rain turned into a violent storm
     and began to flood the entire forest.

The fox was hit by a wave
and dragged into the swirling current
and then pulled under the water.

According to Prince (1973), this passage should definitely be considered a story. However, Mandler and Johnson (1977) would not classify this passage as belonging to the story category, because it contains no reference to the protagonist's emotional response and unplanned action.

The next type of passage in this cluster included a series of events corresponding to the description of a complete episode in all story grammars. Thus it should be considered a story according to Stein and Glenn's (1979) as well as Mandler and Johnson's (1977) goal-based definition. The following is an example of a *complete one-episode story*, with all categories included:

(6) One day Alice was playing in the sand
     when the tide came in very fast.
     Suddenly the waves came on the shore
     drenching Alice and her beach clothes.
     Alice got very scared,
     so she gathered up her things
     and was able to escape from the face of the waves.
     Alice was relieved and happy.

Although this sequence contains all the parts of a story, according to Stein and Glenn (1979) and Mandler and Johnson (1977), it does not necessarily contain a novel goal path or an obstacle in the path of a protagonist. Thus, a *multiple-episode passage* was written where the initial goal path of a protagonist was explicitly blocked. The following is an example of one such text:

(7) Once there was a girl named Judy
     who saw a beautiful doll house in a store window.
     She decided to make one for herself
     so she asked her father for a hammer and saw.
     But her father would not give them to her.
     Judy was very determined to build the doll house,
     so she went to her grandmother for the hammer and saw.
     Judy's grandmother went to the store that day
     and got Judy a hammer and saw.
     Judy took the tools
     and then built herself the most beautiful doll house.

According to Labov and Waletsky (1967) and Kintsch (1980), only this final passage should be considered a story because it is the only one where an obstacle blocks the goal path of the protagonist and forces the protagonist to construct a new plan of action.

A final variation was included in this cluster of materials. For the animate reactive sequence, the complete episode, and the multiple-episode sequence with an obstacle, two versions were written. One version had an ending where the protagonist suffered negative consequences, and the other was written so that positive consequences resulted.

Results: Children's Data.   The proportion scores and the scale scores for Cluster 2 appear in Table 4.4. All data in this cluster were collapsed across sets because of the lack of any significant difference in scores between sets. Also, no differences were found when the types of endings in the causal passages were assessed. Including positive and negative endings did not affect scores given to any of the passages, and, therefore, these data will not be discussed further.

On the Yes–No task, three passages were considered to belong to the story category: the multiple episode with an obstacle included; the single episode; and the animate reactive sequence. There were no significant differences among the proportion scores for these three types of passages, with a mean proportion score of .85 given for the multiple episode, .79 for the single episode, and .80 for the reactive sequence. These data showed that children include both nongoal-based and goal-based passages in their definitions of a story. However, the nongoal-based passages had to include an animate protagonist in order to be classified as a story.

Passages corresponding directly to Prince's definition (e.g., a physical causal sequence without an animate protagonist) were not included in the story category. Neither were passages that had only a partial listing of features from any of the three definitions. The proportion scores on these *incomplete* passages signifi-

TABLE 4.4
Cluster 2: Mean Proportion Scores and Mean Scale Scores

Passage Type	Yes–No Task Mean Proportions		Seven-Point Scale Mean Scores	
	Children	Teachers	Children	Teachers
1. Multiple-episode	.85	.95	4.10	4.70
2. Single-episode	.79	.90	3.40	4.30
3. Reactive sequence	.80	.80	3.60	3.95
4. Action sequence	.62	.71	2.90	3.29
5. Physical causal sequence	.55	.50	3.06	3.10
6. Animate descriptive sequence	.53	.25	3.10	2.10
7. Inanimate descriptive sequence	.21	.22	1.95	1.89

cantly differed from those passages thought to be a story. The mean proportion score for passages not containing reference to an animate protagonist and not including causal connections among events was .57. The fact that the proportion scores on these passages were at approximately the .50 level indicated a large amount of disagreement among children as to whether or not these *incomplete* texts were stories. There was a much larger consensus, however, on the physical descriptive sequence, which contained none of the features of any story definition. Only 21% of the children judged this to be a story. Thus, a significant majority of children rated this text as not a story.

The results from the seven-point scale task were similar to the Yes–No task. The correlation between the goodness rankings and proportion of subjects accepting each passage as a story was .84. Although subjects completing the Yes–No task were not explicitly asked to rank the goodness of a passage, the rankings, in terms of the amount of consensus among children's story judgments, directly paralleled the degree of goodness attributed to each passages on the seven-point scale task.

On the Yes–No task, there was a linear relationship between the number of story features included in a text and whether or not the text was included in the story category. The more story features in a text, the more likely subjects were to include it in their concept of a story. The increase in the number of story features also increased the goodness ranking of the text on the seven-point scale rating task.

One difference did emerge when the Yes–No task and the scale task were compared. On the seven-point rating scale task, only the multiple-episode passage was given a rating of 4 or above, indicating that this passage was the only one definitely included in the story category. The single episode and animate reactive sequences were given mean ratings of 3.4 and 3.6, respectively. These scores fell just below the 4.0 level. The differences in the scores for the multiple episode as compared to the single episode and animate reactive sequence were found to be significant at the $p < .01$ level.

The differences in those texts that were included in the story category on the two tasks could be attributed again to different criteria used on the two tasks. However, it should be noted that approximately 65% of the children on the scale task gave a score of 4 to both the animate reactive sequence and the one-episode passages. These proportion scores indicate a significant proportion of children are classifying both the one episode and animate reactive sequence passages as stories, despite the fact that the mean score fell just below the 4.0 level on the scale task.

The scale scores for those passages containing partial listings of story features or none of the features of any definition were similar to those found on the Yes–No task. None of these passages was considered to be a story, but passages containing a partial listing of features, however, were more likely to be included in the story category than passages containing none of the features of any definition.

Results: Teachers' Data.   There was a high degree of similarity between the results obtained on the Yes–No and rating scale task. The similarity pertained to both the rankings of passages along a continuum of goodness and to those passages included in the story category.

On the Yes–No task, four passages were considered to belong to the story category: the multiple episode, the single episode, the animate reactive sequence, and the animate action sequence. The same results were found on the scale task, except that the animate action sequence was not judged to be a story. The animate action sequence contains a partial listing of features in terms of the three definitions, whereas the other three texts match at least one definition. Thus, like children, teachers appear to use both goal-based and nongoal-based definitions of a story. However, the non-goal-based passages had to include an animate protagonist.

Passages corresponding directly to Prince's definition (e.g., the physical reactive sequence without an animate protagonist) were not included in the story category on either task. On the scale task, the mean score was 3.10; on the Yes–No task, the mean proportion was .55. As indicated by the results from these tasks, this type of passage evoked the greatest amount of disagreement among teachers as to whether or not these passages were stories. The same amount of disagreement was found when scores were assessed from those passages containing a partial listing of features of any one definition.

Passages containing only descriptions of either an inanimate or animate object were classified as definitely not stories on the Yes–No task. On the scale task, these passages were also rated as nonstories, receiving the lowest mean score of any of the passages. The animate descriptive sequence received a mean scale score of 2.10 and the physical descriptive sequence a score of 1.89.

When the rankings of goodness on the two tasks were compared, a correlation of 1.00 was found, indicating a perfect degree of correspondence. On both tasks, there was a direct linear relationship between the number of story features included in a text and whether or not the text was considered to belong to the story category. The more features in the text, the more likely it was included in the story category. Similarly, the more features in a text, the higher it was ranked along a continuum of goodness.

Comparisons between Children and Teachers.   When the rank ordering of the proportion scores on the Yes–No task was compared across children and teachers, the correlation coefficient was found to be .96, indicating an almost perfect correspondence between the two rankings. On the rating scale task, the correlation was .82, again indicating a significantly high degree of agreement among children and teachers. Both groups always chose the passage representing the most complex definition as the best example of a story. Passages with none of the features of any definition were always chosen as the worst example, whereas those texts containing a partial listing of features were ranked in between the best and worst examples.

The criterion for deciding the absolute boundaries of a story category were similar across the two groups. However, there were some important differences. First, teachers included more passages in the story category than children did. This finding generalized across both tasks. Teachers also judged more texts as definitely *not* belonging to the story category than children did. That is, there was more consensus among the teachers group when asked to make judgments about passages with none of the features or only a partial set of features of any story definition. A greater majority of teachers was more likely to classify these texts as not belonging to the story category than children were.

Cluster 3

Description of Materials. The passages contained in this cluster were all goal-based. These materials were used to test the descriptive adequacy of the goal-based definitions of Stein and Glenn (1979) and Mandler and Johnson (1977). As Table 4.1 indicates, the primary difference between the two goal-based definitions is that Mandler and Johnson require an ending to be attached to a single-episode story, whereas Stein and Glenn do not. Therefore, the first passage in this cluster contained all of the relevant parts of a story, except the ending or reaction category. The following is an example of this type of passage:

> Once there was a fox
> who was playing outside
> when it started to pour.
> Suddenly a huge river formed
> pulling the fox into the current.
> The fox became frightened
> but managed to swim fast enough
> to get out of the current
> and save his life.

According to Mandler and Johnson (1977) this passage does not contain an ending (e.g., He felt relieved and was careful never to let that occur again.) and, therefore, should not be rated as a story. However, Stein and Glenn (1979) do not require an ending. If the episode contains all of the other categories, it will still be included in the story category, primarily because the reaction or ending can easily be inferred by the comprehender. Indeed, the reaction or ending category is often omitted during story recall, even at the end of a multiple-episode story.

The other four types of passages in this cluster were variants of the first passage. Each passage omitted a different episodic category from the text, so that the four types of passages resulted in the following category sequence:

1. Setting-internal response-attempt-consequence.
2. Setting-initiating event-attempt-consequence.
3. Setting-initiating event-internal response-consequence.
4. Setting-initiating event-internal response-attempt.

According to Mandler and Johnson, none of these four passages should be considered stories, because all of them are missing an ending category. Stein and Glenn (1979), however, do not require an ending category and additionally claim that either the initiating event or the internal response can be omitted if the other categories are included in the text sequence. Therefore, sequences one and two should be included in the story category, as well as the passage containing all categories with the exception of the ending (reaction) category.

Results: Children's Data.   The data were consistent across both tasks and are provided in Table 4.5. On the Yes–No task, only one type of passage was included in the story category: the sequence with all categories except the reaction or ending. On the seven-point rating scale task, none of the passages were judged to belong to the story category. Three of the five passages were given mean ratings of approximately 3.3, indicating that children thought these passages were similar to stories but still missing something, whereas two of the passages were given lower scores of 2.2.

Results: Teachers' Data.   Teachers' responses on the Yes–No task indicated that two passages were thought to belong to the story category: passages deleting

TABLE 4.5
Cluster 3: Mean Proportion Scores and Mean Scale Scores

Passage Type	Yes–No Task Mean Proportions		Seven-Point Scale Mean Scores	
	Children	Teachers	Children	Teachers
1. Episode with reaction deleted	.70	.85	3.2	4.0
2. Episode with internal response and reaction deleted	.58	.79	3.4	3.6
3. Episode with initiating event and reaction deleted	.49	.55	2.1	2.8
4. Episode with attempt and reaction deleted	.48	.60	2.3	2.7
5. Episode with consequence and reaction deleted	.56	.32	3.2	2.6

the reaction category and passages deleting both the internal response and reaction category. The data from the seven-point rating scale task indicated that passages deleting reactions were considered stories. The passages deleting both the internal response and reaction were given a mean scale score of 3.6, indicating that this passage was almost a story but was still missing something to be fully included in the story category.

Comparisons Between Children and Teachers.   Data from both groups, presented in Table 4.5, indicated that the final episodic category, the reaction or ending, is not necessary for a text to be classified as a story. The results from the teachers' data support this hypothesis more strongly than the children's data. Teachers rated episodes without endings to be stories on both tasks, whereas children judged this type of passage to be a story only on the Yes–No task.

Teachers also included passages with both the internal response and reaction categories deleted in their concept of a story. This result, however, was found only on the Yes–No task. On the seven-point rating scale task, this type of passage was not included in the story category by either teachers or children. Thus, again teachers included more types of passages in the story category than children.

The rank ordering of passages within this cluster, however, was highly similar across groups of subjects. Table 4.6 contains the mean proportion and scale scores for all passages, including the scores from texts containing complete single episodes described in Cluster 2. On the Yes–No task, the rank order correlation was 1.00 across groups, whereas on the rating scale the correlation was .80. These results indicate that the two groups have similar criteria in mind when they decide whether or not a passage is a story and where on the goodness

TABLE 4.6
Mean Proportion and mean Scale Scores on All Single Episodes,
With and Without Category Deletions

	Yes–No Task Mean Proportions		Seven-Point Scale Mean Scores	
Passage Type	Children	Teachers	Children	Teachers
1. Single-episode, with all categories	.79	.90	3.4	4.3
2. Single-episode, Reaction deleted	.70	.85	3.2	4.0
3. Single-episode, internal response and reaction deleted	.58	.79	3.4	3.5
4. Single-episode, with other categories plus the reaction deleted	.51	.49	2.5	2.7

continuum each passage should be placed. The single episode with all categories was given the highest ranking, the ending deleted episode the next highest, and the internal response and ending deleted episode the next highest. All other episodes received lower ranks.

Cluster 4

Description of Materials.   Passages in this cluster were devised to investigate whether subjects could adequately discriminate between procedures, as described by Black and Wilensky (1979), and texts that actually included all parts of a story, according to the Stein and Glenn (1979) or Mandler and Johnson (1977) grammars. As we indicated in the introduction, although Black and Wilensky consider the procedure to contain all parts of the story, it does not. Three of the five episodic categories are missing, as well as mention of a specific animate protagonist. Thus subjects should never rate procedures as stories, especially since the procedure is missing both the attempt and the consequence categories. Passages including these categories and a specific animate protagonist should be judged as stories. In order to test this hypothesis, two passages were constructed: a procedure and a story with all of the parts described in the grammars. Both passages had the same semantic content. The procedure was written in the future tense, indicating a possibility of results if suggestions were followed. An example of a procedural text was the following:

Procedure

Here's how a farmer
can get his stubborn
horse into the barn.
The farmer can go into the barn
and hold out some sugar
to get the horse to come and eat.
But if the horse does not like sugar,
he will not come.
Here's another thing he can do.
Suppose the farmer has a dog.
He can get the dog to bark at the horse.
This may frighten the horse
and make him run into the barn.

The story text, however, included a specific animate protagonist, an attempt and consequence, and was written in the past tense. The following is an example:

Story

Once there was a farmer
who wanted to get his stubborn

horse into the barn.
The farmer went into the barn
and held out some sugar
to get the horse to come and eat.
But the horse did not like sugar
and he did not come.
The farmer tried something else.
The farmer had a dog.
He got the dog to bark at the horse.
This frightened the horse
and made him run into the barn.

In order to ensure generalizability, a second set of passages was constructed similar to the set just described. All subjects made judgments on all four passages.

Results: Children's Data.   The results, as indicated in Table 4.7, are unambiguous. On both tasks children clearly discriminate stories from procedures; the scores for stories and procedures are significantly different from one another. On the Yes–No task, the story passage was considered to belong to the story category, whereas the procedure was not. The scores for this passage were at the .50 level falling in between the cut-off point for a story or nonstory. The scores on the seven-point rating scale showed the mean score for the story to be just on the border of the story category, with a mean rating of 3.8. The procedure was clearly outside of the story category with a mean rating of 2.9.

Results: Teachers' Data.   The results from both tasks were unambiguous. Only the story passages were accepted as stories. The procedure was not included in the story category. On the Yes–No task the mean proportion score for the procedure was .37, indicating almost significant consensus among teachers that the text was definitely not a story. The mean proportion score for the story was .91. On the seven-point rating scale task, the mean score for the procedure was 2.7, whereas the mean score for the story was 4.52.

TABLE 4.7
Cluster 4: Mean Proportion and Mean Scale Scores

Passage Type	Yes–No Task Mean Proportions		Seven-Point Scale Mean Scores	
	Children	Teachers	Children	Teachers
Stories	.89	.91	3.70	4.52
Procedures	.50	.37	2.90	2.70

Comparison Between Children and Teachers.   The data show strong similarities when children's and teachers' judgments are compared. Subjects in both groups clearly discriminate between the two passage types, with both groups rating the story passage as a story and the procedure as not being included in the story category. The only difference in the scores across the groups was that there was more agreement among teachers than children that the story text was definitely a story and that the procedure was definitely not a story.

DISCUSSION

Three issues are discussed in this section. First, the adequacy of nongoal-based and goal-based definitions is considered in relationship to both children's and teachers' judgments. Second, the concept of a *good* story and its many meanings is discussed, Third, the relationship between children's and teachers' knowledge of stories is explored with reference to the educational implications of these relationships.

The Concept of a Story

The results from this study showed that nongoal-based passages, as well as goal-based passages, were accepted as stories. However, Prince's definition was not adequate in describing the type of nongoal-based passage that was considered to belong to the story category. The data showed that a story passage had to contain reference to a specific animate protagonist, as well as including a change of state in the physical environment of the protagonist.

Even if the features of an animate protagonist were included in Prince's nongoal-based definition, it would still not be adequate to capture all judgments made about stories and nonstories. Passages containing emotional state changes of a protagonist, with an intervening event causing the change, were not considered part of the story category by children or teachers. Thus, it is clear from our data that no one definition captures all of the judgments made about stories and nonstories.

We can, however, say two things about the conceptual knowledge of stories acquired by both children and teachers. First, an animate protagonist and some type of causal relationship among events are almost always expected in any passage considered to be a story. Children always rejected texts that did not contain a causal sequence when they were asked to judge the story quality of a text. Teachers accepted only one instance of a noncausal sequence as belonging to the story category, but this judgment did not generalize across tasks. Thus, we can say that texts must include at least an animate protagonist and some type of causal sequence in order to be considered a story.

Our second comment concerns the criteria used for determining when goal-directed behavior has to be in a story text and when it can be excluded. We proposed that because goal-directed behavior is the expected norm in social interaction (e.g., children learn at the very early age of 2½ that other people's behavior is governed by internal desires; Huttenlocher, Smiley, & Charney, 1983) in most stories, this type of behavior would also be the expected course of action.

We suggested, however, that there were social situations where goal-directed actions were not possible and that these situations would also be reflected in stories. In particular, we referred to those situations that present novel, fortuitous, or threatening events where the protagonist has no control over the physical environment and often no time to generate a plan. If the sequence of events in the story made it clear that no available plan of action could be generated or that intentional behavior was not possible or probable, then this type of passage would be considered a story.

The data from both groups of subjects supported this hypothesis. On both tasks, teachers clearly rated our animate reactive sequences, containing no goal-based action, as belonging to the story category. Children also included this type of passage in the story category. Stein & Kilgore (1981) have also replicated this finding on three groups of college students, using both Yes–No and seven-point rating scale tasks as methods of assessment.

In considering the acceptability of nongoal-based passages, however, we argued that these texts had to contain an unambiguous reference to whether or not goal-directed behavior was possible. If the text did not contain an unambiguous reference to the possibility of implementing goal-directed behavior or an explanation for why the set of circumstances or state changes occurred in a passage, then the text would not be considered a story.

The fact that internal emotional state changes with the inclusion of an intervening event are not considered stories offers some initial support for this hypothesis. When children and teachers were asked to judge whether or not these types of passages were stories, both groups rejected these texts as definitely belonging to the story category. Although a majority of teachers included this type of text in their story category (62%), this proportion was not quite large enough to reach the 95% level of responding on the Yes–No task. Furthermore, almost all teachers (98%) excluded this type of text from the story category on the scale task ratings. Clearly, then, some type of critical information was perceived to be missing from these passages relating emotional state changes where the intervening event was not necessarily goal-based (e.g., John was sad; then he found his toy; as a result, he was happy).

A possible interpretation could be based on the length of the passages that children and teachers had to rate. The nongoal-based passages with emotional state changes were only three lines in length, whereas the passages containing physical events and state changes (e.g., animate reactive sequences) were seven lines in length. Both children and teachers could have used the length of a passage to guide their judgment.

This explanation, however, does not hold up under further scrutiny in examining data from this study or the study completed by Stein and Kilgore (1981) on college students. In the Stein and Kilgore (1981) study, college students rated passages similar to the ones used in this study. However, both the length and the content of each passage were controlled. All passages were exactly 12 statements in length and the content was similar across passages.

The results from the Stein and Kilgore (1981) study were the same as those in this study. College students included the same types of nongoal-based passages in their concept of a story and also excluded from the story category the same types of nongoal-based passages, as subjects did in our study. Thus, length is not the critical factor determining whether or not a passage is classified as a story. It should also be noted that teachers in the present study ranked seven-line passages containing only descriptions of objects far lower than three-line passages containing an emotional state change. Future research is necessary to determine more exactly the reasons for the variation in judgment on nongoal-based stories.

The results from our study, however, showed that the added features of more complex definitions, such as Labov and Waletsky (1967) or Wilensky (1980) advocate, are not necessary for a text to be considered a story. Thus, Black and Wilensky's criticism that the grammars do not contain enough detail has not been substantiated. The results showed that fewer features than those proposed in the grammars can be included in story texts. Thus, their assertion that texts exist having all of the features of stories but not being included in the story category is not substantiated. What was found was that there are texts not containing all the features of stories, as described in the grammars, that are included in the story category.

We also found that not all constituents of a goal-based episode need be included in a text for it to be classified as a story. In particular, the ending category of the episode can be deleted, as well as both the internal response and ending categories in some stories. These findings do not support Mandler and Johnson's (1977; Johnson & Mandler, 1980) claim that an ending has to be included in one-episode stories. Their deletion rule concerning the ending category can now be extended to single-episode stories, as well as multiple-episode passages (see Johnson & Mandler, 1980). In order to test the validity of Johnson and Mandler's (1980) other deletion rules, a more systematic test will be necessary. This should be done, especially in the light of Black and Wilensky's criticisms about their deletion rules. Black and Wilensky (1979) claim that any one episodic category could be omitted from a text, and the text would still be classified as a story.

Mandler and Johnson (1980) have argued against Black and Wilensky's claim, stating that although inferability is an important factor in determining permissible deletions, there are other factors of importance too. A second factor is the frequency with which each category is deleted when stories are read or told. From an analysis of many different types of folk tales, two types of deletions predominate: internal responses and endings (reactions) of episodes other than the final episode in the story.

Our data showed, however, that both children and teachers accepted as stories one-episode passages without an ending, despite the fact that this type of deletion rarely occurs in oral and written tales. We should also note that from pilot studies in our laboratory, college students also accept as stories one-episode sequences with any one category deleted, with the exception of the consequence or outcome of an episode. This suggests that story pasages can be written so that information in any one category can be made highly inferable and therefore deletable. However, deletions of information do affect the goodness rating of a story, as we soon discuss.

The Concept of a Good Story

The second set of hypotheses considered in this study concerned the concept of a good story. We argued that if story knowledge is organized along similar principles as natural object categories, then some types of instances should be more frequent and therefore more representative of the story category than other instances. In particular, we argued that although some forms of nongoal-based passage would be considered a part of the story category, they would not be judged to be as good or representative of the story category as goal-based passages. In turn, goal-based passages without obstacles would not be considered as good as those passages containing an obstacle in the goal-path of a protagonist.

The data from both children and teachers supported this hypothesis. There was almost a perfect correlation between the number of features included in a text and the goodness ranking of the text. Also, the number of story features in a text was related directly to the proportion of subjects willing to accept the passage as a story. Similar types of results were found when different types of goal-based stories were assessed. Those passages with all of the parts of an episode were always rated higher than those passages containing permissible deletions of any category information. Some of the controversy over which definition is the correct one can easily be resolved if we consider the difference between a story and a good story. As we illustrated, no one definition captures all of the decisions made about stories and nonstories. This includes the more recent definition offered by Brewer and Lichtenstein (1981; 1982). However, when the concept of a good story is considered, both children and teachers prefer certain stories over others.

In determining the features of a good story, definitions such as those offered by Labov and Waletsky (1967), Quasthoff and Nikolaus (1981), and Brewer and Lichtenstein (1981) may be more accurate in describing the best example of the story category than the simpler description outlined in the grammars. Dimensions, such as obstacles and conflicts, among protagonists may be necessary elements of a good story, as well as some arousal of affective response in the comprehender.

It must be pointed out, however, that dimensions such as a required affective response from the comprehender may also serve to lessen the goodness rating of a story. If a story arouses too much suspense or fear, a reader or listener may choose not to finish a story, or if forced, will block out parts and consider the story a terrible one. An example of this phenomenon can be seen when children are told scary *ghost* stories. Some children delight in these tales, whereas others wish that this type of story never existed. If children were confronted with the question: Does this story arouse suspense, fear, etc.? Almost all would agree that *ghost* stories do. However, some children might rank the story as poor because it aroused too much fear or suspense.

Our point in discussing different affective responses to the same story is to highlight the role of the comprehender in terms of attitudes, needs, and prior knowledge brought to the task at hand. Individual differences in responses to stories also suggest that attempting to understand what is meant by a "good" story deserves further consideration. Although subjects in this study were asked to judge passages in terms of the representative nature of the story category, we cannot say that these were the only factors regulating goodness judgments. Other factors, such as the degree of liking the story, whether or not anything was learned from the story, and whether the story was *realistic,* may play important roles in goodness judgment. This study did not explore this issue, but certainly future studies should.

Developmental Differences in Story Knowledge

When teachers' and children's judgments were compared, highly similar patterns emerged. The goodness ranking of passages was almost perfectly correlated when the two groups were compared, Thus, children and teachers rated the same passages as the best story and the poorest story.

There were, however, some important differences between the two groups. On the whole, teachers accepted more passages as belonging to the story category than did children. This was especially true when teachers had to consider whether or not goal-based episodes containing deletions were stories and whether or not passages containing emotional state changes with an intervening event were also included in the story category. In all cases, teachers more readily included these passages in the story category than did children. In addition, teachers, but not children, included an animate action sequence with only temporal connectors in their concept of a story.

These differences were somewhat different than we predicted. From our generation studies (Stein & Glenn, 1982; Stein, Glenn, & Jarcho, 1982), we know that children in the age range from five to seven sometimes generate nongoal-based passages when asked to tell good stories. This type of storytelling slowly decreases as the child gets older. Thus, we proposed that the story concept, in certain respects, would also narrow in terms of the acceptability of including nongoal-based behavior in stories. Apparently, for these second-grade children, goal-based stories were always preferred over nongoal-based stories, and in most instances, nongoal-based passages were not considered to be stories.

Two explanations for these findings must be considered before our original hypothesis is discarded. If the concept of a story was studied from a truly developmental viewpoint with children in the early preschool years, we might find that these children include almost any type of text in their concept of a story. Thus, both goal-based and nongoal-based passages would be included in their story category.

Instructional implications must also be considered in assessing the knowledge children acquire about stories. The initial concept of a story may differ depending on the quality of input the child receives regarding the story concept. In some environments, the word *story* is used so generally that it becomes difficult for the child to abstract out any consistent set of features that defines this class of discourse. We have seen the word *story* used with children when teachers want to increase attention to a particular word or phrase, as well as to an individual sentence. Indeed, some teachers even use the word *story* when they are beginning to teach children about different discourse structures, like the exposition (e.g., a procedure for how to do something). Many teachers believe that stories are easier for children to learn and that if an exposition is incorporated into a story format, it too will increase in comprehensibility.

This belief may be true; however, the broad use of the word *story* is quite misleading for the child who must try to write an example of a good story. Some children, however, may be exposed to systematic training in telling *good* stories from an early age. If this were the case, then even young children may have a concept of a story similar to that of adults, especially regarding the types of nongoal-based stories included in their story concept. However, we suspect that even if children were to acquire the adult concept of a *good* story very quickly, children would still have more difficulty than adults accepting passages that either deleted or inverted category information within the episodic structure. Only future research will determine the accuracy of these predictions. However, it is clear that the quality of input in the formulation of a story concept is a necessary area for investigation.

ACKNOWLEDGMENTS

The research presented in the chapter was supported in part by a grant from the Sloan and Benton Foundations to Nancy L. Stein. The authors were also supported in part by National Institute of Education grants NIE-G-77-0018 and NIE-G-79-0125 to Tom Trabasso. We would like to thank Jim Mosenthal and Tom Trabasso for their helpful comments and insights during the completion of this manuscript.

REFERENCES

Abrams, D. C., & Sutton-Smith, B. The development of the trickster in children's narrative. *Journal of American Folklore*, 1977, 90, 29–47.

Anglin, J. M. *Word, Object and Conceptual Development*. New York: W. W. Norton and Company, 1977.

Applebee, A. N. *The child's concept of a story*. Chicago, ILL: University of Chicago Press, 1978.

Ausubel, N. *A treasury of Jewish folklore*. New York: Bantam Abridged Edition, 1980.

Baker, A., & Greene, E. *Storytelling: Art and technique*. New York: R. R. Bowker Co., 1977.

Beaugrande, R.de , & Colby, B. W. Narrative models of action and interaction. *Cognitive Science*, 1979, 3, 43–66.

Bettelheim, B. *The uses of enchantment: The meaning and importance of fairy stories*. New York: Random House Vintage Books, 1977.

Black, J. B. *Story memory structure*. Unpublished doctoral dissertation, Stanford University, 1977.

Black, J. B., & Bower, G. B. Story understanding as problem solving. *Poetics*, 1980, 9, 223–250.

Black, J. B., & Wilensky, R. An evaluation of story grammars. *Cognitive Science*, 1979, 3, 213–230.

Botvin, G. J., & Sutton-Smith, B. The development of structural complexity in children's fantasy narratives. *Developmental Psychology*, 1977, 13, 377–388.

Bowerman, M. The acquisition of word meaning: An investigation of some current concepts. In N. Watson, & C. Snow (Eds.), *The development of communication*. New York: J. Wiley and Sons, 1978.

Bremond, C. *Loqique du recit*. Paris: Sevil, 1973.

Brewer, W. F., & Lichtenstein, E. H. Event schemas, story schemas, and story grammer. In A. D. Baddeley, & J. D. Long (Eds.), *Attention and performance, IV*. Hillsdale, N.J.: Lawrence Erlbaum Associates, 1981.

Brewer, W. F., & Lichtenstein, E. H. Stories are to entertain: A structural affect therapy of stories. *Pragmatics*, 1982, 6, 5–6, 473–486.

Calvino, I. *Italian folktales*. New York: Random House, 1980.

Colby, B. N. A partial grammar of eskimo folktales. *American Anthropologist*, 1973, 75, 645–662.

Gentner, D. Verb semantic structures in memory for sentences: Evidence for componential representation. (Technical Report No. 151). Center for the study of Reading, University of Illinois, Urbana-Champaign, 1979.

Goffman, I. *Frame analysis*. Cambridge, Ma.: Harvard University press, 1974.

Goldman, S. Knowledge systems for realistic goals. *Discourse Processes*, 1982, 5, 279–303.

Hoover, N. L. *An investigation of the developmental level of story schema as a factor in beginning reading*. Paper presented at the National Reading Conference, San Diego, December 1980.

Hunt, M., & Hunt, B. *The divorce experience*. New York: New American Library, 1977.

Huttenlocher, J., Smiley, P., & Charney, R. The emergence of action categories in the child: Evidence from verb meanings. *Psychological Review*, 1983, 90, 1, 72–93.

Johnson, E., Sickels, E. R., Sayers, F. C., & Horovitz, C. *Anthology of children's literature*, 5th Edition. Boston, Mass.: Houghton Mifflin Co., 1977.

Johnson, N. S., & Mandler, J. M. A tale of two structures: Underlying and surface forms in stories. *Poetics*, 1980, 9, 51–86.

Kintsch, W. Learning from text, levels of comprehension, or: Why anyone would read a story anyway. *Poetics*, 1980, 9, 87–99.

Labov, W., & Waletsky, J. Narrative analysis: Oral versions of personal experience. In J. Helan (Ed.), *Essays on the verbal and visual arts*. Seattle, Wa.: University of Washington Press, 1967.

Leondar, B. Hatching plots: Genesis of storymaking. In D. Perkins & B. Leondar (Eds.), *The arts and cognition*. Baltimore, Md.: Johns Hopkins Press, 1977.

Levi-Strauss, V. The structural study of myth. In T. A. Sebeck (Ed.), *Myth: A symposium*. Bloomington, Ind.: Indiana University Press, 1955.

Mandler, J. M., & Johnson, N. S. Remembrance of things parsed: Story structure and recall. *Cognitive Psychology*, 1977, *9*, 111–151.

Mandler, J. M. & Johnson, N. S. On throwing out the baby with the bathwater: A reply to Black and Wilensky's evaluation of story grammars. *Cognitive Science*, 1980, 305–312.

Mervis, C. B. Category structure and the development of categorization. In R. Spiro, B. C. Bruce, & W. F. Brewer (Eds.), *Theoretical issues in reading comprehension: Perspectives from cognitive psychology, linguistics, artificial intelligence and education*. Hillsdale, N.J.: Lawrence Erlbaum Associates, 1981.

Mervis, C. B., & Pani, J. R. Acquisition of basic object categories. *Cognitive Psychology*, 1980, *12*, 496–522.

Mervis, C. B., & Rosch, E. Categorization of natural objects. *Annual Review of Psychology*, 1981, *32*, 89–115.

Morgan, J. L., & Sellner, M. B. Discourse and linguistic theory. In R. J. Spiro, B. C. Bruce, & W. F. Brewer (Eds.), *Theoretical issues in reading comprehension: Perspectives from cognitive psychology, linguistics, artificial intelligence and education*. Hillsdale, N.J.: Lawrence Erlbaum Associates, 1981.

National Association for the Preservation and Perpetuation of Storytelling. Jonesborough, Tenn., 37658, Fall, 1980.

Prince, G. *A grammar for stories*. The Hague: Mouton, 1973.

Progoff, I. *At a journal workshop*. New York: Dialogue House, 1977.

Propp, V. *Morphology of the folktale*. Vol. 10. Bloomington, Ind.: Indiana University Research Center in Anthropology, Folklore, and Linguistics, 1958.

Quasthoff, U., & Nikolaus, K. What makes a good story. Paper presented at International Symposium on Text Processing, Friburg, Switzerland, September 1981.

Rainer, T. *The new diary*. Los Angeles: J. P. Tarcher, Inc., 1978.

Rosch, E. Universals and cultural specifics in human categorization. In R. Brislin, S. Bochner, & W. Lonner (Eds.), *Cross-cultural perspectives on learning*. New York: Halsted Press, 1975.

Rosch, E., & Mervis, C. B. Family resemblances: Studies in the internal structure of categories. *Cognitive Psychology*, 1975, *7*, 573–605.

Rumelhart, D. E. Notes on schema for stories. In D. G. Bobrow & A. Collins (Eds.), *Representation and understanding*. New York: Academic Press, 1975.

Rumelhart, D. E. Understanding and summarizing brief stories. In D. LaBerge & J. Samuels (Eds.), *Basic processes in reading: Perception and comprehension*. Hillsdale, N.J.: Lawrence Erlbaum Associates, 1977.

Stein, N. L. How children understand stories: A developmental analysis. In L. Katz (Ed.), *Current topics in early childhood education* (Vol. 2). Norwood, N.J.: Ablex, 1979.

Stein, N. L. What's in a story: Interpreting the interpretation of story grammars. *Discourse Processes*, in press.

Stein, N. L., & Glenn, C. G. An analysis of story comprehension in elementary school children. In R. O. Freedle (Ed.), *New Directions in Discourse Processing*, Volume 2 in the series, *Advances in Discourse Processes*. Norwood, N.J.: Ablex, 1979.

Stein, N. L., & Glenn, C. G. Children's concept of time: The development of a story schema. In W. Friedman (Ed.), *The developmental psychology of time*. New York: Academic Press, 1982.

Stein, N. L., Glenn, C. G., & Jarcho, H. Children's stories: A method for describing the structural complexity and thematic content of generated stories. Unpublished manuscript, University of Chicago, 1982.

Stein, N. L., & Kilgore, K. M. The concept of a story. Paper presented at Psychonomics Society Convention, Philadelphia, Pa., 1981.

Sutton-Smith, B. The importance of the storytaker: An investigation of the imaginative life. *The Urban Review,* 1976, *8,* 82–95.

Sutton-Smith, B., Botvin, G., & Mahoney, D. Developmental structures in fantasy narratives. *Human Development,* 1976, *19,* 1–13.

Thorndyke, P. W. Cognitive structures in comprehension and memory of narrative discourse. *Cognitive Psychology,* 1977, *9,* 77–110.

Wilensky, R. *Points: A theory of story content.* Memorandum No. UCR/ERL M80/17, 1980.

5 Learning to Read Versus Reading to Learn: A Discourse-Processing Approach[1]

Robert de Beaugrande
University of Florida

Learning to read subsumes all settings in which written texts are processed with the dominant (though not exclusive) goal of rehearsing, improving, or organizing the processes themselves. *Reading to learn,* on the other hand, subsumes all settings in which texts are processed with the dominant (though not exclusive) goal of acquiring knowledge about the topic domain underlying the text in use. One could make a similar definition for learning to listen versus listening to learn. So far, the tendency has been to consider the spoken mode unproblematic, probably because it is acquired fairly well outside the schools.

Despite significant advances in educational technology, the major instructional vehicle continues to be the didactic text. Familiar examples include the lecture and the textbook. The didactic text is defined according to its function rather than to its format. It is intended not to expand its domain of knowledge in any absolute sense (e.g., what society overall knows about physics), but rather to present a domain to a group of comparative novices (e.g., to introduce a college undergraduate to physics). Of course, didactic texts imply that the domain itself is stable (that its facts are well-established, that all experts agree, that the central notions are uniformly defined, and so on). The didactic text can at best indicate the background of agreement against which continual discussions and disputes are staged. The text presents the domain as more coherent than it really is or has been (cf. Kuhn, 1970).

There are signals that the methodology which centers schooling around the didactic text may not be very successful. The classroom lecture appears to be

---

[1]This paper was shortened by the editors, and a section on experiments was removed. Footnote 8 summarizes the results reported in that section.

159

ineffective (cf. Kintsch & Bates, 1977). Schools encounter a rate of partial failure that industry or business would not tolerate. Obviously, some improvements are needed in the area of design, where *design* is defined by Rosenstein, Rathbone, and Schneerer (1964) as "an iterative decision-making process which is employed to develop means for optimizing the value of resources" [p. 3]. As Bormuth (1975) has suggested, design improvements can take place either in the materials—text design—or in the learner's skills—process design. We could set up as theoretical constructs the end points of these design directions as the optimal text and the optimal processor, respectively. Though I am not claiming that these end points are actually attainable in practice, this chapter is concerned with the conditions for describing and approaching them.

The well-structuredness of an object of inquiry depends on our abilities to perceive and describe structures in terms of prevailing theories. This has been striking in linguistics and in language psychology. An enduring achievement in linguistics, and one often borrowed by other disciplines, has been the development of techniques for structural analysis, i.e., the classifications of items or of relationships between or among items according to a taxonomic scheme. The notions propagated by this focus—binary oppositions, distinctive features, markers, grammars, transformational rules, embedding, recursion, etc.—have become familiar watchwords among students of language and communication.

Historically, one central enterprise of linguistics has been to increase the well-structuredness of language by adding theoretical substrates of structure. Harris (1952) invented the notion of "transformation" to increase the "equivalences" in discourse samples; Chomsky (1957) greatly expanded the notion into a rule apparatus that would, in effect, establish the uniform well-structuredness of every possible sentence of English. What appeared to many as a "revolution" was rather a continuation of a strong tradition via some new theoretical mechanisms.

Descriptive linguistics had mistrusted the categories of traditional school grammars and tried to find more formally defined grammars. The "distributional" approach (Harris, 1951) undertook to classify items according to the positions they could occupy in language strings. Chomskyan grammarians adopted a more benevolent stance toward traditional grammar, although their classification procedures were tied to the formal arrangement of strings. Both approaches entailed a serious difficulty: professional linguists assumed a kind of well-structuredness that the object domain didn't necessarily possess. Martinet (1962) surmised that the structures were "nothing but a frame invented by the linguist in order to help him classify the data [p. 58]." In other words, a structuralist is not one who *discovers* structures, but one who *makes* them.

This enterprise is, in itself, productive, provided researchers are aware of what they are doing and do not imagine the structures to have a definitive, independent existence in the objects of inquiry. This awareness seems to have been lost when *structural analysis* was incautiously extrapolated as the basic analogy for *language comprehension*. This attitude was adopted variously for immediate constituent analysis (Johnson, 1965), transformational grammar (Mehler, 1963), and many other trends in linguistics (cf. survey in Clark & Clark, 1977). Three important reservations should be made here: (1) that ordinary language users are claimed to hold a level of analytical sophistication equivalent to professional linguists with specialized training; (2) that surface parsing is viewed as being uniform for all communicative occasions; and (3) that the formal analysis placed in the center of investigation abridges the meaning and purpose of discourse, apparently because these concerns are not deemed sufficiently well-structured.

These reservations can be illustrated with the notion of a "well-formed sentence." Linguistic methodologies are frequently based on this notion and use it as a starting point for their studies. In immediate constituent analysis, the sentence is dissected, whereas in transformational grammar, the sentence is assigned a derivational history. But in either case, the structures, discovered or created, *presuppose* the sentence as the basic unit. It is only natural when researchers posit precisely the same precondition for human language users. According to McNeill (1970): "virtually everything that occurs in language acquisition depends on prior knowledge of the basic aspects of sentence structure. The concept of a sentence may be part of man's [sic] innate mental capacity [p. 2]." The motive for such a claim is easy to see if we replace "language acquisition" with "linguistic analysis." The appeal to "innateness" is the only escape from the impasse of how children could know sentence structure (and hence do the analysis) before they start to learn the language.

An enduring empirical problem for linguistics has been the failure to show that the concept of *sentence* has, among average language users, the same degree of well-structuredness required by most theories. These users have trouble distinguishing consistently or uniformly between well-formed sentences and ill-formed ones. Apparently, people are heavily influenced by contexts in which a given sample sentence might or might not be likely to occur (cf. Greenbaum, 1977). Grammarians reacted to this problem by isolating their added theoretical substrate of structure ("competence") from empirical matters ("performance") (Chomsky, 1965).

In retrospect, it appears strange that, with so much concern for well-structuredness, so few researchers thought of seeking it in *processes,* rather than in *artifacts.* It is readily obvious that a text or sentence exists only insofar as it is used (produced or received) in communication, and not because a linguist elects to analyze it. Yet the usual practice was to take the sentence as a given, as an independent object whose arrival on the scene was not recognized as an interesting issue (cf. Morgan, 1975). In effect, the processes that act upon sentences were being carried out *by the investigators themselves* without clear acknowledgement. Thus, it is difficult to tell if anyone's "grammar" is indeed the same as anyone else's.

The story of readability formulas is in many ways comparable (cf. surveys in Klare, 1963, 1974–75). The desire for well-structuredness led to reliance on tabulating three quasi-formal gradients: length, frequency, and complexity of surface units (word, phrase, clause, or sentence). These gradients were construed as good predictors of readability, so that children's readers should progress along these gradients from one grade level to the next. Here again, several reservations must be made.

First, it is far from certain that *structural* factors must correspond directly to *experiential* ones. For example, the relative complexity of a sentence may be experienced quite differently, according to the number and extent of competing demands upon processing in that context. Yet, a measure that counts words in clauses or sentences has no way of representing larger contexts.

Second, the structural measures imply that the processing of the surface text is a constant value in all instances of reading comprehension. No provision is made for varying degrees of approximation, such as the "fuzzy" parsing apparently used in skim-reading (cf. Schank, Lebowitz, & Birnbaum, 1978; Masson, 1979). Learning to read should exert different demands on surface processing than reading to learn. A child not yet in possession of a detailed language model may approach the surface text quite differently from one at a more advanced stage when more detailed distinctions are made.

Third, the correlation between surface structure and the content and purpose of reading is still opaque. Thus, even if the traditional surface-based formulas are good predictors for readability, we have no account of why they should be so. Rothkopf (1976) remarks that the formulas take no notice of vividness, concreteness, exposition, organization, and content. It hardly seems plausible that these factors could be derivable from the frequency and complexity of words and phrases. Yet it seems equally implausible that these factors should play no role in readability. Hence, the usual readability formulas, like the linguist's notion of "competence," are unduly specialized, uniform, and incomplete.

Schooling has a duality of functions: that children should learn specific knowledge and, at the same time, practice their tactics for learning. The question is whether the same measures work for both learning to read and reading to learn. On the face of it, readable texts should also be the best vehicles for learning their content. But here also, an intuitively plausible correlation demands a theoretical account. In particular, it seems unclear whether reading difficulties share the same processes and obstacles as learning difficulties. It is hard to create learning measures that promote the same kind of well-structuredness as the surface-based readability formulas. In earlier times, verbatim recall was often taken as a clear testimonial of learning. Children who could recite from memory extended textbook passages were singled out as supremely gifted, and test answers containing the exact wording of textbook definitions were generally given the best grades. Educators later came to mistrust verbatim reproductions as a possible mask for the child's failure to understand and digest the materials. Yet other measures of learning will not offer the same degree of well-structuredness (and thus not fall into line with readability formulas) until we can define the orderly structure of *discourse processing:* comprehension, memory storage, inferencing, recall, and so on. Nor can we determine how to create the most favorable conditions for learning to read and reading to learn. In this view, the importance of research on language processes, as opposed to the structural analysis of language artifacts, is pressingly evident.

LEARNING TO READ AND READING TO LEARN: DISCOURSE-PROCESSING AS MODEL-BUILDING

Whereas linguistic and psycholinguistic research have been characteristically *analytic,* discourse processing is characteristically *synthetic.* Whereas structural analysis requires a *formally* defined set of categories, discourse processing requires an *operationally* defined set of categories. Hence, to understand the nature of some entity, researchers in the former approach create and define formal features that assign entities a unique place in a taxonomy. Researchers in the latter approach build a model in order to reconstruct the functions assumed by the entity within a working system. There is no guarantee that the entity must be strictly, even uniquely, classified by its features before it can serve the relevant function—it must simply be able to assume that function sufficiently well to support the operational organization of the domain.

Another significant difference between structural analysis and discourse processing is that the latter can be carried out as model-building at any stage of knowledge or experience, whereas the former cannot begin until all categories are defined equally well. We saw above how this consideration inspired grammarians to argue that children have "innate" knowledge of "sentence structure." In a model-building approach, we assume that a child learns a language (or any other domain of skill or knowledge) by building a series of approximative models, each one evolving out of its predecessor (cf. de Beaugrande, 1982). Whatever knowledge a child may have of "sentence structure" is not innate, but a result of building partial models of word order as a pool for conventional discourse patterns. What is innate is this predilection to understand the world by building models of what goes on in it. The fact that syntactic patterns generally become more expanded and complex as the child grows older reflects the increasing need for differentiation and self-expression within a more elaborated role in human interaction.

By the same token, no one human being is in full possession of the complete language system, though some users to attain a huge store of expertise. The dangers of claiming to "describe English" as if linguists or psychologists could have the entire set of data in their heads, were not adequately appreciated. The explosion of theories made it apparent that there can be as many "grammars" of

English as there are grammarians. Of course, different people's personal language models obviously overlap, since communication does succeed quite extensively. Still, this success is not guaranteed by a uniformity of *grammars,* but by a uniformity of *processing outcomes*—the same basis humans use in order to understand the world at large.

Let us grant for the sake of argument that learning to read is a progression where the child builds and refines models of the ways for getting at meaning and purpose from written discourse, and that reading to learn hinges partly on one's model of reading and partly on one's capacities for building models of knowledge domains. Thus, reading to learn subsumes, but extends far beyond, learning to read. Let us also grant that, in both areas, there is a large number of possible discourse and knowledge models that a child might construct, some of them decisively more strategic than others. It is then obvious that educational programs should seek to guide the evolution of children's models toward the more strategic designs. Such an enterprise can scarcely succeed without much more explicit theories than we now have of how cognitive processes evolve in the acquisition of language and knowledge. Emphasis has traditionally been placed on the accepted structure of knowledge domains themselves, not upon the ways in which such domains can be digested into a learner's model. Above all, the role of *approximation* in provisional models has been inadequately recognized, in part because an approximation must seem an "error" as long as it it not diagnosed as a productive, essential stepping-stone toward the desired state of knowledge (Papert, 1980). In fact, the intolerance of errors is likely to discourage learning in all domains where errors are natural,even necessary prerequisites for progress. Reading is certainly one such domain, as miscue analysis has shown (Goodman & Burke, 1973).

The less organized an educational approach is, the harder its tasks will appear to the learners. In effect, learners are required not only to learn the content of the knowledge domain but also to hit upon, by happy coincidence, the proper strategies for organizing that content in a readily learnable mode. Too often, schools blame failure on a child's personal "aptitudes" and leave their own methods out of scrutiny. "Aptitudes" measured in schooling might be a chance distribution of the possibilities of children arriving at a strategic discourse and knowledge model from among the very large set of possible models. If so, "aptitudes" are being *created* as much as *registered* by school performance, and hence shaped decisely by developmental events that the schools cannot reliably influence without some means to represent cognitive transitions from model to model. Otherwise, schooling can only presuppose these events or attempt to intervene via training whose impact upon cognitive organization is barely explored.[1a]

[1a]Posner (1978, p. 340) observes: "We should not get in the habit of thinking that the organization of the brain is something innate and fixed in time. Teaching does reprogram the brain. It provides new organization, information flow, and temporal patterns. The fact that individuals differ in brain

In exploring the means for optimizing processes, we should not rely on premature conclusions about the nature of processing. In the past, some researchers tried to adopt formal logic as a model of what human thought processes are or should be: conclusive, non-contradictory, fact-based, and provable through strict methods of deduction and entailment. Instead of the large, messy "encyclopedia" of world knowledge, a neat, well-structured, logically complete and foolproof "lexicon" was seen as the guarantee and arbiter of language meaning. Discourse was treated as "predication," i.e. the assigning of "arguments" to "predicates" to form "propositions" (Jarvella, 1977; Miller, 1970). It may be alluring to regard the human mind in this light. But the well-structuredness is bought at a high price: all the important reasoning processes that logic excludes. There is no place left for the intuitions, inferences, defaults, and approximations that are especially crucial in children's reasoning and learning processes (cf. Collins, 1978; Papert, 1980; Piaget, 1976).

If allowed to prevail, the view that formal reasoning is the best model of learning and knowing has decisively inhibiting effects on education. Seymour Papert (cited in McCorduck, 1979; cf. Papert, 1971, 1976) remarks:

> We all know that we have all these horrible moments of confusion when we begin a new project, that nothing looks clear and everything looks awful, that we work our way out using all sorts of odd little rules of thumb, by going down blind alleys and coming back again, and so on, but since everyone else seems to be thinking logically, or at least they *claim* they do, then we figure we must be the only ones in the world with such murky thought processes. We disclaim them, and make believe we think in logical, orderly ways, all the time knowing we don't. And the worst offenders are teachers who present crisp, clean batches of knowledge to their students, and look as if they themselves learned that knowledge in a crisp, clean way [pp. 290ff].

This wishful thinking about thinking discriminates against everyday reasoning, so that students "resist a model" of learning "that allows understanding to occur gradually, through a process of additions, refinements, debugging, and so on"; unable to live up to the formal-logical ideal, students "feel hopelessly dumb," and "a child who considers himself dumb has lost all incentive for learning, for adapting to new situations, for shaping his world with any sort of will of his own" (Papert cited in McCorduck, 1979).

We should therefore not hastily adopt formal reasoning as the optimal processor—as a logically perfect machine for acquiring and storing secure, clearly defined facts. Formal reasoning is just one special case among many ways of learning. Rather, the optimal processor is the one that can recognize what learn-

---

processes should not necessarily be thought to imply that such differences are immutable." The problem, as I see it, is that teaching has been "reprogramming the brain" without a realistic, encompassing model of how and why.

ing mode is likely to succeed in a given context and can adapt accordingly. In particular, such a processor must not be at a loss if knowledge domains appear messy, unordered, and unmanageable; it should be able to impose order and coherence on such domains through an evolution, however lengthy, of approximative models. This procedure should be defined and rated in terms of its outcome. We should not judge in advance how much time or how many approximations each child might require. We must respect individual differences in the *rate of learning* if we hope to reduce individual differences in the *end results*.

To understand discourse processing and the learning it enables, we will have to begin, like the children described above, by building and steadily refining our model. As a starting point, discourse processing should conform to the general processing constraints imposed by the organization and limitation of cognitive resources like attention, memory, and motor control. Much of the evidence gathered about these resources was observed from brief, simple tasks in controlled settings, whereas discourse processing is a long-range, complex task in variable settings. Three interpretations of this discrepancy might be made. First, we might claim that discourse processing is *more difficult* than standard experimental tasks, provided that difficulty rises linearly with complexity. Second, we might claim that discourse processing is *less difficult* than standard experimental tasks, because it is a natural activity well supported by stores of knowledge and experience, whereas laboratory tasks are typically novel, artificial, and meaningless (Neisser, 1967); here, difficulty does not increase linearly with complexity to the degree that the latter factor imposes richer constraints and order on a task. Third, we might claim that discourse processing is *inherently difficult* because of its complexity, but it has been steadily redesigned (trained, self-organized, streamlined, compacted, etc.) over a long time, so that it seems deceptively easy to those who have traversed this progression, but forbiddingly hard to those who have not. Here, difficulty correlates linearly with complexity only to the degree that the latter is not so designed as to integrate subprocesses into strategic operational packages.

The third interpretation may now be pursued as the best account of individual differences in text learning aptitudes. Reading and writing are evidently difficult, because they are not adequately manageable only on the basis of skills in listening and speaking. To borrow a catch phrase, reading and writing are "unnatural" (cf. Gough & Hillinger, 1980; Raymond, 1980) in the sense that they require intricate process design; however, they are "natural" (Goodman & Goodman, 1979) in the sense that this design is based upon general human capacities for constructing operations and constraining complexity (cf. Beaugrande, 1982). In between the two poles lies the range of probabilities for better or worse process design—the concern of educational programs.

According to Norman and Bobrow (1975), limitations can be anchored either in the processor (resource limitations) or in the materials to be processed (data limitations). Only the former kind can be overcome with increased concentration and training. The substantial occurrence of errors (both mechanical and conceptual) in reading and writing indicates that these activities do run with a heavy draw on resources; but different limitations could be more acute at a given stage. During learning to read, the written mode is still relatively unfamiliar and should present severe data limitations that fall away when the mode becomes fluently manageable. Then, during reading to learn, the acquisition of a new content domain encounters resource limitations upon one's capacity to organize the domain. Finally, data limitations take over again when the learner reaches the limits of how much content one's processing can obtain from the written text as a medium. It follows that education should focus on text design for the early and advanced learning stages (to alleviate data limitations) and on process design in the broad middle stage (to alleviate resource limitations).

Processing has been shown to operate on distinctive levels or depths (cf. Bobrow & Bower, 1969; Craik & Lockhart, 1972; Craik & Tulving, 1975; Mistler-Lachman, 1974; Treisman & Tuxworth, 1974). The experimental literature demonstrates how different task assignments will call forth particular concentration on various levels. Tasks centering on the *shallower* levels (those more closely dependent on the *surface text*), e.g., watching for spelling or for stipulated sounds and letters, result in poorer learning of the *deeper* levels of content organization. This trade-off supports the view that the various levels are normally processed in parallel, not in a series (cf. Marslen–Wilson, 1975; Woods, 1978), because the demands of the levels evidently compete. When one level is allotted processing dominance, the others run at reduced rates, but are not actually shut down. In Fig. 5.1, we see this scheme graphically, with the arrow intended to suggest a potential migration of dominance. Dominance is assumed to go to only one level at a time. There are, however, at least two ways in which this assumption could be refined. First, a processor might make nearly even distributions among two or more levels if the occasion required it. Second, dominance might be shifted about so rapidly as to create a *time-sharing* effect— the illusion that the several levels are being equally attended to simultaneously.

To model reading,[2] we can designate the various levels or depths in terms of the kind of recovery they are concerned with, where *recovery* denotes an interaction of bottom-up attending to the presented text with a top-down supplying of stored knowledge and emergent expectations. The materials are divided up as shown into letters/sounds, words (or expressions), phrasings (the linearity of syntax), concepts/relations (including meaning and reference), ideas (conceptual control centers), and goals (intention, purpose, etc., of the communicative interaction). The recovery procedure itself is another case of model-building, where a reader postulates what a text is for or about and tries to refine hypotheses

---

[2]For discussion of these various notions, see de Beaugrande (1982, 1983 a, 1983 b). Due to my operational orientation, terms vary slightly, depending on which processing mode (reading, writing, speaking, etc.) we are dealing with.

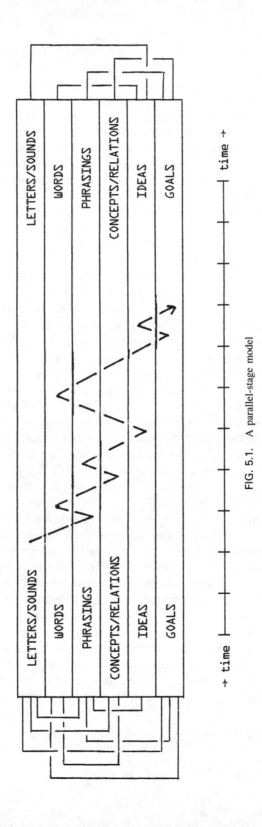

FIG. 5.1. A parallel-stage model

with the actual input. Consequently, the cognitive correlate of a text in the processor's mind could be called a *text-world model* (Beaugrande, 1980 a) containing both the bottom-up content explicitly activated by text expressions and the top-down content supplied from the reader's store of world-knowledge.

The interaction of bottom-up and top-down contributions to recovery signals the vital importance of the *time continuum* in text processing. There must be stages: (1) the perception of the current text; (2) the retrospective representation of the prior text; and (3) the predictive representation of the subsequent text. If we add these three stages to our graphic, we obtain Fig. 5.2. The perception of current text must rely on the memory store known as short-term sensory storage, which works with a fairly direct trace of the surface input of sounds, letters, and words (cf. Crowder, 1978; Crowder & Morton, 1969; Neisser, 1967; Posner, 1978; Sperling, 1960). Research generally suggests that the retrospective retention of short-term sensory storage is only on the order of 1 to 2 seconds. The mental representations are handled in short-term memory (about 20 seconds' duration) plus long-term memory (of apparently unlimited duration). In absence of conclusive evidence, I am assuming that predictive memory is essentially symmetrical with retrospective. In the time line shown at the bottom of Fig. 5.2, the zero point is the exact locus of processing the surface text; past events are to the left and future ones to the right.

Though the several memory stores have been discussed for some time, (Atkinson & Shiffrin, 1968; Waugh & Norman, 1965), their differential contributions to text processing are still relatively underdefined. It seems clear enough that the actual trace of the surface text is largely restricted to short-term sensory storage, so that some organization at least in terms of words and phrases must be very rapidly imposed before the trace fades too far or gets masked by another perception (cf. McClelland, 1976). Breitmeyer (1980) suggests that the eye saccade disposes of sensory images from prior text, lest current text be masked. Some such mechanism seems necessary, because the eye moves on after fixation times averaging only 200 msec (Just & Carpenter, 1980), as compared to the 1 or 2 seconds that visual sensory storage persists. The provisional organization allows the materials to survive into short-term memory where they undergo further treatment that determines what enters long-term memory (cf. Keele, 1973; Kintsch, 1974).

Because the levels must interact to some degree, it seems plausible to envision a *specialization* of the stories, rather than an exclusively *fixation*. Dot shadings are introduced in Fig. 5.3 to indicate these specializations. Short-term sensory storage would be specialized toward sounds/letters and words; short-term memory toward syntactic phrasings and local concept/relation configurations; and long-term memory toward main ideas and goals. Experiments show that memory for syntax fades much faster than memory for meaning (cf. Anderson, 1974; Begg, 1971; Begg & Wickelgren, 1974; Garrod & Trabasso, 1973). But there is no obvious reason why memory stores must be strictly cut up according to

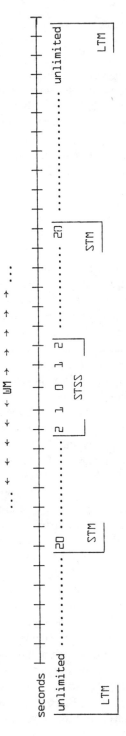

FIG. 5.2. LTM: Long-term memory; STM: Short-term memory; STSS: Short-term sensory storage; WM: Working memory

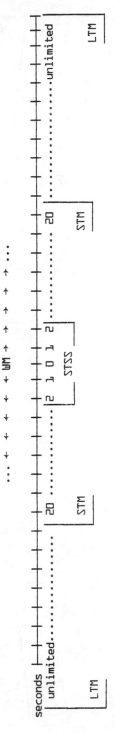

FIG. 5.3. LTM: Long-term memory; STM: Short-term memory; STSS: Short-term sensory storage; WM: Working memory

171

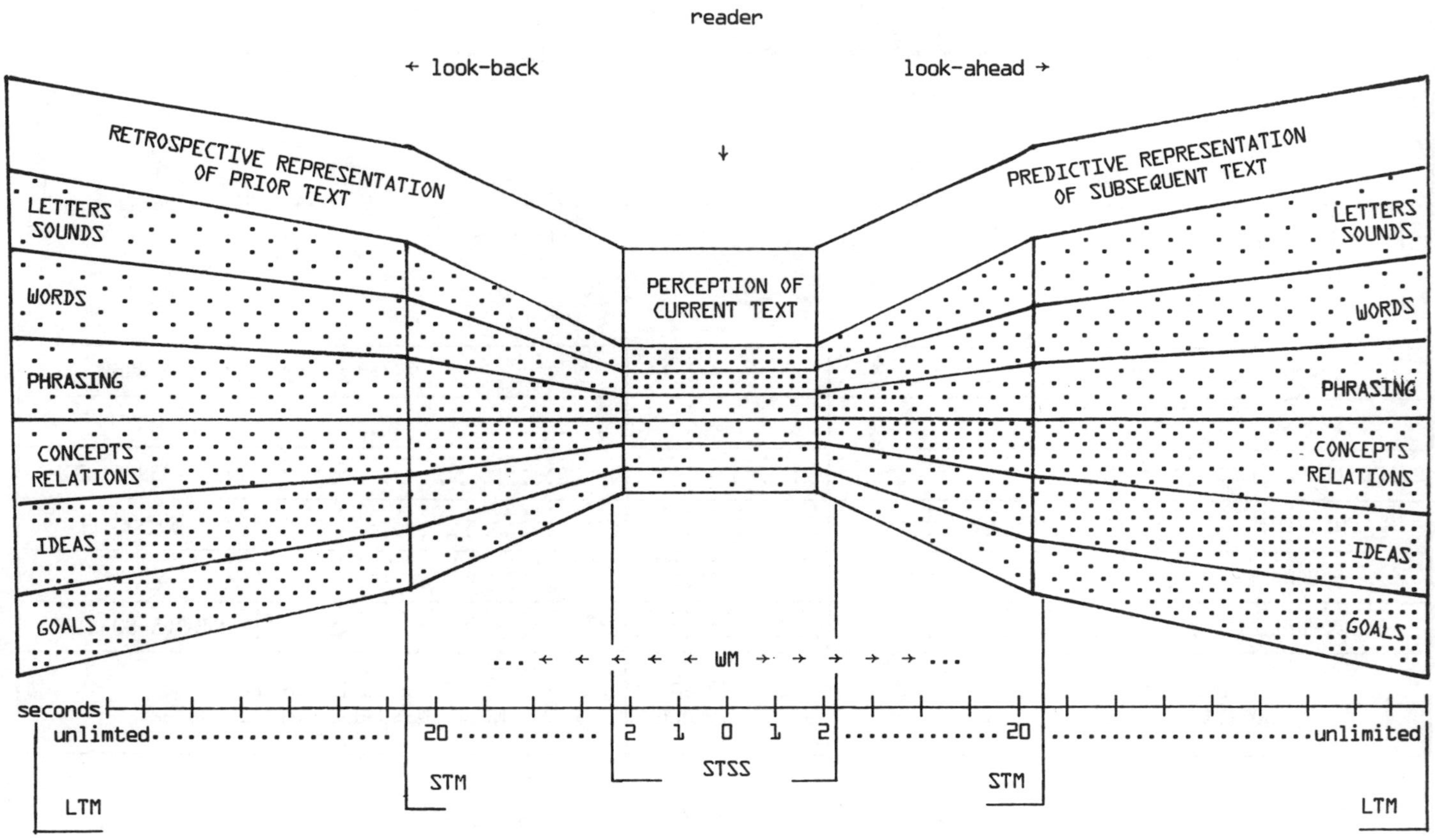

FIG. 5.4. LTM: Long-term memory; STM: Short-term memory; STSS: Short-term sensory storage; WM: Working memory

language levels, considering how many other uses are made of memory. More likely, language-level effects are a special case of the more general capabilities and predilections of the various memory stores.

There is already some evidence that specialization is more probable than fixation. First, some immediate access of perception to conceptual meaning has been found (Raser, 1972; Shulman, 1970). Second, some sensory traces of the surface are retained in long-term memory, whether the language items were presented in the acoustic or the visual mode (Bray & Batchelder, 1972; Hintzman, Block, & Inskeep, 1972). Thirdly, the shallower processes would be explosively uncontrolled without steady guidance from the deeper levels. We know that letters are better perceived inside words than inside nonword strings (Miller, Bruner, & Postman, 1954; Reicher, 1969; Wheeler, 1970). Words are processed better inside meaningful sentences than elsewhere (Miller & Isard, 1963; Tulving, Mandler, & Baumal, 1964; Schuberth & Eimas, 1977). Sentences are better processed if they fit the context of a story than if they do not (O'Connell, Kowal, & Hörmann, 1969). Such findings indicate that shallow processing not only feeds input into deeper processing, but also takes its directions from the latter. It would follow that each memory store has at least a marginal presence of the levels outside its specialization.

An important point is the correlation between *range of decay* and *capacity*. The shorter-range stores also have the more limited capacities. The squeezed graphic in Fig. 5.4 could represent this consideration. Short-term sensory storage gets crowded more easily than short-term memory, and the latter more easily than long-term memory. Yet it is not immediately clear why these proportions should obtain. It is conceivable (though apparently not true) that a brief store could accept large amounts of raw materials precisely because they can enter without prior analysis (cf. Keele, 1973). For the time being, the possibility of a working memory expressly defined in terms of its capacity rather than its range has been left open. Working memory may be a clearinghouse or a buffer (or set of buffers) whose contents may come from any of the three stores defined by their rate of decay. For example, the findings of Spilich, Vesonder, Chiesi, and Voss (1979) indicate that working memory does contain some macro-structures that should be assignable to long-term memory. It has been traditionally supposed that working memory holds about seven chunks (Miller, 1956); recent findings indicate that this capacity might vary depending on where processing is situated within a task—larger in early stages and smaller later on (Kintsch & Polson, 1979). At present, it is by no means established what might function as a single chunk during text processing. An increase both in reading and learning skills should be obtainable by improving one's chunking operations.

Whatever operations occur during text processing must not only reflect the nature of memory, attention, and processing levels; they must also account for the essentially linear character of the language modes themselves. Seven principles of linear organization that would oversee processing in an intelligent (rather than simply mechanical) way are found in Beaugrande (1983 a). These principles apply interactively to all levels of processing and to all scales from global to local.[3] The *core-and-adjunct principle* deals with relations between central and peripheral elements (or configurations of elements). On the *phrasing* level, we have for example the local distinction between heads versus modifiers and the more global one of main clause versus dependent clause. On the *conceptual* level, we have for example the local distinction between primary concepts (action, event, object, situation) and secondary concepts (location, time, cause, etc.) (cf. listing in Beaugrande, 1980 a, pp. 80–84) and the more global one of topic concepts versus associated details. On the *goal* level, we have the distinction between main goals and intermediary sub-goals (cf. Beaugrande, 1980 b).

The *pause principle* allows for a slowing or suspending of processing in the linear sequence. Here also, various levels and scales participate. A pause may reflect a constituent boundary, e.g., the end of a clause or sentence. It may serve as an interval to consolidate processing outstanding from prior text or to plan out processes impending for subsequent text. A pause may also become necessary because at some point, processing undergoes a noticeable overload, whether or not the current item in the sequence is responsible. Just and Carpenter (1980) suggest that the time spent on fixating a word with the eyes is exactly the time spent processing that word; however the correlation must be less immediate because of the partially non-linear organization of underlying processes, many of which are not directly triggered by any word in the surface text.

The access between current text and the retrospective and predictive representations is handled by the *principles of look-back* and *look-ahead,* respectively. The processor could of course scan the surface text backwards or forwards, but eye-movement studies like those of Just and Carpenter (1980) show that this opportunity is not too commonly used. Instead, the processor seems to look back or ahead at the mental representation whose format is not necessarily like the surface text (cf. Beaugrande, 1983 a). The need for look-back and look-ahead is obvious on all levels and scales precisely because single words are not usually meaningful (sometimes not even identifiable) except in their contexts of occurrence; the same is true for concepts and goal steps. There is no clear limit on the distance that can be scanned in this way; probably, though, looking very far would require the search-directed item to be somehow important (memorable, marked, salient, high-up in a hierarchy, etc.). For example, a pronoun can look back to a very remote noun if the latter corresponds to a topic concept (Beaugrande, 1980 a, pp. 91–92).

The *heaviness principle* subsumes such factors as informativity, importance, focus, emphasis, involvement, salience, or surprise. The term *heaviness* should suggest that these factors create a *heavier* load on processing when they rise. Although speaking can signal heaviness with a rich range of modulations in

---

[3]On the design implications of levels versus scales (often confused in structural analysis), see Beaugrande (1983 a).

voice, reading can be cued only with the more limited means of typographic emphasis (italics, bold type) or focus-creating word patterns (e.g., active versus passive, cleft versus non-cleft constructions, etc.).[4] These methods can indicate the relative heaviness of underlying conceptual configurations and their relationship to what readers already know or anticipate.

The *disambiguation principle* applies to all cases where two or more possible organizations compete. The most obvious case is multiple word-meanings being reduced to a single text sense (cf. Coseriu, 1955–56; Beaugrande & Dressler, 1981 a, b). But there are more subtle instances where two entirely different readings of an extended passage would require their own assignments of several categories, for example, for this newspaper headline (*Birmingham Post-Herald,* March 28, 1977):

(1) Child teaching expert to speak

Either three-word subject noun + infinitive (intended reading) or one-word subject noun + participial verb + direct object noun + infinitive verb going with the object (unintended reading) is possible. The less probable reading may attract notice because it is heavier (e.g., more surprising and amusing) than the intended one and hence draws resources toward itself.

The *listing principle* is responsible for all cases where a set of elements (or of configurations of elements) is enumerated. Syntax has the local listing of words as well as the global listing of phrase structures (known as "parellelism"). On the conceptual level, it is expected that listed items will be conceptually comparable. Unintended readings can arise if two possible listings compete, as in another newspaper headline (*Seattle Post-Intelligence,* September 27, 1980):

(2) Milo and Pat Magnano in the kitchen of their Queen Ann home with Milo
    Jr. beating eggs and little brother Tony.

where "Tony" might be listed either with "Milo Jr." (intended reading) or with "eggs" (unintended reading). The following passage is a listing of the interests of a member of the University of Colorado Psychology Department (1976–77 brochure):

(3) Current efforts are directed toward a new, simple technique for discover-
    ing and changing misconceptions in hospitalized mental patients and in
    college students.

Conceptual compatability suggests an odd view of "college students" as akin to "mental patients," but commonsense prefers a neutral reading.

These seven principles seem necessary both for linearly organized behavior at large and for language processing in particular. Even one-word utterances may need to be processed with a look-back and/or look-ahead within a non-verbal context, or with an estimate of relative heaviness. The most common linguistic rules deal with syntactic structures that operate via core-adjunct, disambiguation,

---

[4]On some implications of the differences between spoken and written language, see Beaugrande (1983b). These differences have been neglected in many discussions of transfer between print and sound in reading skills (e.g., Beck & Block, 1979).

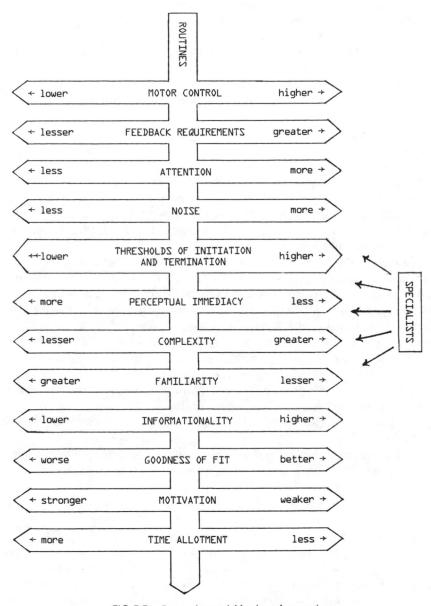

FIG 5.5. Processing variables in task operations

pause, look-back or look-ahead within constituents, and so on. The procedural rules for computer simulation in natural language understanding programs (Hayes, 1977; Schank, Goldman, Rieger, & Riesbeck, 1975; Winograd, 1972; Woods, Brown, Bruce, Cook, Klovstad, Makhoul, Nash-Webber, Schwartz, Wolf, & Zue, 1976) are necessarily constructed in terms of these principles. The principles seem to be necessary, though not sufficient conditions for linguistic rules of any abstraction; considerable further specification may be needed from case to case.

The next step in designing process models should be to determine what gradients affect the *expenditure of cognitive resources*. We can start off by postulating a distinction between *operational routines* that apply to the most common and useful processes, plus *communities of specialists* called in to oversee detailed, on-line processing factors that cannot be exactly predetermined (cf. Minsky, 1979; Winograd, 1972). The most pressing purpose of the specialists would be to prevent processing variables and contingencies from overloading or disorienting the processor. Some of the specialists would be *heterarchical*, so that each one would make minimal assumptions and simply watch for its own triggering conditions (cf. Winston, 1977, p. 99); others would be *hierarchical*, so that the triggering of a superordinate operation would automatically trigger all its subordinates. Communities of specialists might interact or intersect so strategically as to create elaborated complexes of activity that conscious, introspective planning could hardly set up with comparable speed or efficiency. In this perspective, a context-sensitive task might indeed be simpler than a context-deprived laboratory task—provided that the organization of the specialists was appropriately well-designed. A context-deprived task couldn't draw on an already programmed interaction of specialists.

Figure 5.5 illustrates some plausible gradients that influence processing demands. The set shown here is not intended to be exhaustive. Also, the several gradients might interact. But in theory at least, these gradients can be independently raised or lowered. The designations used here are: (1) *motor control* (for the execution of physiological acts, e.g. forming sensory traces of visual patterns); (2) *feedback requirements* (the processor's need to monitor what it's doing); (3) *attention* (expenditure of resources such that other tasks at the same time encounter interference, as opposed to automatization); (4) *noise* (competing events extraneous to the task); (5) *thresholds of initiation and termination* (the criteria used to trigger or end a process, respectively); (6) *perceptual immediacy* (the degree to which the task is close to versus remote from perceived sensory input); (7) *complexity* (organization and mutual integration of part-whole relationships); (8) *familiarity* (extent to which the same task has been done before by the same processor and how often); (9) *informationality* (ratio between repetition

---

[5]In earlier work (e.g., de Beaugrande, 1980 b), I used the term "informativity" for both "familiarity" and "informationality," but I now see the need to distinguish between them for operational motives. They may of course interact.

or equivalence versus change or contrast);[5] (10) *goodness of fit* (degree to which any entity must match a stored feature configuration in order to meet current specifications); (11) *motivation* (why the task is being done; expected rewards/punishments, etc.); and (12) *time allotment* (how long the processor has, or supposes it has, to get through the task).

Figure 5.5 is intended to suggest that when there is a rise on the upper end as labeled, the ongoing processes of any task will impose a heavier draw upon resources. Ideally, the specialists (top of Fig. 5.5) would react by distributing this draw throughout the system, so that there would be no significant strain in one area. However, wide variations in performance, both for different persons and for the same person on differing occasions, demonstrate that this ideal is often not upheld and degradation ensues. It may require a high degree of skill to impose an equitable redistribution of increments in processing load. Failing that, there would be a partly selective and partly random reduction over several areas; in extreme cases, brown-outs or even black-outs might result. For instance, the reader stops and realizes that nothing in the passage has been understood so far.

Possibly, there is some general, neutral degree of processing load for a given person. Or, the neutral degree must be set or re-set for any specified task. As greater skill develops, the task would run better and better with the neutral allotment rather than with heavy loading. The whole structure of the task could be reconstituted by such measures as creating automatic packages for operations that had required attention before; combining from various levels those tasks that have a compatible or parallel structure of components; or rescheduling successive operations into simultaneous ones.

Empirical evidence for these processing load gradients might be hard to obtain because of the dangers of confounding them. For example, familiarity depends on the processor's past experience with the task, whereas informationality depends on how the task itself is internally constituted with one part resembling or else contrasting with a previous part; yet unfamiliarity would naturally create the impression of higher informationality, because the unrehearsed steps would not be easily recognizable as comparable. A low motivation would naturally encourage the processor to relax attention and goodness of fit. If perceptual immediacy were comparatively remote, there might well be a decrement in feedback requirements.

Such considerations lead to a significant conclusion regarding research procedures. Traditional experiments are factored in order to have few dependent variables, if possible only one. The dependent variable was seen in a direct causality with any observed variances. In complex processing, it seems unlikely that a single causality should obtain between a unique processing event and a unique observed variable, at least not within any realistic setting such as reading or learning. Rather, there will be families of candidate processes that could engender the event, often in intricate interactions. The solution may not be to factor out large sets of variables in order to keep the theory or model on the same plane of simplicity. Rather, theories and models should expressly incorporate all candidate processes; we may then manipulate each of them independently to see if the effect can be detected. If so, we can demonstrate a potential causality between a process (or process type) and observable data. We will not, however, normally be able to prove that a given spontaneous event in a natural setting must be attributable to one single cause from among the set identified by experimental manipulation (cf. Perfetti & Lesgold, 1979). At most, realistic process models will be relatable to real-world activities via a steady elaboration of distributed probabilities.

READING AND LEARNING IN SCHOOLS
VERSUS IN REAL LIFE

Readability formulas appear to be inadequate in several ways. The statistical measures address only some aspects of familiarity and complexity among surface items or item configurations. Familiarity of words is undoubtedly a contributor to reading ease because they are easier to access from memory. Yet the statistical frequency of a word does not itself decide its familiarity for a given reader, nor its processing difficulty. An unfamiliar word is much easier to process if it appears inside a familiar story (Wittrock, Marks, & Doctorow, 1975). A familiar word may have very few or very numerous possible senses and hence be more or less demanding to process according to the determinacy of the context (Swinney, 1979; Tanenhaus, Leiman, & Seidenberg, 1979). The statistical counting of words throughout the language (Kučera & Francis, 1967) misses these factors.

Readability measures directed to the length and complexity of clauses or sentences are also insensitive. They imply that working memory is filled with single words, so that load increases linearly with clause length. Evidence shows instead that readers vary considerably in their abilities to use limited memory space for smaller or larger text chunks (Daneman & Carpenter, 1980). Hence, the mere number of words does not determine the effort readers actually expend.

We might want to retain the older formulas, while altering our interpretation of them: not as *complete* measures of *readability*, but as *partial* measures of *reading ease* alongside such determinants as the graphemes, sound blends, and letter formations classified by Coleman (1970). Other things being equal, frequent words and short, simple clauses are easier to read than their opposites. What remains to be done is to explore the ways in which other things are often *not* equal; only this added step will create powerfully predictive readability measures. Finally, having uncovered the additional factors, we can develop ways to manipulate them such that a progression of reading tasks can be developed which really does control the demands steadily being imposed and increased on the learner.

Klare (1971, p. 47) lists three additional ways to estimate readability: reading speed, expert judgments, and performance on follow-up tests. Each of these measures entails its own difficulties if they are applied without a process model of what they may gauge or represent. Speed may reflect many things besides absolute readability. Perfetti and Lesgold (1979, p. 63) note that speed may be only a "by-product" of facility for recognizing words in contexts; or it may reflect the acuteness of a "bottleneck" created when word-recognition, insofar as it is not yet automatized, has to compete with other operations. Also, skilled reading might be slower, because a high degree of feedback requirements, goodness of fit, and motivation would naturally elicit a compensatory increase in time allotment, irrespective of the characteristics of the text itself. Speech experiments even suggest that speed is partly a factor of personal rhythm mechanisms that happen to extend to linguistic processes among other things.

Judgments given by literacy experts may be accurate enough, but we have no way of knowing why they should or should not be so. Recent debates have brought into question the reliability of verbal reports (cf. Ericsson & Simon, 1980, vs. Nisbett & Wilson, 1977). Whichever side we take, we can hardly deny that verbal reports are vastly underdifferentiated, especially regarding detailed operations running largely automatically at high speeds. Moreover, verbalizing one's experiences can scarcely keep from imposing upon them an additional layer of organization, namely that required by text production operations (cf. Beaugrande, 1983b). And finally, experts' judgments are only a gross measure that may be additionally contaminated by the exigencies of verbal reporting and by the need to enact the public role of expert.

Retention testing would be a direct measure of readability only if there are no significant distinctions between learning to read and reading to learn. Learning to read suffers from data limitations, and reading to learn suffers more from resource limitations. Reading to learn includes one's model of reading plus one's capacities for modeling knowledge domains. Retention testing is therefore a valuable corrective to the structural analysis measures, but we must account for the ways in which it doesn't gauge the same things, depending on the kind of testing used. In normal learning situations, verbatim memory for a text is not the main goal. Multiple-choice tests are not very reliable (Pyrczak, 1972): they can often be performed merely by reasoning about the probabilities of candidate answers. Weaver and Bickley (1967) reported test persons achieving 67% right answers without even having seen the reading selection. These reasoning skills indicate advances in learning, but are not too revealing about reading or text design.

Testing must be sorted out according to the dominances of *recognition* versus *recall*. Recognition effects can apply to surprisingly large amounts of fairly superficially processed materials (cf. McCormack, 1972). The more active processes of recall demand "deeper," better designed operations, and thus yield vastly more limited effects. It is far from clear that a text design which supports recognition must also support recall or vice versa. Recognition might in fact be aided by bizarre, barely comprehensible passages, such as the reader had seldom seen before. Recall demands thorough comprehension, supported by the reader's prior knowledge (Voss, Vesonder, & Spilich, 1980). This knowledge could make it difficult to decide which facts were actually in one sample text, so that good recall would appear alongside poor recognition.

Imagine for a moment that text design principles could be found so as to control the resource gradients of Fig. 5.5 during text processing. Would better methods result for learning to read and reading to learn? Certainly, a change in the outlook of publishers and educators would also be necessary. The application of new text design principles would be more demanding than that of the simplistic readability formulas. Textbook editors would have to set and uphold new priorities that would increase the time and effort needed to put materials on the market. More importantly, schools would have to realize and respond to the very delicate balance between prior skills/knowledge and those that learners are to acquire at any stage. Before children can be expected to absorb whatever is considered a complete, accurate model of some knowledge domain (physics, mathematics, etc.), we need reliable ways for approaching the domain through a succession of provisional models. On the one hand, easy reading can aid learning by streamlining the processes whereby content is organized, compacted, and stored. On the other hand, undue ease can degrade attention and motivation, leading to monotony, boredom, and loss of interest. These outcomes promote a system-wide reduction of cognitive resources, thereby impeding rather than assisting memorability, learning, and performance. The correlation between reading ease and learning effects is much more likely to be curvilinear rather than linear (Groeben, 1978). The schools must accordingly be aware of a child's current model in order to find the most strategic level of difficulty.

Papert (1980) argues that school learning tends to become "denatured" by failing to recognize and respect children's own models. Children are handed one "fact" after another and expected to digest it whole, irrespective of its relationship to prior knowledge. In grading, approximations are judged as errors and discouraged. Children see their stepping-stones disqualified and conclude that the knowledge domain is simply too hard for them to grasp. Sometimes a fragmented jumble of mutually unrelated "facts" is learned at least long enough to recite on a test; yet the child sees no enduring usefulness for the facts. According to Papert (1971) perhaps the whole alienation of schooling starts here:

> It is usually considered good practice to give people instruction in their occupational activities. Now, the occupational activities of children are learning, thinking, playing, and the like. Yet we tell them nothing about those things. Instead we tell them about numbers, grammar, and the French Revolution; somehow hoping that from this disorder the really important things will emerge all by themselves. And they sometimes do. But the alienation-drop out-drug complex is certainly not less frequent [cited in McCorduck, 1979, p. 290].

Jean Piaget uncovered the vital role of the provisional models children build (cf. discussion in Papert, 1980, pp. 132–134). For example, when asked what causes wind, one child answered that trees do so by waving their branches. Though the explanation is factually incorrect, it testifies to significant reasoning processes on the child's part: an observed correlation between the presence of wind and the waving of branches, plus experiments in making air currents by waving one's hands. A whole forest of trees, it follows, could easily create high winds. The proper step here is not to puncture the child's theory, but to offer more occasions for gathering evidence, so that the child will revise the theory without outside intervention. Papert (1980) remarks that "educators distort Piaget's message by seeing his contribution as revealing that children hold false beliefs which they, the educators, must overcome," so that "children are being force-fed 'correct' theories before they are ready to invent them [p. 133]."

If we study learning as *on-line processing* rather than as *sets of results,* approximations can be viewed in terms of resource allotments. I surmised above that a heavy draw on one resource gradient requires compensation elsewhere in the system. For example, the child's theory of wind illustrates a way to raise familiarity and perceptual immediacy by incorporating what the child had experienced most directly. An explanation in terms of physical laws, on the other hand, would at that age seem unmanageably unfamiliar and complex. Thus, goodness of fit (between the child's theory and the prevailing theory) is being traded for the rehearsal of important learning strategies that render knowledge easier to access and integrate from experience—the most convincing source of knowing. A failure to compensate in this way elicits processing overload and damages learning.

The intransigence of some educators toward "wrong" theories may be due to a general striving for well-structuredness. The finished, correct theory defines what we are disposed to consider orderly, whereas an incomplete, approximate one looks messy. The desire to spring over the latter and devote all one's respect to the former is only natural, but engenders a sterile unrealistic notion of what it means to learn something. The transition from a rough model toward a refined one is replete with guesswork, falterings, and blind alleys. If these decisive fumblings are ignored or scorned, children devalue their own thought processes and are shy about revealing their results. They offer their answers as "probably wrong," and pose what they call "stupid questions" to clear up a difficulty. They are most confident when a task is small, so that the right answer is attained almost at once. Large, extensive tasks appear threatening because they cannot be mastered in one leap, and the child often gives up before trying.

As educators, we would be less intransigent if we would bear in mind how insecure the "facts" are that are so insistently and confidently fed to children at the expense of the children's own theories. Endel Tulving (1979, p. 9) recently remarked: "There is every reason to believe that all current ideas, interpretations, explanations, and theories are wrong in the sense that sooner or later they will be modified or rejected [p. 9]." Our concern is thus not with what we take or accept as facts right now, but with how we discover, constitute, and eventually discard facts. What is allowed for the scientist should surely be allowed for the child: the freedom to design a managable, coherent world in terms of what is currently, (not ideally) possible.

ONGOING EXPERIMENTATION

What we know most about in reading deals with the surface text: recognition of letters/sounds, words, and phrases (cf. Beck & Block, 1979; Sticht, 1979; Venezky & Massaro, 1979). We know less about the deeper areas of organizing and compacting conceptual content and of relating content to human goals. This discrepancy may account for some disagreements about the role of meaning in reading instruction. Glass (1971) has contended that "decoding" the surface text was a skill to be taught entirely separate from meaning and context. Kintsch (1979, p. 328) surmised that the current literacy crisis is due to such a heavy emphasis on "decoding" that the deeper levels of reading are very poorly programmed or practiced in the schools.

In my view, the notion of "decoding" is far less useful than has been widely realized. Strictly defined, "decoding" is a mechanical interchange of symbols between one code and another, where "code" is a limited, unambiguous set of arbitrarily constructed symbols. A natural language cannot be said to constitute a "code," nor can a text be "decoded," except in the more narrow sense of working from sounds over to letters or vice versa. The view that communication is the "sending" of a "message" from an "encoder" to a "decoder" encourages theory and research to focus on shallow-level issues. Conceptual meaning is not a "code," but a *processing outcome* whose substance is a context-dependent configuration of knowledge constituted during comprehension.

If we concede that reading equals "decoding" only in transitions between print and sounds, the main issues for reading research shift. What kind of a working model can a reader develop that operates from a visual or acoustic modality within an elaborate interactive multi-level system for conveying content and pursuing goals? How does the organization of the surface coding interface with that of the non-code levels? What correlations are involved, and how do different readers navigate the operations involved? How can schooling influence those operations so that children will be proficient not just in decoding, but in reading and learning in the widest sense? Reasoning from the better-known processes toward the lesser-known ones that run alongside them may help us answer these questions.

Since the surface text is accessible, we can manipulate it directly. Alternative versions of the same text might elicit interesting effects on learning and retention. We can consult a model that stipulates how a text is "chunked" into propositions that are integrated in a complex knowledge structure (Beaugrande, 1980 a; Frederiksen, 1977; Just & Carpenter, 1980; Meyer, 1977; Miller &

Kintsch, 1980, van Dijk, 1979). Since propositions are not themselves words, phrases, or clauses, the manipulation of the surface text should have some impact on these deeper processes. We need a much clearer view of what occurs during the actual on-line reading with the intention to learn and not just to "decode."

In the overall scheme of text learning, text design constitutes a *variable,* not a *constant.* Non-strategic text design might impel text receivers to adopt one of three strategies. First, they may ignore the disturbances or even overlook them by relying on top-down methods (cf. Marslen-Wilson & Welsh, 1978; Warren, 1970). Evidence for this strategy is also found in the misperceptions that arise from top-down operation in the written mode (Goodman & Burke, 1973) and in the spoken (Bond & Garnes, 1980). Second, receivers may marginally notice disturbances but see no need to deal with them, as was apparently the case for Gough's test subjects reading passages with missing letters (cf. Gough, 1972). Third, receivers may notice and explicitly deal with the disturbances, moving away from top-down reliance and doing explicit problemsolving (cf. Beaugrande, 1980 a; Frederiksen, 1979). Only if noticing triggers this additional processing does poor text design significantly raise resource demands along such gradients as motor control (eye-scan, trace formation, and if reading aloud, articulation), feedback, goodness of fit, and noise. Otherwise, reading and learning would be only marginally impaired if at all. It follows again that text design is especially crucial for early stages of reading and learning where top–down processing is not yet secure (Samuels, 1979 b, p. 356). There should be a broad middle space where the immediate impact of better or worse text design is not by itself a constant determinant of text learning, provided process design is powerful and adaptable.

In this connection, such process design must be selective about the sections of the text that deserve concentrated treatment. The von Restorff effect (cf. Wallace, 1965)[6] is one way of controlling this selectivity. In view of tests on print displays cued with upper case or colors (Hershberger & Terry, 1965; Rundus, 1971), it is worth exploring whether manipulating the visual contours of texts might be useful for learning (cf. Klare, Mabry, & Gustafson, 1955; Coles & Foster, 1975; Crouse & Idstein, 1972; Fowler & Barker, 1974; Rickards & August, 1975; Annis & Davis, 1978; Glynn, 1978).[7] By and large, improved

---

[6]Note that von Restorff (1933) couched her "effect" in terms of the *inhibition* caused by the similarity of items; in the literature, the effect is often couched in terms of *facilitation* caused by the markedness of items (Keele, 1973, p. 6). The latter view is the logical converse of the former one only if we add overall memory limitations more stringent than those assumed by von Restorff herself, whose orientation was Gestaltist.

[7]Most of these studies of learning from text-cueing used underlining, rather than size and color (cf. review in Glynn, 1978). Learning improved if readers did their own underlining, perhaps because this activity increased the time they spent working on the text (Annis & Davis, 1978; Rickards & August, 1975). If study time remained constant, underlining often made no difference (Idstein & Jenkins, 1972).

retention of marked items is traded off against a decrement for unmarked ones. Still, as Keele (1973) remarks, "proper cueing may improve the organization of material to be learned or may help differentiate some material from other, thereby improving recall [p. 38]."

The von Restorff effect might be explicated in terms of the resource gradients shown in Fig. 5.5 It would raise attention and informativity in general, but perceptual immediacy only for concepts associable with size or color. If used randomly or excessively, it would be likely to increase noise and thereby offset any gains from increased attention. The effect would cancel itself through overuse, because markedness would itself become a monotonous routine. It follows that print display effects would work best if used on strategic words or phrases in brief texts.[8]

Manipulating print might assist on-line processing without necessarily affecting long-term memory storage. Uniform print might require more processing effort to get the same results. Fluent readers can offset disadvantageous print displays, such as obscured word boundaries (Hochberg, 1970)—we all know this from having had to read bad handwriting. But the added effort is wasted, and for longer, more difficult passages, would sooner or later go against learning, e.g., by squeezing the gradients of motivation and time allotment.

CONCLUSION

Conventional models of language and learning suffer from an overemphasis of structural analysis and from a neglect of discourse processing factors. Lengthy disputations about how print is "decoded" into sound or vice versa remain inconclusive until deeper processing is properly investigated. No doubt fluent reading and text learning demand automatic decoding abilities (Samuels, 1979 a); however, far too little concern has been devoted to what lies beyond that necessary first step. Researchers who advocate repetitive drills for learning to read (Samuels, 1979 b) must explain why drills should promote overall comprehension processes. Repetition will lead to the automatization only if accompanied by cognitive reorganization (Mandler, 1979). For example, in "semantic satiation," repetition has just the opposite effect, namely to block coherent

---

[8]We ran some reading and recall tests intended to probe the effects depicted by von Restorff (1933) and Stroop (1935). We manipulated the size and color of print and generally found that such manipulations are not in themselves extremely influential. Words printed in black upper-case print enjoyed a slight advantage in immediate recall, but none after five minutes' delay. Size plus color-cueing elicited a larger and more lasting advantage, but only for words naming objects readily associable with the same color as the print—in line with the "Stroop" effect. However, readers with very poor recall did tend to favor the marked items, though readers with good recall did not do so. Much research is still needed to see if new styles of print might affect processing dispositions reliably.

meaning (Lambert & Jakobovits, 1960). Repetition might also increase the monotony of materials and thereby decrease learning—a finding in the original work of von Restorff (1933). Limitations and differentiations within automatized text processing should be recognized before it can be a sound rationale for rote drills.

The "decoding" approach to reading can at best measure effects such as facilitating it with color-cuing (cf. Popp, 1972) or impeding it with bizarre word-spacing (cf. Hochberg, 1970). But to understand what would constitute a workable approximation during learning to read or reading to learn, we must find out much more about effects that concern deeper content organization both in on-line processing gradients and in long-term memory storage or access. Obviously, much refinement and specification is required to fill in the modeling of process design and to correlate it with text design. Still, it is to be hoped that a discourse-processing approach may eventually provide the theoretical and methodological groundwork for significant advances in text learning.

ACKNOWLEDGMENTS

For running various experiments on text processing, I am grateful to Walter Kintsch and Althea Turner of the University of Colorado and to Charles Hall, Richard Hersh, and John Pieters of the University of Florida. Some results are reported in Beaugrande (1980 a, pp. 221–240).

REFERENCES

Anderson, J. R. Verbatim and propositional representation of sentences in immediate and long-term memory. *Journal of Verbal Learning and Verbal Behavior*, 1974, *13*, 149–162.

Annis, L., & Davis, J. K. Study techniques and cognitive style: Their effect on recall and recognition. *Journal of Educational Research*, 1978, *71*, 175–178.

Atkinson, R. C., & Shiffrin, R. M. Human memory: A proposed system and its control processes. In J. Spence & K. Spence (Eds.), *The psychology of learning and motivation*. New York: Academic Press, 1968.

Beaugrande, R. de. The pragmatics of discourse processing. *Journal of Pragmatics*, 1980, *4*, 15–42. (a)

Beaugrande, R. de. *Text, discourse, and process*. Norwood, N.J.: Ablex, 1980. (b)

Beaugrande, R. de. General constraints on process models of language. In J.-F. le Ny, & W. Kintsch (Eds.), *Language and comprehension*. Amsterdam: North Holland, 1982.

Beaugrande, R. de. The linearity of reading: Fact, fiction, frontier? In J. Flood (Ed.), *Issues in Reading Comprehension*. Newark, N.J.: IRA, 1983. (a)

Beaugrande, R. de. *Text production: Toward a science of composition*. Norwood, N.J.: Ablex, 1983. (b)

Beaugrande, R. de, & Dressler, W. *Introduction to text linguistics*. London: Longman, 1981. (a)

Beaugrande, R. de, & Dressler, W. *Einführung in die Textlinguistik*. Tübingen: Niemeyer, 1981. (b)

Beck, I. L., & Block, K. An analysis of two beginning reading programs: Some facts and some opinions. In L. Resnick, & P. Weaver (Eds.), *Theory and practice of early reading*. Hillsdale, N.J: Lawrence Erlbaum Associates, 1979.

Begg, I. Recognition memory for sentence meaning and wording. *Journal of Verbal Learning and Verbal Behavior,* 1971, *10,* 176–181.

Begg, I., & Wickelgren, W. Retention functions for syntactic and lexical versus semantic information in recognition memory. *Memory and Cognition,* 1974, *2,* 353–359.

Bobrow, S., & Bower, G. H. Comprehension and recall of sentences. *Journal of Experimental Psychology,* 1969, *80,* 455–461.

Bond, Z. S., & Garnes, S. Misperceptions of fluent speech. In R. Cole (Ed.), *Perception and production of fluent speech.* Hillsdale, N.J.: Lawrence Erlbaum Associates, 1980.

Bormuth, J. Reading literacy: Its definition and assessment. In J. B. Carroll & J. S. Chall (Eds.), *Toward a literate society.* New York: McGraw-Hill, 1975.

Bray, N. & Batchelder, W. Effects of instruction and retention interval on memory of presentation mode. *Journal of Verbal Learning and Verbal Behavior,* 1972, *11,* 367–374.

Breitmeyer. 1980.

Chomsky, N. *Syntactic structures.* The Hague: Mouton, 1957.

Chomsky, N. *Aspects of the theory of syntax.* Cambridge, Mass.: MIT Press, 1965.

Clark, H. H., & Clark, E. *Psychology and language.* New York: Harcourt, Brace, & Jovanovich, 1977.

Coleman, E. B. Collecting a data base for a reading technology. *Journal of Educational Psychology,* 1970, *61,* 1–23.

Coles, P., & Foster, J. Typographical cueing as an aid to learning from typewritten text. *Programmed Learning and Educational Technology,* 1975, *1,* 102–108.

Collins, A. M. Fragments of a theory of human plausible reasoning. *TINLAP 2,* 1978, 194–201.

Coseriu, E. Determinación y entorno. *Romanistisches Jahrbuch,* 1955–56, 7, 29–54.

Craik, F. I. M., & Lockhart, R. S. Levels of processing. *Journal of Verbal Learning and Verbal Behavior,* 1972, 11, 671–684.

Craik, F. I. M., & Tulving, E. Depth of processing and the retention of words in episodic memory. *Journal of Experimental Psychology: General,* 1975, *104,* 268–294.

Crouse, J. H., & Idstein, P. Effects of encoding cues on prose learning. *Journal of Educational Psychology,* 1972, *63,* 309–313.

Crowder, R. Sensory memory systems. In E. Carterette & M. Friedman (Eds.), *Handbook of Perception VIII.* New York: Academic Press, 1978.

Crowder, R., & Morton, J. Precategorical acoustic storage. *Perception and Psychophysics,* 1969, *5,* 365–373.

Daneman, M., & Carpenter, P. A. Individual differences in working memory and reading. *Journal of Verbal Learning and Verbal Behavior,* 1980, *19,* 450–466.

Ericsson, K. A., & Simon, H. A. Verbal reports as data. *Psychological Review,* 1980, *87,* 215–251.

Fowler, R. L., & Barker, A. S. Effectiveness of highlighting for retention of text material. *Journal of Applied Psychology,* 1974, *59,* 358–364.

Frederiksen, C. H. Semantic processing units in understanding text. In R. Freedle (Ed.), *Discourse production and comprehension.* Norwood, N.J.: Ablex, 1977.

Frederiksen, C. H. Discourse comprehension and early reading. In L. Resnick, & P. Weaver (Eds.), *Theory and practice of early reading.* Hillsdale, N.J.: Lawrence Erlbaum Associates, 1979.

Garrod, S., & Trabasso, T. A dual-memory information processing interpretation of sentence comprehension. *Journal of Verbal Learning and Verbal Behavior,* 1973, *12,* 155–167.

Glass, G. G. Perceptual conditioning for decoding. In B. Bateman (Ed.), *Learning disorders: Reading.* Seattle, Wash.: Special Child Publications, 1971.

Glynn, S. M. Capturing readers' attention by means of typographical cuing strategies. *Educational Technology,* November 1978, 7–12.

Goodman, K., & Burke, C. *Theoretically-based studies of patterns of miscues in oral reading performance.* Washington, D.C.: U.S. Dept. of HEW, 1973.

Goodman, K., & Goodman, Y. Learning to read is natural. In L. Resnick & P. Weaver (Eds.), *Theory and practice of early reading*. Hillsdale, N.J.: Lawrence Erlbaum Associates, 1979.

Gough, P. One second of reading. In J. Kavanagh, & I. Mattingly (Eds.), *Language by ear and by eye*. Cambridge, Mass.: MIT Press, 1972.

Gough, P., & Hillinger, M. Learning to read: An unnatural act. *Bulletin of the Orton Society*, 1980, *30*, 179–196.

Greenbaum, S. (Ed.). *Language and acceptability*. The Hague: Mouton, 1977.

Groeben, N. *Die Verständlichkeit von Unterrichtstexten*. Münster: Aschendorff, 1978.

Harris, Z. S. *Methods in structural linguistics*. Chicago, Ill.: University of Chicago Press, 1951.

Harris, Z. S. Discourse analysis. *Language*, 1952, *28*, 1–30 and 474–494.

Hayes, P. *Some association-based techniques for lexical disambiguation by machine*. Rochester, N.Y.: University of Rochester Computer Science Technical Report 25, 1977.

Hershberger, W., & Terry, D. Typographical cuing in conventional and programmed texts. *Journal of Experimental Psychology*, 1965, *49*, 55–60.

Hintzman, D., Block, R., & Inskeep, N. Memory for mode of input. *Journal of Verbal Learning and Verbal Behavior*, 1972, *11*, 741–749.

Hochberg, J. Components of literacy: Speculation and exploratory research. In H. Levin, & J. P. Williams (Eds.), *Basic studies on reading*. New York: Basic Books, 1970.

Idstein, P., & Jenkins, J. R. Underlining vs. repetitive reading. *Journal of Educational Research*, 1972, *65*, 321–323.

Jarvella, R. From verbs to sentences. In S. Rosenberg (Ed.), *Sentence production*. Hillsdale, N.J.: Lawrence Erlbaum Associates, 1977.

Johnson, N. F. The psychological reality of phrase-structure rules. *Journal of Verbal Learning and Verbal Behavior*, 1965, *4*, 469–475.

Just, M. A., & Carpenter, P. A theory of reading: From eye fixations to comprehension. *Psychological Review*, 1980, *87*, 329–354.

Keele, S. *Attention and human performance*. Pacific Palisades, Ca.: Goodyear, 1973.

Kintsch, W. *The representation of meaning in memory*. Hillsdale, N.J.: Lawrence Erlbaum Associates, 1974.

Kintsch, W. Concerning the marriage of theory and practice in beginning reading instruction. In L. Resnick & P. Weaver (Eds.), *Theory and practice of early reading*. Hillsdale, N.J.: Lawrence Erlbaum Associates, 1979.

Kintsch, W., & Bates, E. Recognition memory for statements from a classroom lecture. *Journal of Experimental Psychology: Human Learning and Memory*, 1977, *3*, 150–159.

Kintsch, W., & Polson, P. On nominal and functional serial position: Implications for short-term memory models? *Psychological Review*, 1979, *4*, 407–413.

Klare, G. *The measurement of readability*. Ames: Iowa State University, 1963.

Klare, G. Some empirical predictors of readability. In E. Rothkopf & P. Johnson (Eds.), *Verbal learning research and the technology of written instruction*. New York: Teachers' College Press, 1971.

Klare, G. Assessing readability. *Reading Research Quarterly*, 1974–75, *10*, 62–102.

Klare, G., Mabry, J., & Gustafson, L. The relationship of patterning (underlining) to immediate retention and to acceptability of technical material. *Journal of Applied Psychology*, 1955, *39*, 40–42.

Kučera, H., & Francis, W. *Computational analysis of present-day English*. Providence, R.I.: Brown University Press, 1967.

Kuhn, T. S. *The structure of scientific revolutions*. Chicago, Ill.: University of Chicago Press, 1970.

Lambert, W., & Jakobovits, L. Verbal satiation and changes in intensity of meaning. *Journal of Experimental Psychology*, 1960, *60*, 376–383.

Mandler, G. Organization and repetition: Organizational principles with special reference to rote learning. In L. G. Nilsson (Ed.), *Perspectives on memory research*. Hillsdale, N.J.: Lawrence Erlbaum Associates, 1979.

Marslen-Wilson, W. Sentence perception as an interactive parallel process. *Science*, 1975, *189*, 226–228.

Marslen-Wilson, W., & Welsh, A. Processing interactions and lexical access during word recognition in continuous speech. *Cognitive Psychology*, 1978, *10*, 29–63.

Martinet, A. *A functional view of language*. Oxford: Clarendon, 1962.

Masson, M. *Cognitive processes in skimming stories*. Boulder: Univ. of Colorado Institute for the Study of Intellectual Behavior TR 84-ONR, 1979.

McClelland, J. L. Preliminary letter identification in the perception of words and nonwords. *Journal of Experimental Psychology: Human Perception and Performance*, 1976, *2*, 80–91.

McCorduck, P. *Machines who think*. San Francisco, Ca.: Freeman, 1979.

McCormack, P. D. Recognition memory: How complex a retrieval system? *Canadian Journal of Psychology*, 1972, *26*, 19–41.

McNeill, D. *The acquisition of language: The study of developmental psycholinguistics*. New York: Harper & Row, 1970.

Mehler, J. Some effects of grammatical transformations on the recall of English sentences. *Journal of Verbal Learning and Verbal Behavior*, 1963, *2*, 250–262.

Meyer, B. J. F. What is remembered from prose: A function of passage structure. In R. Freedle (Ed.), *Discourse production and comprehension*. Norwood, N.J.: Ablex, 1977.

Miller, G. A. The magic number seven, plus or minus two. *Psychological Review*, 1956, *63*, 81–97.

Miller, G. A. Four philosophical problems in psycholinguistics. *Philosophy of Science*, 1970, *37*, 183–199.

Miller, G. A., Bruner, J. S., & Postman, L. Familiarity of letter sequences and tachistoscopic identification. *Journal of Genetic Psychology*, 1954, *50*, 129–139.

Miller, G. A., & Isard, S. Some perceptual consequences of linguistic rules. *Journal of Verbal Learning and Verbal Behavior*, 1963, *2*, 217–228.

Miller, J. R., & Kintsch, W. Readability and recall of short prose passages. *Journal of Experimental Psychology: Human Learning and Memory*, 1980, *6*, 335–354.

Minsky, M. Plain talk about neurodevelopmental epistemology. *Fifth IJCAI*, 1979, 1083–1093.

Mistler–Lachman, J. L. Depth of comprehension and sentence memory. *Journal of Verbal Learning and Verbal Behavior*, 1974, *13*, 98–106.

Morgan, J. L. Some remarks on the nature of sentences. In R. Grossman, J. San, & T. Vance (Eds.), *Papers from the parasession of functionalism*. Chicago, Ill.: CLS, 1975.

Neisser, U. *Cognitive psychology*. New York: Appleton-Century-Crofts, 1967.

Nisbett, R. E., & Wilson, T. D. Telling more than we can know: Verbal reports on mental processes. *Psychological Review*, 1977, *84*, 231–259.

Norman, D. A., & Bobrow, D. On data-limited and resource-limited processes. *Cognitive Psychology*, 1975, *7*, 44–64.

O'Connell, D., Kowal, S., & Hörmann, H. Semantic determinants of pauses. *Psychologische Forschung*, 1969, *33*, 50–67.

Papert, S. *Teaching children thinking*. Cambridge, Mass.: MIT AI-Lab Memo 247, 1971.

Papert, S. *Some poetic and social criteria for education design*. Cambridge, Mass.: MIT AI-Lab Memo 373, 1976.

Papert S. *Mindstorms: Computers, children, and powerful ideas*. New York: Basic Books, 1980.

Perfetti, C. A., & Lesgold, A. M. Coding and comprehension in skilled reading and implications for reading instruction. In L. Resnick, & P. Weaver (Eds.), *Theory and practice of early reading*. Hillsdale, N.J.: Lawrence Erlbaum Associates, 1979.

Piaget, J. *The child and reality*. New York: Penguin, 1976.

Popp, H. M. *Test project for the LRDC beginning reading program, "Stepping stones to reading."* Urbana, Ill.: ERIC Report No. ED 070040, 1972.

Posner, M. I. *Chronometric explorations of mind*. Hillsdale, N.J.: Lawrence Erlbaum Associates, 1978.

Pyrczak, F. Objective evaluation of the quality of multiple-choice test items designed to measure comprehension of reading passages. *Reading Research Quarterly*, 1972, *8*, 62–71.

Raser, G. A. Recoding of semantic and acoustic information in memory. *Journal of Verbal Learning and Verbal Behavior*, 1972, *11*, 692–697.

Raymond, J. C. *Writing (is an unnatural act)*. New York: Harper & Row, 1980.

Reicher, G. Perceptual recognition as a function of meaningfulness of stimulus materials. *Journal of Experimental Psychology*, 1969, *81*, 274–280.

Restorff, H., von. Über die Wirkung von Bereichsbildung im Spurenfeld. *Psychologische Forschungen*, 1933, *18*. 299–342.

Rickards, J. P., & August, G. J. Generative underlining strategies in prose. *Journal of Educational Psychology*, 1975, *67*, 860–865.

Rosenstein, A., Rathbone, R., & Schneerer, W. *Engineering communications*. Englewood Cliffs, N.J.: Prentice-Hall, 1964.

Rothkopf, E. Z. Writing to teach and reading to learn: A perspective on the psychology of written instruction. *Yearbook of the National Society for the Study of Education*, 1976, *75*, 91–129.

Rundus, D. Analysis of rehearsal processes in free recall. *Journal of Experimental Psychology*, 1971, *89*, 63–77.

Samuels, S. J. How the mind works when reading. In L. Resnick, & P. Weaver (Eds.), *Theory and practice of early reading*. Hillsdale, N.J.: Lawrence Erlbaum Associates, 1979. (a)

Samuels, S. J. The method of repeated reading. *The Reading Teacher*, 1979, *32*, 403–408. (b)

Schank, R. C., Goldman, N., Rieger, C., & Riesbeck, C. *Conceptual information processing*. Amsterdam: North Holland, 1975.

Schank, R., Lebowitz, M., & Birnbaum, L. *Integrated partial parsing*. New Haven, Conn.: Yale Dept. of Computer Sciences Research Report 143, 1978.

Schuberth, R. E., & Eimas, P. D. Effects of context on the classification of words and nonwords. *Journal of Experimental Psychology: Human Perception and Performance*, 1977, *3*, 27–36.

Shulman, H. G. Encoding and retention of semantic and phonetic information in short-term memory. *Journal of Verbal Learning and Verbal Behavior*, 1970, *9*, 499–508.

Sperling, G. The information available in brief visual presentations. *Psychological Monographs*, 1960, *74*, 1–29.

Spilich, G. J., Vesonder, G. T., Chiesi, H. L., & Voss, J. F. Text processing of domain-related information for individuals with high and low domain knowledge. *Journal of Verbal Learning and Verbal Behavior*, 1979, *18*, 450–466.

Sticht, T. G. Applications of the audread model to reading evaluation and instruction. In L. Resnick, & P. Weaver (Eds.), *Theory and practice of early reading*. Hillsdale, N.J.: Lawrence Erlbaum Associates, 1979.

Stroop, J. R. Studies of interference in serial verbal reactions. *Journal of Experimental Psychology*, 1935, *18*, 643–662.

Swinney, D. Lexical access during sentence comprehension: (Re)consideration of context effects. *Journal of Verbal Learning and Verbal Behavior*, 1979, *18*, 645–659.

Tanenhaus, M., Leiman, J., & Seidenberg, M. Evidence for multiple stages in the processing of ambiguous words in syntactic contexts. *Journal of Verbal Learning and Verbal Behavior*, 1979, *18*, 427–440.

Treisman, A., & Tuxworth, J. Immediate and delayed recall of sentences after perceptual processing at different levels. *Journal of Verbal Learning and Verbal Behavior*, 1974, *13*, 38–43.

Tulving, E. Memory research: What kind of progress? In L. G. Nilsson (Ed.), *Perspectives on memory research*, Hillsdale, N.J.: Lawrence Erlbaum Ass., 1979.

Tulving, E., Mandler, G., & Baumal, R. Interaction of two sources of information in tachistoscopic word recognition. *Canadian Journal of Psychology*, 1964, *18*, 62–761.

van Dijk, T. A. *Macrostructures*. Hillsdale, N.J.: Lawrence Erlbaum Associates, 1980.

Venezky, R., & Massaro, D. The role of orthographic regularity in word recognition. In L. Resnick

& P. Weaver (Eds.), *Theory and practice of early reading.* Hillsdale, N.J.: Lawrence Erlbaum Associates, 1979.

Voss, J. F., Vesonder, G. J., & Spilich, G. T. Text generation and recall by high-knowledge and low-knowledge individuals. *Journal of Verbal Learning and Verbal Behavior,* 1980, *19,* 651–667.

Wallace, W. Review of the historical, empirical, and theoretical status of the von Restorff phenomenon. *Psychological Bulletin,* 1965, *63,* 410–424.

Warren, R. M. Perceptual restoration of missing sounds. *Science,* 1970, *167,* 392–393.

Waugh, N. A., & Norman, D. A. Primary memory. *Psychological Review,* 1965, *72,* 89–104.

Weaver, W., & Bickley, A. Sources of information for responses to reading test items. *Proceedings of the 75th Annual Convention of the American Psychological Association,* 1967, *2,* 293–294.

Wheeler, D. D. Processes in word recognition. *Cognitive Psychology,* 1970, *1,* 59–85.

Winograd, T. A. *Understanding natural language.* New York: Academic, 1972.

Winston, P. H. *Artificial intelligence.* Reading, Mass.: Addison-Wesley, 1972.

Wittrock, M. C., Marks, C., & Doctorow, M. Reading as a generative process. *Journal of Educational Psychology,* 1975, *67,* 484–489.

Woods, W. A. Generalizations of ATN grammars. In W. Woods & R. Brachman, *Research in natural language understanding.* Cambridge, Mass.: BBN Technical Report 3963, 1978.

Woods, W. A., Brown, G., Bruce, B., Cook, C., Klovstad, J., Makhoul, J., Nash-Webber, B., Schwartz, R., Wolf, J., & Zue, V. *Speech understanding systems.* Cambridge, Mass.: BBN Technical Report 3438, 1976.

6

On Learning and Learning from Text

James F. Voss
University of Pittsburgh

Two or three decades ago, the psychological study of human learning was dominated by associationism, a conceptual framework that provided a relatively stable, if somewhat restrictive, theoretical environment. The research of that period, primarily consisting of the memorization of lists of verbal items and the methods of paried-associate and serial learning, was widely used to study the acquisition, retention, and transfer of such material.

With the emergence of cognitive psychology, the study of human learning has undergone a number of changes. One is concerned with *what* is assumed to be learned. In classical associationism, learning consisted of forming and strengthening associations between two verbal units (McGeogh & Irion, 1952). Furthermore, although it was assumed that the links forming associations could differ quantitatively (in strength), they were not assumed to differ qualitatively. Today, relations among verbal units are generally assumed to be learned, and thus the links may differ qualitatively.[1] A second change in the study of human learning relates to *how* something is learned. In the classical view, associations were assumed to be developed and strengthened via the operation of the "laws" of association, the most important being contiguity and frequency. Today, the associative laws are generally regarded as an insufficient explanation for learning, primarily because, as traditionally interpreted, they do not provide for the acquisition of relations and the development of organized structures. However,

---

[1] A number of years ago some individuals did argue that developing associations consisted of forming relations, e.g., Asch (1968) and Koffka (1935).

although contemporary theory suggests that learning, at least in part, takes place by the construction of relations and the development of organized structures, mechanisms by which such construction takes place are yet to be firmly established. A third change in human-learning research has been in the experimental paradigms used to study the learning process. The paired-associate and serial-learning procedures, which essentially assume the operation of contiguity and frequency (both methods involve the simultaneous or successive presentation of items over a number of trials), are used much less frequently today than a few decades ago. Indeed, there are relatively few experiments reported in the contemporary human-learning literature that employ any multiple-trial procedure. (As a corollary, there has been a corresponding reduction in the use of the "learning curve" to describe the learning process.) With respect to contemporary research, there is no specific paradigm that is widely accepted as a basis for the study of learning.[2]

The changes just described point to a difficulty in the current study of human learning. Namely, there is not a well-developed theoretical framework that provides for the systematic study of the learning process, both in relation to theoretical mechanisms and experimental paradigms. Furthermore, this state of affairs is especially germane to the present volume, for if there currently is no generally accepted theoretical approach to the study of human learning, then the issue of how a person learns from text cannot be considered as a special case of a more general theory. The investigator interested in how people learn from text is thus confronted by a challenge and an opportunity. The challenge is to develop a theory of learning from text; the opportunity is to contribute to the development of a more general theory of learning via establishing a theory of learning from text.

Although a theory of learning from text is not presented in this chapter, the contents are concerned with how text-processing research is related to more general issues of learning. In the next section, a sketch is presented of the evolution that has occurred in the study of human learning. The section concludes with a statement of why there currently may not be a generally accepted theory of learning and how the concept of learning may need to be reevaluated, especially in relation to the learner's knowledge. The subsequent section summarizes some research we have conducted on how knowledge of a particular subject matter domain influences learning from text, and the chapter concludes with a statement regarding how such research may contribute to a more general theory of learning.

---

[2]The issue of how learning is measured in contemporary research is complicated. Most paradigms involve a single presentation of the stimulus materials and a single test (recall or recognition). However, although the storage-retrieval metaphor works well for this paradigm, such a paradigm does not separate learning and retention in the traditional sense.

ON THE EVOLUTION OF THE STUDY OF HUMAN
LEARNING

Classical associationism, following British empiricism, assumed that what we learn is essentially a copy of the stimulus material. In human-learning experimentation, this assumption was operationalized by measuring acquisition in terms of the amount of and rate at which the presented material was acquired. Moreover, the experimental subject was not tested to determine whether anything had been acquired in addition to the presented material and was not asked about the strategies that may have been used during learning.

The assumption that what is learned is a copy of what was presented was the first issue questioned in the evolution that was taking form (Voss, 1979). More specifically, it was argued that we are "active processors" learning what we attend to, rather than "passive recipients" of the presented material. Indeed, even within verbal learning research per se, the study of stimulus selection and the distinction between the nominal and the functional stimulus attested to this concern (Underwood, 1963).

The next step in the evolutionary process was to argue that the learner not only selects the information to be learned but also does something to it. Thus, the learner may code the input in a number of ways (Melton & Martin, 1972), including elaboration and transformation. Elaboration may take place, for example, by developing associations between verbal items via the use of natural language mediators (Montague, Adams, & Kiess, 1966). Transformations may take place, for example, by enhancing the organization of stimulus materials (Bousfield, 1953). Indeed, the study of the recall of categorized word lists helped the concept of organization become an integral part of theory development in human learning and memory (Postman, 1975).

As the work on coding proceeded, the jargon of the field was also changing. The influence of the computer metaphor was being felt, and the terms storage and retrieval became popular (Melton, 1973). Storage denoted that information had gone into memory, whereas retrieval denoted the process by which the information in memory could be sought and obtained. Moreover, information was taken to be stored in relation to how it had been encoded, and the argument was made that successful retrieval required some component of the information that was present during encoding to be present at retrieval (Tulving & Pearlstone, 1966).

Another step in the evolutionary process occurred when it was argued that the capacity for processing-input information was restricted by the limitations of the human system. The most influential model maintaining this view, that of Atkinson and Shiffrin (1968), assumed that the input was processed in a short-term memory buffer and a particular amount of such processing was necessary to transfer the information to and store it in long-term memory. Processing in short-term memory was presumed to occur, moreover, via the operation of rehearsal and/or by use of control processes. Correspondingly, some information was not acquired because it was not sufficiently processed in the short-term memory buffer.

The next major step consisted of arguing that the quality, not the quantity, of processing is what produces storage (Craik & Lockhart, 1972; Jenkins, 1974). Craik and Lockhart, for example, advocated a view termed ''depth-of-process-ing,'' which posited that processing could be relatively shallow or deep, e.g., processing in terms of the sounds of words or the semantic relations of the words, respectively. More recently, this line of inquiry has emphasized not levels but the uniqueness and/or elaboration with which an item is encoded (Craik, 1979).

Taken as a whole, the evolution in human-learning research described earlier has focused upon what the learner does with the presented material that enables learning to take place. Yet, despite this important shift in perspective, it is this writer's opinion that this emphasis has not been pushed far enough. A more general learning theory will be developed only when the emphasis upon how the individual processes information takes into account the cumulative nature of learning.

Human-learning research, even in the most recent years, has almost ex-clusively concentrated upon how verbal items (or lists of such items) are pro-cessed, and such research generally does not provide for determining how the knowledge and skills the learner brings into the learning situation enable the learner to process and store the information. Thus, although theoretical develop-ments based upon item learning have been substantial and although such devel-opments would be expected to apply to more complex learning situations, (it is difficult to envision a theory of learning that does not include mechanisms such as discrimination and generalization), such research typically minimizes the need to take into account prior learning. However, if one considers what we generally mean when we speak of ''learning,'' as for example in the classroom situation, we find that human learning is highly semantic in nature, with knowledge ac-quisition and utilization being critical aspects of the learning process. Thus, the argument is that much learning consists of using current knowledge to acquire new information, and a more general theory of learning must take into account this knowledge component. Interestingly, text-processing investigators were led to this conslusion quite quickly.

Considering the question of how individuals learn from text, the process typically does not consist of being able to recall, essentially verbatim, the con-tents of the text. Instead, the individual develops a representation or what van Dijk (1980) called ''a global structure of the text contents,'' and this provides the reader with a coherent structure of the main components of the text. Thus, to understand how individuals learn from text requires the investigator to study how text representations are constructed and how knowledge is utilized in the con-structive process.

Not only is it important to expand the base of research on human learning by studying the role of prior knowledge in learning, there is also a related need to reevaluate the concept of learning. Specifically, for many situations, learning should be viewed as transfer. If learning is viewed as a process in which the individual acquires new information via the effective utilization of what the person already knows, then the learning paradigm consists of the *Learn A, Learn B* transfer paradigm in which *Learn A* is the knowledge the individual has when entering the *Learn B* situation (Melton, 1950; Voss, 1978). Viewed in this context, traditional verbal-learning research in general and list learning in particular has endeavored to study *Learn B* with only minimal reference to *Learn A*. The present position is that to develop a comprehensive understanding of the learning process, research and theory must be expanded to include how the learning of *A* influences *Learn B,* where *A* may consist of knowledge and/or skills germane to the learning of *B*.

Incidentally, the position stated here is not meant as pleading a case for the importance of either ecological validity or the study of individual differences. Although the more complex learning situations are generally those found in the "real world," the argument is that the traditional study of human learning, at least to the present, has had theoretical and methodological constraints and that the understanding of the learning process will be facilitated by coming to grips with issues such as knowledge acquisition and utilization. Naturally, such study quite likely will involve research on real world problems. With respect to individual differences, although the present position may be consistent with studying how learning differs in individuals or populations of individuals, this is secondary to the primary argument.

KNOWLEDGE OF SUBJECT MATTER AND LEARNING FROM TEXT

Preliminary Considerations

In order to provide some "setting" information for this section, a description of the components of text processing is presented, at least as they are viewed in this research.

The individual, in acquiring information from text, typically has a goal that is assumed to influence how the text is processed, e.g., processing may be different in reading a mystery or a professional article. While reading, the individual is assumed to interpret the text contents in terms of his or her own knowledge, interests, and attitude. During the interpretive process the individual develops a representation of the contents of the text. Learning is thus presumed to involve the storage of information via the development of the representation. Furthermore, as a text representation is developed, the information involved may modify one's existing knowledge structure. Indeed, new information may "merge" with one's existing knowledge in such a way that it may be difficult to determine at a later time whether particular information stored in memory was or was not from some specific source (Sulin & Dooling, 1974).

Taken as a whole, a substantial amount of research on text processing has been focused upon the nature and use of the knowledge that is utilized in developing the representation of the text. For example, story grammar research (Mandler & Johnson, 1977; Stein & Glenn, 1979; Stein & Trabasso, 1981) has been aimed at demonstrating that individuals have knowledge of prototypical text structures and that they use such knowledge in processing instances of the particular class of text. Thus, for simple narratives, the prototypical structure consists of a relatively small set of categories (e.g., SETTING, INITIATING EVENT, INTERNAL RESPONSE, or OUTCOME) and connectives that enable the categories to be related (e.g., AND, OR, or CAUSE).

Similarly, work by van Dijk (1980) and Kintsch and van Dijk (1978) also emphasizes the development of higher-level text structures. These authors make a distinction between text micro-structure and macro-structure. The former consists of a set of propositions that may be derived from the surface structure of the text and that are presumed to be the underlying components of the text structure that are stored by the individual.[3] The macro-structure of the text is a higher-level version of the text that is presumed to be generated by the reader via the application of macro-rules (van Dijk, 1977, 1980). Such rules include deletion, in which the less important text contents are not incorporated into the macro-structure, and construction, in which a new proposition is constructed that summarizes a relatively large amount of text contents.

In general, the construction of the higher-level representation of text and the processing of the lower level of the text are not independent. Thus, although being able to comprehend each sentence of a passage is generally requisite to the understanding of text as a whole, it does not follow that comprehending each sentence necessarily provides a global understanding of the text. Furthermore, as pointed out by van Dijk (1980), the representation being constructed as the passage is being read may also influence the interpretation of particular sentences.

Knowledge of Baseball and Learning from Text

An Artificial Intelligence Model of Baseball.   Soloway (1978) developed a computer simulation model of baseball. This model is especially informative because it provides an idea of the knowledge required to understand the game of baseball. The model has nine levels. Among the lower levels is knowledge of

---

[3]The issue of how well the surface structure of text is remembered has been the object of investigation (Bates, Masling, & Kintsch, 1978; Kintsch & Bates, 1977; Sachs, 1967).

physical relations, e.g., knowledge of direction and rate of movement of a flying or rolling ball, and knowledge of competitive games, including the objectives of such games. Knowledge of baseball is then described at a higher level in terms of the positions and functions of players. The system then simulates the play of the game by essentially following the ball during a particular game episode and storing the actions and state changes related to that episode.

Of special interest is how the system learns. When a particular episode has occurred, it is stored. Upon subsequent occurrence of a similar action, the representation of the earlier action is activated, and a representation of the new action is stored in close relation to the old action, thus enabling classes of episodes to be stored. Soloway thus refers to learning as "interpretation + generalization." In other words, new actions are interpreted in terms of past actions, and interpretations are generalized across actions. Furthermore, although the description of the events is essentially bottom–up, the system, as it learns, develops top–down components that enable it not only to interpret subsequent actions but also to anticipate what will happen. Soloway's model thus indicates that knowledge of the real world, i.e., knowledge of relatively common physical events and knowledge of social interaction as found in competitive games, must be presumed if the system is to work. Moreover, such learning, based upon this knowledge, is a gradual process by which the system interprets the input in terms of its accumulating experience.

As one would expect, much of the learning that is required for the system to develop a substantial knowledge of the game involves how the particular episodes of the game are related to the goals of the game, and how the conditions under which goal-related activities may occur become established. Thus, as the system develops knowledge of the game, the relatively low-level (physical relations) and high-level structures (goals of competitive games as applied to baseball) develop early. The more complicated process involves relating the physical events to the game conditions and the game conditions to the goals.

There are a number of issues raised by Soloway's model that are not addressed within the system per se. One is the effect of the hierarchical structure upon the processing of input. If, for example, a high-knowledge individual constructs a representation of the important events of the game, is lower-level information processed in a manner similar to a low-knowledge individual? The model proposed by Thibadeau, Just, and Carpenter (1982) suggests that information is processed at all levels upon being read and data are presented later in this chapter that are consistent with this notion.

A second issue raised by Soloway's model is how the individual monitors the information that is important to the cumulative aspects of the game. An account of a baseball game is a narrative, and prior events are related to particular subsequent events. Soloway's model involves a more "static" representation without taking into account a working-memory type of component. This issue is also considered in greater detail later in the chapter.

The third issue involves what constitutes a novice and an expert within the model's framework. Although Soloway's system does not include knowledge of the game's strategies, such knowledge no doubt is contingent upon knowledge of the conceptual relations of the game. Thus, a system having a complete understanding of baseball would likely include a few more levels based upon the goal structure of the game and the strategies used to achieve the goals. The expert, of course, would likely know all such information from which virtually any game action could be interpreted and any potential action could be anticipated. Indeed, the question probably most debated by sports enthusiasts involves which strategy should or should not be used under particular conditions. (Baseball has a finite set of rules and strategies, and it is possible for an expert to know virtually all of these, except perhaps for more technical rules that seldom apply. In many other subject matter domains, however, near-complete knowledge of a domain is virtually impossible. Expertise in such domains thus becomes relative.)

The novice category is a matter of degree. A quite naive novice may watch a baseball game and see only the physical activity of the game and the crowd reaction. A more sophisticated novice may know what constitutes winning and losing in baseball and is able to understand some of the physical actions in reference to the highest-level goals of the game. Finally, a person with more knowledge may have an understanding of some of the game terminology and how specific actions relate to particular subgoals, but such knowledge will likely have gaps, and knowledge of strategies may be minimal. Interestingly, this view of novice development suggests that the problem of becoming an expert largely involves acquiring the information that is required to "fill in" between the simplest physical activity and the highest-level goals, both of which are understood initially as part of the real world. The data presented below are consistent with this view.

Text Processing and Domain-related Knowledge.   Our work on how specialized knowledge influences learning from text has involved use of the contrastive method, i.e., performance differences are examined for individuals who have either high or low knowledge in the particular domain. (Baseball knowledge was determined by a series of sentence completion items designed to test knowledge of the terminology, rules, and principles of the game. The high- and low-knowledge groups were equated on a verbal comprehension task.) Although this type of research is basically correlational and must be interpreted accordingly, the research, nevertheless, provides the opportunity not only to distinguish characteristics of expert and novice performance but also to provide some idea regarding the means by which expertise is acquired.

In an initial text-processing study, a passage was presented that consisted of a segment of a fictitious baseball game (one-half inning). It was a standard description of a baseball game and included not only an account of the game but also contained information that is not directly a part of the game, e.g., weather conditions. After receiving the description, individuals were asked to recall the contents of the text. After recall, they received a set of text-related completion questions.

Although knowledge was related to greater recall, the more interesting findings involve the pattern of recall. High-knowledge individuals recalled more information directly related to the goal structure of the game, whereas there was little performance difference of the groups in recalling information unrelated to the game. Low-knowledge individuals tended to recall the teams, weather, and the first batter coming to bat, but recall of the subsequent events of the game was infrequent and not systematic (Spilich, Vesonder, Chiesi, & Voss, 1979; Voss, Vesonder, & Spilich, 1980).

The recall data were fit by a series of models that were extensions of the Kintsch and van Dijk (1978) theory of text comprehension. This model assumes that as individuals process a text they develop a micro-structure and a macro-structure representation of the text. The micro-structure consists of a set of propositions that, in part, is a function of what the processor is assumed to carry over in working memory as the text is being processed. The macro-structure consists of a set of propositions assumed to be generated via the application of the previously described macro-rules. The important point for present purposes is that we assumed that macro-structure development was a function of the knowledge of the goal structure of the game. Furthermore, the best-fitting model was based upon the assumption that macro-structure information is carried over in a memory buffer as long as it is germane to the goal structure of the game. To illustrate, when a given player is "at bat," events happen (balls and strikes) that are important as long as that particular player is "at bat." However, when the next player is "at bat," the events that occurred when the previous batter was "at bat" are irrelevant to the remainder of the game. This type of *temporary relevance* occurs in various ways in a baseball game. The best-fitting model for both high- and low-knowledge individuals assumed that information was maintained in a buffer only when it was germane to the game, with the high-knowledge individuals being able to carry over more information in the buffer. Thus, these findings indicate that the pattern of recall was best described by a model that was consistent with the game. (It should be noted that the low-knowledge subjects were not "no knowledge" and they did have an understanding of at least some goals of the game.)

Another finding was that high-knowledge individuals were able to recall information on the completion test that was not stated during free recall. Such information was typically not important to the game. This result suggests that high-knowledge individuals encoded the text contents in a hierarchical manner in which the more salient game information was stored at higher levels. The data, of course, do not preclude a retrieval interpretation, although other data presented later in the chapter support the emphasis upon encoding.

In a second study (Voss, Vesonder, & Spilich, 1980), high-knowledge and low-knowledge individuals generated their own segment of a baseball game, and two weeks later they were asked to recall the specific text they themselves had generated. The recall of high-knowledge individuals was again superior despite the fact that the text was self-generated.

Detailed analyses of the data obtained in both studies revealed that although high-knowledge individuals were adept at recalling the sequences of game events, low-knowledge individuals were especially poor in this regard. Like most games, baseball consists of a sequence of alternating game states and actions, i.e., a game state exists and an action produces a change in the game state, followed by another action producing a state change, and so forth. Moreover, some state changes are more important than others with respect to the goals of the game. The results of Voss et al. (1980) indicated that high-knowledge individuals tended to recall the actions of the game and the related changes in game states. Low-knowledge individuals, however, seldom recalled actions, and when recalling game states, they sometimes confused the order of their occurrence. These data were interpreted as showing that because the result of an action is typically a state change, the detailed recall of the actions enabled the high-knowledge individuals to recall the state–by–state sequence of the game.

As stated, the texts in the Voss et al. (1980) study were self-generated and given the recall differences that have been described, it was expected that the texts generated by high-knowledge and low-knowledge individuals should differ. Specifically, text generated by high-knowledge individuals should provide better descriptions of the actions and related state changes of the game than text generated by low-knowledge individuals. Indeed, this result was obtained by Voss et al. (1980). Moreover, it was found that low-knowledge individuals could not recall text generated by high-knowledge individuals as well as high-knowledge individuals could, as one would expect. However, for text generated by low-knowledge individuals, there was little difference in recall by high-knowledge and low-knowledge individuals. This latter result indicates that better recall of baseball-related text is thus not an intrinsic property of high knowledge but that knowledge enhances recall when the particular text provides for the opportunity to utilize that knowledge.

The studies discussed thus far have involved lengthy narrative text. The results of two experiments are now considered in which the length of the text was varied from one to nine sentences in one case and from one to three sentences in the second case.

Chiesi, Spilich, and Voss (1979, Experiment III) presented a sentence memory span with high- and low-knowledge individuals. A sequence of one, three, five, seven, or nine sentences was presented, followed immediately by a recall test. There were three types of materials, an event sequence of a baseball game, an event sequence of neutral material, and a sequence of scrambled baseball events. The important result was that a significant knowledge and length interaction was obtained for baseball material. High-knowledge and low-knowledge individuals differed relatively little in recall performance on short passage lengths (no difference at a length of one sentence), but as length of passage increased, recall of low-knowledge individuals decreased more than recall of the high-knowledge individuals.

A second study (Chiesi, Spilich, & Voss, 1979, Experiment V) not only showed a similar effect but also indicated how low-knowledge performance may deteriorate when input information is not integrated. Without going into the specific design, the basic finding was that if single baseball-related target sentences are presented, there is no significant difference in free recall for high- and low-knowledge individuals. However, if one or two related sentences precede the target sentences at input, and later recall of the target sentences is obtained *without* the preceding sentences being presented (and serving as cues), high-knowledge performance is significantly better than that of low-knowledge individuals. In other words, as the number of context sentences increased *at input,* target-sentence recall became greater for high-knowledge individuals than when target sentences were presented by themselves, even without the context sentences being present at recall. However, for low-knowledge individuals, as the number of sentences preceding the target sentence at input increased, that is, zero, one, or two, recall of the target sentences, without the context sentences being presented at recall, deteriorated significantly.

These findings were interpreted in the following way. When high-knowledge individuals are presented with a meaningful sequence of domain-related sentences, they integrate the sequence. Subsequently, at recall, retrieval of the contents of any sentence in the sequence is able to generate the entire sequence. Low-knowledge individuals are not readily able to integrate the sentence sequence, and the sentences are thus processed as separate bits of information that interfere with each other, probably at input.

Finally, an interesting aspect of these findings is that in two experiments, recall performance did *not* vary with knowledge when only a single sentence was presented at input. The result suggests that the encoding of single sentences has little relation to knowledge, a finding considered later in the chapter.

The findings of the previously mentioned Spilich et al. (1979) study suggested that high-knowledge individuals are able to carry over more information in a working memory buffer than are low-knowledge individuals. Furthermore, one would also expect on intuitive grounds that high-knowledge individuals access the information being carried over more quickly than do low-knowledge individuals. This hypothesis assumes that the information carried over is organized better and requires less search time for high-knowledge than for low-knowledge individuals. Similarly, high-knowledge individuals would be expected to have a well-developed baseball schema, and as a game proceeds, they should be able monitor the game's events and update the appropriate parameter values more readily than low-knowledge individuals. These and related ideas were tested in a series of four unpublished studies that are now briefly described.

In the first two experiments, a complete (fictitious) baseball game was presented on a computer terminal one sentence at a time. The game was a "play–by–play" account as given on the radio, and the account included commercials as well as usual game-related information. The entire description contained 900 sentences. Throughout the game, probes were presented. Each probe consisted of a simple sentence, and individuals were asked to press one of two buttons to indicate whether the information stated in the particular probe was or was not correct in relation to the previously presented text. The information contained in the sentence verification task was related to various aspects of the' game as well as to the neutral material of the text. In general, the probe sentences were quite similar to the original text.

In the first experiment, the category of probe information was varied. Based upon the recall data of Spilich et al. (1979), two categories in which little performance difference was expected between high-knowledge and low-knowledge individuals were nongame information and setting. Nongame information referred to that found in commercials, whereas setting information was general, e.g., teams playing, weather conditions, or specific, as information about particular players. Five other probe categories were used, four of which were expected to produce performance differences in the two knowledge groups. Two of these involved information about the game actions and game states, respectively, whereas the other two tested for game-related information after relatively long periods of time. The final category, integration, consisted of probe items given after the game. To answer these questions, knowledge of information of different parts of the game was necessary. The type of information contained in the probe was such that, although related to the game, it is not typically found in the schema of baseball games. This condition was included in an effort to break down the anticipated advantage of the high-knowledge individuals. In the second experiment, two major modifications were made. First, lag (number of intervening sentences between presentation of information and probe test on that information) was not controlled in the first experiment, and, where possible, lag was manipulated by presenting the probe either "near" or "far" from the preceding text in the second experiment. The second manipulation involved having context information presented immediately before the probe. The information that immediately preceded the target information in the text was presented immediately prior to the probe for one-half of the probes.

The results of these experiments, although providing partial support for the hypotheses, raised some questions. To illustrate, in the first experiment, game action and game state probes were identified correctly significantly more often for high-knowledge (HK) than low-knowledge (LK) individuals. The p(Hit) $-$ p(False Alarm) means for game actions were HK $=$ .73 and LK $=$ .48 and for game states were HK $=$ .68 and LK $=$ .56 (borderline significance). However, the mean verification times (msec) were not significantly different in either case, HK $=$ 2605 and LK $=$ 2827 for game actions and HK $=$ 2356 and LK $=$ 2329 for game states. As anticipated, nongame and setting information yielded no significant differences for either measure. There was some evidence that high-knowledge individuals performed better when tests occurred after a considerable number of sentences, but the differences were not significant for either measure. Finally, the integration probes produced poor performance in both conditions, ρ(Hit) $-$ ρ(False Alarm) $=$ .24 for high-knowledge and $-$.07 for low-knowledge individuals.

The second experiment produced similar results. One interesting finding, however, was that presentation of the context sentence prior to the probe facilitated correct response performance for the low-knowledge but not the high-knowledge individuals, p(Hit) $-$ ρ(False Alarm): Context Present, HK $=$ .74, LK $=$ .62; Context Absent, HK $=$ .70, LK $=$ .47. However, context-facilitated ($p<$.07 for the interaction) probe-verification time for high-knowledge more than for the low-knowledge individuals, verification time (msec): Context Present, HK $=$ 2011, LK $=$ 2594; Context Absent, HK $=$ 2397, LK $=$ 2775. These findings suggest a more organized structure for high-knowledge individuals, because the context sentence yielded a Haviland & Clark (1974) type of effect. In addition, the results suggest that when a context sentence is not presented, the high-knowledge individuals essentially supply their own context, an idea considered later.

A possible reason for the general lack of performance differences in verification time is that if the high-knowledge individuals are indeed carrying over more game-related information than are the low-knowledge individuals, then the high-knowledge individuals may have a set-size problem. Specifically, verification could take longer for high-knowledge individuals, because there is more information through which they must search. We tested this hypothesis using a modified Sternberg paradigm in which one, three, five, or seven sentences were presented serially. Subsequently, individuals were tested with a probe sentence, being asked to indicate whether the probe sentence was a member of the immediately preceding stimulus set. One-half of the sentence sets contained information, and one-half contained neutral information. For sets greater in length than three sentences, one-half of the sets consisted of related sentences, and one-half consisted of unrelated sentences. Relatedness and subject matter were orthogonal. Pronouns were avoided, and the related sentences from different sets were used to form the unrelated sentence sets. Thus, what was expected were slopes of lower magnitude for high-knowledge individuals than for low-knowledge individuals but of such a differential magnitude that it would take, for example, high-knowledge individuals about the same time to verify a sentence from a seven-sentence set as it would a low-knowledge person to verify a sentence from a three- or a five-sentence set.

Both groups performed at a relatively high level of accuracy, which was desired. However, the results indicated no significant differences in verification time in interactions involving knowledge, including those involving the variable of number of sentences. The set-size effect hypothesis was thus not supported.

At this time it was realized that in each experiment, the probe information was closely related to the actual statements of the text even when such information was important to the goal structure of the game. What was not tested for was information that should be generated in the construction of the text macro-structure, even though it may not be explicitly stated in the text. Therefore, the 900-sentence fictitious game was modified and probe items were presented specifically constructed to test for information found in the text as well as for information presumed to be generated in the text macro-structure. The probes included nongame information and internalizations (players' or fans' reactions to events) game actions, game states, summarizations, memory update, and again integration questions. Memory update refers to the monitoring of game parameters when the information is presented in the text but a specific update statement is not presented. For example, assume the text states that "Winslow scored another run for the Sharks," but the resulting score is not mentioned. Subsequently there is a probe stating the score. Summarization involved similar probes, but the probes required more integration of information. For example, at the end of an inning, the probe may state, "The Sharks scored two runs in the inning."

The results indicated a general advantage for high knowledge on game-related information and no advantage for nongame information. The p(Hit) $-$ p(False Alarm) data indicated, for high-knowledge and low-knowledge groups, respectively, means of .85 and .84 for nongame information and .75 and .75 for internalizations. For game actions, there was borderline significance, HK = .79, LK = .63, but, of necessity, this information was again closely related to the text contents. For memory update, the means were significantly different, .79 and .56 and for summarization the significantly different means were .91 and .66. The integration probes showed no significant differences, .29 and .25. With respect to verification time, high-knowledge individuals were faster on "Hits" for all categories. (Length of sentence and base reading time for each individual was partialed out.) Of particular interest is that there was relatively little difference in mean verification time of high-knowledge individuals: nongame, 439; internalization, 323; game action, 516; memory update, 510; and summarization, 452. However for low-knowledge individuals, the corresponding values were 1059, 1101, 1908, 2419, and 2066. For the integration category, the mean values for "Hits" were 2105 and 2703 for high- and low-knowledge groups, respectively.

Two results should be noted. First, the data support the hypothesis that high-knowledge individuals are more adept at constructing the macro-structure from the text than are low-knowledge individuals. Second, high-knowledge individuals verified macro-structure probes as rapidly as they verified probes more directly related to the specific text information. This finding thus suggests that the macro-structure representation is being constructed while reading the text. Furthermore, this result is even more remarkable, because the probes closely related to the text information were usually presented shortly after the information occurred in the text, whereas information found in summarization probes was usually presented over larger spans of the text. Finally, for low-knowledge individuals, performance accuracy is lower for macro-structure probes than for game-related information and verification times are greater for "Hits" of the macro-structure probes than for the nongame information probes. This result suggests at best a weaker macro-structure development for low-knowledge than for high-knowledge individuals. At worst, it suggests little if any macro-structure development and the need for low-knowledge individuals to search for the appropriate text information in order to answer the macro-structure probe items correctly.

The results of the probes studies also provide an interpretation of the Spilich et al. (1979) findings with respect to carry-over information. High-knowledge individuals are especially adept at constructing a macro-structure for the game, and this process continues throughout the entire game with updating and summarizing of pertinent information. Furthermore, for the high-knowledge individuals, this macro-structure would be expected to be hierarchical in nature, the hierarchy based upon the goals of game. The present findings thus support the idea that this hierarchical structure is used as a basis of retrieval as suggested by Spilich et al (1979).

Another aspect of the present findings involves why the first three experiments in the series failed to reveal verification-time differences as a function of knowledge, even for schema-related items. A possible reason is that the information tested was found in the text and testing usually came shortly after the information was presented. Thus, low-knowledge individuals were able to access information explicitly stated in the text, even if it was game-related. However, being able to respond to probes when the target information is presented does not mean that low-knowledge individuals construct a macro-structure. Indeed, the present findings taken with the poor recall by low-knowledge individuals in the Spilich et al. (1979) study suggest that low-knowledge individuals do not construct a macro-structure even if they understand the germane information on a sentence–by–sentence basis. On the other hand, high-knowledge individuals construct the macro-structure whether or not the macro-structure propositions are explicitly presented in the text.

The findings on the role of knowledge in text processing suggest that a major component of learning from text involves the construction of representations that take into account the most salient features of a text. This, moreover, is apparently done as the text is being processed. However, to construct such representations, the individual, much as Soloway's system, must have knowledge of the cogent physical and social factors relevant to the text contents and also have knowledge of the concepts of relations found in the text. Finally, learning from text is likely influenced by the experience the individual has had in developing representations when the text involves a prototypical structure such as that found in the account of a baseball game. Such experience is taken to help in selecting and organizing the text contents. Interestingly, this description is quite similar to that which has been postulated regarding the role of knowledge of story structure in learning from text (Mandler & Johnson, 1977; Stein & Glenn, 1979).

An additional point is that in the present research the mechanisms of representation construction may be assumed to be a joint function of domain-related knowledge and the macro-rules employed to construct macro-structures, as suggested by van Dijk (1980). Although both the high-knowledge and low-knowledge individuals of college age would be expected to be able to employ macro-rules, only the high-knowledge individuals would be expected to apply the rules in order to construct an appropriate game representation.

Knowledge and Attitude in the Processing of Text

Research such as that described in this chapter has been primarily concerned with the cognitive factors that influence learning from text. Despite the concern of Bartlett (1932) regarding the role of attitude, factors that have received little attention in the study of learning from text are those of emotion, attitude, motivation, and interest. These factors have received more attention in some European research found in the United States, with European research related to a view known as action theory (Mandl, Schnotz, & Ballstaedt, 1980). A basic concept in the theory is that of Tatigkeit, and although this term lacks precision, the concept refers in general to mental activity carried out with a particular purpose in mind.

In the interest of studying the role of attitudinal factors in the processing of text, Tyler and Voss (1982) conducted the following study. Individuals were obtained from introductory and advanced undergraduate political science classes and were given tests designed to assess their knowledge of and attitude toward the Soviet Union. In the second stage, individuals were asked to rate on a six-point scale the general state of international relations that exist between the Soviet Union and each of 18 countries. Six countries were western, six were in the Soviet bloc, and six were neutral, although three may be regarded as leaning toward the Soviet Union and three leaning toward the West. Thus, this rating provided a measure of perceived relations of the Soviet Union and each of the countries.

In the third stage, a series of 18 passages was presented with one passage referring to each of the 18 respective countries. Individuals were instructed to regard the passage as though it came from *Pravda*. Actually, the passages were reasonably authentic, having been constructed by a graduate student in political science who reads *Pravda* routinely.

There was also a between-subject manipulation with respect to the passage contents. In one condition, termed Congruent, the contents of the passage related to a particular country were in agreement with the general posture of the Soviet Union toward that country. However, in the Incongruent condition, the statements made about the particular country were generally the opposite of what one would expect. Congruent and Incongruent passages were respectively presented to two groups under instructions to rate the contents of the passage with respect to aggressiveness with each individual rating each of the 18 passages.

Finally, the last two phases of the experiment consisted of giving a previously unannounced cued-recall test followed by a recognition test. In the former, the cues were the names of each of the 18 countries, and the instructions were to state whatever could be remembered from the text about each respective country. The recognition test consisted of presenting a statement from each passage along with the names of four countries, the correct country, a country of the same bloc, of the different bloc, and one country not in the 18-country set of the study.

With respect to the results in general, attitude was related more than knowledge to recall in the Congruent condition (with knowledge effects partialed out), whereas knowledge was related to recall in the Incongruent condition (with attitude effects partialed out). These findings, combined with those of Weldon and Malpass (1981), indicate that attitude and knowledge may be viewed as parts of the same system and attitude may be assumed to be related to recall when the information processed is relatively simple and consistent with one's expectations. Whole knowledge dominates when the information is new and/or when it is inconsistent with expectations. Although this work on the role of knowledge and attitude in text processing is exploratory, the results at least suggest that attitude and knowledge may both be important in developing an appropriate representation of the text contents. However, the relative contribution of each is a function of the relation of the text contents to the individual's knowledge and expectations.

LEARNING FROM TEXT AND LEARNING IN GENERAL

Earlier in this chapter, the point was made that the study of learning from text may help to provide a better understanding of the process of learning in general. The following comments are made in relation to this observation.

Learning from text involves the development of a representation that provides a reasonable and coherent interpretation of the text contents. Furthermore, selection of what goes into the representation is based upon importance, and the individual uses various forms of knowledge to determine what is important. These forms include:

1. Knowledge of the concepts and relations found in the text including those of the particular subject-matter domain.
2. Knowledge of the nature of the information that typically goes into global structures, as the structures relate to the topic or domain in question.

An important issue that is raised in reference to how knowledge is used in learning from text is how the knowledge is acquired. After all, one could argue, what has been presented is that if one has the knowledge, input may be mapped onto it; in baseball, for example, high-knowledge individuals, in part, construct macro-structures by binding and updating variables in a schema based upon the game's goal structure. This also permits them to store the text information hierarchically with the actions related to state changes serving to enhance one's memory of the state changes.

The answer to how individuals acquire knowledge is, of course, a critical issue, and in the contemporary literature, the theory most directly related is that of Anderson (1982). Although Anderson's model refers to skill learning, the fact is that becoming an expert in a particular domain and being able to process new information of that domain is a skill, and as most skills, it takes a long time to develop. Anderson's model suggests that individuals acquire declarative knowledge and that with experience the knowledge becomes proceduralized, i.e., becomes incorporated into procedures that permit access to the information under specified conditions. The findings described in the present chapter, when viewed in the context of this model, suggest that knowledge acquisition is a gradual process in which new concepts and relations are constructed if they are not identified as components of the knowledge structure. Through experience, patterns of such relations are constructed, forming structures usually referred to as schema. Also, with experience, the individual proceduralizes information by acquiring patterns of event contingencies. In baseball and probably in most other domains, these patterns are probabilistic in the sense that the individual knows what event, *B,* will likely follow event *A* and how it could occur. But the individual also knows that some other events could follow *A* and knows how they could occur. Thus, from this point of view, knowledge acquisition is a process of pattern learning that is based upon knowledge of concepts and conceptual relations. (Pattern learning refers to both relations that tend to exist jointly in a schema as well as sequential patterns.)

In order to understand how such learning occurs, it probably will be necessary to design experiments that are a longitudinal design rather than the expert–novice cross-sectional paradigm. The longitudinal studies will require appropriate measures of knowledge acquisition as well as training procedures that provide for the testing of hypotheses concerning knowledge acquisition. Such experimentation is of course costly and difficult. But for a general theory of learning to be developed, such research is likely critical.

ACKNOWLEDGMENTS

The research reported in this paper was supported by the Learning Research and Development Center of the University of Pittsburgh, which is supported in part by the National Institute of Education (NIE) or Advanced Research Projects Agency (ARPA), an office under the Secretary of Defense. The opinions expressed do not necessarily reflect the position or policy of NIE and ARPA, and no official endorsement should be inferred. The author wishes to thank Tom Trabasso, Nancy Stein, and anonymous reviewers for their comments on an earlier draft of this manuscript.

REFERENCES

Anderson, J. R. Acquisition of cognitive skill. *Psychological Review,* 1982, *89,* 369–406.

Asch, S. The doctrinal tyranny of associationism: Or what is wrong with rote learning. In T. R. Dixon & D. L. Horton (Eds.), *Verbal behavior and general behavior theory.* Englewood Cliffs, N.J.: Prentice-Hall, 1968.

Atkinson, R. C., & Shiffrin, R. M. Human memory: A proposed system and its control processes. In K. W. Spence & J. T. Spence (Eds.), *The psychology of learning and motivation* (Vol. 2). New York: Academic Press, 1968.

Bartlett, F. C. *Remembering.* London: Cambridge University Press, 1932.

Bates, E., Masling, M., & Kintsch, W. Recognition memory for aspects of dialogue. *Journal of Experimental Psychology: Human Learning and Memory,* 1978, *4,* 187–197.

Bousfield, W. A. The occurrence of clustering the recall of randomly arranged associates. *Journal of General Psychology,* 1953, *49,* 229–240.

Chiesi, H. L., Spilich, G. J., & Voss, J. F. Acquisition of domain-related information in relation to high- and low-domain knowledge. *Journal of Verbal Learning and Verbal Behavior,* 1979, *18,* 257–274.

Craik, F. I. M. Levels of processing: Overview and closing comments. In L. S. Cermak & F. I. M. Craik (Eds.), *Levels of processing and human memory.* Hillsdale, N.J.: Lawrence Erlbaum Associates, 1979.

Craik, F. I. M., & Lockhart, R. S. Levels of processing: A framework for memory research. *Journal of Verbal Learning and Verbal Behavior,* 1972, *11,* 671–684.

Haviland, S. E., & Clark, H. H. What's new? Acquiring new information as a process in comprehension. *Journal of Verbal Learning and Verbal Behavior,* 1974, *13,* 512–521.

Jenkins, J. J. Remember that old theory of memory? Well, forget it! *American Psychologist,* 1974, *29,* 785–795.

Kintsch, W., & Bates, E. Recognition memory for statements from a classroom lecture. *Journal of Experimental Psychology: Human Learning and Memory,* 1977, *3,* 150–159.

Kintsch, W., & van Dijk, T. A. Towards a model of discourse comprehension and production. *Psychological Review,* 1978, *85,* 363–394.

Koffka, K. *Principles of Gestalt psychology.* New York: Harcourt Brace, 1935.

Mandl, H., Schnotz, W., & Ballstaedt, S. P. *Learning from text seen from the perspective of action theories.* Paper presented at the 22nd International Congress of Psychology, Leipzig, Germany, July 1980.

Mandler, J. M., & Johnson, N. S. Remembrance of things parsed: Story structure and recall. *Cognitive Psychology,* 1977, *9,* 111–151.

McGeogh, J. A., & Irion, A. L. *The psychology of human learning.* New York: Longmans Green, 1952.

Melton, A. W. Learning. In W. S. Monroe (Ed.), *Encyclopedia of Educational Research,* New York: Macmillan, 1950.

Melton, A. W. The concept of coding in learning–memory theory. *Memory and Cognition,* 1973, *1,* 508–512.

Melton, A. W., & Martin, E. (Eds.), *Coding processes in human memory.* Washington, D. C.: Winston, 1972.

Montague, W. E., Adams, J. A., & Kiess, H. O. Forgetting and natural language mediation. *Journal of Educational Psychology,* 1966, *72,* 829–833.

Postman, L. Verbal learning and memory. *Annual Review of Psychology,* 1975, *26,* 291–335.

Sachs, J. S. Recognition memory for syntactic and semantic aspects of connected discourse. *Perception and Psychophysics,* 1967, *2,* 437–442.

Soloway, E. M. *"Learning = Interpretation + Generalization": A case study in knowledge-directed learning.* Unpublished doctoral dissertation, University of Massachusetts, 1978.

Spilich, G. J., Vesonder, G. T., Chiesi, H. L., & Voss, J. F. Text processing of domain-related information for individuals with high- and low-domain knowledge. *Journal of Verbal Learning and Verbal Behavior,* 1979, *18,* 275–290.

Stein, N. L., & Glenn, C. G. An analysis of story comprehension in elementary school children. In R. O. Freedle (Ed.), *New directions in discourse processing* (Vol. 2). Norwood, N.J.: Ablex, 1979.

Stein, N. L. & Trabasso, T. What's in a story: An approach to comprehension and instruction. In R. Glaser (Ed.), *Advances in instructional psychology* (Vol. 2). Hillsdale, N.J.: Lawrence Erlbaum Associates, 1981.

Sulin, R. A., & Dooling, D. J. Intrusion of a thematic idea in retention of prose. *Journal of Experimental Psychology,* 1974, *103,* 255–262.

Thibadeau, R., Just, M. A., & Carpenter, P.A. A model of the time course and content of reading. *Cognitive Science,* 1982, *6,* 157–203.

Tulving, E., & Pearlstone, Z. Availability versus accessibility of information in memory for words. *Journal of Verbal Learning and Verbal Behavior,* 1966, *5,* 381–391.

Tyler, S. W., & Voss, J. F. Attitude and knowledge effects in prose processing. *Journal of Verbal Learning and Verbal Behavior,* 1982, *21,* 524–538.

Underwood, B. J. Stimulus selection in verbal learning. In C. N. Cofer & B. S. Musgrave (Eds.), *Verbal behavior and learning: Problems and processes.* New York: McGraw Hill, 1963.

van Dijk, T. A. *Text and context: Explorations in the semantics and pragmatics of discourse.* London: Longman, 1977.

van Dijk, T. A. *Macro-structures: An interdisciplinary study of global structures in discourse, interaction, and cognition.* Hillsdale, N.J.: Lawrence Erlbaum Associates, 1980.

Voss, J. F. Cognition and instruction: Toward a cognitive theory of learning. In A. M. Lesgold, J. W. Pellegrino, S. D. Fokkema, & R. Glaser (Eds.), *Cognitive psychology and instruction.* New York: Plenum, 1978.

Voss, J. F. Organization, structure, and memory: Three perspectives. In R. C. Puff (Ed.), *Memory, organization, and structure.* Hillsdale, N.J.: Academic press, 1979.

Voss, J. F., Vesonder, G. T., & Spilich, G. J. Text generation and recall by high-knowledge and low-knowledge individuals. *Journal of Verbal Learning and Verbal Behavior,* 1980, *19,* 651–667.

Weldon, D. E., & Malpass, R. S. Effects of attitudinal, cognitive, and situational variables on recall of biased communications. *Journal of Personality and Social Psychology,* 1981, *40,* 39–52.

7

Learner, Text Variables, and the Control of Text Comprehension and Recall

Peter Michael Fischer
Heinz Mandl
Deutsches Institut für Fernstudien
an der Universität Tübingen

The learning that occurs in classes is regulated and guided by the instructor through the use of direct instructions as to information and references. The influence of the instructor ranges from the arrangement of the yet to be learned material into manageable tasks or portions. Also the diagnosis, assessment, advancement, and guiding of the learning process is under the control of the instructor. What remains to be done by the learner is the execution of the given instructions, allowing for correction or regulation. Within the framework of school learning, the execution of homework and assignments is, as a rule, also managed, easily surveyed, and corrected by the instructor.

On the contrary, the requirements demanded of a learner in a self-study program accompanied with written instructions are more severe and far-reaching. The command of learning techniques and learning strategies is often tacitly assumed. It is expected that the learner will manage the material given in written form at a self-pace. Further, the learner must realize his own learning success and adjust to the learning goal. The learner must have at his/her disposal the competence to maintain interest and motivation over longer periods of time without the intervention of outside help. It comes, therefore, as no surprise that learning problems or difficulties are reported regardless of whether this occurs in the university, in the upper classes in high school, or in adult education.

Examination is limited to those learning demands that originate with the processing of written learning material. Focus is placed on the actual process of the reading of the written material, its diagnosis, and regulation.

TASK ANALYSIS OF LEARNING FROM TEXT

Learning from text calls for some elementary literacy and skills in processing written materials. The major goals of learning are to work out the core information contained in texts, to reduce it to its main information, to comprehend it, and to integrate it with the learner's existing body of prior knowledge. Additionally, the newly acquired knowledge should be retrievable quickly and without effort at the right time and place. This task of comprehending and storing a text's core information is subdivided further into concrete subgoals. The learner must be able to plan learning by some overview of the text's structure and content, to identify a text's macro-structure and segmentation, to allot study time so as to not neglect the text's most important passages, to monitor and check comprehension, in short, to orchestrate and to regulate the course of learning.

Although there is agreement about complex interactions between orienting tasks, subjects, criterial tasks, and materials (Jenkins, 1979, tetrahedral model of learning), common learning programs (Fischer & Mandl, 1980b, 1981a) neglect the complexity of the demands with which the learner is confronted. There is little differentiation between learning goals according to their cognitive functions such as comprehension and/or memorization, or according to their text dimensions, such as understanding and/or memorizing the core information of the text versus its details. The techniques offered are general and are not tailored to circumscribed, definite learning tasks; there is also no differentiation according to formal and structural versus content area and domain-specific characteristics. Rather, an average text of common difficulty and familiarity is presupposed. The *average learner* is also fictitiously presupposed for narrative or scientific texts, and no distinction is made as to prior knowledge or learning competence. The tasks of learning and control of learning are not separated. The given recommendations for learning are styled according to some Kantian *categorical imperative:* "Look out for important text passages."!"Underline them."!"Review your understanding.!" Such advice is seldom transformed into manageable processing steps.

In contrast, recent instructional models based on cognitive science, however, do differentiate between the tasks of the learning: to learn by using prior knowledge and one's learning competence on the one hand, and to monitor, control, and orchestrate learning on the other.

Levin (1982) argues that learning is dependent on the task. Learning at the *information level* may be directed either at the macro-structure (main ideas, topics, or themes) or at micro-propositions (smaller text units, details, or facts). A further distinction refers to the *focus* of learning: Is the text to be processed for comprehension and/or for storage of the information? Four types of learning strategies result. The first is *comprehension-directed macro-structure strategies* and consists of overviewing the text, skimming for main ideas or concepts, comprehending the main ideas, and paraphrasing larger units through note taking. The second, *memory-directed macro-structure strategies,* involves analysis of the text, such as constructing a hierarchical representation of the text; concretizing the main ideas through pictorial representations, maps, graphs, or flowcharts; writing summaries of the text; underlining and identifying the important ideas; and directing higher-order questions to those concepts that require inferences. The third, called *comprehension-directed micro-structure strategies,* entails concretizing factual details, making analogies, and paraphrasing smaller text units. Finally, *memory-directed micro-structure strategies* involves rereading and reviewing, and answering questions about and memorizing the factual details. These comprehension and memorization strategies of Levin (1982) are depicted in Fig. 7.1.

Levin's heuristic requires some "cybernetic control mechanism." Strategic monitoring is defined by Levin (1982) as follows:

> Strategic monitoring is viewed as a cybernetic process, with effective monitoring providing information concerning the effectiveness of strategy implementation. That is, the degree of effective monitoring is assumed to have a direct effect on the amount of text comprehended and remembered . . . (Strategic monitoring) consists of student's metacognitions, how successfully they process a text, reflected by the student's monitoring of their comprehension of and memory in which they are studying. "Do I or don't I understand this information?" and "Will I be able to remember it?" are the relevant questions here" [p. 6].

In trying to understand Levin's model as being a cybernetic system, a series of concerns is raised. Does strategic monitoring mean more than self-questioning? What are the consequences of strategic monitoring? What does the learner do when he/she experiences the results of his self-control? How does the learner use that information to further control learning? How conscious is the strategic monitoring? What mode of learning regulation is implied? Must we think of deliberate learning criteria against which the results of self-questioning are matched? What role do learner's qualities play, such as skill endowment or *monitoring ability?* Is the learner skilled enough to supervise learning? Which role is played by prior knowledge? Is *metaknowledge* necessarily implied? And what is it like? Levin does not address these questions, but then, his interest does not lie in the strategic control of learning but rather in the implementation of pictorial mnemonic aids. In their essence, his learning strategies represent a rough sketch of what the learner might do when preparing a text.

Levin (1982), himself, gives reason to doubt his usage of the term *strategy.* If monitoring per se deserves this label, the underlining of important text units certainly would not. The kinds and types of activities Levin recommends are thus heterogeneous in nature and differ widely in their psychological implications. Unless one adopts some level-of-processing notion, there is no reason to view underlining as a rehearsal strategy. The same holds true for the directing and

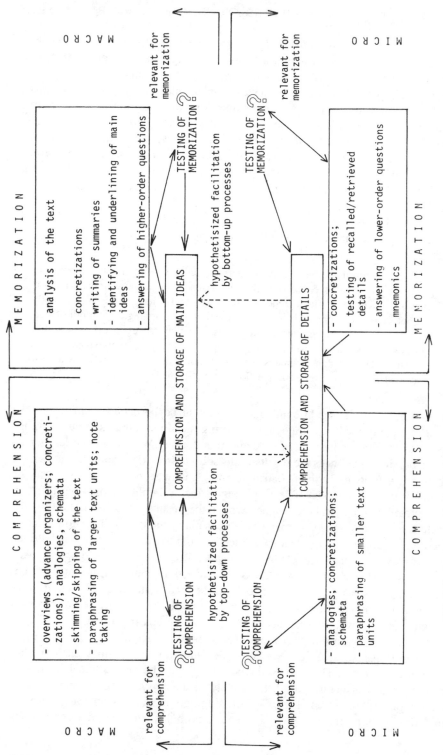

FIG. 7.1. Levin's (1982) learning strategy heuristics. The question marks denote the entry points for strategic or metacognitive monitoring.

answering of questions that principally function as a monitoring strategy in the service of cybernetic feedback. What else does *strategic monitoring* mean if not the checking of one's own understanding or recall? The lack of differentiation between the asking of questions and strategic monitoring shows the necessity to define fuzzy concepts precisely. Metacognitive terminology serves here as some kind of "deus ex machina" mechanism.

MAIN APPROACHES TO "METACOGNITIVE" REGULATION OF LEARNING AND THINKING

The rediscovery of metacognition, defined as *cognizing about cognition* in the late 1960s, may be viewed as the christening ceremony of a phenomenon that was known but not termed long ago. As Brown (1982) points out, metacognitive phenomena were known since the beginnings of Greek philosophy and have been a part of philosophical tradition from Plato, Aristotle, Strato, Galen, Plotin, Spinoza, and Locke. This tradition was continued in psychology: James' (1890) "tip-of-the-tongue" phenomenon, Binet's (1903) "pensee," Ach's "self-awareness" (1910), Huey (1908), Gard (1907), Kuhlmann (1907), Lindley (1897), Baldwin (1909), Dewey (1910), or Thorndike (1917). These pioneers all thought of self-reflexive elements of thinking and its control as indispensable. As Cavanaugh and Perlmutter (1982) in their recent critical examination of metacognitive theory point out, both the levels-of-processing approach of Craik and Lockhart (1972) and the contextualist and constructivist view of cognitive activity require thinking about thinking.

The term *metacognition* elliptically refers to both *knowledge about knowledge* as well as to the usage of that knowledge in the service of control of thinking.

Metacognitive Knowledge: Flavell's Approach

Flavell's first notions about *thinking about thinking* were wholistic in essence and were based on observations about children's memorial processing. Metacognitive activities of the child were described as the child's strategic behavior, foresight in planning activities, and *self-testing* activities in mnemonic tasks (Flavell, 1970). Further terms were introduced in Flavell, Friedrichs, and Hoyt (1970), namely, *monitoring* and *self-testing* of one's mnemonic behavior. However, when Flavell and co-workers focused on the development of metacognitive activities, they studied *metacognitive knowledge* by means of interviews rather than observation or experimentation (Kreutzer, Leonard, & Flavell, 1975). Flavell's last broad-scope mention of metacognition was done in 1976(b), when he outlined *metacognition* as the active monitoring and regulation and orchestration of information processing in the service of goals.

Early experimental findings yielded evidence for some *strategic conscious-*

ness and planfulness in the memory behavior of older children or of children with better memorization skills (Masur, McIntyre, & Flavell, 1973). Modulated by the sampling of verbal answers to questions about hypothetical memorization situations, the focus shifted to the predominance of metacognitive knowledge as the switchboard for any cognitive enterprise. The swing was from doing to knowing according to Flavell (1976b):

> The growing child has much to learn about how, where, and when to store information, and how, where, and when to retrieve it, as means to a variety of life goals. The *"how"* includes a variety of storage and retrieval *strategies.* The *"where"* refers to a variety of storage and retrieval resources . . . (The "when" refers to the sensitivity to situation in which deliberate processing would likely prove useful). The *"when"* refers to the child's growing *sense* that such-and-such situations call for active, deliberate attempts to learn and to store, and that this and that situation calls for active, deliberate attempts to retrieve and apply what is in store [p. 233].

While the earlier, functional description of metacognition focused on *active monitoring* and *orchestration and regulation,* the janus-faced term sensitivity refers to a not really behavioral but rather an attitudinal category. Flavell is Hegelian in that consciousness plays the dominant part in the actual change of behavior. In contrast, Brown's (1977) thinking, discussed later, is more *materialistic,* metaphorically speaking, because cognitive control is not based upon the conscious, deliberately acting thinker but rather upon the doing itself, which is regulated by the means of an *auto-pilot* executive mechanism.

Flavell and Wellman's (1977) taxonomy of metacognitive knowledge marks a transition. The taxonomy of metacognitive knowledge contains two main categories: *sensitivity* and a group of *variables,* which are depicted in Fig. 7.2.

Sensitivity is variously referred to as *feeling, sensing, sense of,* or *being attuned to* situational demands. Sensitivity is a hybrid of actually experiencing a processing demand and knowledge-dependent learning from earlier experience with a task similar to the current one. It retrieves information concerning processing demands from the metacognitive store. Sensitivity may refer to an attitude to be conscious to the task at hand.

Sensitivity, according to Flavell and Wellman (1977) is illustrated as follows:

> The child could come to learn which situations do and which situations do not call for intentional memory-related behavior . . . (He may learn) to be attuned to and responsive to those occasions, when it is adaptive either to try to retrieve something right now, or to prepare himself and/or his environment for effective future retrieval, for example deliberately try to store or memorize it [p. 3].

The calibration of relevant memory behavior was dependent on the quality and content of the variables. The person subcategory was further subdivided into a person trait category that referred to knowledge of what the self and others are

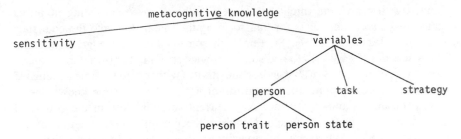

FIG. 7.2.   Taxonomy of metacognitive knowledge according to Flavell and Wellman (1977).

generally like as memorizers. This subcategory referred to the ability and disposition to monitor and interpret one's immediate mnemonic experiences in specific memory situations and the recognition that engaging in such activities can be adaptive.

Flavell is Hegelian in that manipulation of practice is to take place by means of manipulation of consciousness. Thus, training in behaving strategically is arranged by expansion of consciousness. According to Flavell (1976b), training was influencing the learner's consciousness:

> Is there anything . . . that children could be taught that would improve their ability to assemble effective problem-solving procedures from already available cognitive components? Perhaps they could . . . be taught to produce and respond to some very general imperatives and questions when problem solving. Here are some possible candidates: Examine task features carefully. Is there a problem here? Is the problem I just solved the one I had originally in mind to solve, or is it only a subproblem or even an irrelevant one? If I don't succeed initially in solving the problem I should keep trying. When trying to solve a problem, search both internal and external sources for solution-relevant information and procedures. . . Keep track of past solution efforts, their outcomes, and the information they yielded using external resources if it makes sense to do so . . . actively "remember" to remember, monitor and update information, and actively bring this information to bear on the problem [p. 121].

There are questions left open concerning the nature of *metacognitive regulation*. Are they self-instructional commands in the sense of Meichenbaum's (1976a,b,c) "self-talks"? Do they have their *inner* counterpart in thought regulation?

Flavell and Wellman (1977) differentiated between the *basic hardware of memory*, which referred to the activities and operations of the memory system as inaccessible to consciousness. Apart from these two categories *knowing how to know* and *knowing about knowing* were thought to be a part of general knowledge, which the individual deliberately might use if necessary. Persons confronted with a problem might construct a problem space consisting of initial state, goal state, and means for transforming the initial state into the goal state (Flavell & Wellman, 1977). Starting with some initial knowledge of the item characteristics (task variable) and some knowledge of his/her own current memory state (person state variable and/or sensitivity) with regard to some anticipated goal state (task solution), the person might use his/her strategic knowledge to devise means for transformation. Any current solution state in the course of processing then could be matched against the person's representation of the end/goal state, making use of his awareness of task demands and the fitting of current state to final state with regard to the task demands. In essence the development of intelligence was thought of as the development of a growing sensitivity as well as an accumulating knowledge about the world. But there was no mention made about the command structure of the whole system. There was no conceptualization about how the knowledge of cognitive functioning might gain regulative power to control processing. In fact, Flavell and Wellman (1977) cautioned against premature speculations about plausible functional connections between metamemory and actual memory behavior.

Regardless of this cautioning, there grew a widespread assumption concerning the relationship between metacognitive awareness and its regulatory power of thinking. The more a learner knew the person, task, or strategy variables, the more efficient the learning should be in regulating cognitive activity. Thus knowledge about cognitive facts, as assessed by self-statements or by thinking-aloud protocols or by questionnaires, were thought to be ideal predictors of cognitive efficiency. Competence in regulatory power was to foster cognitive functioning by means of schooling. Making a child sensitive to cognitive states could enable him to behave cognitively in an adult, expert-like fashion. The problem is that no training measure can be devised according to Flavell's notion with regard to control of behavior. Flavell and Wellman (1977) speculate about the generality of metacognition as a device for general problem solving and reference Brown's (1977) work as well as the executive processes conceptualized by her. They conclude that Flavell's (1976a) list of *categorical metacognitive imperatives* such as *"Examine task features carefully"* and the like, are analogous to executive monitoring and control procedures. How these commands might be translated mentally is left unspecified.

Flavell's later work (1978a,b,c, 1979a,b,c,d) was concerned with metacognitive awareness, a combination of knowledge and self-awareness. Flavell focusses on *metacognitive ideas, thoughts, feelings,* or *sensations* that are consciously and deliberately read out and interpreted during the course of processing. Cognitive monitoring is seen as using a switching station to call other cognitive functions into service. Figures 7.3 and 7.4 serve to illustrate Flavell's more recent metacognitive systems.

Figure 7.4 illustrates the time-dependent character of the interactions illustrated in Fig. 7.3.

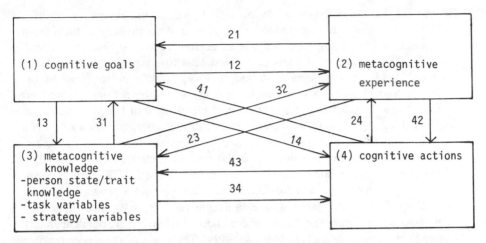

FIG. 7.3.   Flavell's (1978a) model of cognitive monitoring.

In Fig. 7.3, *cognitive goals* refers to any instigating event that leads to a cognitive enterprise, or which originates in the service of a subgoal during processing, or is called upon by a metacognitive experience. *Metacognitive experiences* are conscious experiences, ideas, thoughts, sensations, or feelings related to cognitive enterprise. Cognitive monitoring seems to be a special subclass of metacognitive experience that is already processed, elaborated, and interpreted. Cognitive monitoring is different from metacognitive experiences by its elaborated, highly conscious, and deliberate nature. Cognitive monitoring could be considered as the activity of scanning one's experiences in the service of controlling thought. *Metacognitive knowledge* is a data base needed to activate information concerning person, task, and strategy variables in order to reach one's goals. They are both *tactics* in the service of the strategies and activities of the mental machinery. The arrows in Fig. 7.4 represent interrelations among the four main variables. Cognitive goals may interact with metacognitive experience

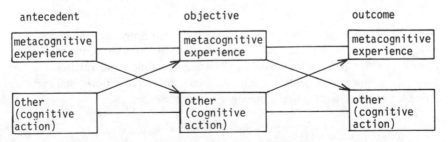

FIG. 7.4.   Possible antecedents, objectives, and outcomes of cognitive actions (based on Flavell, 1978b).

(interaction 12) when the formation of a goal leads to the experience of difficulty. Such experiences may lead to a clarification of the problem in the light of metacognitive knowledge concerning task, person, or strategy aspects (interaction 23). The formation of goals also could lead to metacognitive knowledge (interaction 13), which helps to define, clarify, or reformulate goals of the calling upon of cognitive actions (interaction 34). Cognitive actions for their part may lead to some sensation or experience of puzzlement or trouble (interaction 42), which again then is focused by assistance of metacognitive knowledge. If a person is confronted with a cognitive task, this does not necessarily lead to any sensation, but it might lead directly to the help of metacognitive knowledge, which in turn calls up some cognitive action (interaction 34). There is no planning structure that could schedule elementary actions into a program, because Flavell's (1978b) model does not have an executive. It is, in essence, an orchestra without a conductor. The data flow in a chain reaction but are not deliberately scanned, processed, or analyzed by a monitor. The place of the leader remains unclear. Does the thinker coincide with the *executive* in the sense of Brown (1977)? Are metacognitive processes to be thought of as highly conscious, fully aware, and rational operations?

The sensations, experiences, and reflections that originate during thinking and give rise to executive decisions about the processing, flanked by long-term information about the three variables, are not controlled in the sense that the thinker controls them but happen within or even control the thinker. Flavell's (1978a) description of the temporal nature of the process and the interactions within underlines that fluent, happening nature:

> Cognitive monitoring can appear to be an exceedingly complex affair, particularly if viewed over the course of an extended cognitive enterprise. For instance, a cognitive action may lead to a metacognitive experience, which may instigate another action, which may produce another experience, and so on; cognitive goals and metacognitive knowledge will also play antecedent and outcome roles in such cycles. In other words, the arrows in Figs. 7.3 and 7.4 should be visualized as flashing on and off, simultaneously and in rapid alternation with one another [p. 29].

It is hard to imagine how a process such as that above can be canalized or brought under control for means of academic education. One of the most recent Flavell (1979c) publications tries to illustrate the functional relationships between the major components of cognitive goals, cognitive actions, and metacognitive knowledge with actual metacognitive experience:

1. (ongoing) action(s) $\bigl\langle$ metacognitive knowledge
   metacognitive experience(s)

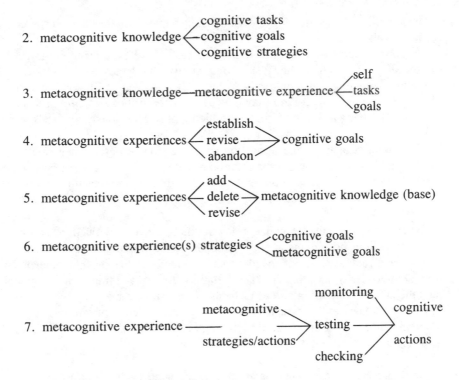

1. Ongoing cognitive actions/enterprises may be preceded, followed, or give rise to metacognitive experience(s) of one's own doing, which then call up metacognitive knowledge for interpreting the actual experience in terms of person × task × strategy knowledge.

2. Metacognitive knowledge can guide and control the selection and scheduling of appropriate cognitive goals and strategies once the task the learner is confronted with has been identified, classified, and analyzed.

3. Metacognitive knowledge is used to interpret and process some actual metacognitive experience in terms of states and traits of the self or relevant aspects of tasks or goals. It thus serves as a frame of reference for the analysis of data stemming from metacognitive experiences or deliberate cognitive monitoring.

4. The actual feeling of progress, facing of difficulty, or facing of a change in the progressing rate may directly (or mediated through the knowledge base) lead to corrections of the problem space and to a reformulation of the cognitive goals established in the process of task analysis.

5. Similar to Piagetian thinking and his notion of assimilation and accommodation, metacognitive experience(s) developmentally may lead to changes in the metacognitive knowledge base, which then gradually may be attuned to the

characteristics of the growing individual and features of the tasks he is confronted with.

6. In the course of actual processing, metacognitive experience(s) may lead to the deliberate call up and usage of cognitive strategies in the service of conscious scanning and monitoring of one's own as well as of solution states. The mode of cognitive control may thus be switched from some *auto-pilot state* into some *debugging state* of control, which highly consciously proceeds stepwise from bottom to up sensations.

7. Cognitive actions and allocation of processing resources then might be deliberately distributed across the solution process, which now, according to the very definition of metacognition, is the object of thinking. Metaactions may now be used to monitor and control actions.

The very fluent, interchanging roles of the antecedent, objective, and outcome conditions prevent the model from being tested empirically. One can never use an antecedent as an independent variable and predict the outcome if the model to be tested rules this out. The inflation of mays and mights in the model and the large number of interdependencies make it impossible to draw any valid, testable conclusion. Additionally Flavell (1977) lists factors of interference that may prevent metacognitions from becoming effective so that testability is further restricted:

> In some cases, metamemory could not possibly influence behavior because no metamemory "occurs" on that occasion. (I wish I knew exactly what I should mean by "occur" here. Become psychologically active? Become partly or fully conscious? The question must remain unsettled for the present). For example, the situation might automatically stimulate only nonstrategic, incidental-memory type processing. Something is nondeliberately encoded and stored, or something is unintentionally retrieved. There is little if any conscious memory activity or output in these instances, let alone anything like conscious metamemory [p. 25].

Overlearned, skilled, *automatic* strategic behavior may bypass metacognitive processes. Metacognitive processes may be aroused but not be developed well enough to influence behavior because of attentional capacity shortcomings. Nevertheless, Flavell (1978a) concludes:

> If children could be gotten to monitor their speaking and listening efforts (in the case of metacommunication), the quality of these efforts would generally be improved. . . (We) could consider teaching children to become aware of and maintain in awareness their communicative goals . . . Such heightened awareness could help them choose means to these goals, evaluate the effectiveness of these means, and generally monitor their progress in the . . . endeavour . . . The fostering of metacognitive experiences and associated cognitive actions is an educational objective that may possess the (attributes of being a highly useful one, efficacious,

broadly applicable, and easy to implement) . . . Metacognitive experiences can be deliberately sought out and evoked by metacognitive strategies. They can also occur as nondeliberate outcomes of cognitive strategies—and be no less useful for being nonintended. Having occurred they may instigate new goals, new metacognitive strategies; these in turn may yield new metacognitive experiences. Finally, concrete metacognitive experiences and associated actions can provide input to permanent metacognitive knowledge, which in turn will influence future experiences and actions [p. 30].

Flavell consequently argues for training children in self-awareness or introspection, in attending to introspections, and in interpreting sensations of that kind in terms of metacognitive knowledge. A critical test of Flavell's assumptions, would be to devise some measure of metacognitive activity and to assess it concomitantly with performing some academic task. The intensity and differentiatedness of a subject's metacognitive knowledge should be directly related to performance in a variety of scholastic tasks. Correspondingly the first experiment presented here tried to test this assumption.

Executive Performance as Prerequisite of Efficient Thinking: Brown's "Executive Pandemonium"

Whereas Flavell generally did emphasize the role of metacognitive experience concomitant to performing a cognitive task, placing heavy stress on the metacognitive knowledge by which such experience is interpreted, Brown (1977) stresses the role of executive behavior in the very act of performance. Although Flavell tends to localize differences between good and poor learners in terms of metacognitive knowledge, poor performers, according to Brown's executive model since 1978, are monitoring and controlling their cognitive actions to a lesser degree than the good performers. The central role is given to the *executive*, which is conceptualized as the central processing unit (CPU), in models of artificial intelligence or information-processing devices. The executive analyzes task requirements, selects, and schedules appropriate actions to reach the goal of criterion fulfillment. Furthermore, it scans and picks up data about the system's states continually, tests and evaluates the intermediate results, matches them against certain criteria, and evaluates any possible differences between current and final state in terms of possible corrections until the end state is reached. The executive is a hierarchy of plans to execute and control plans in the sense of Miller, Galanter, and Pribram's (1960) "metaplans." The developing human organism is seen as gradually shifting from external control to internalized conscious control, until the control of thinking ultimately proceeds in an automatic and routine manner. The central mechanism of the executive is capable of intelligently evaluating his own operations. According to Brown (1977), some kind of self-consciousness and explicit knowledge about one's own functioning is

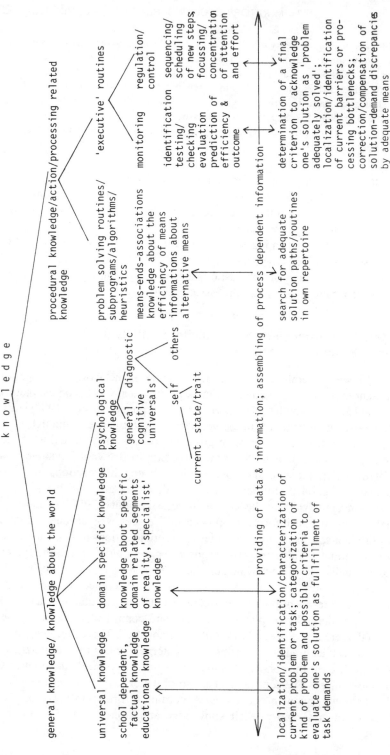

FIG. 7.5. Retrieval of static knowledge and access to dynamic process-related information according to Brown (1977, 1978).

essential for efficient problem solving. The executive serves several important functions in the system: It is capable of predicting capacity limitations of the system, of knowing its repertoire of heuristic routines and their appropriate usage, of characterizing and identifying a problem at hand, and of planning and scheduling appropriate actions to solve a given problem. It is also able to monitor, check, and evaluate current actions and their efficiency and to make stop-and-go decisions until the solution is reached. According to this notion, maturity can be equated with the capability to use one's knowledge at the right place and time. Maturity then, in essence, is reducible to executive decisions in regard to the calling up of operations and data concerning any intermediate state of the system.

Brown's executive model (e.g., 1978) is summarized in Fig. 7.5. To control and regulate efficient, intellectual behavior, an elaborate knowledge base is needed. Within the knowledge base, no differentiation is made between declarative and procedural knowledge. Correspondingly no assumptions are made about the format in which knowledge of both kinds may be coded and stored. The person is master of general knowledge about the world and about the self as a person and as a thinker. The latter knowledge is a subclass of general knowledge, termed *psychological knowledge*. In addition, problem-solving algorithms, routines, and programs are available and are informative and orienting in character. Although much of general knowledge is schooled, learned knowledge, and skills, the *executive routines* are learner dependent, stemming from *learning-to-learn* experiences of the learner. These executive routines govern the process of thinking and problem solving. They pick up relevant knowledge or action when needed, and they supervise and control the flow of action. To a restricted degree, differences in the static knowledge base explain the differences in learning efficiency. Rather, the activity of the executive assembler is more responsible for the quality and degree of performance. Thus, differences between efficient and less efficient learners are seen mainly as differences in executive functioning. Furthermore, these differences are open to training and to intervention. The central role of executive monitoring and control naturally leads to a less prominent role of knowledge. Whereas Flavell's approach centers on the dominant role of highly-conscious, deliberate self-attention by the thinker, Brown's control of thinking does not seem to happen consciously at all. Ordinarily, thinking proceeds along routinized paths, is automatic, and is self-acting until a problem arises. Then, but only then, *auto-pilot regulation* is abandoned, and control is switched over into the *debugging state*. Actions and problem-solving routines now are planned and executed step by step. Efficiency control and outcome evaluation are then deliberately undertaken. Scanning and analysis of the relevant aspects of the task are performed in a controlled, stepwise manner. Then, and only then, would the individual be able to sense (and report) some state of heightened consciousness. Brown does not search for the cognitive map in the head of the learner, as does Flavell. Brown (cf. Brown & Day, 1981) found in comparisons between experts and novices that the experts were able to verbalize their cognitions impressionistically and intuitively. If experts are not able to report about their inner world in terms of deliberately selected actions, then it appears that knowledge expansion is not crucial to thinking control. According to Brown's notion, one has to foster skills, but not the knowledge. Performance of the *act of thinking control* rather than the *knowledge about thinking control* is assumed to help learners to become more efficient.

Instead of assessing learner's cognitions and inner worlds via verbal statements, problem-solving tasks are analyzed in terms of an ideal, normative solution and control program. Such an a priori program could then be tested against the real procedure as used by experts. It relies on *inner control statements* by experts. Such statements can be found in solutions and thinking-aloud protocols (Dörner, 1978; Simon, 1975; Sternberg, 1979). Ideally, a priori processing and the actual processing by experts could yield a matching standard. This standard then could be compared with the processing of people with less expertise. The executive guidance of action is the factor by which successful and less successful learners differ. Poor comprehenders (readers or memorizers) do not allocate their attention to the most important aspects. They do not adequately monitor and control what they are doing. Lacking the feeling of noncomprehension (or *secondary ignorance*) they do not look out for misunderstandings or comprehension failures, and they do not try to assess their own understanding by the means of self-testing and self-questioning. Without the information they would get by self-diagnosis, they are unable then to schedule, organize, and start strategies for the bypassing of comprehension bottlenecks. Monitoring and control are identical with executive functioning and are very deficient in the performance of poor learners. If a learner is given all the strategies needed to solve the task, he consequently should have all necessary building blocks at his disposal. *Executive training* means that the learner is trained in the usage of executive control strategies *on-line,* in the course of processing, especially in the continual monitoring, testing, and checking of intermediate results. If learning is controlled by self-monitoring and self-diagnostic data, the learner becomes attuned to task requirements. This attuning yields both flexibility and transfer by control procedures. It is the transsituational, nonspecific nature of the executive control mechanism that guarantees generalizable, intelligent, flexible use of strategies. Brown's training concepts are principally based upon *learning by doing*—by performing an act and by monitoring and testing its efficiency, the learner acquires all the rules needed for flexible handling in a variety of tasks and learning situations. Flavell tries to foster learning efficiency by enriching the cognitive map of the learner via informing him about cognitive functioning. Brown, on the other hand, seems to say: "Don't tell the learner what he has to do (or why), but rather tell him how he might proceed (and give him feedback about his efficiency after he has done it)." Flavell appears to try to influence the (metacognitive) knowledge base of the learner. He hopes to change behavior by changes in the attitudinal system. Brown, in contrast, is concerned with behavior change through the intervention and manipulation of the behavior itself.

In the following paragraphs, some typical training procedures of Brown and her colleagues shall be sketched. Brown often does comparison studies with retardates against normals or with younger versus older subjects. Performance by less successful subjects is compared with performance of the more mature subjects. The differences are interpreted often in terms of insufficient monitoring and control behavior. If training in self-monitoring and control strategies leads to the leveling of performance differences, executive behavior is explained retrodictively to have been built up or strengthened. Studies done by Bisanz, Vesonder, and Voss (1978), Brown (1978), Masur, McIntyre, and Flavell (1973), and Rogoff, Newcombe, and Kagan (1974), showed that younger children and retardates were able to recognize recallable vs. unrecallable items but were not successful in allocating their learning time or study effort on the items not yet recalled. A composite training in selective rehearsal and discrimination of the more difficult items was successful in fostering performance. Wellman (1977a,b), Posnansky (1978), and Brown and Lawton (1977) likewise were able to show that feeling-of-knowing and tip-of-the-tongue experiences could be used as means to strengthen the learner's sensitivity for the control of his learning. Strategies to look for important text units, to make use of text cues, and to process information differently, could be chained into efficient processing programs for complex narrative texts (Brown & Smiley, 1977(a,b), 1978; Brown, Smiley, Day, Townsend, & Lawton, 1977; Brown, Smiley, & Lawton, 1978; Yussen, Mathews, Buss, & Kane, 1980).

Brown and Smiley (1978), Brown, Smiley, and Lawton (1978), Yussen et al. (1980) were successful in training children in the identification and use of important text units as retrieval cues and as cues to prompt recall. Likewise, Brown (1978), and Brown, Bransford, Ferrara, and Campione (1983), and Danner (1976), were successful in building up complex learning strategies, based upon the learner's self-monitoring and deliberate use of self-testing data in the programming of further learning steps. Besides such complex strategies, training of the self-diagnostic component of monitoring was very efficient as a cornerstone of intelligent learning regulation. Belmont, Butterfield, and Ferretti (1980), Brown and Barclay (1976), Brown and Campione (1977a,b), Brown, Campione, and Barclay (1979), and Brown, Campione, and Murphy (1977), trained children in task-independent, domain, nonspecific monitoring and self-testing procedures in an effort to teach a learning set that might enable transfer and maintenance of learning or performance. After training, the children were able to monitor and control their learning regardless of the type of memory task or material to be memorized. It is especially this latter type of domain- and task-nonspecific training that seems promising. Training according to Brown, especially that of school relevant tasks, neglects the installing of specific criteria dependent on a special type of task. The same learner trained with the two types

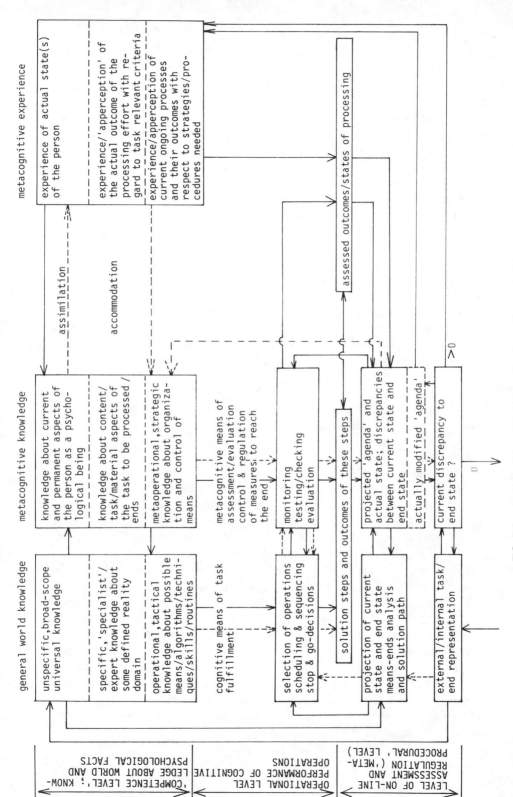

FIG. 7.6. An integrative representation of metacognitive regulation.

of tasks, however, might acquire inconsistent, even contradictory rules. Suppose a learner is to be trained in selective rehearsal of a prose passage. The learner may acquire the following rule(s): *Try to recall the passage. Look for those items you were not able to recall. Look at those items you have just recalled. You will notice that those recalled refer to the most important segments of the text. Since you have to recall also the less important items, go on, but now look out for the less important ones, study them selectively, until your next self-test produces evidence that you are able to recall them as well.* What is acquired is a focus on the less important segments of the text. But what if the same learner not only has to recall the core and the factual, micro-level information of the text but to summarize also its major content? In this case the rule would be: *Look out for the most important text segments. Try to delete trivia and combine several minor statements into a macro-proposition. You will have to invent one if one does not exist. But in any case delete all the less important information.* Both strategies, the one for selective rehearsal and the latter for summarization of text core content were investigated separately (Brown, 1978; Brown & Day, 1981; Brown & Smiley, 1977a,b, 1978; Brown, Smiley, Day, Townsend, & Lawton, 1977; Brown, Smiley, & Lawton, 1978; Day, 1980), but never in combination. What would happen if the two tasks were to be combined, as is the case in ordinary academic text-processing tasks, where the focus is placed on summarization as well as on factual details? What might—what should—one and the same learner do to cope with that complex task? Without some *metacognitive task variable* knowledge that could help the learner to look for cues for selection of appropriate strategies, he/she might not perform very well. This may hold true especially for handicapped learners. How could a disabled learner cope with contradictory sets of rules? Possibly the sacrifice of insight and the neglect of the learner's *meta-knowledge* restrict possibilities for an efficient chaining of several diverse and even incompatible substrategies into one and the same complex learning program. An integration of the two approaches is depicted in Fig. 7.6. Taken literally, the approaches appear to lead to different and perhaps contradicting predictions concerning the learner's efficiency.

According to Flavell the best predictor of a learner's actual performance is his/her cognitive competence, by which he/she is able to calibrate and attune learning according to the person, task, and situational parameters. Knowing about the person, task, and situation, coupled with heightened consciousness, should result in control of learning. An adequate assessment of the learner's metacognitive knowledge suffices to explain for the learning results.

Flavell does not rule out the case that a learner may perform well without metacognitive knowledge of the task. Additional explanation might then be made in terms of routinized, automatized behavior. This, however, strikes us as an ad-hoc explanation. How would one explain a behavior that was deficient in terms of a learner's assessed metacognitive knowledge? If the learner knows more than he does, *bottlenecks* in processing capacity or some kind of interference between the metaprocedural and the procedural levels might be used to explain the data.

According to Brown, differences in the monitoring and regulative behavior of the learners are the decisive factors in explaining for performance differences. It is, however, difficult to localize a performance deficit in terms of insufficient executive control, because one could not rule out the possibility that the learner actually assessed his/her *secondary ignorance* but was not able to overcome this difficulty, because the learner's world knowledge or procedural knowledge was insufficient. Without additional data regarding the learner's knowlege relevant to the task and to the current problem–solution state, one could never rule out such an alternative explanation.

METACOGNITIVE COMPONENTS OF ADULT PROCESSING OF INSTRUCTIONAL TEXTS

According to the tetrahedral model of text processing (Brown, Campione, & Day, 1981), four major groups of variables determine the course and efficiency of reading. The first group is the *characteristics of the learner;* the learning prerequisites in terms of general and domain-specific knowledge, the available learning strategies and knowledge concerning self with respect to the characteristics of the text to be processed. The second group of variables includes *text characteristics,* the domain area as well as text structure variables (coherence, structuredness, explicitness vs. implicitness of style, the text's difficulty, and its abstractness vs. concreteness). The third group, *learning goals,* contains the overt and covert aims of learning, for example, verbatim vs. recall of main content of comprehension vs. recall. The last group, the actualized *learning strategies* cover the activities of the reader in the processing of the text, ranging from strategy usage, rule application, or use of more elementary learning techniques to deliberate executive monitoring and control. The tetrahedral model specifies complex interactions between the four variables that not only are held to be valid for any complete model of reading, but also, direct the mature learner's understanding of the reading task.

Learner Characteristics and Text Features

In an explorative study, learner characteristics, learning activities, and text features were investigated (Fischer & Mandl, 1980b, 1981b). Metacognitive differentiatedness should explain variation in the performance of good vs. poor readers under the Flavell model. According to Brown, text features that guide executive monitoring and control, together with the learner's overall strategic behavior, should be decisive. Data from both comprehension and recall were obtained, as well as data on self-perception and self-awareness, by measuring verbal statements of the subjects.

METHOD

Text Variables.   To rule out domain-specific prior knowledge, a social science text about the development of morality according to Piaget and Kohlberg was given to students of the department of biology. They were expected to have only rudimentary, nonspecific knowledge about the domain in question. If so, differences between the learners would be restricted to procedural knowledge and metaprocedural learning skills. Two text versions were constructed: a basic text that contained about 1700 words and was not graphically structured in any way; and a second, adapted version containing additional marginals, headings, and attention-guiding cues with respect to its formal structure, organization, and sequencing. These markers pertained to important text aspects and to the comparative structure of the two main sections (Piaget vs. Kohlberg). The adapted version was expected to guide reader's processing and to give hints for the monitoring and control of comprehension and recall. According to a procedure derived from Kintsch and van Dijk (1978), the source text was analyzed in terms of five text hierarchy levels: level 5, 1 unit (most abstract, highest level); level 4, 4 units; level 3, 18 units; level 2, 13 units; and level 1, 4 units (most concrete, lowest level). Average hierarchical level of the text was 2.63 (Standard deviation, SD = .88). According the distribution of the text units per hierarchical level, multiple choice questions were constructed. An examination of the topical structure of the text revealed the discrepancy that the text, although the title referred to the comparison of the positions of Piaget vs. Kohlberg, was not structured in two equivalent segments (referring to the two positions in question). Inasmuch as it was structured unequally, only nine of 40 thematic units referred to Piaget's position, whereas 22 units referred to Kohlberg. The last nine units contained critical and referential statements by the author.

The assignment of headlines and marginals with regard to content could have been misleading for the subjects in that their assignment was not equally distributed according to topic, and thus produced an inherent, diverging, topical organization. Headlines and marginals could serve only as hints about the themes of the text. The learner would have to construct and code text information according to its actual organization. In a sense, then, the text cues of the adapted version served as attention allocating hints but could not be used in a straightforward manner as retrieval cues.

Subjects.   Subjects were 24 students from the department of biology at the University of Tübingen. They were paid for participation. The procedure required about 2 hours, 30 minutes for the interview, approximately 40–45 minutes for text preparation, and approximately 20 minutes for the multiple-choice test and the free-recall test. Subjects were tested individually.

Experimental Conditions.   Recall was delayed for half of the students to allow for evocation of metacognition. The design is illustrated in Table 7.1.

TABLE 7.1
Experimental Design: Study 1

	Recall Condition	
Delayed		*Immediate*
Text: Adapted Source		*Adapted Source*
Task Order:		
1. Text preparation		Text preparation
2. Interview		Free recall
3. Free recall		Multiple-choice
4. Multiple-choice		Interview

The student was instructed as follows: As a student you are used to working through instructional material. When studying it is quite normal to prepare a text in order to catch its main ideas for the later partaking in courses or discussion groups. Imagine that you had to refer to and discuss the information contained in the text I'll hand out to you now. Time for preparation of the text is unrestricted.

Following the instructions, the two experimenters unobtrusively observed the subject's study behavior with the text, registered the time spent per page of the text, and recorded forward and backward jumps in the text booklet. When the subject had finished reading, either the interview or the free-recall test was administered. The interview started with a free report by the subject about what he had done with the text. Additional questions were then asked regarding some observed study behavior. The focus was then shifted to the subject's more general study habits.

Scoring Procedure.   The transcribed interviews were content analyzed by two independent scorers who had been trained extensively in the use of the content analytic schema. The schema was structured according the temporal course of reading. It was also subdivided according to the nature of the statements. The statements were separated in that they were referred to as procedural vs. metaprocedural topics.

1. Preparation phase/prereading
   activities } "on-line" activities < procedural / metaprocedural
2. Reading phase/text-processing
   activities)
3. Postreading activities; "off-line" activities < procedural / metaprocedural

The absolute number of statements per category per person was normalized by the total number of scored units per person. The percentages of statements per category were then averaged over the subjects.

Text recall scores were assigned according to the precision of recall. Four points were scored for conservation of meaning, but not verbatim recall; 3, 2, and 1 points were scored for any reproduction of the original units according to our preceding text analysis; 3 points for mainly correct, 2 points for partially correct, and 1 point for fragmentary but correct recall. Comprehension points were scored for each totally correct answer to a multiple-choice question (2 points). There were maximally 105 points for recall of complete hierarchical structure of the text plus additionally 160 points for perfect recall. The maximal comprehension score was 20 points. In a second analysis, an economy measure was calculated, relating performance to reading time needed. Niveau- and speed measures were then transformed into z-values; an average z-value ultimately represented a subject's total performance.

Distribution of the Subjects into Groups.   According to their overall performance in the niveau- and speed measures, all subjects were then grouped into the following three groups: percentile rank < 25, poor readers; percentile rank ≥ 25 < 75, average readers; and percentile rank ≥ 75. good readers. The content-analyzed interview statements were then compared for the two extreme groups of good versus bad readers. The analytic categories as well as the averaged percentages over the subjects are shown in Fig. 7.7.

RESULTS

Differences in Metacogitive Thinking

There was no overall effect in amount and intensity of metacognitive self-awareness between the more and the less efficient students. Poor readers did not produce less metacognitions; rather they allocated them at other points in the course of processing. In any case, there is no such thing as "high versus low metacognitioners." Poor readers did, however, show a discrepant pattern of self-monitoring and control. Although the good readers used their time to clarify the concrete learning task and task-specific criteria (A1.1–1.1433), they did not go into details concerning some anticipatory assessment of text characteristics (A1.22–1.2232). Rather, they focused on planning and scheduling of their learning (A2.5–2.55). On the contrary, the poor readers spent more time with orientation to text features (A1.22–1.2232), then turned back introspectively to inspect their capabilities as learners (A2.1–2.15). Also, they neglected concrete planning of their activities (A2.5–2.55). They monitored their intermediate progress to a somewhat higher degree (B2.1–2.14) but scored less in criteria matching (B2.2–2.55). The good readers showed more flexible and adaptive learning consequences (B2.41–2.416) and were able to identify obstacles and difficulties at a fine-grain level (B2.42–2.4292). The poor readers scored higher at intuitive

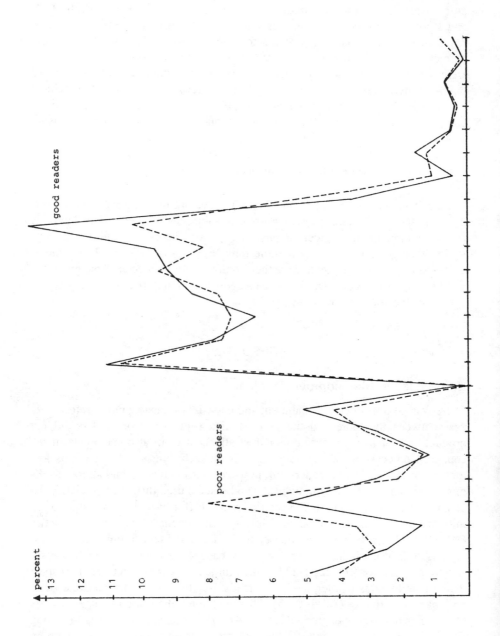

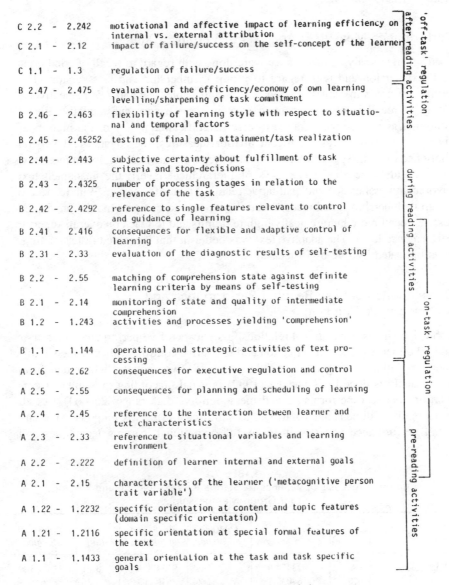

C 2.2 -	2.242	motivational and affective impact of learning efficiency on internal vs. external attribution
C 2.1 -	2.12	impact of failure/success on the self-concept of the learner
C 1.1 -	1.3	regulation of failure/success
B 2.47 -	2.475	evaluation of the efficiency/economy of own learning levelling/sharpening of task commitment
B 2.46 -	2.463	flexibility of learning style with respect to situational and temporal factors
B 2.45 -	2.45252	testing of final goal attainment/task realization
B 2.44 -	2.443	subjective certainty about fulfillment of task criteria and stop-decisions
B 2.43 -	2.4325	number of processing stages in relation to the relevance of the task
B 2.42 -	2.4292	reference to single features relevant to control and guidance of learning
B 2.41 -	2.416	consequences for flexible and adaptive control of learning
B 2.31 -	2.33	evaluation of the diagnostic results of self-testing
B 2.2 -	2.55	matching of comprehension state against definite learning criteria by means of self-testing
B 2.1 -	2.14	monitoring of state and quality of intermediate comprehension
B 1.2 -	1.243	activities and processes yielding 'comprehension'
B 1.1 -	1.144	operational and strategic activities of text processing
A 2.6 -	2.62	consequences for executive regulation and control
A 2.5 -	2.55	consequences for planning and scheduling of learning
A 2.4 -	2.45	reference to the interaction between learner and text characteristics
A 2.3 -	2.33	reference to situational variables and learning environment
A 2.2 -	2.222	definition of learner internal and external goals
A 2.1 -	2.15	characteristics of the learner ('metacognitive person trait variable')
A 1.22 -	1.2232	specific orientation at content and topic features (domain specific orientation)
A 1.21 -	1.2116	specific orientation at special formal features of the text
A 1.1 -	1.1433	general orientation at the task and task specific goals

FIG. 7.7.   Percentage of statements per analytic category.

evaluation of their efficiency (B2.44–2.443). They also did less task attainment testing (B2.45–2.4552).

Performance Measures: Analysis of Variance Data

Two separate analyses of variance were done with regard to recall of conditions and text version and with regard to group membership and text version. The results are given in Tables 7.2 and 7.3, and in Tables 7.4 and 7.5, respectively. Delay of recall is not sufficient to explain the variance substantially. Recall condition as a main factor failed to reach significance in any of the nine measures. Text version was significant in four measures; the adapted text version shortened the time spent with reading and preparing the text. Although more text units could be recalled (regardless of hierarchical level), the unadapted text favored comprehension and qualitative recall of text information. With respect to group membership, good readers were better able to comprehend the unadapted text, to recall more hierarchically high text units and to reach on overall superior performance level. The adaptive text was better in that it enabled faster reading, as is indicated by five of 13 measures.

Correlations between Reading Performance and Metacognitive Thinking

Table 7.6 shows correlational relationships between five performance measures and 10 dimensions of self-reflection and executive control. Although the significant correlations averaged to $r = .38$ (SD = .19), which in the light of data from a metaanalysis done by Schneider (1982) is usual (according to Schneider correlations between performance and metacognitive data range .25–.64), not all metacognitive dimensions contribute to significant effects. Comprehension and recall performance covary with usage of operational learning techniques and

TABLE 7.2
Summary Analysis of Variance (A Stands for Text Version and B Stands for Group Membership)

Measure	Source	Sum of Squares	Degrees of Freedom	Mean Sum of Squares	F-Ratio	Level of Significance
Reading time	A	923470.9	1/24	923470.9	3.81	p < .063 s.
	B	64033.1	1/24	64033.1	.26	p > .615
	AB	383993.4	1/24	383993.4	1.58	p > .221
	within	5820381.9	24	242515.9		
Comprehension	A	11.6	1/24	11.6	3.66	p < .068 s.
	B	64.8	1/24	64.8	20.50	p < .00014 ss.

(continued)

TABLE 7.2
(Continued)

Measure	Source	Sum of Squares	Degrees of Freedom	Mean Sum of Squares	F-Ratio	Level of Significance
	AB	.1	1/24	.1	.03	p > .864
	within	75.9	24	3.2		
Comprehension	A	.018	1/24	.018	1.52	p > .230
points per min.	B	.1	1/24	.1	7.21	p < .013 s.
reading time	AB	.027	1/24	.027	2.24	p > .148
	within	.3	24	.012		
Recall precision	A	1.3	1/24	1.3	.02	p > .889
	B	1695.7	1/24	1695.7	22.04	p < .00009 ss.
	AB	555.4	1/24	555.4	7.22	p < .013 s.
	within	1846.7	24	76.9		
Recall precision per	A	.4	1/24	.4	6.44	p < .018 s.
min. reading time	B	1.5	1/24	1.5	22.33	p < .00008 ss.
	AB	.1	1/24	.1	2.00	p > .170
	within	1.6	24	.1		
Recall hierarchy	A	12.8	1/24	12.8	.26	p > .615
points	B	1537.6	1/24	1537.6	31.79	p < .000008 ss.
	AB	465.0	1/24	465.0	9.61	p < .005 s.
Recall H-points per	A	.5	1/24	.5	5.19	p < .032 s.
min. reading time	B	1.4	1/24	1.4	14.66	p < .0008 ss.
	AB	.1	1/24	.1	.89	p > .414
	within	2.4	24	.1		
Total recall points	A	22.1	1/24	22.1	.09	p > .767
	B	6459.8	1/24	6459.8	27.61	p < .00002 ss.
	AB	2038.8	1/24	2038.8	8.71	p < .007 s.
	within	5615.4	24	234.0		
Total recall points	A	1.9	1/24	1.9	6.01	p < .022 s.
per min. reading	B	5.8	1/24	5.8	18.88	p < .00022 ss.
time	AB	.4	1/24	.4	1.24	p > .277
	within	7.4	24	.3		
Number of recalled	A	0	1/24	0	0	p < .000005 ss.
thought units	B	295.8	1/24	295.8	33.85	p < .009 s.
	AB	70.2	1/24	70.2	8.04	
	within	209.7	24	8.7		
Average hierarchy	A	.2	1/24	.2	2.79	p > .108
level	B	1.6	1/24	1.6	18.50	p < .00025 ss.
	AB	.1	1/24	.1	.85	p > .366
	within	2.1	24	2.1		
Comprehension +	A	66.6	1/24	66.6	.28	p > .602
recall points	B	7815.9	1/24	7815.9	32.77	p < .000007 ss.
	AB	2022.1	1/24	2022.1	8.48	p < .008 s.
	within	5724.6	24	238.5		
Total points per	A	2.3	1/24	2.3	6.07	p < .021 s.
min.	B	7.3	1/24	7.3	19.72	p < .0002 ss.
	AB	.2	1/24	.2	.57	p > .458
	within	8.9	24	.4		

TABLE 7.3
Significant Differences between Means for Prepared Text (FS),
Normal Text (N), Good Readers (GR), and Poor Readers (PR)

Measure	*Main Effects*		
	Text	Group	Interaction
Reading time:	FS > N-text	—	—
Comprehension points	N > FS-Text	GR > PR	—
Comprehension points per min. reading time	—	GR > PR	—
Recall precision	—	GR > PR	text × reader interaction
Recall precision per min. reading time	FS > N-text	GR > PR	—
Recall hierarchy points:	—	GR > PR	text × reader interaction
Recall hierarchy points per min. reading time	FS > N-Text	GR > PR	—
Total recall points	—	GR > PR	text × reader interaction
Total recall points per min. reading time:	FS > N-text	GR > PR	—
Number of recalled thought units	—	GR > PR	text × reader interaction
Average hierarchy level of recalled units	N > FS-text	GR > PR	—
Comprehension + recall points	N > FS-text	GR > PR	text × reader interaction
Comprehension + recall points per min. reading time	FS > N-text	GR > PR	—

strategies, adaptive regulation in the course of processing, fine-grain learning regulation, awareness of task fulfillment and subjective certainty about goal attainment, and number of processing cycles undertaken. Interestingly, comprehension strategies, comprehension monitoring, and comprehension testing fail to reach significant correlations.

DISCUSSION

Utterances concerning metacognitive or executive control by the good readers mainly focused on instrumental and regulative aspects of text processing. Those aspects that related to identification of comprehension problems and decisions with regard to coping with intermediate difficulties were prominent. In contrast, the poor readers focused on self-related, state-oriented aspects of themselves as learners, and failure-oriented monitoring of current progress. These were not followed by adequate regulatory decisions or actions. This self-monitoring picture, as it is revealed by the group of the poor readers, resembles the one we got in an earlier, preliminary study (Fischer & Mandl, 1980a). It is thus possible that the poor, failure-oriented learners process self-diagnostic information affectively, in terms of an affirmation of failure expectations, which prevents them from overcoming intermediate difficulties. A fostering of metacognitive self-attention might have detrimental consequences. Since the poor learners had an equal number of learning techniques at their disposal (as compared with the more successful students), their poor performance can be described as a disposition to give up. Thus it seems incorrect to postulate learning-training programs in order to foster a global, higher degree of metacognitive awareness. On the contrary, such programs should guide the learner's attention to the *functional* parts of the

TABLE 7.4
Summary Analysis of Variance (A Stands for Text Version and B Stands for Recall Condition)

Measure	Source	Sum of Squares	Degrees of Freedom	Mean Sum of Squares	F-Ratio	Level of Significance
Reading time	A	2222850.7	1/20	2222850.7	6.169	p < .022
	B	3408.2	1/20	3408.2	.0095	n.s.
	AB	120416.6	1/20	120416.6	.3342	n.s.
Comprehension	A	10.011	1/20	10.011	1.568	p < .225
points	B	.011	1/20	.011	.017	n.s.
	AB	3.761	1/20	3.761	.589	n.s.
Comprehension	A	.038	1/20	.038	2.077	p < .165
points per	B	.002	1/20	.002	.109	n.s.
min. reading time	AB	.002	1/20	.0183	.109	n.s.
Recall precision	A	10.666	1/20	10.666	.073	n.s.
points	B	0	1/20	0	0	n.s.
	AB	700.669	1/20	700.669	4.802	p < .04
Recall hierarchy	A	26.041	1/20	26.041	.228	n.s.
points	B	3.375	1/20	3.375	.030	n.s.
	AB	459.337	1/20	459.337	4.025	p < .059
Total recall	A	70.041	1/20	70.041	.135	n.s.
points	B	3.374	1/20	3.374	.007	n.s.
	AB	1962.044	1/20	1962.044	3.789	p < .066
Total recall	A	2.156	1/20	2.156	3.828	p < .0645
points per	B	.009	1/20	.009	.016	n.s.
min. reading time	AB	.504	1/20	.504	.895	n.s.
Number of re-	A	1.041	1/20	1.041	.049	n.s.
called	B	2.041	1/20	2.041	.096	n.s.
thought units	AB	70.044	1/20	70.044	3.290	p < .085
Average hier-	A	.095	1/20	.095	.556	n.s.
archy level of	B	.254	1/20	.254	1.487	n.s.
recalled units	AB	.007	1/20	.007	.041	n.s.

TABLE 7.5
Significant Differences Among Means for Immediate Recall (I),
Delayed Recall (DR), Prepared Text (FS), and Normal Text (NS)

Measure	Text	Recall Condition	Interaction Text × Recall Condition
Reading time	FS > N	–	–
Comprehension	N > FS	–	–
Comprehension/time	–	–	–
Recall precision	–	–	+
Recall hierarchy	–	–	+
Total recall points	N > FS	–	–
Total recall points/time	FS > N	–	–
Number thought units	–	–	+
Average hierarchy level or recalled units	–	–	–

reading progress. That is, it is not enough to say "Be self-aware," but rather, the less able learner must be shown where he/she might concentrate his/her attention. A second study was done with this goal in mind.

A Text-processing Study-aid Package with Guided Self-assessment

Poor learners did not seem to be less adept at monitoring their study behavior than better learners. Instead of processing the self-assessment data functionally for the control of further learning, they interpreted learning difficulties inadequately, as if these affirmed their failure expectancies. The results, then, are dysfunctional with regard to reading performance or self-worth, in general. Study-aid packages should then orient learning concomitant with self-assessment as the functional parts of monitoring. Additionally, one should not restrict such aids to mere information about where difficulties in processing exist. One should give the learner a means for coping with difficulties. Therefore, a study-aid package was developed that contained learning techniques and strategies on the one hand, and control signals for necessary self-assessment on the other hand. Any single learning aid or control signal was exemplarily introduced, illustrated, and generalized to enable spontaneous transfer. The study-aid package for text processing contained the following parts:

(A) Reading for Comprehension/Understanding
    1. Overview: skimming the text for an orientation to the text structure and content.
    2. Preparation of the Text Surface: underlining, highlighting, marking of important text segments with respect to specified learning goals or criteria.

3. Reading for Understanding: construction of content-related elaborations, activation of domain-specific prior knowledge, directing and answering of higher- and lower-order questions, clarification of missing information.

4. Fixing the Result of Reading: making excerpts from the text, preparation of an outline, mappings, graphs, writing up of summaries reducing text information.

(B) Storage and Retrieval

1. Memorization: cumulative rehearsal as a means for controlled information storage (check recall against outline or summary; focus on difficult topics and memorize again).

2. Reconstruction: unfolding of condensed information by making inferences.

(C) Monitoring/Self-Testing

1. Clarification of Goals: analyzing the learning task.

2. Clarification of Content/Text Goals: analyzing text specific, content-related learning goals and criteria for self-testing.

3. Comprehension Self-testing

4. Recall Self-testing

5. Installing of Learning Cycles: understanding of reading as repetitive reading, testing, and cycles.

(D) Enduring Learner Traits and Learning Competence Self-rating

1. Learning ability self-efficacy rating.

2. Learning competence with respect to strategic endowment.

3. Diagnosis of learning problems.

The study-aid package was styled as a booklet and contained practical, illustrative examples as well as exposition about the usefulness and reason for the aid and tasks for exercise and transfer.

METHOD

Text Versions

The experimental text was prepared in two versions. The source version of 3181 words dealt with man's environmental influences on the devastation of natural and biological resources. The source text was analyzed according to Kintsch and van Dijk's (1978) hierarchical text level analysis. Topical units as well as compounds of topical units in the adapted text version were interspersed with attention guiding hints of the following kinds:

1. Clarify the learning Aims and text specific Goals (CAG)
2. Reflect upon the goals stated implicitly and explicitly in the text.

TABLE 7.6

Summary Results for Analyses using Parabolic (p), Cubical (c), and Linear (l) Regression

(Dependent measures are listed in rows on right; Metacognitive strategies are listed in columns on bottom)

Measure		1	2	3	4	5	6	7	8	9	10
Level of comprehension per unit processing time	p	.06	.10	.241	.261	.283	.241	.326	.346 *	.345	.245
	c	.22	.20	.46 *	.32	.17	.35 *	.39 *	.26	.53 **	.28
	l	−.037	+.033	−.156	+.047	+.130	+.134	+.299	−.222	−.323	+.048
Level of comprehension regardless processing time	p	.40 *	.32	.20	.173	.221	.481 **	.498 **	.141	.548 **	.03
	c	.42 *	.33	.32	.17	.35 *	.49 **	.53 **	.17	.56 **	.20
	l	+.398 *	+.301	−.222	−.152	−.124	+.263	+.484 **	−.121	−.500 **	+.029
Level of recall per unit processing time	p	.10	.10	.20	.134	.20	.045	.265	.352 *	.241	.141
	c	.10	.17	.20	.35 *	.22	.44 *	.26	.47 *	.32	.22
	l	+.004	−.069	−.168	+.096	+.067	+.021	+.209	−.334	−.241	+.032

244

Level of recall regardless processing time			Combined weighted speed & level overall comprehension and recall performance			*p < .05 **p < .01	
p	c	l	p	c	l		
.34 *	.33	+.329	.24	.35 *	+.233		Operational and strategic activities of text processing
.10	.10	+.062	.141	.17	+.057		Comprehension processes and strategies
.173	.26	-.159	.259	.32	-.247		Comprehension monitoring
.141	.28	-.087	.03	.26	+.013		Matching of state of comprehension against learning criteria; self-testing/ self-checking
.274	.35 *	-.083	.293	.36 *	-.058		Evaluation of learning states
.184	.53 **	+.138	.155	.48 **	+.093		Activities of adaptive learning regulation with regard to learning state
.457 *	.44 *	+.406 *	.41 *	.41 *	+.382 *		Awareness of/knowledge about task features and fine-grain learning regulating activities
.217	.42 *	-.192	.313	.47 *	-.278		Number of processing cycles with regard to task relevance
.359 *	.37 *	-.314	.365 *	.37 *	-.349 *		Awareness of task fulfillment and subjective certainty of goal reachment with regard to stop decisions
.10	.14	+.005	.10	.10	+.047		Objective testing/checking of task fulfillment/goal reachment

3. Identify or construct possible criteria for the testing/checking of your learning, comprehension, and memory state.
4. Test your Comprehension/Understanding (TCU) of the text content with regard to the specified learning goals and criteria.
5. Test your Memory/Recall (TMR) of the text information.

Monitoring assessment, and learning, regulatory strategies were explained, illustrated, and practiced in the study-aid package. The experimental group, familiarized with monitoring and control of learning in the training phase, was expected to make deliberate use of these hints.

Procedure.   The study was done in three phases. In the *first phase,* learning prerequisites were assessed by a battery of tests, consisting of verbal intelligence, ability, and reasoning skills, and domain-specific tasks about technical, biological, chemical, physical, and geographic knowledge. The subjects had to write an essay about the target content area (man and environment). Finally, all subjects had to fill out a questionnaire concerning their learning ability, competence, and problems.

On the basis of their verbal intelligence, prior knowledge, and essay scores (the essays were analyzed for hierarchical structure according to Kintsch and van Dijk (1978), and were evaluated according to the richness of concepts contained), the subjects then were subdivided into a high- or low-ability group. Half of each group was then randomly assigned to a treatment or a placebo group.

Additionally, a separate analysis was done on the learners' self-efficacy ratings. Half of the low as well as half of the high scorers were not able to rate their learning efficiency consistently with their real ability, so that 50% of the subjects over- or underestimated their real learning ability. To rule out any bias stemming from the inconsistent self-efficacy rating of the subjects, this variable was additionally taken into consideration when grouping the subjects. After grouping of subjects the second, *training phase,* was undertaken.

In the *training phase,* the high- and low-ability subjects of the treatment group (HT and LT, respectively) were given the learning-aid package and a text of about 10 pages of print. They had to prepare excerpts, summaries, and elaborations, as well as written recall. The high- and low-ability subjects of the placebo group (HP and LP, respectively) were given a distractor task. They had to work through a text in the manner to which they were accustomed and to prepare themselves for a multiple choice test. None of the texts in the placebo and in the treatment group referred to topics related to the domain, which was given as text in the third, experimental phase. All students, placebo subjects as well as experimental subjects were instructed to work profoundly with the material handed out.

In the final, *experimental phase,* the subjects (in homogeneous groups of six to eight students) were handed the two text versions. While the placebo subjects received the source version without monitoring hints, the experimental subjects received the adapted version. Instructions were as follows: As all of you know it is the usual goal of text preparation in everyday university learning to comprehend the information of instructional texts and to keep that part of information in memory that is important enough to be reported later on in group discussions or examinations. Please prepare now the text as you usually do (placebo group)/as we have told you to do in the study-aid booklet (treatment group)— preparation time is unrestricted.

After approximately 2 hours of preparation, most of the subjects signaled that they had finished. Immediately after finishing reading, the subjects were administered a written, free-recall test of the material they had just read. After completing the free recall, subjects were then given a multiple-choice comprehension test. Multiple-choice items were selected in such a way that all hierarchical text levels were represented according to their distribution in the source text. Finally, the subjects were retested on the self-efficacy questions of the first phase.

Scoring.   Besides the self-ratings, three kinds of measures were obtained:

1. Number of topics recalled, weighted according to text hierarchy level and their degree of cohesion.
2. Number of correctly answered multiple-choice questions weighted according to their text hierarchy level.
3. Type, number, and adequacy of spontaneously produced study techniques and reading techniques.

The raw scores of all the measures were transformed into z-values to make the subjects comparable to each other.

RESULTS

Analysis of Variance Data.   The z-values of 15 dependent measures were then analyzed by the ANOVA-design, illustrated by Table 7.7. The analysis of variance data of the 36 subjects, who were all law students in their first two or three semesters, are shown in Table 7.8.

TABLE 7.7
Design of Study 2

	Learning Prerequisites	
	High Ability	*Low Ability*
Condition:		
Placebo	HP	LP
Treatment	HT	LT

TABLE 7.8
Statistical Summary of Comparisons of High (H) and Low (L) Ability with Placebo (P) and Treatment (T) Conditions

Dependent measures/ Performance Tested	Main Effect A: Ability Level		Main Effect B: Treatment Cond.		Interaction A × B: Ability × Treatment		Comparison of Group Means
	F_A	p	F_B	p	F_{AB}	p	
Comprehension score	2.252 ≥	.148	1.262 ≥	.273	1.161 ≥	.293	HP > HT > LP > LT
Free-recall score	15.688 ≥	.001	.085	—	.026	—	HT > HP > LT > LP
Cohesion of recalled units	1.798 ≥	.195	.279	—	2.522 ≥	.127	HP > LT > HT > LP
Combined comprehension & free recall score	14.278 ≥	.001	.436	—	.858 ≥	—	HP > HT > LT > LP
% comprehended units (CUs) at level 4	3.275 ≥	.08	.797	—	.385	—	HT > HP > LT > LP
% CUs at level 3	1.353 ≥	.257	.161	—	1.354 ≥	.257	HT > HP > LP > LT >
% CUs at level 1	2.532 ≥	.126	1.010 ≥	.326	1.750 ≥	.199	HT > HP > LP > LT
% Recalled units (RUs) at level 4	2.441 ≥	.132	.005	—	.005	—	HT > HP > LP > LT
% RUs at level 3	6.012 ≥	.023	4.733 ≥	.041	1.621 ≥	.216	HT > HP > LT > LP
% RUs at level 2	.003 ≥	—	.007	—	3.720 ≥	.067	HP > LT > LP > HT
% RUs at level 1	4.470 ≥	.046	.789	—	.029	—	LP > LT > HP > HT
Average hierarchy level of recalled units	6.399 ≥	.019	.980	—	.513	—	HT > HP > LT > LP
Use of reading strategies in experimental phase	1.518 ≥	.231	.261	—	2.067 ≥	.165	HP > LT > HT > LP
Use of reading strategies in training transfer situation	3.591 ≥	.071	16.818 ≥	.0005	6.345 ≥	.02	LT > HT > HP > LP
Self-efficacy rating after strategy implementation	.454 ≥	—	4.491 ≥	.042	.386	—	HT > LT > HP > LP

RESULTS AND DISCUSSION

The following two pairs of hypotheses with regard to learning achievement after training on the one hand, and with regard to a change in self-efficacy rating on the other hand, have been formulated:

1. Learning achievement after training:
   HT ≥ HP and LT ≥ LP; LT = HT?
2. Self-efficacy judgment after training:
   HT ≥ HP and LT ≥ LP; LT = HT?

As expected, the high-ability subjects excelled the low-ability subjects, regardless of training condition. The influence of learning ability, high verbal intelligence, and domain-specific, knowledge-related, learning prerequisites is large enough to rule out even most of the possible beneficial effects of the treatment. High-ability subjects profited considerably from training, as is revealed by the stable pattern of superior HT means, which exceeded any other group mean in 10 out of 15 comparisons. But there is evidence, too, that the LT subjects did profit from the treatment. They immediately follow the HT subjects in seven of 15 measures. Interestingly enough, some of the training subjects did not use the trained strategies. This may be explained in light of the fact that 10 days of training with a complex package of reading techniques surely is not enough to stabilize its use and to assure its transfer to new learning situations, especially if the time to work with the new strategies is limited by experimental constraints.

The HT subjects made a very different use of the mnemonic and comprehension strategies as compared with the LT subjects. Whereas the HT subjects focused attention on hierarchically higher text units in comprehension and recall, LT subjects tried to focus on all text hierarchy levels. Thus they may have suffered some information overload. High-ability, spontaneous users of the strategies were most efficient.

With respect to the self-efficacy ratings, the treatment subjects scored higher and showed more consistency with respect to an objective diagnosis of their own learning efficiency. Their efficacy judgments heightened achievement orientation, and reduced fear of failure, which may have resulted in better, functionally oriented self-monitoring. An additional analysis of the questionnaire data of the HT subjects and the LT subjects showed that the effects of intensified self-monitoring may be bidirectional. Failure-oriented subjects, regardless of their ability level, tended to react on self-diagnostic data affectively. Feedback, which is originally intended to lead to error identification, may be interpreted in terms of punishment. Two studies of Stapf and Mix (1979) and by Stapf and Degner (1981) give evidence that instructional feedback might be interpreted by the learner not only in terms of information about erroneous performance but also in terms of positive and negative reward. The motivational consequences of feedback, then, might also lead to consequences interfering with performance. Self-diagnostic monitoring and feedback exclusively have been restricted conceptually to their informational value. The present study suggests that they should be conceptualized in terms of affective and motivational consequences. The frame of metacognitive research needs to be broadened to include motivational factors.

GENERAL COMMENTS

Current learning-aid packages rely on the learner's competence in self-assessment. They are not explicit nor precise enough about what "metacognitive self-monitoring" might mean, however. Theorizing about metacognitive aspects of thinking has been done within the framework of two paradigms. Whereas Flavell, centrally, does emphasize the role of metacognitive or, more generally, of "psychological knowledge," which makes up the learner's competence for intelligently solving intellectual problems, in contrast, Brown favors the role of an executive control program. The latter, in the course of processing, continually calls for learning concomitant monitoring data, which then are tested against solution criteria and serve as standards for the regulation of thought processes. Correlations between metacognitive self-statements and performance data generally range between .25 and .64 (Cavanaugh & Borkowski, 1980; Hagen, 1975). Current researchers feel there may be a necessity for some theoretical reformulation, a clarification of the concept (Brown, 1982; Flavell, 1982). Wellman (1981) has pleaded not to repudiate the concept prematurely but rather to further elaborate it. Educational practice seems to support Wellman's pleading, because the many practice oriented studies done by Brown and coworkers have shown the fruitfulness of the approach despite vagueness of theory.

Furthermore, the data presented here support an information-processing integration of Brown and Flavell's ideas. Because Flavell's metacognitive thinker knows a lot but has no executive device to make use of knowledge and Brown's executive does much but does not know much, a theoretical synthesis seems to be necessary.

REFERENCES

Ach, N. *Über den Willensakt und das Temperament*. Leipzig: Quelle & Meyer, 1910.

Baldwin, M. J. How children study. *Archives of Psychology*, 1909, *12*, 65–70.

Belmont, J. M., Butterfield, E. C., & Ferretti, R. P. *To secure transfer of training, instruct self-management skills*. Unpublished manuscript, Medical Center of the University of Kansas, Kansas City, Kansas, 1980.

Binet, A. *L'etude experimentale de l'intelligence*. Paris: Schleicher Frères, 1903.

Bisanz, G. L., Vesonder, G. T., & Voss, J. F. Knowledge of one's own responding and the relation of such knowledge to learning. *Journal of Experimental Child Psychology*, 1978, *25*, 116–128.

Brown, A. L. Development, schooling, and the acquisition of knowledge about knowledge. In R. C. Anderson, R. J. Spiro, & W. E. Montague (Eds.), *Schooling and the acquisition of knowledge*. Hillsdale, N.J.: Lawrence Erlbaum Associates, 1977.

Brown, A. L. Knowing when, where, and how to remember: A problem of metacognition. In R. Glaser (Ed.), *Advances in instructional psychology*. (Vol. 1). Hillsdale, N.J.: Lawrence Erlbaum Associates, 1978.

Brown, A. L. Metakognition, Ausführungsbeherrschung, Selbststeuerung und andere, noch geheimnisvollere Mechanismen. In R. Kluwe & F. E. Weinert (Eds.), *Metakognition, Motivation und Lernen*. Stuttgart: Kohlhammer, 1982.

Brown, A. L., & Barclay, C. R. The effects of training specific mnemonics on the metamnemonic efficacy of retarded children. *Child Development*, 1976, *47*, 71–80.

Brown, A. L., Bransford, J. D., Ferrara, R. A., & Campione, J. C. Learning, remembering, and understanding. In J. H. Flavell & E. M. Markman (Eds.), Cognitive development. In P. Mussen (Ed.), *Handbook of child psychology*. (Vol. 1). New York: Wiley, 1983.

Brown, A. L., & Campione, J. C. Memory strategies in learning: Training children to study strategically. In H. Pick, H. Leibowith, J. Singer, A. Steinschneider, & H. Stevenson (Eds.), *Application of basic research in psychology*. New York: Plenum Press, 1977. (a)

Brown, A. L., & Campione, J. C. Training strategic study time apportionment in educable retarded children. *Intelligence*, 1977, *1*, 94–107. (b)

Brown, A. L., Campione, J. C., & Barclay, C. R. Training self-checking routines for estimating test readiness: Generalization from list learning to prose recall. *Child Development*, 1979, *50*, 501–512.

Brown, A. L., Campione, J. C., & Day, J. D. Learning to learn: On training students to learn from texts. *Educational Researcher*, 1981, *10*, 14–21.

Brown, A. L., Campione, J. C., & Murphy, M. D. Maintenance and generalization of trained metamnemonic awareness in educable retarded children. *Journal of Experimental Child Psychology*, 1977, *24*, 191–211.

Brown, A. L., & Day, J. D. Strategy and knowledge for summarizing texts: The development and facilitation of expertise. Unpublished manuscript, University of Illinois, Center for the Study of Reading, 1981.

Brown, A. L., & Lawton, S. C. The feeling of knowing experience in educable retarded children. *Journal of Developmental Psychology*, 1977, *13*, 364–370.

Brown, A. L., & Smiley, S. S. *The development of strategies for studying prose passages*. Tech. Rep. 66. Urbana, Ill.: University of Illinois, Center for the Study of Reading, 1977. (a)

Brown, A. L., & Smiley, S. S. Rating the importance of structural units of prose passages: A problem of metacognitive development. *Child Development*, 1977, *48*, 1–8. (b)

Brown, A. L., & Smiley, S. S. The development of strategies for studying texts. *Child Development*, 1978, *49*, 1076–1088.

Brown, A. L., Smiley, S. S., Day, J. D., Townsend, M., & Lawton, S. C. Intrusion of a thematic idea in children's recall of prose. *Child Development*, 1977, *48*, 1454–1466.

Brown, A. L., Smiley, S. S., & Lawton, S. C. The effects of experience on the selection of suitable retrieval cues for studying texts. *Child Development*, 1978, *49*, 829–835.

Cavanaugh, J. C., & Borkowski, J. G. Searching for metamemory-memory connections: A developmental study. *Journal of Developmental Psychology*, 1980, *16*, 441–453.

Cavanaugh, J. C., & Perlmutter, M. Metamemory: A critical examination. *Child Development*, 1982, *53*, 11–28.

Craik, F. I. M., & Lockhart, R. S. Levels of processing: A framework for memory research. *Journal of Verbal Learning and Verbal Behavior*, 1972, *11*, 671–684.

Danner, F. W. Children's understanding of intersentence organization in the recall of short descriptive passages. *Journal of Educational Psychology*, 1976, *68*, 174–183.

Day, J. D. Training summarization skills: A comparison of teaching methods. Unpublished doctoral dissertation, University of Illinois, 1980.

Dewey, J. *How we think*. Boston: Heath, 1910.

Dörner, D. Theoretical advances of cognitive psychology relevant to instruction. In A. M. Lesgold, J. W. Pellegrino, S. D. Fokkema, & R. Glaser (Eds.), *Cognitive psychology and instruction*. New York: Plenum Press, 1978,

Fischer, P. M., & Mandl, H. Metacognitive components of study behavior. Short Rep. 80/6. Deutsches Institut für Fernstudien, Hauptbereich Forschung, Tübingen 1980. (a)

Fischer, P. M., & Mandl, H. *Selbstwahrnehmung und Selbstbewertung beim Lernen. Metakognitive Komponenten der Selbststeuerung beim Lernen mit Texten*. Forschungsbericht Nr. 10. Deutsches Institut für Fernstudien, Hauptbereich Forschung, Tübingen, Oktober 1980. (b)

Fischer, P. M., & Mandl, H. Selbstdiagnostische und selbstregulative Aspekte der Verarbeitung von Studientexten: Eine kritische Übersicht über Ansätze zur Förderung und Beeinflussung von Lernstrategien. In H. Mandl (Ed.), *Zur Psychologie der Textverarbeitung*. München: Urban & Schwarzenberg, 1981. (a)

Fischer, P. M., & Mandl, H. *Metakognitive Regulation von Textverarbeitungsprozessen. Aspekte und Probleme des Zusammenhangs von metakognitiven Selbstaussagen und konkretem Leistungsverhalten*. Forschungsbericht Nr. 15. Deutsches Institut für Fernstudien, Hauptbereich Forschung, Tübingen, November 1981. (b)

Flavell, J. H. Developmental studies of mediated memory. In H. W. Reese & L. P. Lipsitt (Eds.), *Advances in child development and behavior*. (Vol. 5). New York: Academic Press, 1970.

Flavell, J. H. *The development of Metacommunication*. Paper given at the 21st International Congress of Psychology. Paris, 1976. (a)

Flavell, J. H. Metacognitive aspects of problem solving. In B. C. Resnick (Ed.), *The nature of intelligence*. Hillsdale, N.J.: Lawrence Erlbaum Associates, 1976. (b)

Flavell, J. H. *Metacognitive development*. Paper presented at the NATO Advanced Study Institute on Structural/Process Theories of Complex Human Behavior. Banff, Alberta Canada, June 20–30, 1977.

Flavell, J. H. *Cognitive monitoring*. Paper prepared for the Conference on Children's Oral Communication Skills. University of Wisconsin, 1978.(a)

Flavell, J. H. *Metacognition*. Paper presented at the meeting of the APA. Toronto, 1978. (b)

Flavell, J. H. Metacognitive development. In J. M. Scandura & C. J. Brainerd (Eds.), *Structural process theories of complex human behavior*. Alphen a.d. Rijn: Sijthoff & Noordhoff, 1978. (c)

Flavell, J. H. The development of metacognition. Grant application. Stanford University, 1979. (a)

Flavell, J. H. *Kognitive Entwicklung*. Stuttgart: Klett–Cotta, 1979. (b)

Flavell, J. H. Metacognition and cognitive monitoring: A new area of cognitive-developmental inquiry. *American Psychologist*, 1979, *34*, 906–911. (c)

Flavell, J. H. *Monitoring social-cognitive enterprises: Something else that may develop in the area of social cognition*. Paper prepared for the Social Science Research Council Committee on Social and Affective Development During Childhood. January 1979.(d)

Flavell, J. H. Annahmen zum Begriff Metakognition sowie zur Entwicklung von Metakognition. In R. Kluwe & F. E. Weinert (Eds.), *Metakognition, Motivation und Lernen*. Stuttgart: Kohlhammer, 1982.

Flavell, J. H., Friedrichs, A. G., & Hoyt, J. D. Developmental changes in memorization processes. *Cognitive Psychology*, 1970, *1*, 324–340.

Flavell, J. H., & Wellman, H. M. Metamemory. In R. V. Kail & J. W. Hagen (Eds.), *Perspectives on the development of memory and cognition*. Hillsdale, N.J.: Lawrence Erlbaum Associates, 1977.

Gard, W. L. A preliminary study of the psychology of reasoning. *American Journal of Psychology,* 1907, *18,* 490–504.

Hagen, J. W. Commentary (on Kreutzer, Leonard & Flavell). *Monographs of the Society for Research in Child Development,* 1975, *40* (159), 59–61.

Huey, E. B. *The psychology and pedagogy of reading.* Cambridge, Mass.: M. I. T. Press, 1968. (Originally published, 1908).

James, W. *The principles of psychology.* (Vol. 1). New York: Holt, 1890.

Jenkins, J. J. Four points to remember: A tetrahedral model and memory experiments. In L. S. Cermak & F. I. M. Craik (Eds.), *Levels of processing in human memory.* Hillsdale, N.J.: Lawrence Erlbaum Associates, 1979.

Kintsch, W., & van Dijk, T. A. Toward a model of text comprehension and production. *Psychological Review,* 1978, *85,* 363–394.

Kuhlmann, F. On the analysis of the memory consciousness for pictures of familiar objects. *American Journal of Psychology,* 1907, *18,* 389–420.

Kreutzer, M. A., Leonard, C., & Flavell, J. H. An interview study of children's knowledge about memory. *Monographs of the Society of Research of Child Development,* 1975, *40,* (159), 1–60.

Levin, J. R. Pictures as prose-learning devices. In A. Flammer & W. Kintsch (Eds.), *Tutorials in text processing.* Amsterdam: North Holland Publishing Company, 1982.

Lindley, E. G. A study of puzzles. *American Journal of Psychology,* 1897, *8,* 431–493.

Masur, E. F., McIntyre, D. W., & Flavell, J. H. Developmental changes in apportionment of study time among items in a multitrial free recall task. *Journal of Experimental Child Psychology,* 1973, *15,* 237–246.

Meichenbaum, D. Cognitive factors as determinants of learning disabilities: A cognitive functional approach. In R. Knights & D. Bakker (Eds.), *The neuropsychology of knowing disorders: Theoretical approaches.* Baltimore: University Park Press, 1976.(a)

Meichenbaum, D. Teaching children self-control. In B. B. Lahey & A. E. Kazdin (Eds.), *Advances in clinical child psychology.* (Vol. 2). New York: Academic Press, 1976. (b)

Meichenbaum, D. Toward a cognitive theory of self-control. In G. E. Schwartz & D. Shapiro (Eds.), *Consciousness and self-regulation.* (Vol. 1). New York, 1976. (c)

Miller, G. A., Galanter, E., & Pribram, D. H. *Plans and the structure of behavior.* London: Holt, Rinehart, & Winston, 1960.

Posnansky, C. J. Age- and task-related differences in the use of category size information for retrieval of categorized items. *Journal of Experimental Child Psychology,* 1978, *26,* 373–382.

Rogoff, B., Newcombe, N., & Kagan, J. Planfulness and recognition memory. *Child Development,* 1974, *45,* 972–977.

Schneider, W. Developmental trends in the metamemory-memory behavior relationship: An integrative review. Unpublished manuscript. Max-Planck-Institut für Psychologische Forschung, München, 1982.

Simon, H. A. The functional equivalence of problem solving skills. *Cognitive Psychology,* 1975, *7,* 268–288.

Stapf, K. H., & Degner, U. *Experimentelle Untersuchungen verschiedener Rückmeldungsmodalitaten beim Lernen.* Berichte aus dem Psychologischen Institut der Universität Tübingen, Nr. 5, 1981.

Stapf, K. H., & Mix, R. *Zur relativen Wirksamkeit positiver und negativer Rückmeldung. Eine Latenzzeit-Analyse.* Berichte aus dem Fachbereich Psychologie der Philipps-Universität Marburg/Lahn, August 1979.

Sternberg, R. J. Compounds of human intelligence. Tech. Rep. 19. Yale University, Department of Psychology, October 1979.

Thorndike, E. L. Reading as reasoning: A study of mistakes in paragraph reading. *Journal of Educational Psychology,* 1917, *8,* 323–332.

Wellman, H. M. The early development of intentional memory behavior. *Human Development*, 1977, *20*, 86–101.(a)

Wellman, H. M. Tips of the tongue and feeling of knowing experiences: A developmental study of memory monitoring. *Child Development*, 1977, *48*, 13–21.(b)

Wellman, H. M. Metamemory revisited. To appear in: What is memory development, the development of? A look after a decade. *Contributions to human development*, 1981.

Yussen, S. R., Mathews, S. R., Buss, R. R., & Kane, P. T. Developmental change in judging important and critical elements of stories. *Developmental Psychology*, 1980, *16*, 213–219.

8 Instructing Comprehension-fostering Activities in Interactive Learning Situations

Ann L. Brown
Annemarie Sullivan Palincsar
Bonnie B. Armbruster
Center for the Study of Reading
University of Illinois

INTRODUCTION

"Pupils don't learn to comprehend by osmosis (Cushenbery, 1969)." As with any definite statement concerning the acquisition of reading skills, this could be a controversial position, but a main theme of this chapter is that, at least for a sizable number of children, the statement is true. It is also argued that children who need extensive instruction in comprehending written materials most, are least likely to receive it. The latter part of the chapter describes cognitive-skills training studies that have provided extensive practice in comprehension-fostering activities and have resulted in substantial improvements in students' ability to learn from texts.

Resnick (1979) has argued that there are two main biases in reading instruction, namely direct instruction of decoding and informal teaching of comprehension. Those who advocate a heavy emphasis on decoding mechanisms in early reading also tend towards the direct-instruction approach, whereas those who emphasize early attention to language processing, language arts, or comprehension tend also to espouse learner-directed, informal instructional approaches. As Resnick also argued, there is no reason in principle why one cannot have direct instruction in comprehension, or (a little harder to envisage) informal instruction in decoding. In this chapter, concern is with one of the underpopulated cells, relatively direct or explicit instruction in comprehension. Of particular concern is the explicit instruction of comprehension-fostering skills with children at risk for academic failure precisely because they experience unusual difficulties in this arena.

PREREADING EXPERIENCES

Preschool Reading Dyads

Learning to read does not begin when the child enters school; the child brings a history of preschool learning experiences that, to a greater or lesser extent, have prepared the way for a smooth transition. Some of these experiences could clearly be classified as prereading activities; others are more general learning practices with some relevance to reading. Many of these early experiences have taken place in social settings that share pertinent features with common school learning activities. Some children have considerable preschool experience in interactions that are very similar to school reading groups; others have not.

Certain parent–child interactions are ideal practicing grounds for subsequent teacher–child activities that will be of central importance in the early grades. Social settings such as these, where the child interacts with experts in a problem-solving domain, are settings where a great deal of learning occurs in and out of school. Indeed, some would argue that the majority of learning is shaped by social processes (Laboratory of Comparative Human Cognition, in press; Vygotsky, 1978). From this perspective it is claimed that children first experience a particular set of problem-solving activities in the presence of others and only gradually come to perform these functions for themselves. First, the adult (parent, teacher, etc.) guides the child's activity, doing much of the cognitive work herself, but gradually the adult and child come to share the cognitive functions with the child taking initiative and the adult correcting and guiding where the child falters. Finally, the adult allows the child to take over the major thinking role and adopts the stance of a supportive and sympathetic audience.

This developmental progression from social- to individual-cognitive processing (other-regulation to self-regulation) is nicely illustrated in parent–child learning dyads such as those reported by Wertsch (1978). Of particular interest to the argument here are the interactions of mothers and children as they engage in picture-book "reading."

At least in middle-class homes, a stable locus of parent–child interactions is the picturebook task. Ninio and Bruner (1978) observed one mother–infant dyad longitudinally, starting when the child was only 8 months old and terminating (unfortunately) when he was 18 months old. From the very beginning, their interaction can best be described as a dialogue with the timing of mother's and child's behavior following an almost complete alternation pattern strikingly similar to the turn-taking conventions observed in dialogue. The mother initially is very much in command and seduces the child into the ritual dialogue for picture-book reading by accepting any response from the baby as appropriate for his turn in the conversation. Indeed, Ninio and Bruner point out the mother accepts an astonishing variety of responses as acceptable turn-taking behavior interpreting anything as having a "specific, intelligible content." The "imputation of intent and content" to the child's activities constitutes "an important mechanism by which the child is advanced to more adult-like communicative behavior" (Ninio & Bruner, 1978, p. 8).

A dramatic shift in responsibility comes when the child begins to label pictures for himself. Now the mother acts as if she believes the child has uttered words rather than babble. As the mother's theory of the child changes, so does her part in the dialogue. At first she appears to be content with any vocalization, but as soon as actual words can be produced the mother steps-up her demands and asks for a label with the query "what's that?" The mother seems to increase her level of expectation, first "coaxing the child to substitute a vocalization for a nonvocal sign and later a well-formed word for a babbled vocalization." Initially, the mother does all the labeling because she assumes that the child cannot. According to Ninio and Bruner (1978):

> Later, the mother starts a cycle with a label *ONLY* if she thinks that the child will not label the picture himself, either because he does not yet know the correct word or he is not attentive enough to make the effort at labeling. If circumstances seem more favorable for labeling to occur, she will usually start the cycle with a *"What's that?"* question [p. 14].

Responsibility for labeling is transferred from the mother to the child in response to his increasing store of knowledge, finely monitored by the mother. During the course of the study, the mother constantly updated her inventory of the words the child had previously understood and repeatedly attempted to make contact with his growing knowledge base. For example:

1. You haven't seen one of those; that's a goose.
2. You don't really know what those are, do you? They are mittens; wrong time of year for those.
3. It's a dog; I know you know that one.
4. We'll find you something you know very well.
5. Come on, you've learned "bricks."

DeLoache (1983) has repeated many of these observations in a cross-sectional study of mothers reading to their children. The children ranged from 17–38 months. The mothers of the youngest children point to the objects and label them sometimes providing some additional information. In the middle age group, the children are much more active. Their mothers ask them to point to and label objects and to provide other information about the picture. These children often spontaneously provide labels ("There's a horsie.") or ask the mothers for labels ("What's this?") In the oldest group studied, more complex stories were introduced, and the mothers do much more than simply label objects. They talk about the relation among the objects in the picture and relate them to the child's experience (e.g., "That's right, that's a bee hive. Do you know what bees make? They make honey. They get nectar from flowers and use it to make honey, and then they put the honey in the bee hive."). When the child can recognize the pictures and knows something about them, the mother uses the material to provide the child with a great deal of background information only loosely related to the actual pictures. It is not simply that the amount of help changes as the child becomes more competent, but the quality of help is finely geared to the child's current level.

In both the Ninio and Bruner and DeLoache dyads, the mother is seen functioning repeatedly in the child's "region of sensitivity to instruction" (Wood & Middleton, 1975) or "zone of proximal development" (Vygotsky, 1978). As the child advances so does the level of collaboration demanded by the mother. The mother systematically shapes their joint experiences in such a way that the child will be drawn into taking more and more responsibility for the dyad's work. In so doing the mother not only provides an optimal learning environment, she also models appropriate comprehension-fostering activities such as elaboration, activating appropriate background knowledge, and questioning strategies. These crucial activities are thereby made *overt* and *explicit*.

Inadequate Early Mediated Learning

It has been argued that parent–child interactions such as the social-reading experiences just described are important preparations for early school success. It has also been argued that a severe lack of such interactive experiences is a primary source of academic retardation. A leading advocate of this position is Feuerstein (1979, 1980), who argues that cognitive growth is very heavily dependent on the quality of *mediated learning* that the child experiences. According to Feuerstein (1979): "Mediated learning is the training given to the human organism by an experienced adult who frames, selects, focuses, and feeds back an environmental experience in such a way as to create appropriate learning sets [p. 6]." These mediated-learning experiences are an essential aspect of development beginning when the parent selects significant objects for the infant to focus on and proceeding throughout development with the adult systematically shaping the child's learning experiences. Feuerstein believes that this is the principal means by which children develop the cognitive operations necessary for learning independently. By interacting with an adult, who models and guides problem-solving activities and structures learning environments, children gradually come to adopt structuring and regulating activities of their own. It is argued that cognitive skills, including those of comprehension-fostering and monitoring, develop normally via a process whereby the adult models and prompts their use and the children gradually adopt such activities as part of their own repertoire.

Feuerstein believes that the principal reason for the poor academic performance of many disadvantaged students is the lack of consistent instruction by parental models in their earlier developmental histories because of parental apathy, ignorance, or overcommitment. Quite simply, parents in disadvantaged homes were often themselves disadvantaged children and cannot be expected to teach what they perhaps do not know; large family size and the need for a working mother do not leave a great deal of time for Socratic dialogue games. In addition, interactive styles of continually questioning and extending the limits of knowledge that are typical of middle-class social-interaction patterns (Ninio & Bruner, 1978) may even be alien to some cultures (Au, in press; Bernstein, 1971).

Mediated-learning activities, however, are exactly what occur in schools, and the middle-class child comes well-prepared to take part in these rituals. Not only does the disadvantaged child lack sufficient prior exposure, but there is evidence that teachers give less experience in this learning mode to those who, because of their lack of prior experience, need it most.

SCHOOL READING EXPERIENCES

Teachers as Models of Reading Strategies

Ideally when the child reaches school, teachers take over some of the mediating functions acting as models and promotors of comprehension-fostering activities. In schools, effective teachers are those who engage in continued prompts to get children to plan and monitor their own reading activities. Effective teachers model many forms of critical thinking for their students (Collins & Stevens, 1982). Thus, Collins and Smith's (1982) recent call for teachers to model comprehension-monitoring activities is timely but not novel. In a recent review of the literature, Bird (1980) traces the history of this idea and points out that it is a recurrent theme in the reading-education literature. For example, Lorge (1957) stressed that the teacher should model active-comprehension processes and direct the child's attention to the thinking and reasoning processes that he/she engages in while reading for meaning. Smith (1961) also called for teachers to ask questions that stimulate the drawing of inferences, the making of predictions and of comparisons, and the use of cause and effect reasoning. This theme was repeated by King (1967) and Gantt (1970), who described programs of teacher-directed questioning by which children are led through the sequence of thinking necessary to understand the passage. Similarly, Schwartz and Scheff (1975) suggested that teachers encourage active reading by demonstrating their own curiosity, posing questions, reasoning, predicting, and verifying inferences and conclusions.

Good teachers do this, of course. Even teachers who refrain from such activities in Reading Group do demonstrate them in, for example, reading a story to the whole class (Griffin, 1977). In their discussion of why teachers are easier to understand than texts, Schallert and Kleiman (1979) identified four main activities that teachers use to help children understand. They tailor the message to child's level, activate relevant background knowledge, focus student attention on main points, and force comprehension monitoring by probing and question asking aimed at testing the degree of understanding.

The main theme of all this work is that the ideal teacher functions as a model of comprehension-fostering and monitoring activities largely by activating relevant knowledge and questioning basic assumptions. These are the essential features of the teaching style referred to variously as Socratic, case, or inquiry methods. Collins and Stevens (1982) have examined a variety of teachers and developed a taxonomy of tactics that are commonly used by outstanding teachers, notably the "entrapment ploys" of counterexamples and invidious generalizations, the "extension ploys" that force students to apply their newfound knowledge broadly, and the "debugging ploys" that force students to correct their misconceptions (Collins & Stevens, 1982).

Collins and Stevens point out that a main goal of such dialogues is not to convey the content of a particular domain; if this were the aim, the method would be inefficient due to the low rate of information transfer; more points can be conveyed in a lecture than can be discussed in a Socratic dialogue. If the method is successful, it is because it teaches students to think scientifically, to make predictions, to question and evaluate. An effective aid to knowledge building and revision is the ploy of forcing learners to make their theories explicit and to defend them to others.

In order for these activities of questioning, predicting, hypothesis generation, testing and revision to be of service to the child, it is necessary that they are transferred from the teacher to the child in such a way that they form part of the learner's battery of comprehension-fostering skills. A common problem with all these approaches, as pointed out by Jenkinson (1969) and Gall (1970) is that they presuppose that children witnessing these activities will come to employ them on their own. This is the problem of *internalization*, how the child comes to use personally activities that were originally social (Vygotsky, 1978). We return to this point later.

Reading Groups and Reading Status

Not all children are exposed to gifted teachers, and even the same teachers may offer different learning environments to those viewed as good or poor readers (Brown, Palincsar, & Purcell, in press). The selection of a curriculum is itself the selection of a particular reading environment. Bartlett (1979) claimed that disadvantaged children are most likely to be exposed to early-reading programs with a heavy emphasis on decoding such as Distar, whereas middle-class children receive earlier exposure to programs that emphasize comprehension such as Open Court. Bartlett goes on to compare the types of questions featured prominently in

Distar exercises to those recommended by Open Court. In general, the Distar questions tend to focus on locating and remembering specific information, whereas the Open Court questions promote reflection upon and the questioning of the meaning of the text. Hence, a different type of instruction is aimed at children who enter school differentially prepared for the experience.

Even if the curriculum and classroom placement do not differ, there remains evidence that the reading environment is not equal for all children. For example, detailed observations of reading groups (Allington, 1980; Au, 1980; Cazden, 1979; Collins, 1980; McDermott, 1978) have shown that good and poor readers are not treated equally. Good readers are questioned about the meaning behind what they are reading, and they are asked to evaluate and criticize material frequently. A considerable amount of time in the good reading group is "on task", i.e., reading-related activities occur, and a sizable amount of the group activities are of an optimal "comprehension-fostering" type. In the good reading group, the teacher adopts the procedure of asking every child to read in turn; but in the poorer reading group, turn-taking is at the teacher's request, and the really poor readers are not called upon to perform to save everyone embarrassment (McDermott, 1978). Precious little time in the poor reading group is spent doing comprehension-fostering activities; the lion's share of activities involve the establishment of such rituals as turn taking and hand raising. When and if they are required to read, poor readers receive primarily drill in pronunciation and decoding. Rarely are they given practice in qualifying and evaluating their comprehension (Allington, 1980; Collins, 1980). A case could even be made that the poorest readers receive little formal reading-comprehension instruction in these groups (McDermott, 1978)!

Children who come to school inadequately prepared for reading, for whatever reason, tend to end up on the bottom reading groups and are, therefore, exposed to different reading experiences. The emphasis is clearly on decoding and not on comprehension. If as a result of their initial failure and subsequent treatment these children are singled out for special education, they run the risk of an intensive version of this same treatment; for special education in reading problems has an even heavier emphasis on decoding skills at the expense of reading-comprehension instruction.

A strong emphasis on direct instruction in basic skills permeates resource rooms and special-education classrooms, perhaps an understandable reaction to the "lack" of these skills demonstrated by the students. Special-education classes are more likely to provide step–by–step instruction for students in basic skills (decoding, etc.) and rarely allow the students to figure out meanings or question their assumptions. Heavily programmed and guided learning of this type may be a practical and efficient means of getting less successful students to perform better on a particular task, i.e., word recognition. But it is the teacher, not the child, who is making all the learning decisions. Such experience is less likely to be the appropriate procedure for promoting insightful learning. Students may learn something about a particular task, but they are less likely to learn how to learn from reading (Brown, 1982).

Of course we are not arguing against the practice of direct instruction in decoding per se. As Resnick (1979) has pointed out, there is a great deal of evidence to support the success of reading programs that favor early direct instruction of decoding. We do argue, however, that instruction in comprehension can and should be offered in addition (Tharp, 1982). Because the current state of affairs is that poor readers, particularly those labeled as learning disabled or mildly retarded, are unlikely in the present system to develop adequate reading-comprehension skills. Decoding is mastered eventually, but reading-comprehension scores remain low and possibly permanently and severely depressed. Many factors may be responsible for this typical pattern, but one that is rarely addressed is the simple explanation of practice. Practice makes possible; if so, perhaps we should not be surprised to find a cumulative deficit in comprehension skills in those who are systematically denied extensive experience in comprehension-fostering activities.

In summary, following repeated experience with experts (parents, caretakers, teachers, etc.) who situate, elaborate, evaluate, and extend the limits of their experience, many students develop a battery of school-relevant autocritical skills (Binet, 1909; Brown, in press) that include comprehension-fostering activities ideally tailored for reading. These skills are essential acquisitions if students are to learn how to learn independently. If for some reason the child is deprived of a constant history of such interaction in and out of school, the development of an adequate battery of self-regulatory skills for performing independently on academic tasks may be impeded.

Given this argument, an appropriate training experience would be to attempt to mimic naturally occurring interactive-learning settings as a context for instruction. In a subsequent section a series of experiments is reviewed that may have promise for improving comprehension skills precisely because they attempt to help children adopt for themselves questioning and monitoring activities that they experience initially in interactive settings.

Comprehension-Fostering Activities

Before proceeding to a discussion of instruction, an attempt is made to be somewhat more explicit about the nature of the comprehension processes involved in effective reading. We concentrate on those that promote comprehension and lead to effective comprehension monitoring, i.e., activities engaged in by readers to ensure that comprehension is proceeding smoothly. Although far from a detailed task analysis of reading comprehension, there are several overlapping skills that have been mentioned repeatedly as prime comprehension-fostering activities in a variety of recent theoretical treatments (Baker & Brown, in press-a, in press-b; Brown, 1980; Collins & Smith, 1982; Dansereau, 1980; Markman, 1981). These activities include:

1. Clarifying the purposes of reading, i.e., understanding the task demands, both explicit and implicit.
2. Activating relevant background knowledge.
3. Allocating attention so that concentration can be focused on the major content at the expense of trivia.
4. Critical evaluation of content for internal consistency and compatibility with prior knowledge and common sense.
5. Monitoring ongoing activities to see if comprehension is occurring by engaging in such activities as periodic review and self-interrogation.
6. Drawing and testing inferences of many kinds, including interpretations, predictions, and conclusions.

All of these activities appear as academic tasks in their own right; for example, it is a common practice to call on children to concentrate on the main idea, to think critically about the content of what they are reading, to summarize or answer questions on a passage. But, in addition, these activities, if engaged in while reading, serve to enhance comprehension and afford an opportunity for the student to check whether it is occurring. That is, they can be both *comprehension-fostering* and *comprehension-monitoring* activities if properly used. Self-directed summarization is an excellent comprehension-fostering and monitoring technique (Brown & Day, 1983; Brown, Day, & Jones, 1983; Day, 1980; Linden & Wittrock, 1981). Monitoring one's progress while reading, to test whether one can pinpoint and retain imporant material, provides a check that comprehension is progressing smoothly. If the reader cannot produce an adequate synopsis of what is being read, this is a clear sign that comprehension is *not* proceeding smoothly and that remedial action is called for.

Similarly, self-directed questioning concerning the meaning of text content leads students to a more active monitoring of their own comprehension (André & Anderson, 1978-79). Thus, closing one's eyes (metaphorically) and attempting to state the gist of what one has read and asking questions of an *interpretive* and *predictive* nature (Collins & Smith, 1982) are activities that both improve comprehension and permit students to monitor their own understanding. These are also the kinds of active and aggressive interactions with texts that poor readers do not engage in readily; the need for explicit instruction in comprehension-enhancing activities is particularly acute for the slow-learning student (Brown & Palincsar, 1982).

INSTRUCTING READING COMPREHENSION

Teaching Settings and Reading Strategies

In this section a series of successful training studies is described which attempt to combine a knowledge of effective teaching settings and appropriate learning activities in order to improve comprehension (Palincsar & Brown, 1983). We have argued that many students lack sufficient practice in interactive-learning situations where comprehension-fostering activities are modeled and promoted. If this were true, then an obvious compensatory strategy would be to design instruction where practice in the essential skills is embedded within an interactive-learning situation that mimics the idealized mother–child, teacher–child dialogues previously described.

The particular skills selected for training were *summarizing* (self-review), *questioning, clarifying* and *predicting*. There is a large literature connected with each activity. A considerable amount is known about the use or nonuse of these activities in isolation, especially in response to direct instruction. But considerably less is known about the spontaneous orchestration of a battery of such activities in the face of different forms of comprehension failure. For example, high-school and junior-college students have a great deal of trouble writing adequate synopses of texts (Brown & Day, 1983); although well-designed training can improve these skills (Day, 1980). Very little is known, however, about the use of self-directed paraphrasing as a method of periodic review or as a means of monitoring comprehension when the text gets difficult. Also, young and poor readers have difficulty evaluating texts for clarity, internal consistency, or compatibility with known facts (Markman, 1981), and training helps here too (Markman & Gorin, 1981). But again, little is known about where and when and with what actual processes the reader will engage in such monitoring spontaneously. Similarly, students often fail to generate questions and can be trained to perform better on these skills in isolation (André & Anderson, 1978-79), but little is known about the spontaneous use of questioning as part of a concerted, personally-designed and coordinated plan of attack in the face of comprehension difficulties. Therefore, in this series of studies the four activities of self-directed summarizing (review), questioning, clarifying and predicting are combined in a package of activities with the general aim of enhancing understanding. Each ''separate'' activity, however, was used in response to a concrete problem of text comprehension. Clarifying occurred only if there were confusions either in the text (unclear referent, etc.) or in the student's interpretation of the text. Summarizing was modeled as an activity of self-review; it was engaged in in order to state to the group what had just happened in the text and as a test that the content had been understood. If an adequate synopsis could not be reached, this fact was regarded *not* as a failure to perform a particular decontextualized skill but as an important source of information that comprehension was not proceeding as it should and remedial action (such as re-reading or clarifying) was needed. Questioning, similarly, was not practiced as a teacher-directed isolated activity, but as a concrete task—what question would a teacher or test ask about that section of the text. Students reacted very positively to this concrete detective work, rather than the more typical isolated skills–training approach as we will see.

We embedded these activities within a training procedure that was very similar to the interactive mother–child, teacher–student dyads described earlier. The procedure was also similar to that of reciprocal questioning. Manzo (1969) introduced a variant of this with his *ReQuest* procedure. Teachers and small groups of remedial-reading students took turns asking themselves questions about what they were reading. Questions followed every sentence, a procedure that would not encourage synthesis across larger segments of text. And the types of questions modeled and generated were not necessarily optimal. For example, one teacher modeled the question, ''What was the third word in the first sentence?'' Even so, Manzo reported significant improvement in standardized reading-comprehension scores. Frase and Schwartz (1975) also had college students taking turns generating or answering questions. Regardless of which role the students assumed, they performed better than when engaged in silent reading. Even though training was not extensive and again there was no attempt to ensure adequate quality of questions, the intervention produced a modest but reliable effect. Given these promising precursors, a reciprocal teaching method was adopted where, in addition to question generation, the activities of reciprocal paraphrasing, clarifying, and predicting were added.

Instructing Comprehension-Fostering by Reciprocal Teaching

So far three studies have been completed (Palincsar & Brown, 1983). The first two are laboratory studies with an experimenter (Palincsar) interacting with individual children or with pairs of students. The third study was conducted in the classroom by regular classroom teachers. The students in all three studies were seventh graders with average decoding skills but seriously deficient comprehension scores.[1]

Study 1

In Study 1, four students served as subjects in an extensive training experiment (for full details see Palincsar & Brown, 1983). Each subject served as his or her own control. After completing the decoding and comprehension tests that made them eligible for the study, the students received a period of baseline assessment, on each day of which they read a 500-word expository passage and then attempted to answer 10 comprehension questions independently. This baseline procedure of reading and answering questions on a novel assessment passage each day was also followed during maintenance and long-term follow-up periods. During training periods the students also read and answered questions on a

---

[1]The students were of low-normal intelligence (mean IQ 84) and low socio-economic status. Their decoding was judged adequate as they could read grade-appropriate texts at a rate of 80–100 wpm with no more than two errors per minute. Their standardized reading comprehension scores averaged 3 years delayed.

novel assessment passage, but the assessment stage was preceded by interactive training sessions on still different passages. All data reported are percent correct from the daily independent-assessment test, *not* from the interacted-upon texts.

There were 6–8 days of initial baseline, 10 days of reciprocal teaching, followed by 6 days of maintenance and then a further 3 days of reciprocal teaching. Six months later, the students were retested for 8 days, 4 days of untreated maintenance followed by 2 days where reciprocal teaching was reintroduced, which was followed in turn by a final 2 days of maintenance.[2]

During the reciprocal-teaching intervention, the investigator and the student engaged in an interactive-learning game that involved taking turns in leading a dialogue concerning each segment of text. If the passage were new, the investigator called the student's attention to the title, asked for predictions based upon the title, and discussed the relationship of the passage to prior knowledge. For example, if the passage were entitled *Ship of the Desert,* the investigator and student would speculate about what the passage might concern and would review what they knew about the characteristics of the desert. If the passage were partially completed, the investigator asked the student to recall and state the topic of the text and several important points already covered in the passage.

The investigator then assigned a segment of the passage to be read (usually a paragraph) and either indicated that it was her turn to be the teacher or assigned the student to teach that segment. The investigator and student then read the assigned segment silently. After reading the text, the teacher for that segment summarized the content, discussed and clarified any difficulties, asked a question that a teacher or test might ask on the segment, and finally made a prediction about future content. All of these activities were embedded in as natural a dialogue as possible with the teacher and student giving feedback to each other.

Throughout the interventions, the students were explicitly told that these activities were general strategies to help them understand better as they read and that they should try to do something like this when they read silently. It was pointed out that being able to say in your own words what one has just read and being able to guess what the questions will be on a test are sure ways of testing oneself to see if one has understood.

At first the students had difficulty taking their part in the dialogue, experiencing particular difficulties with summarizing and formulating questions. The adult teacher helped with a variety of prompting techniques such as "What question did you think a teacher might ask?"; "Remember, a summary is a shortened version, it doesn't include detail"; "If you're having a hard time summarizing, who don't you think of a question first?"

---

[2]In Study 1, another group of students received a second intervention, locating information (see Palincsar & Brown, 1983, for details), where they were trained to answer comprehension questions by using the text intelligently. These students did improve from their starting level of 15% to approximately 50%, but they never reached the level of the reciprocal-teaching group, and they failed to maintain this level over time.

The adult teacher also provided praise and feedback specific to the student's participation: "You asked that question well; it was very clear what information you wanted"; "Excellent prediction, let's see if you're right"; "That was interesting information. It was information that I would call detail in the passage. Can you find the most important information?" After this type of feedback, the adult teacher modeled any activity that continued to need improvement: "A question I would have asked would be . . ."; "I would summarize by saying . . ."; "Did you find this statement unclear?"

Initially, then, the experimenter modeled appropriate activities, but the students had great difficulty assuming the role of dialogue leader when their turn came. The experimenter was sometimes forced to resort to constructing paraphrases and questions for the students to mimic. In this initial phase, the experimenter was modeling effective comprehension-monitoring strategies, but the student was a relatively passive observer.

In the intermediate phase, the students became much more capable of playing their role as dialogue leader and by the end of 10 sessions were providing paraphrases and questions of some sophistication. For example, in the initial sessions, 46% of questions produced by the students were judged as nonquestions or as needing clarification. By the end of the sessions only 2% of responses were judged as either needing clarification or nonquestions. Unclear questions drop out and are replaced over time with questions focusing on the main idea of each text segment. Examples of questions judged to be needing clarification, main idea, and detail are shown in TABLE 8.1

A similar improvement was found for summary statements. At the beginning of the sessions, only 11% of summary statements captured main ideas, whereas at the end 60% of the statements were so classified. Examples of summary statements are shown in TABLE 8.2.

With repeated interaction with a model performing appropriate questioning and paraphrasing activities, the students became able to perform these functions on their own. Over time the students' questions became more like the tutor's, being classified as *inventions*, that is, questions and summaries of gist in one's own words, rather than selections, repetitions of words actually occurring in the text (Brown & Day, 1983). For example, an early occurring form of question would be to take verbatim from the text "plans are being made to use nuclear power" and append the question with the inflection "for what?" Later forms of questioning were more likely to be paraphrases of the gist in the students' own words. For example, reading a passage about fossils, one student posed the following question: "When an animal dies, certain parts decay, but what parts are saved?" This question was constructed by integrating information presented across several sentences. Given the steady improvement on the privately read texts, it would appear that students internalize these activities as part of their own repertoire of comprehension-fostering skills. In support of this statement are the data from peer tutoring sessions taken at the termination of the study. Trained

TABLE 8.1
Examples of Student-Generated Questions During
Reciprocal Teaching

Main Idea Questions

Why don't people live in the desert?
Why are the grasslands of Australia ideal for grazing?
What does the light on the fish do?
What did these people (the Chinese) invent?
Plans are being made to use nuclear power for what?
What are three main problems with all submarines?
Is there just one kind of explosive?
What are one of the things people used explosives for?
What are the Phillipine officials going to do for the people?

Questions Pertaining to Detail

How far south do the maple trees grow?
What color is the guards' uniforms?
How many years did it take to build the Great Wall?
What are chopsticks made out of?
Tell me where the cats hide?
What was the balloon material made of?
What (on the fish) overlaps like shingles on a roof?
How far can flying fish leap?
What is the temperature along the southern shores of Australia?

Questions Requiring Clarification
(and Suggested Appropriate Questions Regarding the Same Material and Ideas)

What was uh, some kings were uh, about the kings? (Why is it that kings did not always make
   the best judged?)
What were some of the people? (What kinds of people can serve on a jury?)
What was the Manaus built for? Wait a minute. What was the Manaus built for, what certain
   kind of thing? Wait a minute. O.K. What was the Manaus tree built for? (Why was the city of
   Manaus built?)
What does it keep the ground? (What effect does snow have on the ground?)
What are the Chinese people doing today, like . . . What are they doing? (Why are the Chinese
   people rewriting their alphabet today?)
There's you know, like a few answers in here and one of my questions is, uh, anything that
   burns and explodes can be fast enough to . . . See, they got names in here. O.K.? (Name
   some explosives.)
In Africa, India, and the Southern Islands where the sun shines what happens to the people? You
   know, like . . .? (Why do people who live in Africa, India and the Southern Islands have dark
   skin?)

TABLE 8.2
Examples of Student-Generated Summary Statements During
Reciprocal Teaching

Main Idea Statements

It says if a man does his job real good, then he will do better in his next life.
I learned that they have different kinds of Gods, not just Brahman, every family has their own.
It tells us about the two kinds of camels, what they are like and where they live.
My summary is that the part of the earth that we live on and see and know is the top layer, the
  crust.
This paragraph talks about what happens when people perspire or sweat. They lose a large
  amount of salt and they get weakness.

Detail Statements

It is a pair of fins which look like legs.
The sea horse always swims head up.
There were large lizzards and four eyed fish and 30 foot dandelion.
What I learned is that a submarine went around the world in 84 days.
I learned that Cousteau's first artificial island was in the North Sea.
Professor Charles went 27 miles and rose 2,000 feet in his balloon.
They (the aborigines) don't wear much clothes on.
They (Egyptians) made bread a long time ago.

Incomplete Statements and Corresponding Text Segment

They talk about it was the richest island; but it didn't have something, o.k., it was the richest
  island but didn't have everything. They didn't have something. (Although this was a very rich
  land, no people lived there.)
If you pick a cherry branch in the winter you will have luck hoping they will bloom early. (If
  you pick a cherry branch in the winter, you will have no luck with it blooming.)
And uranium can be making explosion that equals a skyscraper. (A small amount of uranium can
  cause an explosion as great as a skyscraper full of dynamite.)

Examples of Student-Generated Critical/Evaluative Comments

"Boy, the paragraph sure is a mess. It is all over the place."
"I don't see how they can say "heat lightning occurs on hot summer days.' How could you see
  it?"
"It says here 'cloud to cloud' then 'cloud to earth.' Wouldn't that be the same thing?"
"The word 'meter' throws me off in this sentence."
"What's the difference between soap and detergent anyway?"
"At first I didn't get this because I thought the word 'pumping' was 'bumping.' "
"I don't know what 'omitting' is."
"I have one, what do they mean by 'far away dreams?' "

tutees faced with naive peers did attempt to model main idea paraphrase and questions (Palincsar & Brown, work in progress).

In addition to the qualitative changes in the students' dialogues, there was a gratifying improvement in the level of performance on the daily assessment question–answering score. The students averaged 15% correct during baseline. After the introduction of the reciprocal teaching, the students reached accuracy levels of 80–90% correct. This level was durable across both the maintenance and brief reintroduction of the intervention. After the 6 month delay, the students averaged 60% correct without help, significant savings over their original level of 15%. After only 1 day of renewed reciprocal teaching, the performance of two students returned to 80% and for the the remaining students it reached 90% correct; again, the levels were maintained when the intervention was removed. Remember that these scores were obtained on the *privately read* assessment passages, i.e., different texts that the students read independently after their interaction with the instructor. What was learned during the instructional sequence was used independently by the learners.

Generalization to Classroom Settings.   Throughout the study a series of five probes was made in the social studies classroom setting to see if the students would show any improvement on the identical task of answering 10 comprehension questions on a test. The students were not told that these tests, administered by the classroom teacher, had anything to do with the intervention. All seventh graders took the social studies tests as part of their regular classroom activity. The experimental students began the study below the 15th percentile on this task compared with the remaining seventh graders in their school. Performance fluctuated widely, which was not surprising as little was done to promote generalization to the classroom, e.g., the classroom teaching did not encourage the use of strategies and the students received no feedback regarding classroom performance. However, the following mean gains in percentile ranks were obtained between the baseline and final probes: Student 1 = 20, Student 2 = 46, Student 3 = 4, and Student 4 = 34.

In summary, students in Study 1 showed a dramatic improvement in their ability to answer comprehension questions on independently read texts. This improvement was durable in the resource-room setting and showed some tendency to generalize to the classroom setting. In addition, qualitative improvement in the students' dialogues reflected their increasing tendency to concentrate on questions and summaries of the main idea. The reciprocal-teaching procedure was a powerful intervention for improving comprehension.

Study 2

Encouraged by the success of the initial study, it was decided to replicate the main features of the successful reciprocal-teaching procedure with six additional students, in three groups of two. In addition to group size, the second study also differed from the first in that (1) a criterion level of 75% correct on 4 out of 5 consecutive days was established; (2) students received explicit (graphed) knowledge of results; and (3) tests of transfer were included.

The tests of transfer were selected because it was believed that they tapped the skills taught during the reciprocal teaching, and, pragmatically, because a considerable body of prior work has established "normal" levels of performance for seventh graders. Two of the four transfer tests were measures of the two most frequently engaged in activities during the reciprocal-teaching sessions, *summarizing* (Brown & Day, 1983) and *predicting questions* that might be asked concerning each segment of text. In addition, two other tests were used as measures of general comprehension monitoring, *error detection* (Harris, Kruithof, Terwogt, & Visser, 1981; Markman, 1981), and *rating importance of segments of narratives* (Brown & Smiley, 1977).

There were four phases to the study. As in Study 1, each student was given a daily assessment passage on which he/she answered 10 comprehension questions, and this was all that occurred on baseline and maintenance days. On intervention days the assessment passage was preceded by the reciprocal-teaching intervention, identical to that described in Study 1. The phases of Study 2 were as follows:

1. *Variable baseline* consisting of 4 days for Group 1, 6 days for Group 2, and 8 days for Group 3.
2. *Reciprocal-teaching intervention* consisting of approximately 20 days.
3. *Maintenance* consisting of 5 days of testing at the termination of training.
4. *Long-term follow-up* that took place 8 weeks later (3 days).

All students were appraised of their progress on a daily basis. They were shown graphs depicting the percentage correct for the previous day's assessment.

The data from the daily assessment passages are shown in FIG. 8.1. The six students of Study 2 had baseline accuracy not exceeding 40% correct. They proceeded to make stepwise progression towards means in excess of 75%. Four of the six students reached a stable level of 80% for 5 successive days, taking 12, 11, 11, and 15 days respectively to do it (Students 1, 3, 4, and 6). Student 5 reached criterion of 75% correct in 12 days. Student 2 was the only "failure"; she progressed from a baseline of 12% correct and reached a steady level of 50% correct in 12 days, a significant improvement, but she never approached the criterion level of the remaining five students. All students maintained their improved level of performance on both short- and long-term maintenance tests.

A similar improvement in the quality of the dialogues over time was found in Study 1 and Study 2 (see Palincsar & Brown, 1983, for details). At the outset, students required more assistance with the dialogue, asked more unclear and detailed questions, and made more incomplete/incorrect or detailed summaries

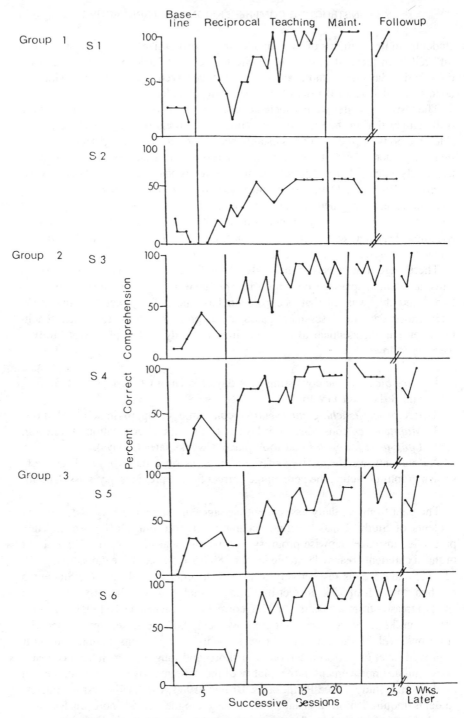

Fig. 8.1. An example of the daily data from individual subjects during baseline, intervention, maintenance and long-term follow-up. These data are taken from the six experimental subjects of Palincsar & Brown (1983), Study 2.

than they did on the last intervention day. Both main-idea questions and para-phrases increased significantly over time.

Students improved at differential rates. For example, Student 6, a minority student whose Slossen test indicated an IQ of 70, made steady but slow progress as indicated by the dialogues shown in TABLE 8.3. The data are taken from Days 1 to 15, the day on which he reached criterion. From a very slow start, this student did achieve an acceptable level of performance both on the dialogues and on his daily assessment passages.

Generalization probes taken in the classroom setting resulted in variable performance but did show clear evidence of improvement. Probes were taken in two settings, social studies and science. At baseline on the social studies probe the range of percentile rankings was .9–43, with four students at or below the fifth percentile. The percentile rankings were typically higher in science with a range of 2–47, four students scoring at or below the 25th percentile. Although performance on these probes was variable, the total mean change in percentile rankings (combined across settings and phases) were: Student 1, 47; Student 2, −.5; Student 3, 26; Student 4, 35.5; Student 5, 40.6; and Student 6, 36. Excluding Student 2, at the conclusion of the study, the range of subjects' mean percentile ranks was 49–76. All students, except Student 2, demonstrated con-siderable generalization to the classroom setting. Student 2 was also the only student who did not reach criterion during the intervention.

Transfer tests were conducted in a pre- and post-test format. It would be impossible to go into all the details of the transfer probes here (see Palincsar & Brown, 1983 for details). Briefly, three of the four tests showed a significant improvement: writing summaries, designing questions to be asked on a test, and error detection using the Harris et al. (1981) procedure. The students did not improve on the Brown and Smiley (1977) task of rating narratives for variations in importance; although they did improve in their ability to select important elements in their summary writing.[3]

To give only the flavor of the transfer results, we consider one test, the question-prediction task. The ability to generate important and clear questions was a skill that received considerable focus during training. A transfer measure was included to assess the accuracy with which students could identify and construct "teacher-like" questions. The students were given four randomly as-signed passages, two prior and two following the study. They were asked to predict and write 10 questions a classroom teacher might ask if testing the student's knowledge of the passage.

---

[3]In Study 2 and 3, there were treated and untreated control groups consisting of students matched with the experimental subjects for decoding and comprehension scores, as well as IQ, standardized tests, and class placement. These students demonstrated no significant change on their performance on the baseline, maintenance and follow-up stages of the study. Neither did they improve their performance on any of the tests of generalization (to the classroom) or transfer (across laboratory tasks). For full details of the control groups included in Studies 1–3, see Palincsar and Brown (1983).

TABLE 8.3
The Acquisition of Question-Asking by One Seventh-Grade Student

---

Day 1:

S: What is found in the southeastern snakes, also the copperhead, rattlesnakes, vipers—they
    have. I'm not doing this right.
T: All right. Do you want to know about the pit vipers?
S: Yeah.
T: What would be a good question about the pit vipers that starts with the word "why?"
S: (No response)
T: How about, "Why are the snakes called pit vipers?"
S: Why do they want to know that they are called pit vipers?
T: Try it again.
S: Why do they, pit vipers in a pit?
T: How about, "Why do they call the snakes pit vipers?"
S: Why do they call the snakes pit vipers?
T: There you go! Good for you.

Day 4:

S: (No question)
T: What's this paragraph about?
S: Spinner's mate. How do spinner's mate . . .
T: That's good. Keep going.
S: How do spinner's mate is small than . . . How am I going to say that?
T: Take your time with it. You want to ask a question about spinner's mate and what he does,
    beginning with the word "how."
S: How do they spend most of his time sitting?
T: You're very close. The question would be, "How does spinner's mate spend most of his
    time? Now you ask it.
S: How does spinner's mate spend most of his time?

Day 7:

S: How does the pressure from below push the mass of hot rock against the opening? Is that it?
T: Not quite. Start your question with "What happens when?"
S: What happens when the pressure from below pushes the mass of hot rock against the opening?
T: Good for you! Good job.

Day 11:

S: What is the most interesting of the insect eating plants, and where do the plants live at?
T: Two excellent questions! They are both clear and important questions. Ask us one at a time
    now.

Day 15:

S: Wh͵ ͻ scientists come to the south pole to study?
T: Excellent question. This is what this paragraph is all about.

The pre- and post-test scores are shown in FIG 8.2 for the students of Study 2 and 3 and also for an untreated control group. The comparison group on the right of the figure represents the level set by average seventh-grade readers on this task. Training brought the level of performance up to that set by the normal comparison group. The graph is designed to illustrate where the improvement was found. Trained students improved in the overall quality of their questions, in the match between their questions and those actually generated by teachers, in their ability to paraphrase rather than lift questions directly from the text, and in their ability to concentrate on the main ideas.

In summary, the main findings of Study 2 were that students diagnosed as experiencing particular problems with reading comprehension improved considerably as a result of taking part in the reciprocal-teaching sessions. All students reached asymptote within 15 days, and for five of the six the level was at 70–80% correct, comparable to accuracy attained by 13 good comprehenders who acted as control subjects. Only Student 2 failed to reach the normal level, but she did improve from 12 to 50% and maintained that level well. Indeed, all of the students maintained their asymptotic level for at least 8 weeks.

In addition to this dramatic increase on the daily comprehension measures, the students improved their percentile ranking in the classroom, gaining an average of 37 percentile points. The quantitative improvement in the ability to answer comprehension questions on texts read in a variety of settings was accompanied by a qualitative improvement in the students' dialogues. Main-idea statements and summaries came to predominate, and unclear, incomplete, or detail responses dropped out.

There was also encouraging evidence of transfer to new tasks. Reliable improvement was found in the ability to use condensation rules for summarizing, in the ability to predict questions that a teacher might ask concerning a text segment, and in the ability to detect incongruous sentences embedded in prose passages.

Study 3

Given the success of Studies 1 and 2, another replication was attempted, but this time the teacher would be a "real" teacher, not an investigator, and the instruction would take place in naturally occurring groups within the school setting. In Study 3, four groups of students were considered, two classroom reading groups for the poorest readers and two reading groups that met regularly in a resource room. The group size ranged from 4–7 students. In all other respects the study was a replica of Study 2.

The teachers received three training sessions. In the first, they were introduced to the rationale behind the reciprocal-teaching intervention and were shown the results of Study 1. They also viewed a videotape of the investigator employing the technique with a group of students.

In the second training session, the teacher and the investigator practiced the

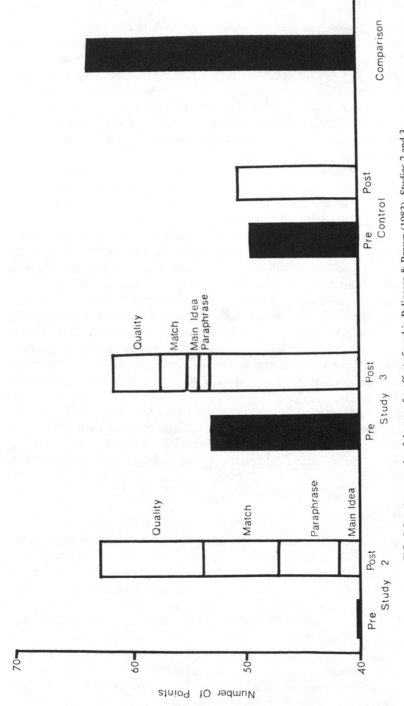

FIG. 8.2. An example of the transfer effects found in Palincsar & Brown (1983), Studies 2 and 3. These data are taken from the Question-Prediction Task. The degree and type of post-test improvement of the experimental subjects is detailed.

procedures privately with the investigator modeling both the teacher's role and behaviors that might be expected from students. Difficulties that could arise were anticipated and discussed such as situations where a student is unable to generate a question or where a student summarizes by reiterating the whole paragraph in detail! Remedial steps were demonstrated.

In the final session, the teacher and the investigator met with a group of seventh graders who were not taking part in the study and practiced the procedure. The investigator modeled how the procedure should be introduced to the students, modeled the four main activities, and the process of feedback. The teachers then assumed responsibility for the group and, as the practice session transpired, the teacher and investigator discussed the proceedings with one another. In addition, the teachers were left with several pages of directions regarding the introduction and daily format of the training sessions. The investigator also checked weekly on the teacher-directed sessions to see if the intervention was being conducted properly. These visits provided further opportunity for discussion and resolution of any difficulties encountered. The students were shown their progress charts on a daily basis during baseline, maintenance, and long-term follow-up and on a weekly basis during intervention, and their improvement was discussed with them. All reciprocal-teaching sessions were tape-recorded.

The four groups of subjects were subjected to different amounts of baseline (from 4–10 days); otherwise, they were treated identically. Individually, the students performed in a manner similar to that found in Study 2 (see Palincsar & Brown, 1983, for full details). All of the subjects in Groups 1–3 individually reached criterion within 15 days. In Group 4, all students reached criteria in 5 days. If one considers the group means, two groups reached criterion in 13 days (Groups 1 and 2) and one in 9 days (Group 3) and one in 5 days (Group 4). It is interesting to note that in Group 4, two of the four students were performing quite well on the first day. The resultant group in some sense consisted of three models, the teacher and the two good students, and two tutees, the remaining two poor students. In this favorable milieu, the poor students rapidly improved, and the entire group reached criterion in 5 days, versus a mean of 12 days for the other groups. Such findings if replicated could have important implications for decisions concerning the composition of the "optimal" reading group. All improvements were maintained over both short- and long-term follow-up sessions.

Quality of Dialogue.   A similar improvement in quality of dialogue was found as in Studies 1 and 2 but was less dramatic in Study 3. In the group settings, the teachers decided to call upon the "better students" in the initial sessions and then gradually to introduce the poorer students into the dialogue as they felt they could handle the responsibility, a natural procedure for experienced teachers. This resulted in a level of student responses that was higher initially and did not improve as dramatically over sessions. The trend was still the same, however, with incomplete or unclear questions decreasing from 20% to 4% and main-idea questions increasing from 57% to 70% across the sessions. Similarly, main-idea summaries increased from 68% to 85% of the total produced by the groups.

Transfer Tests

The same pattern of transfer performance occurred in Studies 2 and 3. Reliable improvements were found on three of the four tests: writing summaries, predicting questions, and error detecting. Again training brought the level of performance up to that set by normal seventh-grade readers.

The Palincsar and Brown series of studies can be regarded as successful for six main reasons:

1. The effect was large and reliable; of the 10 subjects included in Studies 1 and 2, nine improved to the level set by good comprehenders, and all of the subjects in Study 3 met this level.

2. The effect was durable; maintenance probes showed no drop in the level of performance for up to an 8 week period (Studies 2 and 3). Although there was a decline after 6 months (levels dropping from 70–80% to 50–60%), only one session with the reciprocal-teaching procedure was sufficient to raise performance back to the short-term maintenance level (Study 1).

3. The effect generalized to the classroom setting: of the 10 students taking part in Studies 1 and 2, nine showed a clear pattern of improvement, averaging a 36 percentile-rank increase, thus bringing them up to at least the average level for their age mates. Given the difficulty reported in obtaining generalization of trained skills across setting (Brown & Campione, 1978; Meichenbaum & Asarnow, 1978), this is an impressive finding.

4. Training resulted in reliable transfer to dissimilar tasks; summarizing, predicting questions, and detecting incongruities all improved. Again this is an impressive finding given prior difficulty with obtaining transfer of cognitive-skills training (Brown & Campione, 1978; Brown, Campione, & Day, 1981).

5. Sizable improvements in standardized comprehension scores were recorded for the majority of subjects.

6. The intervention was no less successful in natural group settings conducted by teachers than it was in the laboratory when conducted by the experimenter.

TRAINING STUDIES AND THE PROBLEM OF MULTIPLE DETERMINANTS

Let us consider some possible reasons for the success of the Palincsar and Brown studies when so many other attempts have failed to find durability, generalization, and transfer of the effects of training. First, the training was extensive. Second, the activities trained were well-specified theoretically, and well-established empirically as particularly problematic for poor readers. Third, the training was specifically tailored to the needs of these particular students, good decoders but passive comprehenders. Fourth, the skills themselves could reasonably be expected to be trans-situational. Such ubiquitous activities of self-review and self-interrogation are pertinent in a wide variety of knowledge-acquisition tasks.

In addition, a great deal of attention was paid to "metacognitive" variables (Baker & Brown, in press-a): The subjects were fully informed about the reasons why these activities were important; the subjects were given explicit information concerning the generality of the activities and their range of utility; the subjects were trained in self-regulatory activities including the checking and monitoring of their own comprehension; and the skills themselves were general comprehension-monitoring activities applicable in a wide variety of reading/studying tasks.

The reciprocal-teaching mode itself could be responsible for the improvement. The interactive format permits extensive modeling of the target activities in a reasonably natural setting. It also forces the students to participate at whatever level they can so that the teacher can evaluate current states and provide appropriate feedback and assistance (Table 8.3).

Listing all the good points about the Palincsar and Brown studies leads us to the obvious problem of interpretation. The studies are multiply confounded, and this is true to some extent of all of the successful cognitive-training studies to date (Chipman, Segal, & Glaser, in press). For example, would a single activity rather than the package of paraphrasing, questioning, predicting and clarifying have been successful. Component analyses studies currently underway in our laboratory suggest that whereas all of the activities engaged in individually result in improvement, the summary component is the most powerful. The combined package, however, is the most effective intervention.

Similarly, the addition of the metacognitive setting variables may or may not be essential and such variables permit of degrees. For example, in a Ph.D. thesis conducted in our laboratory, Day (1980) trained junior-college students to apply basic rules of summarization and to check that they were using the rules appropriately. The subjects were remedial students who, although of normal reading ability, were diagnosed as having writing problems. There were three main, instructional conditions that varied in how explicit the training was:

1. *Self-Management:* The students were given general encouragement to write a good summary, to capture the main ideas, to dispense with trivia and all unnecessary words—but they were not told rules for achieving this end.
2. *Rules:* The students were given explicit instructions and modeling in the use of the rules of deletion, selection, invention, etc.
3. *Control of the Rules:* The third and most explicit training condition in-

volved training in the rules and additional explicit training in the control of
these rules; i.e., the students were shown how to check that they had a
topic sentence for each paragraph, how to check that all redundancies had
been deleted, all trivia erased, etc., and how to check that any lists of
items had been replaced with superordinates, etc.

An example of the results is shown in Fig. 8.3, where the data from one of the
rules, selection, are shown The degree of post-test improvement was significantly related to the explicitness of training. Merely telling students to stay on
task, be economical, concentrate on main ideas, i.e., the self-management condition, produces significantly less improvement than did direct instruction in
using the specific rules, which in turn was less successful than a combined
package that involved both practice using the task-appropriate rules *and* direct
instruction in monitoring and overseeing their application. In this context it
should be noted that in the Palincsar and Brown studies, the students not only
received modeling of the appropriate comprehension-fostering activities, they
were also explicitly and repeatedly directed to use these activities while reading
on their own.

There is growing evidence that the most successful cognitive-skills training
packages will include three components: (1) *skills* training, practice in the use of
the task appropriate cognitive skills; (2) *self-control* training, direct instruction in
how to orchestrate, oversee and monitor the effective use of the skills; and (3)
awareness training, information concerning the reasons why such strategy use
improves performance and detailed instruction in when and where the strategies
should be used. For practical reasons, interventions should include all these
factors (Brown & Palincsar, 1982), but for theoretical reasons, we need to
conduct component analyses of the separate effect of all three forms of metacognitive settings (Brown, Bransford, Ferrara, & Campione, 1983).

The reciprocal-teaching package is also multiply confounded. Would modeling alone, feedback alone, or just explicit instruction be as effective? Such
component analyses studies are currently underway in our laboratory. Preliminary evidence again favors the combined package (see also Bird, 1980), but
more data are needed.

From a practical standpoint, the results of the required component analyses
would be helpful in permitting the streamlining of the training packages into
efficient and economical units. From a theoretical perspective, we need considerable further research before we can attribute the success of the intervention
appropriately. Of course, it could be that multiply confounded interventions are
needed, because successful reading comprehension is a multiply determined
outcome, i.e., effective comprehension rests on the interaction of a number of
"separate" activities. Given the typically limited outcome of restricted cognitive-skills training studies (Brown, Campione, & Day, 1981), we advocate the
procedure of *first* obtaining an educationally relevant, sizable, durable, and

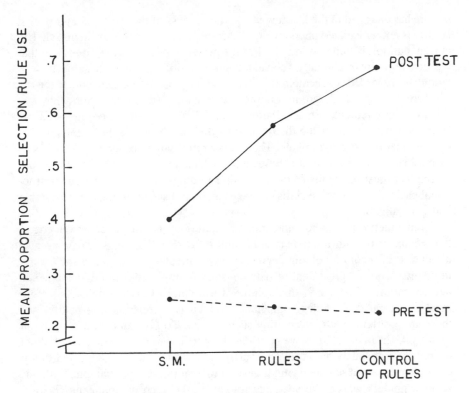

FIG. 8.3. An example of the type of improvement found as a result of the explicitness of training. These data are taken from Day (1980) and depict the pre- and post-test results on the selection rule of summarization.

generalized effect of training and then conducting the necessary investigations to determine the subcomponents that are primarily responsible for the improvement.

THE THEORETICAL AND PRACTICAL STATUS OF TRAINING STUDIES

Until the middle 1970s, the prognosis of worthwhile educational gains from cognitive-skills training studies was poor. Although some success had been achieved in obtaining improvement on a particular skill in isolation, this improvement was often slight and fleeting, and there was very little evidence of transfer. Maintenance over time, generalization across settings, and transfer within conceptual domains was rarely found. The more difficulties the learner experienced initially, the more fleeting and bounded were the effects of training (Brown & Campione, 1978, 1981; Meichenbaum & Asarnow, 1978). But the picture has changed in the last few years; the success of the Palincsar and Brown studies is not an isolated phenomenon (Chipman, Segal, & Glaser, in press). The current outlook is quite optimistic. From a practical point of view, it is clear that we can train instructionally relevant cognitive skills even with subjects who would be regarded as recalcitrant. This training can be carried out under the pressure of normal classroom settings, and it does result in worthwhile and reliable improvements, in the Palincsar and Brown studies bringing students from the very bottom of the distribution of their age peers to the average set by their normal reading classmates. The necessary research needed now consists of extensions across skills and settings and of "clean-up" operations that would permit us to test the limits of these exciting findings and streamline our instructional packages. Cognitive skills can be trained, and such training can be durable and generalizable.

From a theoretical standpoint, training studies are not just exercises in cognitive engineering with immediate applicability to school settings. They are also direct tests of theory involving degrees of experimental manipulation and control in an area where a great deal of data consist of simple one-shot developmental demonstrations (Chapter 9, this volume, for a detailed discussion of this argument). A great deal of developmental research is correlational in nature, and there are problems with interpreting such results. To give an example from our own work, in many studies we consider the performance of students who do or do not spontaneously adopt an appropriate text-processing strategy, and this is often the major variable carrying a developmental trend. For example, fifth and seventh graders who make adequate rought drafts when paraphrasing (Brown, Day, & Jones, 1983) or spontaneously underline or take notes of important text elements, and so on (Brown & Smiley, 1978), perform as well as the majority of twelfth graders, whereas twelfth graders who fail to employ these activities perform more like fifth graders. This pattern suggests that it is the strategy that leads to efficiency, and developmental trends showing improvement with age are created by the increased proportion of strategic subjects. This is a reasonable interpretation, but as the data are primarily correlational, the interpretation is not that simple. It could be that the young, spontaneous strategy users are the more efficient children in general and would perform better than their peers on any task and on the particular task in question without the use of strategies. Even partialling out ability factors such as IQ or reading scores does not totally bypass this problem.

The training study is then an important tool for providing convergent evidence of the importance of the strategy under consideration. First, the theorist speculates about the underlying processes involved in reading comprehension. Next, is the correlational step; students who read well are also found to perform well on the identified underlying processes, whereas poor readers experience particular difficulty on just these activities (Armbruster, Echols, & Brown, 1982; Baker & Brown, in press-a, in press-b; Brown & Palincsar, 1982). Finally, students who are not using the strategy are given training designed to induce the use of processes theoretically specified as key activities underlying efficiency. Others are not. If the theory is correct (and training adequate) and these are the underlying effective processes, trained students' performances should become more like that of spontaneous users. There are nontrivial problems with interpreting the outcomes of training studies (Brown & Campione, 1978, 1981), but they do provide an important manipulative tool to aid theory development. Thus from the point of view of both theory development and successful cognitive instruction, training studies such as these reported here are valuable tools for enhancing our understanding of the mechanism of reading comprehension.

ACKNOWLEDGMENT

The preparation of this manuscript was supported in part by Grants HD06864 and HD05951 from the National Institute of Child Health and Human Development and in part by NIE-C-400-76-0116 from the National Institute of Education.

REFERENCES

Allington, R. Teacher interruption behavior during primary-grade oral reading. *Journal of Educational Psychology*, 1980, *72* (3), 371–377.

André, M. D. A., & Anderson, T. H. The development and evaluation of a self-questioning study technique. *Reading Research Quarterly*, 1978–79, *14*, 605–623.

Armbruster, B. B., Echols, C. H., & Brown, A. L. The role of metacognition in reading to learn: A developmental perspective. *Volta Review*, 1982, *84* (5), 45–56.

Au, K. H. *A test of the social organizational hypothesis: Relationships between participation structures and learning to read.* Unpublished doctoral dissertation, University of Illinois, 1980.

Au, K. H. ETR: Start with the experiences of the minority culture child. *The Reading Teacher*, in press.

Baker, L., & Brown, A. L. Cognitive monitoring in reading. In J. Flood (Ed.), *Understanding reading comprehension.* Newark, Del.: International Reading Association, in press.(a)

Baker, L., & Brown, A. L. Metacognition and the reading process. In P. D. Pearson (Ed.), *A handbook of reading research.* New York: Longman, in press.(b)

Bartlett, E. J. Curriculum, concepts of literacy and social class. In L. B. Resnick & P. A. Weaver (Eds.), *Theory and practice of early reading* (Vol. 2). Hillsdale, N.J.: Lawrence Erlbaum Associates, 1979.

Bernstein, B. *Class codes and control* (Vol. 1). London: Routledge & Kegan Paul, 1971.

Binet, A. *Les idées modernes sur les infants.* Paris: Ernest Flammarion, 1909.

Bird, M. *Reading comprehension strategies: A direct teaching approach.* Unpublished doctoral dissertation, University of Toronto, 1980.

Brown, A. L. Metacognitive development and reading. In R. J. Spiro, B. Bruce, & W. Brewer (Eds.), *Theoretical issues in reading comprehension.* Hillsdale, N.J.: Lawrence Erlbaum Associates, 1980.

Brown, A. L. Learning how to learn from reading. In J. Langer & T. Smith–Burke (Eds.), *Reader meets author, bridging the gap: A psycholinguistic and social linguistic perspective.* Newark, Del.: International Reading Association, Dell Publishing, 1982.

Brown, A. L. Mental orthopedics: A conversation with Alfred Binet. In S. Chipman, J. Segal, & R.

Glaser (Eds.), *Thinking and learning skills: Current research and open questions* (Vol. 2). Hillsdale, N.J.: Lawrence Erlbaum Associates, in press.

Brown, A. L., Bransford, J. D., Ferrara, R. A., & Campione, J. C. Learning, remembering, and understanding. In J. H. Flavell & E. M. Markman (Eds.), *Carmichael's manual of child psychology* (Vol. 1). New York: Wiley, 1983.

Brown, A. L., & Campione, J. C. Permissible inferences from cognitive training studies in developmental research. In W. S. Hall & M. Cole (Eds.), *Quarterly Newsletter of the Institute for Comparative Human Behavior, 1978, 2* (3), 46–53.

Brown, A. L., & Campione, J. C. Inducing flexible thinking: A problem of access. In M. Friedman, J. P. Das, & N. O'Connor (Eds.), *Intelligence and learning*. New York: Plenum Press, 1981. cognitive modifiability. Baltimore: University Park Press, 1980.

Brown, A. L., Campione, J. C., & Day, J. D. Learning to learn: On training students to learn from texts. *Educational Researcher, 1981, 10* (2), 14–21.

Brown, A. L., & Day, J.D. Macro-rules for summarizing texts: The development of expertise. *Journal of Verbal Learning and Verbal Behavior, 1983, 22,* 1–14.

Brown, A. L., Day, J. D., & Jones, R. S. The development of plans for summarizing texts. *Child Development,* 1983.

Brown, A. L., & Palincsar, A. S. Inducing strategic learning from texts by means of informed, self-control training. *Topics in Learning and Learning Disabilities, 1982, 2* (1), 1–17.

Brown, A. L., Palincsar, A. S., & Purcell, L. Poor readers: Teach, don't label. In U. Neisser (Ed.), *The academic performance of minority children: A new perspective.* Hillsdale, N.J.: Lawrence Erlbaum Associates, in press.

Brown, A. L., & Smiley, S. S. Rating the importance of structural units of prose passages: A problem of metacognitive development. *Child Development,* 1977, *48,* 1–8.

Brown, A. L., & Smiley, S. S. The development of strategies for studying texts. *Child Development,* 1978, *49,* 1076–1088.

Cazden, C. B. Learning to read in classroom interaction. In L. B. Resnick & P. A. Weaver (Eds.), *Theory and practice of early reading* (Vol. 3). Hillsdale, N.J.: Lawrence Erlbaum Associates, 1979.

Chipman, S., Segal, J., & Glaser, R. (Eds.). *Cognitive skills and instruction.* Hillsdale, N.J.: Lawrence Erlbaum Associates, in press.

Collins, A. M., & Smith, E. E. Teaching the process of reading comprehension. In D. K. Detterman & R. J. Sternberg (Eds.), *How and how much can intelligence be increased.* Norwood, N.J.: Ablex, 1982.

Collins, A. M., & Stevens, A. Goals and strategies of inquiry teachers. In R. Glaser (Ed.), *Advances in instructional psychology* (Vol. 2). Hillsdale, N.J.: Lawrence Erlbaum Associates, 1982.

Collins, J. Differential treatment in reading groups. In J. Cook–Gumperz (Ed.), *Educational discourse.* London: Heinneman, 1980.

Cushenbery, D. C. Building effective comprehension skills. In J. A. Figurel (Ed.), *Reading and realism.* Proceedings of the 13th annual conference of the International Reading Association, Newark, Del.: 1969.

Dansereau, D. F. *Learning strategy research.* Paper presented at NIE–LRDC Conference on Thinking and Learning Skills, Pittsburgh, October 1980.

Day, J. D. *Training summarization skills: A comparison of teaching methods.* Unpublished doctoral dissertation, University of Illinois, 1980.

Deloache J. S. Mother-child picture book reading as a context for memory training. Paper presented at the Society for Research in Child Development meeting. Detroit, April 1983.

Feuerstein, R. *The dynamic assessment of retarded performers: The learning-potential assessment device, theory, instruments, and techniques.* Baltimore: University Park Press, 1979.

Feuerstein, R. *Instrumental enrichment: An intervention program for cognitive modifiability.* Baltimore: University Park Press, 1980.

Frase, L. T., & Schwartz, B. J. Effect of question production and answering on prose recall. *Journal of Educational Psychology*, 1975, *67*, 628–635.

Gall, M. D. The use of questions in teaching. *Review of Educational Research*, 1970, *40*, 707–720.

Gantt, W. N. Questioning for thinking: A teaching strategy that makes a difference for disadvantaged learners. *The Reading Teacher*, 1970, *24*, (1), 12–16; 22.

Griffin, P. How and when does reading occur in the classroom? *Theory into Practice*, 1977, *16*, 376–383.

Harris, P. L., Kruithof, A., Terwogt, M. M., & Visser, P. Children's detection and awareness of textual anomaly. *Journal of Experimental Child Psychology*, 1981, *31*, 212–230.

Jenkinson, M. D. Cognitive processes in reading: Implications for further research and classroom practice. In J. A. Figurel (Ed.), *Reading and realism*. Proceedings of the 13th annual International Reading Association convention. Newark, Del.: The Association, 1969.

King, M. L. Evaluating critical reading. *Forging ahead in reading*. IRA Proceedings, 1967, *12*, 179–185.

Laboratory of Comparative Human Cognition. The zone of proximal development: Where culture and cognition create one another. In J. Wertsch (Ed.), *Culture, communication, and cognition: Vygotskian perspectives*. New York: Cambridge University Press, in press.

Linden, M., & Wittrock, M. C. The teaching of reading comprehension according to the model of generative learning. *Reading Research Quarterly*, 1981, *16*, (1), 44–57.

Lorge, I. *Reading, thinking, and learning*. International Reading Association Proceedings II, 1957, 15–18.

Manzo, A. V. The ReQuest procedure. *Journal of Reading*, 1969, *13* (2), 123–126; 163–164.

Markman, E. M. Comprehension monitoring. In W. P. Dickson (Ed.), *Children's oral-communication skills*. New York: Academic Press, 1981.

Markman, E. M., & Gorin, L. Children's ability to adjust their standards for evaluating comprehension. *Journal of Educational Psychology*, 1981, *83* (3), 320–325.

McDermott, R. P. Kids make sense: An ethnographic account of the interactional management of success and failures in one first-grade classroom (Doctoral dissertation, Stanford University, 1976). *Dissertation Abstracts International*, 1978, *38*, 1505A. (University Microfilms No. 77–18, 265).

Meichenbaum, D., & Asarnow, J. Cognitive-behavioral modification and metacognitive development: Implications for the classroom. In P. Kendall & S. Hollon (Eds.), *Cognitive-behavioral interventions: Theory, research, and procedure*. New York: Academic Press, 1978.

Ninio, A., & Bruner, J. S. The achievement and antecedents of labeling. *Journal of Child Language*, 1978, *5*, 1–15.

Palincsar, A. S., & Brown, A. L. *Reciprocal teaching of comprehension-monitoring activities*. Technical Report #269, Center for the Study of Reading. Univ. of Illinois January 1982.

Resnick, L. B. Theories and prescriptions for early reading instruction. In L. B. Resnick & P. A. Weaver (Eds.), *Theory and practice of early reading* (Vol. 2). Hillsdale, N.J.: Lawrence Erlbaum Associates, 1979.

Schallert, D. L., & Kleiman, G. M. *Some reasons why the teacher is easier to understand than the text book* (Reading Education Report No. 9). Champaign: University of Illinois, Center for the Study of Reading, June 1979. (ERIC Document Reproduction Service No. ED–172 189).

Schwartz, E., & Scheff, A. Student involvement in questioning for comprehension. *The Reading Teacher*, 1975, *29* (2), 150–154.

Smith, N. B. The good reader thinks critically. *The Reading Teacher*, 1961, *15*, 162–171.

Tharp, R. G. The effective instruction of comprehension: Results and description of the Kamehameha Early Education Program. *Reading Research Quarterly*, 1982, *17* (4), 503–527.

Vygotsky, L. S. *[Mind in society: The development of higher psychological processes]* (M. Cole, V. John–Steiner, S. Scribner, & E. Souberman, Eds. and trans.). Cambridge, Mass.: Harvard University Press, 1978.

Wertsch, J. V. Adult–child interaction and the roots of metacognition. *Quarterly Newsletter of the Institute for Comparative Human Development*, 1978, *1*, 15–18.

Wood, D., & Middleton, D. A study of assisted problem solving. *British Journal of Psychology*, 1975, *66*, 181–191.

9 An Analysis of the Outcomes and Implications of Intervention Research

Joseph C. Campione
Bonnie B. Armbruster
University of Illinois

Over the last decade or so, there has been a major change in the kinds of processes many investigators have begun to study and in the materials used in that research. From an emphasis on learning and recall of sets of words or sentences, work is now seen investigating the comprehension and recall of larger segments of language up to and including texts. Rather than being concerned with how people come to learn and remember bits of information provided in relative isolation, current interests emphasize to a greater extent the processes involved in the comprehension of material that is inherently meaningful, such as simple stories and more complex expository text segments.

Some of the trends in this emerging area are similar to those that appeared in prior work in the broad area of memory development. As investigators come to be more complete and confident in their accounts of the processes involved in text understanding, they initiate research in which the goal is to teach students how to improve their comprehension capabilities. As in the earlier memory work, there are two distinct reasons investigators undertake training studies. One, primarily theoretical, is analogous to computer simulation approaches to the study of cognitive processes. If it is possible to use a theoretical model to develop an instructional program to achieve some desired end, for example, understanding a text, then that result reinforces the theoretical approach adopted. If, according to some theory, activity A is an important component of comprehension, then teaching people who do not do so to employ A should enable them to improve their performance. If it does, the guiding theory is inferred to be correct.

The second reason for conducting such research is more practical. Many students seem to have considerable trouble reading and comprehending texts independently. Because such reading is an essential scholastic activity, it is worthwhile in its own right to attempt to develop curricula or programs that serve to improve the comprehension performance of academically poor students. Here theoretical niceties are less important. It is not implied that these (theoretical and practical) approaches are independent. Adequate, specific theory can certainly help practitioners, and the fact that some program does promote comprehension provides important data for the theoretician. Simply, the emphases in the different types of research are different, different experimental designs tend to be used, and the interpretations that result are also likely to be of different kinds.

As interest in instructional research in the comprehension area increases, it seems worthwhile to review some of what has been learned from a decade or more of training studies aimed at evaluating some hypotheses about the nature of developmental and individual differences in memory performance. Keeping these lessons in mind should facilitate any attempts to use instructional methodologies to inform theory development in other domains including comprehension. In the treatment here, concern is placed on both an analysis of the design and interpretation of intervention studies in general and the implications of that analysis for research aimed at fostering comprehension.

In general, intervention research can be divided into two broad categories according to whether the *major* focus of the intervention is on the *learning materials* or the *activities of the learner*. In the first category, the approach to improving student performance is to modify the learning materials. For example, texts might be rewritten to clarify the organization and to call attention to the most important information. If students have difficulty identifying structure and determining main points, this modification should facilitate learning. Chapter 1 (by Meyer) this volume represents an excellent example.

The second category of intervention research focuses on modifying the activities of the learner. Here the goal is to teach certain strategies or procedures that will help the student learn; a good example of such work can be found in Chapter 8 in this volume by Brown, Palincsar, and Armbruster. In contrast to the *materials* emphasis aimed at facilitating the learning of particular text information, the *activities* approach is aimed at fostering learning to learn (Brown, Bransford, Ferrara, & Campione, 1983).

These two approaches represent different *emphases* and are neither independent nor mutually exclusive. For example, providing clearly structured texts could itself result in modifying the students' learning activities. Having learned from exposure to well-written texts to appreciate the effect of clear organization on understanding, students may search out structure in less well-written texts. As another example, students taught an array of comprehension strategies aimed at discovering or imposing structure on poorly prepared prose may benefit even more than untrained students from well-written materials. The most impressive learning outcomes would most likely result from programs involving both high-quality materials and students prepared with the strategies necessary to take maximal advantage of them.

Because of space constraints, the analysis in this chapter is limited to research emphasizing learning activities. However, the approach should apply as well to intervention studies focusing on the learning materials.

ANALYSIS OF INTERVENTION STUDIES:
A MODAL APPROACH

A typical intervention study found in the literature begins with a demonstration of performance differences between two groups of students, designated as less successful (L) and more successful (M). The L and M groups could be children of different ages, retarded vs. nonretarded groups, normally achieving students vs. students with a specific reading disability, etc.; the argument is essentially the same in all cases. To provide a more concrete example, younger children often perform more poorly than older children on memory tasks. To account for the difference, the researcher frequently tenders two hypotheses. The first is in the form of a theoretical task analysis, a specification of the components of adequate performance. In many cases, the task analysis indicates several learning activities or strategies that are critical to adequate memory performance. The second hypothesis is of the form that the observed differential performance is due to differences in the availability or use of one or more of the essential components; as an example, the researcher may assume that the memory differences are attributable to differences in the use of a *rehearsal* strategy.

The researcher then trains some of the L (younger) students in the hypothesized missing component(s) and compared their posttraining performance with that of *untrained* L students and with *untrained* M students. In this example, a group of younger students is trained to use a rehearsal strategy, and then their performance is compared with that of untrained younger students and untrained older students.

If performance of the trained group then increases significantly, the researcher may infer support for both of the guiding hypotheses. First, rehearsal is inferred to be an important component of task performance, for if it were not, performance would not have improved. Second, it is concluded that the differential use of rehearsal was responsible, at least in part, for developmental differences on this task, because the group of students who were performing poorly to begin with are not performing more similarly to the initially more proficient.

A comparison of the trained L and untrained M students provides some further information about the quality or completeness of the task analysis. If the trained L students' performance is still significantly below that of the M group, this is a clear sign that there are other factors associated with efficient performance and involved in the developmental differences, that is, there are as yet other undetermined sources of developmental differences.

An excellent example of the *modal* approach can be found in Butterfield, Wambold, and Belmont (1973). In that work, retarded adolescents were trained to use a cumulative rehearsal strategy; they would repeat several times the first item after it was presented, the first two after presentation of the second, the first three after presentation of the third, etc. The trained subjects improved but not to the level of an untrained M group (in this case, nonretarded adolescents). This result indicated that the task analysis was incomplete. These researchers were also in an enviable position in that a considerable amount was known about the determinants of memory performance; and in their work, the specific patterns of the subjects' responses provided hints about the other components that might be important. Without going into detail, additional training attempts centering on a specific retrieval plan were then undertaken by Butterfield et al. (1973) with the eventual outcome of bringing the retarded subjects' performance to a level comparable to that of nonretarded adolescents, that is, comparative differences between the groups were "eliminated" via the specific training program.

EVALUATION OF THE MODAL APPROACH

Given that the group differences have been eliminated in this way following instruction, it may then be claimed that the importance of the trained activities to adequate performance of the task at hand has been documented and that a very strong theory about the nature of L–M differences on that task has been demonstrated. That is, it may be argued that this result reinforces both the task analysis and the view of individual or group differences. The question then is how valid those claims are likely to be. It is argued later that neither conclusion is appropriate without additional data. However, before dealing with the evaluations of the theoretical task analysis and the nature of group differences, one other issue is briefly mentioned.

Practically Versus Theoretically Motivated Research

Researchers can differ in terms of the initial motivation for doing research. If the aim were the practical one of improving performance to some desirable level, much of the following would be largely irrelevant. If the training program resulted in the desired gains, further theoretical niceties would be of limited interest. Similarly, if the major goal of the research was simply to demonstrate a degree of plasticity in L learners, the research would already be successful. Additional analyses would be nice but not necessary. In fact, some of the following issues might be almost impossible to implement in many practical situations. However, if the research goal were to develop and evaluate theories about the components of adequate or excellent performance and about individual differences in those components, the results of the modal approach cannot alone enable strong endorsements of either of the guiding theories.

Task Analysis

Returning to the case where instruction has brought the L subjects' performance up to that of the M group, the first conclusion that may be drawn is that the instructed activity (rehearsal, for example) is an important component of performance on the task. The argument is that if it were not important, teaching students to use it would not improve their performance. The problem is that it is possible for the rehearsal training to result in improved performance even if the specific activity taught were not itself important. The training could be effective because it influences some other cognitive process that is in fact responsible for the improved performance. For example, training could lead to increased attention to the task or to heightened motivation, and these could be the factors mediating the improved performance. As this issue has been dealt with in a number of other sources (Butterfield, Siladi, & Belmont, 1980), we can simply note that in the memory area, this has not been an enormous problem, as the theories of many of the experimental tasks employed are quite detailed.

For example, in the case of rehearsal strategies, the problem is relatively minor, because whereas attentional or motivational mechanisms can be expected to produce enhanced performance, the increase should be a somewhat general one. Improvements due to rehearsal, in contrast, can be predicted to take a much more specific form. It is possible to specify in some detail the patterns of accuracy and latency that should emerge following training rather than simply to predict that performance will increase. For example, rehearsal-produced improvements should be particularly large on items presented earlier in a series rather than later. It is also possible to predict that rehearsing subjects will differ from nonrehearsing ones in terms of their patterns of self-pausing during study (Belmont & Butterfield, 1971), their overt production of the strategy (Flavell, Beach, & Chinsky, 1966), and the extent to which their accuracy and speed of response should be affected by variations in list structure (Brown, Campione, Bray, & Wilcox, 1973). In the Brown et al. (1973) experiment, all but one of these measures were used, and they all converged on the same conclusions regarding the importance of rehearsal processes, both in leading to excellent performance and in being partly responsible for differences between ability groups. Butterfield et al. (1980) provide a detailed discussion of the process of relating performance variations to specific changes in processing activities.

The modal training study is simple: Students who do not do so spontaneously are told to carry out some specific activity, and their performance after instruction is compared with their pretraining accuracy. In the best studies, information is available not only about what the subjects are told to do, but also direct evidence exists that they have in fact been doing that correctly (Belmont & Butterfield, 1971; Brown et al., 1973). There is also evidence that the quality of execution of the strategy is strongly related to the level of recall. In addition, there is evidence that the improvements in recall accuracy are precisely what would be expected theoretically from a rehearsing subject. As such, the conclusion that the trained activity is an important component of performance on the task is considerably strengthened.

The reason for emphasizing this point here is that the same problem exists in situations where instruction is aimed at improving comprehension processes. In the area of comprehension, in fact, the problem of attributing improvement to the wrong factor is much more acute than in the memory examples, simply because much less is known about comprehension than about deliberate memorization. The general point to be made (Campione & Armbruster, 1983) is that assessments of both strategy execution and the sequelae of instruction be as detailed as possible.

To cite examples of the ways in which more detailed evaluations can facilitate the analyses, consider the following cases. The first involves the importance of data on the quality of strategy execution. Brown and Smiley (1978) were interested in the extent to which students who underlined or took notes while reading a story would show better recall of that story than those who did not. As it turned out, students who carried out these activities did outperform those who did not but only if the underlining and notetaking were done reasonably. Students who underlined randomly, for example, did not perform any better than those who did not underline at all. As those who underlined randomly were primarily those who underlined in response to instructions to underline, one might have inferred from a simple instructional study that underlining is not a useful comprehension-fostering activity. Information about the quality of underlining and its relation to learning and recall provides a much clearer picture of its role in influencing learning than would have been obtained otherwise.

A slightly different type of example is also relevant. Many of the studies involving instruction in comprehension activities have emphasized target processes more complex or multifaceted than has been the case in the memory research. It is thus possible that a *single* intervention could affect any of a number of different component processes. To illustrate, consider the series of studies reported by Palincsar and Brown (1983) and summarized in Brown, Palincsar, and Armbruster (this volume). They sought to increase students' comprehension scores by teaching them to summarize what they had just read, predict the type of questions a teacher might ask on a subsequent test, note inconsistencies and ambiguities, etc. Training was clearly successful, as performance improved dramatically on 10-question comprehension tests administered after students had read a passage independently.

In addition, the experimental design of Palincsar and Brown allowed them to describe the nature of the process changes underlying this improvement in some detail. The design allowed them to monitor the extent to which students actually improved on the target processes throughout training, and there was correspondence between those measures and comprehension scores. Also, they administered a number of transfer tests following the experiment to obtain additional assessments of the extent to which specific processes had been influenced by the intervention. The instructed students showed reliable (pretest to posttest) improvements in summary writing, question prediction, and their ability to detect incongruities, but not in their ability to judge relative thematic importance. The overall package offered by Palincsar and Brown then not only indicates that the training was effective in bringing about substantial improvement, but it also allows an accurate accounting of the more specific changes underlying the overall improvement. It also indicates some areas where the instruction appears to be less effective, thus leading to suggestions about how it might be improved.

Sources of Group Differences

The more interesting interpretive question associated with the modal training study concerns the inference that group differences were due completely or in part to differential use of the instructed activity. This inference rests on the assumption that training was unnecessary for the M students. Consider again the case where the trained L group performs as well as the untrained M group. Presumably, this is because the only difference between the groups was due to variations in use of the instructed activity, a difference eliminated by instructing the L group. The implicit assumption here is that the M group is already using the instructed activity; as a result, they would not improve if training were provided. Training only the L group is sufficient to *equate* the groups' learning activities.

   To evaluate this questionable assumption, the same instruction must be provided to the M group as was given to the L group; that is, it is necessary to employ an age/ability × instruction factorial design. As will be argued, the use of such a design permits stronger conclusions about developmental/comparative differences; it indicates areas where M students can also benefit from training; and it can also facilitate the attempts to account for some situations where instruction is ineffective. In the next section, possible outcomes of training studies using such a factorial design and the implications of these outcomes for theory and practice are explored.

THE AGE/ABILITY × INSTRUCTION FACTORIAL DESIGN: SOME OUTCOMES AND THEIR IMPLICATIONS

To reiterate, the proposed factorial design involves four groups: an L untrained group, an L trained group, an M untrained group, and an M trained group. The design can result in several possible patterns of outcomes, as shown in Fig. 9.1.

Outcomes

One possible outcome is that training will improve performance of the L group but have no effect on the (nonceiling) performance of M students (see Fig. 9.1,

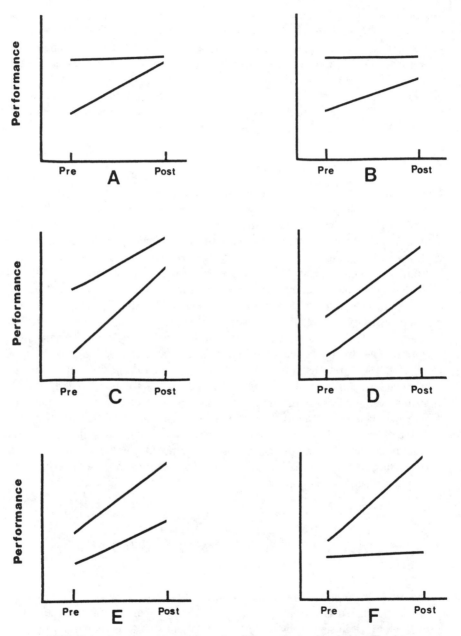

FIG. 9.1. Possible outcomes from the ability × instruction design. The data points on the left of each panel represent performance prior to training; those on the right represent performance following training. The upper curve represents the data of the originally more proficient group; the lower curve depicts the performance of the originally less successful group.

Panel A). This outcome resembles the outcome of the successful modal study discussed previously, but with the factorial design, the interpretation is more straightforward and the conclusion more sound.

Clear examples of the pattern of results represented in Panel A occur in Brown (1973) and Brown, Campione, and Gilliard (1974). In these studies, the tasks involved a judgment of relative recency. Students were shown a series of single pictures followed by a test trial. On the test, two of the previously seen pictures were presented, and the students' task was to indicate which of the two had been seen more recently. If background cues to anchor the temporal series were not provided, younger and older students performed similarly. If background cues were provided, however, the older subjects outperformed the younger, presumably because the older, but not the younger, subjects used the background cues to their advantage. Instruction in how to use the background cues did not change the excellent (but not ceiling) performance of the older subjects, but it did succeed in bringing the younger ones up to a comparable level. This outcome is the strongest possible evidence that differential use of the trained component was a major, if not sole, determinant of developmental differences and that training was largely unnecessary for the older subjects.

Another outcome is displayed in Panel B. In this case, training also affects the performance of the L group, but after training, their performance is still not up to the level achieved by the M group. Training does not improve the performance of the M group. Such a result would indicate that the M subjects were in fact competent with regard to the instructed activity *and* that there are other sources of group differences still to be determined.

Another example of the pattern of results depicted in Panel B comes from research on teaching reading comprehension skills. Hansen and Pearson (1982) trained classroom teachers to provide instruction designed to improve the inferential comprehension ability of good and poor fourth-grade students. One dependent measure was performance on worksheets of literal and inferential questions that accompanied the stories in which the instruction was embedded. Results indicated that the training enhanced the inferential comprehension of poor readers but not of good readers.

Studies reported by André and Anderson (1978–79) provide yet another example of the pattern of results in Panel B. High school students were taught to generate comprehension questions while studying textbook-like prose. The performance of trained students on a constructed response achievement test over a 450-word passage was compared to the performance of untrained students who used a read–reread studying method. Verbal ability, as measured by the Wide Range Vocabulary Test, was used to assign subjects *ex post facto* to three levels. Results revealed a significant treatment × verbal ability interaction: The low-ability trained group scored higher than the low ability untrained group, wheras the high-ability students scored about the same in both the trained and untrained groups.

A third possibility is depicted in Panel C. Both the L and M groups improve following training, but the L group profits from instruction to a greater degree than the M group. One set of possible conclusions from this pattern of results is:

1. The M group was not entirely proficient in the use of the target process (otherwise training would not have helped).
2. Differential use did contribute to the original developmental differences (because equating use did reduce those differences).
3. Other sources of performance variations exist.

A fourth possible pattern, illustrated in Panel D, is that training has the *same* effect on both developmental levels; that is, both the L and M groups exhibit the same increment in performance after training. Although several explanations are possible for such a result, a simple interpretation is that the trained activity was important for performance on the criterion task but that it did not contribute to developmental differences.

As one example, Huttenlocher and Burke (1976) evaluated the hypothesis that developmental differences in digit span were due to the fact that older children grouped the input into richer *chunks*. In a standard condition, they found the usual developmental differences. In a grouped condition, in which the input string was grouped by the experimenter to simulate the chunking presumably done by older subjects, both the younger and older subjects improved and to about the same degree. Thus, the intervention that might have been expected to reduce the developmental difference by being more effective or necessary for the younger group was equally effective for all subjects. Similar effects have been obtained by Lyon (1977) using college students who differed in memory span. Interventions designed to reduce individual differences by providing *expert help* to the lower scorers improved everyone's performance and had no effect on the magnitude of individual differences.

Note that without training the mature students, the results might have been interpreted in the same way as the modal training study. That is, developmental differences would be attributed to differential tendencies to chunk the input, and inducing mature subjects to engage in such chunking would not be deemed necessary or helpful. Both of these conclusions obviously need to be reevaluated. The opinion that the mature students would not benefit from chunking interventions is certainly incorrect, as the effects of the intervention were equal for the mature subjects. Also, if the grouping manipulation does in fact simulate the kinds of organizational processes that are presumed to underlie developmental differences, the parallel improvement result is strong evidence against the chunking hypothesis. Indeed, Huttenlocher and Burke (1976) argued that developmental differences were more likely due to differences in the efficiency with which subjects identified incoming items and/or to the ability to maintain information about order.

The Hansen and Pearson (1982) study mentioned earlier also provides an example of the Panel D pattern of results. Besides worksheets, another dependent measure was performance on literal and inferential questions over a transfer story at a level that could be read by both good and poor readers. For the inference questions, results revealed significant effects for ability and treatment but not for their interaction. In other words, the experimental treatment of inferential comprehension instruction was about as effective for both the good and the poor readers on at least one type of criterion task.

Panels E and F portray variations on another pattern of results, in which the developmental differences are greater *after* training than *before* training. This divergent pattern is rather common in the literature (Cronbach, 1967; Snow & Yalow, 1982). One interpretation of this pattern of results is that the trained routine was not employed efficiently, if at all, by the more advanced students prior to training and that its use requires some additional skills or knowledge before it becomes maximally effective. The first conclusion is straightforward. If the advanced students were proficient when left unaided, instruction should not be particularly beneficial. The second point addresses the relatively weaker effects of instruction on the initially poorer performers. The explanation offered is that the poorer students are also unlikely to have available or to produce other skills that are prerequisite to the one(s) being trained. From the point of view of instruction, this would indicate that the analysis of the task on which the intervention was based was not sufficiently detailed. Without the inclusion of the older/more capable group, a different interpretation could easily have resulted, namely that the task analysis was in error and that the activities being taught or simulated were not important ones. Given this interpretation, the overall approach might then be abandoned rather than refined. That is, the outcome obtained with the older learners influences the interpretation of the null result with the younger ones.

As an example of this pattern of results, consider a number of experiments on the balance beam problem reported by Siegler (1976, 1978). Subjects are shown a series of weight arrangements and asked to predict whether the beam will balance or whether one side or the other will fall if support is withdrawn. Siegler has analyzed the problem in terms of a number of increasingly complex rules that represent a progression toward a full understanding of the principles involved. An early rule, Rule I in Siegler's taxonomy, is based on a consideration of only weight factors. If the amount of weight on either side of the fulcrum is the same, the scale will balance; otherwise, the side with more weight will drop.

An extremely simple type of instruction is to provide examples from which a rule can be inferred. Siegler adopted this approach with groups of 3- and 4-year-olds who had not yet acquired Rule I. Their predictions of balance beam performance were essentially random. Interested in how his subjects might attain that rule, Siegler administered a series of feedback trials. The subjects would first predict what would happen to the beam when supports holding it in place were removed; then the supports were withdrawn, and the subjects were allowed to observe what actually happened. This method simulated the process of formulating hypotheses, obtaining data, and then reevaluating those hypotheses. The main result was that the 4-year-olds tended to induce Rule I, whereas the 3-year-olds did not. Note that if only the young children were included, it would be possible to conclude that leading them to explore the domain in this way was an ineffective way of producing learning.

Subsequent experiments showed that 4-year-olds did in fact encode the relevant weight dimension even though they predicted randomly prior to feedback; the 3-year-olds, however, did not encode the weight dimension. In this sense, one might say that the older children know more about the balance problems (i.e., that weight is a relevant dimension) than the younger children and that this knowledge or competence is necessary for the intervention to produce learning. This conclusion prompted a more detailed training procedure in which 3-year-olds were taught to encode weight before receiving the feedback trials. In this situation, they showed an increased tendency to acquire Rule I.

A second example of this type of result comes from a study reported by Brown and Campione (1977). They were concerned with teaching two groups of retarded children to deploy systematically their study time in a list learning situation. The paradigm, based on a prior study by Masur, McIntyre, and Flavell (1973), involved studying and remembering the labels of a set of 12 pictures. On each trial after the first, the subjects could select only one-half (six) of the pictures for further study. The "ideal" pattern would appear to be to select for study those items that had not been previously recalled, that is, ones that were causing particular problems for the learner; in fact this is what college students do, both in a free recall task (Masur et al., 1973) and in a text studying situation (Brown & Campione, 1979).

The retarded adolescents did not show this strategic selection during a baseline phase of the experiment, and there was no age difference in recall prior to intervention. When both groups were required to study missed items, the older group (who had a mean mental age of 8 years) significantly surpassed the younger group (mean mental age of 6 years), again a divergent effect. The data here indicate that the study time apportionment strategy can help students learn more quickly but that the young sample seemed to lack some other skills necessary for its use. Their recall pattern was informative in this regard. They tended to recall the studied items (one-half the total set) but not the unstudied but previously recalled set. The interpretation preferred was that they failed to continue to attend to or rehearse that set. The failure to produce this essential activity led to the failure of the overall approach. In this case, the pattern of recall provided clues about the specific additional components that needed to be taught to improve the effectiveness of the instructional package.

In a reading comprehension intervention study, Gordon and Pearson (1983) provide a third example of the divergent pattern of results depicted in Panels E and F. Fifth graders of high and average ability received 8 weeks of instruction in one of two procedures designed to increase their ability to make inferences from stories. In one treatment (Content and Structure), students were taught to relate new information to prior knowledge within a structural framework for stories (a simplified story grammar). In the second treatment (Inference Awareness), students were taught, through modeling and feedback, a step-by-step procedure for drawing inferences from the text and evaluating the plausibility of those inferences. Higher-ability students improved their story comprehension (as measured by both experimenter-designed and standardized tests) more as a result of the instruction than did lower-ability students. In addition, higher-ability students showed greater improvement in ability to recall stories after content and structure training than did lower-ability students. Gordon and Pearson speculated that complexity of training procedures or difficulty of training materials may have been responsible for the divergent pattern of results.

In the balance beam and study time examples, the divergent effect indicated that the approach taken was a reasonable one and that more input would need to be provided to make the teaching packages more effective for the L children. Because a considerable amount is known about determinants of performance in both domains, it was possible to develop more powerful procedures. These procedures were based on a detailed analysis of the younger children's response protocols. In the area of comprehension, where the models are not as detailed, this may be more difficult. But the presence of a divergent effect, for example, would at least provide information about the directions future remediation attempts might take, information which simply would not be available if only the younger or poorer group were included in the research.

Although there are other outcomes that are possible, this set is sufficient to show some of the types of additional information that can be obtained by the simple expedient of including instruction for older subjects in an age/ability × instruction factorial design. To add further to the analysis, it is also the case that a number of other factors—specifically the criterion task used to assess the effects of training, and task difficulty—can influence the specific outcome obtained in a particular study.

Criterion Measure

To demonstrate the effects of this variable, consider a series of experiments on teaching self-monitoring skills to mildly retarded children (Brown & Barclay, 1976; Brown, Campione, & Barclay, 1979). The children were required to study a set of items larger than their memory span for as long as they wanted until they were sure they could recall all the items. Baseline performance was poor, and instruction was undertaken. In some conditions, the children were taught both procedures for learning the items and methods for checking on their state of learning. The effects of this strategy plus regulation training for the older (mean age, MA = 8 years) but not the younger (MA = 6 years) children were: immediate beneficial effects of the instruction; maintenance of the strategy over a 1-year period: and evidence for generalization to a quite different task—studying and recalling prose passages. The younger group showed only immediate effects of training; on maintenance probes given a few days after training, they reverted to baseline levels of performance; although mild prompts were sufficient to elicit the trained activities even one year later.

If this age × instruction experiment is considered, which of the various outcomes illustrated in Fig. 9.1 best typifies the results? Note that if adjustments are made for memory span differences, the MA 6 and MA 8 groups did not differ significantly prior to training. Immediately after training, the subjects were given a prompted posttest (on which they were told to continue executing the trained activities); both groups improved significantly, and there was still no reliable difference between them. Given these data, parallel improvement (Panel D) could be said to be the result. When unprompted tests were given a day later, however, the younger group abandoned the trained routines, and their performance reverted to baseline levels. The older subjects, in contrast, continued to perform well, and for the first time, there was a significant difference between the groups. If degree of independent (unprompted) learning is the criterial task, a divergent pattern (Panel F) is obtained. If the fact that the older children demonstrated transfer to a prose recall task is taken into account, the divergent pattern becomes even more pronounced. Thus, studies that produce convergent patterns (Panels A–C) when initial response to instruction is the metric might turn out to produce a divergent effect (Panels F and G) if more demanding criteria, such as maintenance and transfer, are included.

A similar example within the area of comprehension can be found in the Hansen and Pearson (1982) work mentioned earlier. Recall that they obtained either relative convergence (Panel B) or parallel improvement (Panel D) depending on the criterion measures used to evaluate the results of training.

Relative convergence was the result when the criterion measure was performance on worksheets accompanying the stories used during instruction, whereas parallel improvement was the result when the dependent measure was performance on a transfer task.

Difficulty of Trained Activity

To illustrate this issue, consider an experiment by Day (1980) aimed at teaching junior college students strategies for summarizing expository prose passages. The instruction consisted of teaching a set of rules of varying difficulty that could be used to generate adequate summaries (adequate in the sense that they would include the main points of the text and be judged acceptable by college rhetoric teachers). Day also worked with students of varying ability levels: those with no diagnosed reading or writing problems; some with writing problems; and a final group who were receiving remedial help in both writing and reading. Ignoring the details of the different rules, they can be classified into three difficulty categories: easy, intermediate, and difficult. The ability × instruction interaction took different forms depending on this variable. Prior to instruction, the groups did not differ with regard to use of any of the rules. All were proficient when the easiest cases were investigated; hence, training produced no improvement. For the intermediate rules, a pattern of parallel improvement was found; all groups improved to about the same extent. With the most difficult rules, however, a divergent pattern was obtained. The most proficient students showed the largest improvement; those with only writing problems showed some but significantly smaller gains; and the poorest students' rule use was unaffected by instruction.

Although Day's experiment was more complicated than described here, the main point for purposes here is summarized fairly simply. When attention is restricted to one of the teaching procedures, featuring both a detailed description of the various rules and explicit instruction in the management of those rules, the relative effects of that general approach on the different ability groups was systematically related to the difficulty parameter. As the complexity of the specific rule under scrutiny increased, the tendency toward and magnitude of the divergent effect increased.

SUMMARY

In this chapter, the training approach frequently used in the developmental/instructional literature was discussed. This approach involves data from three different conditions. Younger and older (or L and M) students are tested under unprompted conditions to assess the presence and magnitude of some developmental or comparative difference. The L are then instructed, and after a suitable intervention, their performance may improve to the level of the contrast group. It may be inferred that: (1) the activities manipulated during training were important components of adequate task performance; (2) the differential use of those activities was responsible for the original group differences; and (3) with suitably older or more proficient students, the same training programs would have been redundant with what those students were already doing and hence relatively unnecessary.

Although such conclusions were possibly (even probably) correct, more stringent analysis would require additional data of two sorts. First, it would be highly desirable to have data on the quality and extent of production of the target activities by the students during and following instruction; telling students to do something does not guarantee that they do it well or at all. Such data can help in a number of ways. Obviously, if students do not use the activities at all or produce only marginal approximations of what is intended, dramatic effects of the intervention would not be expected. More interestingly, if measures of the topography of students' productions of the activities are available, that information may be used to refine the approach. For example, students who do not improve markedly may produce different or less complete examples of the target activities than do more successful tutees. The specific ways in which the groups' actual activities differ can then be used to modify instruction for those who are not benefiting as much as hoped.

Second, the addition of data from the fourth cell of a hypothetical factorial design was advocated—the performance of M students following the same instruction afforded the L students. From that factorial design, a number of different patterns could and do emerge, ranging from complete or partial convergence through parallel improvement to various degrees of divergence. Although it is not the case that any particular outcome leads to a unique interpretation, it is true that the different outcomes can preclude the strongest interpretation suggested by the modal package and do succeed in constraining significantly the possible interpretations that can be made.

The addition of the fourth cell enables the researcher to evaluate in much more detail hypotheses about the source and nature of developmental or comparative differences in task performance, estimate the presumed competence of more mature subjects, assess the appropriateness and completeness of our task analysis, and derive hints about the directions in which instructional packages need to be modified to increase their power.

In addition, some data make it clear that the outcomes obtained and the resulting interpretations can be influenced by other factors including the criterion measure against which *success* is measured and the difficulty of the skill being taught. The implication is that these factors must be considered carefully when formulating explanations of training studies and that in some cases it may be necessary to include these variables directly in the research program before a clear picture can emerge.

Although the interpretation of training studies is not a simple matter, they represent a significant methodology for attempts to understand the nature of active comprehension and to design instructional programs that can aid students to become more proficient comprehenders. More to the point here, a considerable amount about the strengths, weaknesses, and interpretation of training studies has been learned from work in the areas of memory and problem solving along with more recent attempts in the area of comprehension.

As these lessons are noted and become applied to the area of comprehension, the instructional approach should provide valuable insights into both theories of comprehension and methods of teaching critical comprehension skills. Finally, on a very global level, *comprehension* may be regarded as a more difficult task than *remembering*. If the general conclusions about the effects of task difficulty drawn are correct, divergent effects are likely to be the modal outcome in research addressing the teaching of comprehension-fostering activities. Essentially, this would suggest that advanced students are not nearly as proficient gleaners of meaning as might be assumed and that their performance can be enhanced considerably by the kinds of detailed training procedures that have been developed in the *simple* memory tasks upon which so much attention has been focused.

REFERENCES

André, M. D. A., & Anderson, T. H. The development and evaluation of a self-questioning study technique. *Reading Research Quarterly,* 1978–79, *14,* 605–623.

Belmont, J. M., & Butterfield, E. C. Learning strategies as determinants of memory deficiencies. *Cognitive Psychology,* 1971, *2,* 411–420.

Brown, A. L. Mnemonic elaboration and recency judgments in children. *Cognitive Psychology,* 1973, *5,* 233–248.

Brown, A. L., & Barclay, C. R. The effects of training specific mnemonics on the metamnemonic efficiency of retarded children. *Child Development,* 1976, *47,* 71–80.

Brown, A. L., Bransford, J. D., Ferrara, R. A., & Campione, J. C. Learning, remembering, and understanding. In J. H. Flavell & E. M. Markman (Eds.), *Carmichael's manual of child psychology* (Vol. 1). New York: Wiley, 1983.

Brown, A. L., & Campione, J. C. The effects of knowledge and experience on the formation of retrieval plans for studying from texts. In M. M. Gruneberg, P. E. Morris, & R. N. Sykes (Eds.), *Practical aspects of memory.* London: Academic Press, 1979.

Brown, A. L., & Campione, J. C. Training strategic study time apportionment in educable retarded children. *Intelligence,* 1977, *1,* 94–107.

Brown, A. L., Campione, J. C., & Barclay, C. R. Training self-checking routines for estimating test readiness: Generalization from list learning to prose recall. *Child Development,* 1979, *50,* 501–512.

Brown, A. L., Campione, J. C., Bray, N. W., & Wilcox, B. L. Keeping track of changing variables: Effects of rehearsal training and rehearsal prevention in normal and retarded adolescents. *Journal of Experimental Psychology,* 1973, *101,* 123–131.

Brown, A. L., Campione, J. C., & Gilliard, D. M. Recency judgments in children: A production deficiency in the use of redundant background cues. *Developmental Psychology,* 1974, *10,* 303.

Brown, A. L., & Smiley, S. S. The development of strategies for studying texts. *Child Development,* 1978, *49,* 1076–1088.

Butterfield, E. C., Siladi, D., & Belmont, J. M. Validating process theories of intelligence. In H. W. Reese & L. P. Lipsitt (Eds.), *Advances in child development and behavior* (Vol. 15). New York: Academic Press, 1980.

Butterfield, E. C., Wambold, C., & Belmont, J. M. On the theory and practice of improving short-term memory. *American Journal of Mental Deficiency,* 1973, *77,* 654–669.

Campione, J. C., & Armbruster, B. B. Acquiring information from texts: An analysis of four approaches. In S. Chipman, J. Segal, & R. Glaser (Eds.), *Thinking and learning skills: Relating instruction to basic research.* Hillsdale, N.J.: Lawrence Erlbaum Associates, 1983.

Cronbach, L. J. How can instruction be adapted to individual differences? In R. M. Gagné (Ed.), *Learning and individual differences.* Columbus, OH.: Charles E. Merrill, 1967.

Day, J. D. *Training summarization skills: A comparison of teaching methods.* Unpublished doctoral dissertation, University of Illinois, 1980.

Flavell, J. H., Beach, D. H., & Chinsky, J. M. Spontaneous verbal rehearsal in memory tasks as a function of age. *Child Development,* 1966, *37,* 283–299.

Gordon, C., & Pearson, P. D. *The effects of explicit inference training on students' comprehension and recall* (Tech. Rep. No. 277). Champaign, Ill.: University of Illinois, Center for the Study of Reading, 1983.

Hansen, J., & Pearson, P. D. *An instructional study: Improving the inferential comprehension of good and poor fourth-grade readers* (Tech. Rep. No. 235). Champaign, Ill.: University of Illinois, Center for the Study of Reading, 1982.

Huttenlocher, J., & Burke, D. Why does memory span increase with age? *Cognitive Psychology,* 1976, *8,* 1–31.

Lyon, D. R. Individual differences in immediate serial recall: A matter of mnemonics? *Cognitive Psychology,* 1977, *9,* 403–411.

Masur, E. F., McIntyre, D. W., & Flavell, J. H. Developmental changes in apportionment of study time among items in a multitrial free recall task. *Journal of Experimental Child Psychology,* 1973, *15,* 237–246.

Palincsar, A. S., & Brown, A. L. *Reciprocal teaching of comprehension-monitoring activities* (Tech. Rep. No. 269). Champaign, Ill.: University of Illinois, Center for the study of Reading, 1983.

Siegler, R. S. Three aspects of cognitive development. *Cognitive Psychology,* 1976, *8,* 481–520.

Siegler, R. S. The origins of scientific reasoning. In R. S. Siegler (Ed.), *Children's thinking: What develops?* Hillsdale, N.J.: Lawrence Erlbaum Associates, 1978.

Snow, R. E., & Yalow, E. Education and intelligence. In R. J. Sternberg (Ed.), *Handbook of human intelligence.* New York: Cambridge University Press, 1982.

10 Reading Skills and Skilled Reading in the Comprehension of Text

Marcel Adam Just
Patricia A. Carpenter
Carnegie-Mellon University

Although the flight would constitute an entry into a page of history, the final determination of target location had been made just moments before the launch. Much of the preflight activity involved the programming of the trajectory by the world's most complex assemblage of computational systems. This phase was important because the ballistic flight path could not be altered after take-off. Without a word, the launch in orbit began. Even while maintaining very high velocities the missile continued to transmit optical information collected over the unfamiliar terrain back to the central computational system. At mid-flight, the acceleration propulsion acceded to the deceleration system, bringing the flight to its target exactly as had been planned. As smoothly as it had started, the flight ended, and the eye came to rest on the next word of the history text.

How does a reader progress from making three to five fixations per second, fixating 60–70% of the words, to producing a summary of the text, answering questions about it, or acting on its implications? How does the reader's knowledge of the topic influence the on-going interpretive processes (as in the passage above)? What general features characterize skilled reading? In this chapter, we review the recent progress that has been made in answering these questions and outline the principles that emerge from the research on skilled reading. The paper has three parts. The first discusses some general characteristics of theories of skilled performance, particularly theories of language processing. The second part discusses a specific theory of reading that was developed on the basis of chronometric eye-fixation data and that describes a range of processes, from perceptual-level processes to discourse-level ones. The third part applies this theory to a specialized form of skilled reading, namely rapid reading.

KNOWLEDGE COMPREHENSION

One of the paradoxes of learning from reading is that you must know a lot before you can learn more. You must know the language that is used, the meaning of the words, and something about the topic that is being described. The idea that a large knowledge base is fundamental to language understanding is one area of agreement among language researchers. Beyond this general consensus, there has also been an attempt to refine how the previous knowledge is represented, and how it is used during the comprehension process.

Declarative Knowledge

A useful distinction has been made between two kinds of knowledge. One form, called *declarative knowledge*, refers to static knowledge about concepts and their relations and corresponds to our everyday meaning of knowledge. Declarative knowledge can be thought of as "knowing that . . . ," such as, knowing that Paris is the capital of France, or that gold is a heavy substance, or that some birds can't fly. A large amount of research in the past 10 years has focused on the fact that such knowledge is a necessary component of comprehending even a relatively simple text. Consider Charniak's (1972) example of what you need to know to understand the sentences: *The little girl heard the ring of the ice cream man's bell. She ran inside to get her piggy bank.* Part of what a reader needs to know is that an ice cream man sells ice cream, that he signals his presence by ringing a bell, that to buy something requires money, that money is often kept in piggy banks, and so on. These facts are not explicitly stated, but nevertheless comprehension processes must have access to them to infer the relations among the information that is explicit in the text.

Terms such as *schemas, scenerios, scripts,* and *frames* have been used to refer to the representation of such knowledge (cf. Bartlett, 1932; Minsky, 1975; Norman & Rumelhart, 1975; Schank & Abelson, 1977). These theories were most recently developed to explain the interplay of previous knowledge with understanding a text, particularly texts that describe stereotypic situations, such as an order-eat-pay scenario in a restaurant. In such cases, the text tends to play a lesser role in specifying the relevant information. The various schema theories have some important similarities. They assume that information is stored in an organized way, in which related pieces of knowledge are linked and mutually accessible (with some constraints). They also assume that there are certain default values for some of the goals, actions, objects, and people in a given situation. For example, if the text does not specify the person with whom the order for food is placed, then it may be assumed to be a waiter or waitress by default. By providing default values that are likely to be correct inferences, a schema can provide the information that is necessary to make the mental links among the clauses and sentences.

There have been two main methodological approaches to empirically examining the role of knowledge. One has been to study passages that refer to very well-known events, but are written in a way that prevents readers from realizing what the referent is. Using this approach, Bransford and Johnson (1973) showed that even a passage described a mundane task, like how to do laundry, was much less comprehensible and remembered much less well when the readers were not told the topic beforehand and could not infer it. The explanation is that comprehension requires constructing a referent and using previous knowledge of the referent to infer intersentential relations. In a variant of this type of study, Sulin and Dooling (1974) showed that a passage describing Helen Keller led to different memory performance when the name was changed to Carol Harris, because different knowledge structures were used in the two situations.

The introductory paragraph to this paper provided an analogous illustration of how the referential domain influences the interpretive process. The passage was written to suggest that the topic was a rocket launch, until the last clause specified the true topic—a saccadic eye movement. Rereading with the actual topic in mind leads to an entirely different interpretation of the passage.

A second approach has been to study a domain where there are large individual differences in how much is known about a topic, essentially examining the comprehension processes of experts and novices. One example of this approach has been the work of Voss (this volume) and his co-workers who have examined how readers who are knowledgeable about baseball differ from those who aren't in how they remember and process descriptions of baseball games (Chiesi, Spilich, & Voss, 1979; Spilich, Vesonder, Chiesi, & Voss, 1979; Voss, Vesonder, & Spilich, 1980). Voss has suggested that a crucial aspect of knowledge is the filtering role that it plays during comprehension, allowing the more knowledgeable reader to fit information into a conceptual structure that contains the implications of what might otherwise seem like isolated facts.

Reading teachers have long known the importance of providing background information before having novice readers read a text. What do the schema-related formalisms add beyond this commonsense observation? The contributions of schema theory are largely promissory. Schema theories may:

1. Help specify what information must be recruited in a particular situation.

2. Focus attention on the issue of what evokes the relevant knowledge, as well as which knowledge is evoked.

3. Provide the beginning steps toward constructing a taxonomy of types of knowledge.

4. Focus on the processing implications of knowing about a topic before reading a related text. How does that knowledge decrease the complexity of the comprehension process? Does it alter the temporal parameters for basic processes, such as encoding? Does it decrease the constructive rules that must operate in the absence of previously constructed referents? Does it alter what is attended and how it is coded?

Procedural Knowledge

In contrast to declarative knowledge, procedural knowledge is the knowledge used in performing actions, including mental actions. Procedural knowledge can be thought of as *knowing how to* . . . tie a bow, ride a bicycle, or comprehend a counterfactual sentence. Much of the linguistic knowledge used in reading is usually thought of as procedural. The case for this kind of representation has been strongly made by artificial intelligence researchers, whose natural language understanding programs use procedural knowledge of the language to understand it. For example, in Winograd's program (1972), much of the linguistic knowledge is represented as a procedure to be executed in order to understand a given linguistic structure. Understanding in this and other cases means being able to represent and appropriately use the information in the linguistic structure. The procedural knowledge used in language comprehension often cannot be described in verbal terms, at least not by a layman who may be very proficient at using the procedures. For example, consider the rule that governs the use of the word *either* to conjoin two clauses or phrases. It is difficult to describe the knowledge that correctly produces and comprehends a sentence like *John never travelled and Mary didn't travel, either,* but not one like *John often went and Mary frequently went, either.* This knowledge is implicit in the processes that are used to understand English, although it certainly is not something that can be spontaneously described. More generally, many of the comprehension processes that a reader or listener uses seem to be best described as procedural knowledge.

Reading Comprehension Is Comprehension

A second important feature of reading comprehension models is that most of the interesting computation is not specific to the visual modality. The first stage of reading is obviously visual, but the subsequent stages involve processes and strategies that are likely to be common to both reading and listening and to draw on the same general knowledge. One source of evidence for this conclusion comes from the correlations between listening and reading ability for children of various ages (Curtis, 1980). What correlated best with reading ability before third grade was a measure of phonological coding ability. Presumably, in early reading the visual encoding aspect of reading is a bottleneck and accounts for significant individual differences. However, after third grade, the correlations between listening and reading ability increased and surpassed those between reading ability and coding ability. With adults, listening and reading ability are generally highly correlated (Daneman & Carpenter, 1980; Sticht, 1972). Thus, beyond the early stages of reading, the specifically visual aspects of reading are much less likely to be a bottleneck, and most of the individual differences in reading ability are probably best accounted for by the processes and structures that are common to listening and reading comprehension.

THE PROCESSING COMPONENT

How are the processes and the declarative knowledge base coordinated to accomplish a task as complex as reading? There are several areas of convergence among theories on this issue. We first discuss some general features of the processing environment, and then present a more detailed model that reflects our particular theoretical stance on these features.

Immediacy of Interpretation

As soon as the cognitive system encounters the representations of successive words of a text, it interprets the words one at a time in the order in which they are encoded from the text or discourse. Immediate interpretation can be contrasted with a processing mode in which the cognitive system buffers several words as it encounters them (say three words, a phrase worth's, or a clause) and attempts the interpretation only after the buffer has been filled. If words A, B, and C constitute one buffer's worth, then nonimmediate interpretation would have the interpretive processes wait until all three of the words had been registered by the cognitive system. By contrast, immediacy would have the interpretation of A start and continue to completion (or as far as possible) even before B was input. One strong source of evidence for immediacy of interpretation is that the gaze duration on a given word is clearly influenced by the properties of that word (Dee-Lucas, Just, Carpenter, & Daneman, 1982; Just & Carpenter, 1980). *Interpretation* refers to processes at several levels, from encoding, accessing meanings, determining syntactic status, the conceptual dependency role, its referent, and role in the discourse. Naturally, there are occasions when not all aspects of a word's interpretation can be immediately determined, but the immediacy principle states that such interpretations are attempted and acknowledges that the attempts will sometimes fail and must be postponed.

Activation Levels of Knowledge Elements

It has been useful to think of knowledge being in various states of activation that correspond roughly to levels of confidence. Moreover, some theories treat activation levels as having a continuous distribution, so that the activation level of a given piece of knowledge can gradually change. Activation levels have been used to explain the influence among related knowledge structures, such that highly activated elements also activate elements to which they are linked by some relation. Each knowledge element can accumulate activation from one or more sources. This metaphor can be traced to the connectionism of the 19th century and earlier. However, it has received new attention, due in part to the empirical work on semantic priming (Meyer & Schvaneveldt, 1971) and the theoretical work on semantic networks in psychology and artificial intelligence

(Anderson, 1976; Collins & Loftus, 1975; Findler, 1979). An activation process has a time course such that some time must elapse before activation from one element has some effect on the availability of another (Posner & Snyder, 1975). Thus, the theoretical construct of activation provides a vehicle for considering how knowledge might differ in its availability, the time course of change in availability, and how availability may be modified by mental operations or by the activation of related knowledge.

Functional Parallelism

In a complex but highly practiced, overlearned task like reading, it is likely that psychological processes can temporally co-occur. A computational system is functionally parallel if several processes can be executed concurrently, or executed sequentially but with such a short alternating cycles that it is indistinguishable from parallel processing. The functional parallelism has implications for the processes that may occur within a traditional reading *stage,* such as word encoding. The word encoding *stage* may consist of many subprocesses, which operate together to encode a word. These subprocesses may co-occur, so that feature-level, letter-level, syllable-level, word-level and sometime supraword-level processes co-occur to encode and recognize the visual stimulus. In addition, functional parallelism may occur between processes that are contributing to different analyses. For example, some processes may be computing the syntactic case of a word, while other processes attempt to establish its referent and still other processes attempt to determine its role in the discourse.

If a theory postulates functional parallelism, it must consider how information from various processes is coordinated, which processes can co-occur, and whether (and how) the concurrent processes can influence each other. Early information-processing models were very bottom–up and linear, such that lower-level processes fed their outputs to the immediately following higher-level processes until the successive, cumulated wisdom of all the preceding levels was fed into the highest level. In this view, a reader's major information source was the text itself. But more than that, knowledge accumulated from the previous parts of the text or from the reader's previous knowledge did not influence the bottom–up processes, but were presumably additional sources of information at the higher levels. More recent emphasis on the role of knowledge and the comprehension of mundane texts have lead to more top–down approaches. In this view, the reader knows much of what will be described (e.g., in reading a description of a commonplace restaurant episode) before doing any reading, and the text serves only to provide details. Hence, the top–down information might determine how lower-level processes are executed (see Levy, 1981, for a discussion of these issues). A range of intermediate possibilities exists between these two views. But at each point on this continuum, there must be some form of communication between various stages. One communication question is whether a given stage can be influenced by another after it has begun a major processing cycle, and the other is whether a given stage can produce any useful output before the end of a major processing cycle. Communication to or from a stage during a cycle is sometimes referred to as interaction between stages. Some comprehension models, like HEARSAY, have proposed parallel computation without interaction between stages (Reddy & Newell, 1974), whereas others have proposed parallel computation with feedback between stages (McClelland & Rumelhart, 1981; Thibadeau, Just, & Carpenter, 1980). We return to this question in the second section of the chapter when we describe our own theory of reading.

Automaticity

Skilled performance has many components that are automatic in the sense that they: (1) are evoked by a stimulus without conscious effort; (2) require little processing capacity for execution; (3) allow for functional parallelism; and (4) are not available to conscious introspection. A defining property of automatic processes is that they are evoked by the effective stimulus without any conscious effort to decision (Posner & Snyder, 1975; Shiffrin & Schneider, 1977). In fact, it is difficult to suppress consciously an automatic process, such as the automatic encoding of a familiar word. One example of this kind of stimulus triggering occurs in the Stroop task, in which the subject's task is to name the color of the ink that has been used to print a word. If the word is also the name of a color that mismatches the color of the ink used to print the word, subjects experience considerable interference. They cannot completely suppress the processes that encode, access, and verbally produce the color word even though it is not necessary (in fact, detrimental) to their performance. Similarly, it is very difficult to hear a simple sentence while suppressing the processes that understand it.

The reading processes that are most likely to become automatic are the relatively low-level ones, such as feature and word encoding, programming eye movements, and the language-specific processes, such as those associated with parsing, segmentation, and conceptual dependency analysis. But within each of these "stages," there is a constellation of processes that are also candidates for automatization. Consider for example, "word encoding," which may be conceptualized as a single stage or as a complex series of computations that operate on visual features, letters, syllables, word shape, and words themselves. La-Berge and Samuels (1974) argued that an important aspect of automaticity in word perception is that these codes can be evoked concurrently.

Another feature of automaticity is that the reader is less aware of the nature or execution of automatic processes. To some extent, this is a property of most forms of procedural knowledge. That is, knowledge of *how* to do something is often difficult to express. In reading, there is a great deal of computation that is not available to conscious introspection, and by contrast, the reader is aware of the products of the processes, that is, the semantic and pragmatic import and occasionally, the verbatim content, especially in poetry or literary prose. But we are certainly not aware of how such interpretations are derived or the cues that evoke various expectations or interpretations.

Processes can become automatic only if they are used repeatedly and extensively. The skill literature and the educational research on reading evaluation both suggest that the time spent practicing a task is the overwhelmingly important determinant of speeded, skilled performance. Moreover, Newell and Rosenbloom (1981) showed that the improvement curve in very many skills seems to be best described by a power function. The implication is that there is no asymptote, although there are decreasing gains with higher levels of practice. Thus, skill can continue to increase with practice. This implies that automaticity in reading is not necessarily some end-state, but a point along a continuum whose upper-bound is not known. The applied research in reading supports this theoretical analysis. It has been shown that the time on the task is one of the largest determinants of reading performance and in some large studies has been the only schooling-related variable that does predict achievement (Lerner, 1981).

Perceptual Processes

The number of words that a reader can encode and semantically process while fixating at a given point in a text is relatively small. As a reader fixates on a given location, he can determine the meaning of an adjacent word only if it begins within six letter spaces of the point he is fixating (Rayner, 1975). Generally, long words cannot be encoded without being fixated, although it is possible and likely that readers encode and interpret some short, familiar words without fixating them. The narrow perceptual span implies that readers should fixate the text fairly densely, and the data show that they do. Skilled adult readers fixate a large proportion of the content words (about 80%), and the words that they don't directly fixate tend to be the short function words. Indeed, as normal readers go from left to right in the text, about 90% of the time the next word that is fixated is the adjacent word or the target word immediately following the adjacent word (Carpenter & Just, 1983), although this percentage is drastically reduced if the reader is skimming or speedreading.

In sum, there has been considerable progress in describing the knowledge structures and processes required to characterize skilled reading. Some of these characteristics, such as procedural knowledge, automaticity, activation, and functional parallelism apply to more than just reading, and may be general features of skilled behavior. Other characteristics are obviously specific to language or reading behavior. In the next section, we will describe how we have embodied these features in a particular computer simulation of reading.

A PROCESS MODEL READING SKILL

In this section we describe a particular computer-implemented architecture that has many of the features described in the first section. We describe how we have used this as a framework in which to simulate skilled reading. The model is expressed as a computer program called READER, a computer simulation of human reading (Thibadeau, Just, & Carpenter, 1982). READER has word-encoding processes, lexical-access processes, semantic and syntactic analysis processes, schema-level processes, and model-referent processes that build a model of the world that is being discussed. READER takes as input a 140 word passage about flywheels, processes the text word by word, and constructs an internal representation sufficient to summarize or answer questions about the passage. Moreover, the amount of processing time READER expends on each word corresponds to the human gaze duration on that word during normal reading. READER is a production system that operates within an information-processing architecture or programming language called CAPS that was designed principally by Robert Thibadeau. CAPS embodies many of the properties of human processing described in the first section of this chapter and, consequently, provides a framework for describing a variety of skilled behaviors, including spatial problem solving, deductive inferencing, memory-based performance, such as recall and retrieval, and language understanding, such as reading. The reading simulation program expresses some processes that are general to language understanding and some that are specific to the comprehension of written language. The architecture and the reading simulation were motivated by human experimental work (Just & Carpenter, 1980), and both are described in more detail elsewhere (Thibadeau, Just, & Carpenter, 1982).

The Architecture: CAPS

This section describes the theory of the processing environment called CAPS, an acronym for *C*ollaborative *A*ctivation-based *P*roduction *S*ystem. Production systems provide a convenient way to express procedural knowledge, declarative knowledge, and the central role of working memory in language processing. Production systems are formalisms in which the procedural knowledge is embodied in a set of condition–action rules (Newell, 1980). The condition part specifies what element(s) should be present in (or absent from) working memory to enable an action. For example, a typical production in READER that helps accomplish syntactic parsing has as a condition that a determiner has been encountered and has as an action the creation of an expectation that a noun will be encountered. The form of the actual production is, roughly: (determiner)—(expect noun). Thus, if a reader encounters *the, a,* and so on, he will set up the expectation of a noun phrase, although not a conscious expectation. The procedural knowledge constitutes part of long-term memory and under the appropriate circumstances, this knowledge is used for processing current information.

CAPS also allows for declarative knowledge, which consists of propositional information. These are expressed as *is a* and *has a* propositions that provide the data base on which the productions operate. Each proposition has a specified amount of activation that is expressed numerically, and varies from high positive fractional values (meaning that there has been considerable evidence for the proposition and that it is now in working memory) to lower positive values (meaning that there was less evidence for it) to negative values (meaning that it is negated). When a proposition has a high level of activation, it has the potential to activate productions. Thus, working memory consists of the intermediate and final products of the various computations. The working memory is the site of interaction among productions and knowledge structures.

The productions fire in cycles. At the beginning of a cycle, all the productions scan the elements in working memory, and all the productions whose condition elements are matched to some elements in working memory take their associated action concurrently. Actions consist of adding, deleting, or changing the activation level of a knowledge element in working memory. The changes in working memory initiate a new processing cycle; all the productions again check the contents of the working memory, and there is another evaluate–act iteration. In CAPS, the processing cycle is defined as a primitive unit of processing. Every CAPS cycle is assumed to take the same amount of time, and thus the count of CAPS cycles provides a measure of the duration of the processing activity. If one kind of input requires more cycles than another, the increase can be quantitatively compared to the differences in time that humans spend on the two. This means that caps allows for quantitative comparisons between behavior and the simulation, and hence a fairly fine-grained measure of the fit of the model.

READER makes use of this feature to model some of the detailed chronometric results of gaze durations of human readers. The gaze durations vary as a function of a word's length, frequency, or semantic appropriateness. For example, we found that the time a reader spends on a word increases with the number of characters in the word. Readers spend more time on six-letter words than on five-letter words, and more time on five than on four, and so on. This occurs not only in reading tasks in which a reader normally executes eye movements, but also in tasks where eye movements are unnecessary because each word is presented one at a time, centered at the same position and the reader presses a button to see the next word (Just, Carpenter, & Woolley, 1982). The significance of this is that the length effect seems not to be due entirely to acuity, that is, attempting to get all of the letters within foveal view. This increase in gaze duration in the human reading has its parallel in READER cycles. The simulation spends more cycles on longer words because it serially encodes letters one by one and then continually scans for prefix, suffix, and subword units that can be used to access the lexicon. Thus, the encoding processes of READER have the same quantitative function related to the number of characters as the gaze duration data.

*Functional Parallelism.*The productions can fire in parallel, so more than one may be enabled and fire. In skilled reading, this means that several types of computations may co-occur. For example, if READER encodes a noun, the new knowledge element might activate a syntactic production (that identifies it as the sentence subject) and a referential-level production (that identifies it as having a particular referent) on the same cycle. Generally, each level of processing (such as syntactic analysis) requires several cycles to accomplish its function, so there are often a number of concurrent streams of processing at different levels spanning several cycles.

The number of cycles required to complete each level of processing is not the same for each process or for each word. Each process has some goal, and the number of cycles required to satisfy the goal depends on the strength of the evidence, the specific computations, and the prior context that may facilitate one or another computation. For example, the number of cycles necessary to compute the referent of a particular noun might depend on whether the referent had been established earlier in the text, or how easily it can be inferred from the semantic context. There is no refractory period for CAPS productions. If a production is fired on cycle N, it can continue to fire on successive cycles until something stops it. Typically, a process terminates if its goal is satisfied. For example, the productions associated with lexical access continue until some interpretation of a word reaches threshold. The processing of a particular word terminates when no further productions are satisfied, and then the next word is read. Thus, the total number of cycles spent on a word is determined by the process that requires the most cycles.

One consequence of this concurrent processing architecture is the potential for collaboration among processes. Some recent language understanding systems, such as the HEARSAY program (Reddy & Newell, 1974), have also explored some forms of concurrent processing, but among relatively large modules (such as complete semantic and syntactic analysis). By contrast, CAPS allows for collaboration among individual processes irrespective of the specific computational goal in which each participates. For example, in READER, the knowledge from one level of processing, such as the semantic analysis, can in principle influence another, such as the referential analysis, before the other has been completed. Each process writes its intermediate results on a common scratch pad (working memory), and those intermediate products have the potential to influence other processes. Although the potential for total concurrence and interaction exists, the informational constraints among processes impose some sequentiality. For example, our data suggest that word encoding generally precedes the other processes. Hence, there is orderliness in the type and extent of the interaction, and not all processes interact with all others.

Automaticity in CAPS. Automaticity in a production system can be expressed as a shift to processing that is governed increasingly by its own inputs and partial products, and decreasingly by control (strategic) productions. CAPS (and other production systems) allows for a relatively easy expression of this property of skilled performance because there is no executive and the processes are self-organizing. Unlike a conventional subroutine, productions are not explicitly evoked, but are automatically evoked whenever their enabling conditions are present in working memory. The contrast can be clarified by considering an analogy of building a house. The conventional way of building a house resembles the organization of standard programming formalisms. The events are scheduled by a central executive (general contractor). First, an excavator is called and asked to dig out the space for the foundation; then the cement contractor is asked to pour the foundation; then carpenters are told to put up the frame; then an electrician does the wiring, and so on. A production system takes a very different approach to the organizational issue. It assembles the experts at the building site and expects each of them to keep watch on the building's progress, so that each one performs the appropriate task as soon as conditions permit. Like the productions in CAPS, they self-schedule their activities.

The immediacy assumption follows rather directly from the CAPS architecture. It is instantiated simply as each production firing as soon as its conditions are present. There is no buffering or holding back on processing, because the productions fire whenever they get a chance to. Sometimes certain processes have to be postponed. For example, one might not be able to interpret the first word of a sentence at the schema-level right at the beginning of the sentence. Its role may only be computable at the end of the phrase or clause. In this sense, the system does buffer. But the buffering occurs out of necessity and not out of design.

Automaticity gradually arises when, with enough practice, the processes become better coordinated with each other. With increasing practice, processes that initially could be executed only sequentially, can increasingly overlap in time. One way that the transition from sequentiality to partial concurrence can come about is if the second process can become enabled by a partial product of the first one, rather than by its final product. Better coordination may also arise if processes can be evoked not only by their usual conditions, but by conditions that usually give rise to their enabling conditions. If a production P1 has a condition A and an action B, and another production P2 has condition B and action C, then learning may occur to form a third production P3 with condition A and action C. Both of these forms of automaticity involve the learning of better cues that allow processes to begin earlier and operate concurrently with processes that they used to operate sequentially.

Activation in CAPS. Each knowledge element has an associated activation level that corresponds to the degree of confidence in that knowledge. Generally, only those knowledge elements whose activation levels are above a standard threshold level are capable of satisfying the conditions of productions. The activation level of a knowledge element can increase (or decrease) as supporting evidence is accumulated, so that knowledge grows over time (cycles), somewhat similarly to the way it does in stimulus sampling theory and neural counter theory. What makes the activation level of an element increase is the output of various productions that direct activation from one specific element to one or more specific others. For example, if the knowledge that the current word *the* has a high activation level, then activation is directed to the knowledge that a noun phrase is being read.

Productions increase and decrease the activation levels of knowledge elements (whether they are above or below threshold), in addition to creating new knowledge elements. The productions alter the activation level of some element as follows. When a condition is satisfied, the production takes the activation of its condition elements, multiplies it by some weight, and adds it to the activation level of the action elements. So if the condition is A and the action is B and if the system is confident that A is true, then it increases the confidence in B by some fraction of A.

Productions can also direct activation to themselves. Self-activation of a mental representation is an old concept in psychological theories, from Hartley's "vibrating" ideas (Boring, 1950) to Hebb's reverberating cell assemblies (Hebb, 1949), which has been used to explain the persistence of a mental representation when the external stimulus is no longer present. READER uses self-activation to explain the gradual emergence of a proposition whose growth is initiated by some production, but whose growth is maintained by a self-activation production. Directing activation from a proposition back to itself with some weighting (if the weight is positive and fractional) will gradually increase its activation level to threshold, at which point feedback stops the self-activation process.

An example from READER will clarify how the presence of activation levels allows for context effects. For example, we mentioned a production before that says if there is a determiner, expect a noun. Suppose that the reader encodes the words "The bank . . .". The word *bank* may be a noun or a verb. A production that stores this knowledge may say that when the letters b-a-n-k are encoded, activate concepts corresponding to the nouns and to the verb. However, the expectation of a noun feeds activation to any noun interpretation (and potentially decreases the activation of the verb interpretation) and so it contributes to disambiguate the meaning of this word. Thus, there is a vehicle for linear integration of confidence from different knowledge sources.

Some of the partial products of READER's comprehension processes never reach threshold. This occurs in the case of polysemy or syntactic ambiguity, if different productions increment interpretations that are mutually incompatible. If two or more interpretations are activated, the one that reaches threshold first (accumulates sufficient supporting information fastest) becomes the accepted interpretation, and the other ones are suppressed. In this way, base activation levels (reflecting base frequencies of usage) and contextual information are effectively used to resolve problems of multiple interpretations before the multiple interpretations reach threshold (awareness).

READER was developed to simulate *normal* reading, that is reading in which every word of the text is considered (with the exception of some very predictable function words that READER can skip). However, *normal* reading is not the only kind of skilled reading that can occur. Human readers can read with more or less speed and more or less care. In the next section, we will describe some research that we have done on faster than normal reading and show how with relatively few changes in the basic structure of READER, it is possible to account for these kinds of reading as well.

THE MODEL APPLIED TO RAPID READING

The reading speed of college students is usually about 200–300 words per minute (wpm), but the rate can increase to 600–700 wpm or higher if the students are asked to read rapidly or if they have been trained in a speedreading course. As the reading rate trebles, the pattern of eye fixations must change. The following studies (Just, Carpenter, & Masson, 1981) examined the changes in eye-fixation behavior as reading rate increases. The specific goals were to determine the algorithm that selected which words were to be fixated during rapid reading and to determine what governed the amount of time spent on the fixated words. The interest in the comparison between normal and rapid readers is enhanced by the presence of two kinds of rapid readers in the study, trained speedreaders and untrained subjects who were asked to read rapidly. The latter group will be called skimmers.

The normal readers generally read like the readers in our other studies of normal reading, described earlier. But the speedreaders covered the material three times as fast as the normal readers, and the skimmers were two and a half times as fast. The speedreaders read at 686 wpm, skimmers at 585 wpm, and normal readers at 234 wpm. What did the rapid readers do differently than the normal readers? Three main ways of increasing reading speed have been suggested. The first and most obvious way is simply to look at fewer of the words. Associated with this is a second way, namely processing some words without fixating them, effectively increasing the perceptual span. The third way is to decrease the duration of the comprehension processes by some means. We will show that only the first and third of these means are used by rapid readers.

One remaining aspect of normal reading that might change with increased speed is that the immediacy of processing that is so prevalent in normal reading may not necessarily dominate in rapid reading. If rapid reading produces an encoding of only a small subset of the content words, then the linearity of the written text is lost, and it may be strategically advantageous to delay the interpretation of the sampled words until several of them have been encoded. This strategy of buffering several words before interpreting any of them might make sense, because each word alone would be encoded within a very sparse semantic and syntactic context. Evidence supporting immediacy would be provided if rapid readers' eyes paused immediately on the words that initiated a time-consuming process.

The speedreaders had just completed a speedreading course that involved about 40 hours of practice plus formal training on how to pace their reading using their hand as a guide. The skimmers had no formal training, but during the warm-up period of the testing session, they were given feedback on their reading speed until it approximated the speed of the speedreaders. Each of the three groups had about 11 subjects, and the actual study involved both longitudinal and cross-sectional comparisons to avoid subject selection effects. Each subject read several very long passages. After a passage, the reader gave a 100 word summary and answered 20 true–false questions about it. The analysis of the eye fixations involved two of the passages. One was a 2004-word passage from *Reader's Digest* that described some adventures of John Colter, an early 19th century American frontiersman. The second passage was a 1527-word excerpt from *Scientific American* entitled "The Surface of Mars," which described what had been learned about the Martian surface and atmosphere by various space exploration projects.

Sampling Strategies

Previous data and our own showed that rapid readers are fast, in part, because they fixate a much smaller proportion of words in the text than do normal readers. Speedreaders fixated about 34% of the words and skimmers 40%, whereas the normal readers fixate 64% of the words. The percentages were similar for both passages. To determine how many words readers typically skipped over, we counted the lengths of the runs of successive unfixated words. If the reader fixates two adjacent words, then the length of the run of unfixated words is zero. If the reader skips exactly one word, then the length of the run is one, and so on.

The analysis of the run lengths showed that when the normal readers move their eyes forward in the text from one word to some other word, most of the time (89%) they fixate the very next word or skip over only one word. The density of fixation is generally high, probably because the perceptual span in reading is fairly narrow. This empirical observation contradicts a common stereotype and naive theory of the normal reader as fixating only once every three or four words. Although this stereotype is incorrect for normal readers, it happens to be an accurate description of the speedreaders. Speedreaders and skimmers were less likely to fixate adjacent words and more likely to skip several words between consecutive fixations than normal readers. Where normal readers fixated adjacent words or skipped no more than one word 89% of the time, the corresponding percentages for speedreaders and skimmers were 55% and 67%, respectively. Both rapid reading groups also had a substantial number of runs of four or more unfixated words, whereas normal readers have almost none.

Perceptual Span

As we said earlier, the perceptual span in normal reading is not large. In Rayner's (1975) study, a nonword embedded in a text did not affect readers' eye fixation durations unless the nonword was directly fixated or was within three character spaces to the right of the locus of fixation. But the possibility exists that training in speedreading could expand the perceptual span, enabling a speedreader to encode several words to the right or left of his point of regard. If this were true, a speedreader could encode many more words than those that were directly fixated.

To evaluate the size of the span of the rapid readers, we determined whether they ever learned any fact they did not fixate during their reading of the text. Because the performance of the speedreaders and skimmers was undistinguishable with respect to this issue, the two rapid reading groups were analyzed together. We examined their ability to answer questions about facts that were mentioned in only one place in the text and determined if they ever knew a fact without ever fixating it. They could not. The rapid readers had to look directly at the fact (or within three character spaces) in order to answer questions that interrogated that fact. This result strongly suggests that the speedreaders and the skimmers, like normal readers, have a relatively small span for semantic processing.

Gaze Duration

The third method of increasing reading speed is by decreasing the time taken by elementary psychological processes. In particular, one could imagine that rapid readers lower their threshold or impose some time limit so that they move on before completing the more extensive processing that might occur in normal reading. Indeed, the data show that the two rapid reading groups spent less time on each word than normal readers. Of course, to compare the time on a word for rapid readers to normal readers, it is necessary to take into account the different probabilities of fixating the word. Therefore, we computed the average time on a word conditionalized on the reader having fixated the word. The conditionalized gaze duration was about one-third shorter (100 msec) for speedreaders and skimmers than for normal readers. The speedreaders spent an average of 233 msec, the skimmers 221 msec, and the normal readers 330 msec, for the *Colter* passage, with similar results for the *Mars* passage.

Rapid readers generally show similar effects to those found in normal reading, such as longer fixations on longer words and on infrequent words. However, the effects are attenuated in the case of rapid readers. The fact that rapid readers do pause on the very words that evoke the comprehension process indicates that they are interpreting the words as soon as they fixate them, i.e., they are using the immediacy strategy.

We analyzed the conditionalized gaze duration using a linear regression model. All three groups paused longer on longer words and on less frequent words. Word length is presumed to affect an iterative encoding process whose iterations increase with length, and certainly the time on a word increases with length for all three groups. The normal readers paused for an extra 16 to 18 msec for each additional letter, and the speedreaders and skimmers paused for an extra 6 or 7 msec per letter. Word frequency is thought to affect lexical access, retrieving a word's meaning. The access mechanism we have proposed in READER involves word concepts having base activation levels that are linearly related to the word's normative frequency and an activation mechanism that requires several cycles to bring a concept to threshold, with the number of required cycles decreasing logarithmically as the base level increases. Both normal readers and rapid readers spent less time on more frequent words. There was a decrease of 13 msec per log unit for the normal readers, with smaller but still reliable parameters of 7 and 8 msec for the speedreaders and skimmers, respectively. The *Mars* passage, with its somewhat greater proportion of infrequent words, produced a 17 msec increase in gaze duration per log unit for the normal readers, and 10 and 8 msec for the speedreaders and skimmers, respectively. Thus even rapid readers modulate their pause on each word they fixate by the word's frequency. The fact that the time on a word is related to its properties for all three groups suggests that at least encoding and lexical access show immediacy in rapid reading, as is found in normal reading.

The effects of word length and word frequency on the gaze duration of rapid readers are less than on normal readers, suggesting that something about their basic comprehension processes takes less time. The rapid readers are "faster," but the regression result itself does not specify the source of the speed advantage. Although the mean conditionalized gaze durations are about 100 msec shorter for the rapid readers, only about 23 msec (on average) is attributable to a difference in intercepts, the duration of the processes common to all words, such as planning the next saccade. Much more of the difference is attributable to the particular comprehension processes whose durations are influenced by the independent variables of the regression model, such as word length, word frequency, and end-of-screen wrap-up.

There are several possible explanations for why some of the independent variables produce smaller effects for rapid readers. One possibility is that rapid readers have lower criteria for such processes as word recognition and lexical access. The process model of reading we described above involves the growth of the activation level of an item over psychologically defined processing cycles, until the activation level reaches some threshold. For example, the mechanism proposed to explain the logarithmic function relating normative word frequency and gaze duration is a self-activation process that adds an item's current activation level to itself. The base activation levels of word concepts are presumed to be linearly related to the word's normative frequency, and the number of self-activation cycles required to raise any word concept's activation level to a fixed threshold is logarithmically related to the base level. If the threshold for accepting a word concept is lower for rapid readers, the mechanism proceeds normally, but reaches threshold sooner (after fewer cycles), while retaining the logarithmic characteristic. Having a lower threshold also makes it easier for an incorrect word concept to be accepted as the word's meaning, because there is less opportunity for the preceding context to influence the selection of word meanings. So this model predicts that rapid readers are more likely to interpret words incorrectly. This may account in part for their poorer comprehension performance.

A second explanation for the smaller parameters for the two rapid reading groups is that they are less likely to know which are the important words to understand. This is because they are more likely to have skipped the preceding context that determines relative importance. Hence, they may spend less time on a word trying to interpret it or integrate it with the cumulating representation of the text because they do not know its role. For example, normal readers often spent extra time on the word that gave the unit of measurement after a number, e.g., 1600 *kilometers,* but such words received very short gazes from the rapid readers, perhaps because they were less likely to have processed the context that would indicate the role or importance of the number or they were less likely to want to study the number.

Another reason that rapid readers show smaller effects is that they may set absolute upper bounds on the processing time on any word, regardless of whether all the levels of processing have reached completion. Truncation of all processing beyond some limit may explain why the rapid readers never produce the extremely long gaze durations on difficult words commonly found among the normal readers. This difference between normal and rapid readers was particularly vivid in the 10 words in the *Mars* passage on which normal readers spent the most time. On 20% of the gazes on these words, the normal readers spent more than 1 sec, whereas the rapid readers never did so. Of course, the three explanations for the comprehension processes of rapid readers taking less time are mutually compatible and could operate in concert.

Differences Between Normal and Rapid Reading Comprehension

Both rapid reading groups perform much worse than the normal readers on the comprehension test. The eye fixations suggest several sources of this decrement. The general conclusion from these analyses is that both the speedreaders and skimmers are working from a data base that, relative to normal reading, is impoverished in two respects. Rapid readers have a far sparser sample of the text, because they fixate far fewer of the words. Their sampling is fairly unselective, and their perceptual span processing is sufficiently narrow to make the comprehension of unfixated words (especially longer ones) fairly improbable. Thus, they are more likely to be operating on input that cannot be parsed using the usual syntactic constraints of English. Moreover, they are much more likely to have skipped a word or phrase that may modulate the gist of a sentence or provide information that relates it to earlier information.

The second source of impoverishment is that rapid readers spend about 30% less time than normal readers on the words they do fixate. Although the rapid readers' gaze duration is clearly affected by the properties of the fixated word, the size of the effects is smaller than for normal readers. The fact that rapid readers have much smaller regression weights suggests that basic comprehension processes are modified during rapid reading, probably by lowering the criterion for sufficient confidence in a partial result that is produced by a component of the comprehension process. Thus, some comprehension processes must be truncated or accelerated, probably with an associated loss in quality of the resulting representation.

Differences Between Trained Speedreaders and Untrained Skimmers

The speedreaders performed somewhat better than the skimmers on the comprehension tests that followed the reading of each passage, in spite of the fact that they were reading slightly faster. The speedreader's advantage was localized to questions that probed for relatively high-level information about familiar topics (the *Reader's Digest* narratives). (Although we have analyzed the eye-fixation data for only two passages, this comprehension result applies to many other passages.) We can look to the eye-fixation behavior of the two groups of rapid readers to suggest what might or might not be the source of the speedreaders' advantage.

One obvious difference in the eye fixation behavior of the speedreaders and skimmers was that speedreaders sampled the text fairly uniformly, whereas skimmers read some portions very carefully and skipped other portions entirely. Some of the skimmers had a strong tendency to occasionally skip long sequences of consecutive words. Although skimmers sometimes skipped over large portions of text, they also read some portions in great detail. As mentioned earlier, skimmers fixated two adjacent words or skipped over only one word (i.e., had runs of unfixated words of length 0 or 1) more often, 67% of the time compared to the speedreaders' 55%. Thus, both speedreaders and skimmers skipped more words than normal readers, but the sampling scheme was more uniform for the speedreaders.

The relatively constant rate of sampling might be an important component of the speedreading process. Even when speedreaders encountered important or difficult parts of the text and their reading rate decreased, they were less likely than skimmers to revert to normal reading habits. Instead, they tended to maintain the general characteristics of rapid reading, while making an increment in the sampling density. This procedure of fairly uniform sampling apparently is effective for the goal of obtaining gist information, perhaps because it frees cognitive resources that would otherwise be alternating between two different modes of reading and deciding where to place the next fixation.

Speedreaders were not more likely to fixate important words than were the skimmers, ruling that out as a source of their advantage. To test this, we correlated the probability of fixation with the rated importance of each word (and covaried out word length). For both groups, the correlation between the rated importance of a word and its probability of being fixated was unimpressive, and if anything, the skimmers' correlation was slightly higher (.11 versus .08). Thus, speedreaders are *not* more perceptually selective than untrained skimmers.

*Probable Sources of the Advantage of Speedreaders.*Readers trained in a speedreading course do attain a new rapid reading skill. The speedreaders' advantage over untrained skimmers is probably due to top–down, conceptual processes like making inferences and effectively using previous knowledge of familiar content areas. Unlike normal reading, speedreading requires these conceptual processes to operate very rapidly, and to operate on an impoverished data base consisting of a randomly selected proportion of the words. Top–down processes cannot function effectively unless an appropriate knowledge base exists from which inferences can be drawn so the speedreaders perform better only on high-level *Reader's Digest* test items.

Most readers cannot speedread without extensive practice, usually in the context of a formal instructional situation. Repeated practice at making rapid, extended inferences from an impoverished data base seems to be a prerequisite to comprehension gains during rapid reading. Moreover, even after having had training and practice, experienced speedreaders still report that the process is effortful and difficult to maintain for long periods of time. The strenuousness and repetitiveness of the task might require the discipline imposed by an instructional situation. Thus, there is more to speedreading than just turning pages quickly and making inferences based on previous knowledge. It also involves the very disciplined and rapid use of the information as it is being collected from text in conjunction with previous knowledge.

CONCLUSION

We have outlined some of the major characteristics of skilled reading. Furthermore, we have described one formal model that captures many of these characteristics and provides a reasonable account of skilled reading. One benefit of this approach is that it offers a framework in which to place different types of reading. Reading behavior varies considerably, depending on the task, the reader, and the text. Speedreading is one point in the space of reading behaviors. Our results indicate that speedreading involves changes in the text sampling density and a change in some comprehension processes. For example, a speedreader cannot do a full syntactic analysis of a sentence or clause. But speedreading does appear to make similar use of knowledge structures, as described in the first and second section. Thus, speedreading and presumably other types of reading in the speed–care continuum may require somewhat different specific models of reading, but they certainly can peacefully coexist in the same conceptual framework.

ACKNOWLEDGMENTS

This research was partially supported by Grant G-79-0119 from the National Institute of Education and Grant MH-29617 from the National Institute of Mental Health. Much of the research reported here was done in collaboration with Robert Thibadeau and Michael Masson.

REFERENCES

Anderson, J. R. *Language memory and thought*. Hillsdale, N.J.: Lawrence Erlbaum Associates, 1976.

Bartlett, F. C. *Remembering*. Cambridge, Ma.: The University Press, 1932.

Boring, F. G. *A history of experimental psychology*, 2nd ed. New York: Appleton-Century-Crofts, 1950.

Bransford, J. D., & Johnson, M. K. Considerations of some problems of comprehension. In W. G. Chase (Ed.), *Visual information processing*. New York: Academic Press, 1973.

Carpenter, P. A., & Just, M. A. What the eyes are doing while the mind is reading. In K. Rayner (Ed.), *Perceptual and language processes*. New York: Academic Press, 1983.

Charniak, E. *Toward a model of children's story comprehension*. Cambridge, Ma.: MIT Artificial Intelligence Laboratory, TR–266, 1972.

Chiesi, H. L., Spilich, G. J., & Voss, J. F. Acquisition of domain–related information in relation to high and low domain knowledge. *Journal of Verbal Learning and Verbal Behavior, 1979, 18,* 257–274.

Collins, A. M., & Loftus, E. F. A spreading activation theory of semantic processing. *Psychological Review, 1975, 82,* 407–428.

Curtis, M. E. Development of components of reading skill. *Journal of Educational Psychology, 1980, 72,* 656–669.

Daneman, M., & Carpenter, P. A. Individual differences in working memory and reading. *Journal of Verbal Learning and Verbal Behavior, 1980, 19,* 450–466.

Dee-Lucas, D., Just, M. A., Carpenter, P. A., & Daneman, M. What eye fixations tell us about the time course of text integration. In R. Groner & P. Fraisse (Eds.), *Cognition and eye movements*. Amsterdam: North Holland, and Berlin: Deutscher Verlag der Wissenschaften, 1982.

Findler, N. V. (Ed.) *Associative networks: Representation and use of knowledge by computers.* New York: Academic Press, 1979.

Hebb, D. O. *The organization of behavior: A neuropsychological theory.* New York: Wiley, 1949.

Just, M. A., & Carpenter, P. A. A theory of reading: From eye fixations to comprehension. *Psychological Review,* 1980, *87,* 329–354.

Just, M. A., Carpenter, P. A., & Masson, M. Speedreading and skimming: What eye fixations tell us about rapid reading. Unpublished manuscript. Carnegie–Mellon University, 1981.

Just, M. A., Carpenter, P. A., & Woolley, J. D. Paradigms and processes in reading comprehension. *Journal of Experimental Psychology: General,* 1982, *111,* 228–238.

LaBerge, D., & Samuels, S. J. Toward a theory of automatic information processing in reading. *Cognitive Psychology,* 1974, *6,* 293–323.

Lerner, B. The minimum competence testing movement: Social, scientific and legal implications. *American Psychologist,* 1981, *36,* 1057–1066.

Levy, B. A. Interactive processes during reading. In A. M. Lesgold & C. A. Perfetti (Eds.), *Interactive processes in reading.* Hillsdale, N.J.: Lawrence Erlbaum Associates, 1981.

McClelland, J. L., & Rumelhart, D. E. An interactive activation model of context effects in letter perception: Part 1. An account of basic findings. *Psychological Review,* 1981, *88,* 375–407.

Meyer, D. E., & Schvaneveldt, R. W. Facilitation in recognizing pairs of words: Evidence of a dependence between retrieval operations. *Journal of Experimental Psychology,* 1971, *90,* 227–234.

Minsky, M. A framework for representing knowledge. In P. H. Winston (Ed.), *The psychology of computer vision.* New York: McGraw–Hill, 1975.

Newell, A. Harpy, production systems and human cognition. In R. Cole (Ed.), *Perception and production of fluent speech.* Hillsdale, N.J.: Lawrence Erlbaum Associates, 1980.

Newell, A., & Rosenbloom, P. S. Mechanisms of skill acquisition and the law of practice. In J. R. Anderson (Ed.), *Cognitive skills and their acquisition.* Hillsdale, N.J.: Lawrence Erlbaum Associates, 1981.

Norman, D. A., & Rumelhart, D. E. *Explorations in cognition.* San Francisco, Ca.: W. H. Freeman and Company, 1975.

Posner, M. I., & Snyder, C. R. Attention and cognitive control. In R. L. Solso (Ed.), *Information processing and cognition: The Loyola Symposium.* Hillsdale, N.J.: Lawrence Erlbaum Associates, 1975.

Rayner, K. The perceptual span and peripheral cues in reading. *Cognitive Psychology,* 1975, *7,* 65–81.

Reddy, R., & Newell, A. Knowledge and its representation in a speech understanding system. In L. W. Gregg (Ed.), *Knowledge and cognition.* Potomac, Md: Lawrence Erlbaum Associates, 1974.

Schank, R. C., & Abelson, R. P. *Scripts, plans, goals, and understanding: An inquiry into human knowledge structures.* Hillsdale, N.J.: Lawrence Erlbaum Associates, 1977.

Shiffrin, R. M., & Schneider, W. Controlled and automatic human information processing: Perceptual learning, automatic attending, and a general theory. *Psychological Review,* 1977, *84,* 127–190.

Spilich, G. J., Vesonder, G. T., Chiesi, H. L., & Voss, J. F. Text processing of domain-related information for individuals with high and low domain knowledge. *Journal of Verbal Learning and Verbal Behavior,* 1979, *18,* 275–290.

Sticht, T. G. Learning by listening. In J. Carroll and R. Freedle (Eds.), *Language comprehension and the acquisition of knowledge.* Washington, D.C.: V. H. Winston & Sons, 1972.

Sulin, R. A., & Dooling, D. J. Intrusion of a thematic idea in retention of prose. *Journal of Experimental Psychology,* 1974, *103,* 255–262.

Thibadeau, R., Just, M. A., & Carpenter, P. A. *Real reading behavior.* Proceedings of the 18th annual meeting of the Association of Computational Linguistics, 1980.

Thibadeau, R., Just, M. A., & Carpenter, P. A. A model of the time course and content of human reading. *Cognitive Science*, 1982, *6*, 157–203.

Voss, J. F., Vesonder, G. T., & Spilich, G. J. Text generation and recall by high knowledge and low knowledge individuals. *Journal of Verbal Learning and Verbal Behavior*, 1980, *19*, 651–667.

Winograd, T. A program for understanding natural language. *Cognitive Psychology*, 1972, *3*, 1–191.

11 Elaborations: Assessment and Analysis

Steffen-Peter Ballstaedt
Heinz Mandl
*Deutsches Institut für Fernstudien
an der Universität Tübingen*

ELABORATIVE PROCESSES

In spite of the emphasis placed on the constructive activities of the reader, much research on text processing has until now focussed on the exact reproduction of the contents of a text. Thus, the measuring of recall performance is a widely used method of acquiring information about what occurred during information processing. However, with this task orientation it is easy to overlook constructive activities which Herbart (1816), the proponents of hermeneutics, and especially Bartlett (1932) had already placed in the center of their text processing or comprehension theories: the interaction of the contents of a text with the prior knowledge of the individual reader (cf. Ballstaedt, Mandl, Schnotz, & Tergan, 1981). This level of text comprehension is labeled *elaborative processing* in the framework of the levels of processing approach. The processes that connect the contents of the text and prior knowledge are inferences of various types. During reading, schemata are assumed to be activated in the memory of the reader and are used to draw conclusions beyond the text itself.

Phenomenologically, these elaborative processes appear as ideas, associations, and images during reading. Through elaborative inferences the knowledge structure realized in the text is connected and integrated in a number of ways with existing structures. For example, a reader reads the following sentence: *Many plants contain substances which are of pharmacological use.* Via the activation of different schemata and their subschemata, different readers could form the following ideas or associations:

1. Camomile is a plant that contains substances that are of pharmacological use.
2. My grandmother knew an herbal tea for every ache and pain.
3. Inhumane animal experiments are unnecessarily carried out by pharmacologists.
4. I'm imagining an old herb-seller.
5. *Pharmacological* is a scientific term I don't know.

In elaboration 1, *semantic knowledge* is activated; it is a case of simple specification of the initial statement. With elaboration 2, *episodic knowledge* is evoked; an autobiographical experiential context is supplied. Elaboration 3 contains an *evaluative component* in addition to the activated semantic prior knowledge. Elaboration 4 suggests the existence of *visual imagery* that is verbally communicated. Finally, elaboration 5 represents a *metacognitive statement* about the reader's own processing: He/she found a gap in his/her lexicon.

From these examples the variety and idiosyncratic nature of the elaborative processes which constitute the creative activity during reading can clearly be seen. This is especially valid for the comprehension of literary texts, which are distinguished from expository texts through greater openness for possible interpretations. However, elaborations play a role even for expository texts, which has been underestimated.

The occurrence and effects of elaboration during reading have as yet not been sufficiently examined. Anderson and Reder (1979) proposed the hypothesis that only the number of elaborations is decisive for the retention of the contents of a text: the more elaborations there are, the broader the processing, and the better the retention. Anderson (1980) proposed two theoretical reasons for a better recall performance through elaborative processes. For this, he assumes that knowledge is represented in the form of semantic networks:

1. A node representing a content unit of a text has a greater chance of being retrieved in an elaborated network because it has more connections to surrounding nodes. These connections may serve as possible alternate retrieval routes.

2. If a content unit failed to be stored as a node in memory during reading, it can more likely be inferred or reconstructed from the existing nodes in an elaborated network structure.

The hypothesis of a linear relation between the number of elaborations and retention has been suggested by various findings. It was also shown several times that elaboration techniques or elaborative learning strategies have a positive effect on learning success (Mayer, 1980; Reder, 1980; Weinstein, 1978; Weinstein, Underwood, Wicker, & Cubberly, 1979). Mandl and Ballstaedt (1982) doubt that the relation is linear. They found indications for an inverted, U-shaped relationship. This could be explained in the following manner. If someone elaborates very little, the new information will be insufficiently anchored and *woven* into the knowledge structures. The reconstruction of the contents of the text will have few reference points that can be utilized. As a result, the recall performance will most likely be poor. On the other hand, if someone elaborates very broadly, even though they *interweave* quite extensively, they will have difficulties in reconstructing the original information found in the text due to the large number of activated schemata. A moderate amount of elaborative processing would then seem to be most desirable.

It must, however, be questioned whether the number of elaborations is alone responsible for recall success in text learning. Bransford and his research team (1979) have conducted several experiments whose findings permit the conclusion that not all elaborations facilitate the learning process. They apparently do so only when they provide a relevant and consistent context for the task (Bransford, 1979; Bransford, Franks, Morris, & Stein, 1979; Stein, Morris, & Bransford, 1978). The quality of elaborations is probably of more importance than the quantity.

Methodological problems of collecting and analyzing spontaneously generated elaborations present the most serious hindrance in answering the questions that have been posed. How is one to get at cognitive processes which emerge—as every introspection show—fleetingly and often nonverbally in one's consciousness? And in what manner should the numerous elaboration processes be divided into categories that are meaningful? Which type of elaborations will more likely hinder? Which elaborations will more likely affect certain learning performances in a positive way? Subsequently, we discuss the quantitative and qualitative problems. To begin with, we examine the validity of the *thinking aloud* method in assessing elaborations. Then, three procedures for evaluating verbalization protocols will be presented, which use different meaning units: words, main ideas, and foci of attention. Finally, these same procedures are utilized in an empirical investigation.

ASSESSING ELABORATIONS

On the Method of Thinking Aloud

Thinking aloud while reading presents itself as a promising method by which to reveal elaborative processes. By the *thinking aloud* method, only the direct verbalization of those processes which are occurring at the time in one's consciousness is to be understood (Duncker, 1935; Ericsson & Simon, 1979, 1980). The standard instruction requires that the ideas, thoughts, and associations that appear during the reading of text segments (sentences, sections, units of the reader's own choosing) be spoken aloud. Thereby *thinking aloud* is distinct from introspection, which requires a retrospective verbalization (Bühler, 1907; Ericsson & Simon, 1978; Nisbett & Wilson, 1977). Graesser (1981) lists three advantages of this method for researching text comprehension:

1. Verbal protocols represent qualitatively rich data material in which phenomena can be discovered that as yet have not been registered by any theory. The *thinking aloud* method, then, fulfills a hypothesis generating function.
2. Inferences can be uncovered that serve to help the reader understand the text. This advantage addresses directly the registering of elaborations.
3. This method can be used with ecologically valid texts from actual teaching/learning systems that were not constructed on the researcher's drawing board for a specialized issue under consideration.

These advantages are countered, however, by several problems and criticisms, which cast doubt on the usefulness and validity of the method (Ericsson & Simon, 1979; Huber & Mandl, 1982; Weidle & Wagner, 1982):

1. Anderson and Reder (1979) believe that thinking aloud during reading brings only the "tip of the iceberg" of the processes into view. More is going on in the head of the reader than they can verbalize. There are automated processes that are no longer consciously represented. Furthermore, parallel processes are presumably occurring. From the numerous choices a selection must be made, the criteria of which need not necessarily agree with the interests of the researcher. Thus, verbal protocols are not only *incomplete* but also may contain material that is irrelevant for the issue under discussion.
2. It has not been clarified whether the unusual task of verbalizing has an effect on the ongoing processes. Of course, in normal reading situations, many cognitive processes are accompanied by *internal speech*. However, every reader also knows that verbalizing presents difficulties in itself: One may search for the given words, or one may correct oneself, because a better or more exact expression has been found. Sentences that have already been initiated are stopped, and new ones are started. The transformation of nonverbal ideas presents an additional problem because it may require processes that otherwise would not have occurred. It cannot altogether be ruled out that additional processing capacities may be required, which may cause *interference* with the ongoing processes.
3. Finally, the elicitation of verbalizations occurs in a social situation in which certain communicative conventions are observed. Thus, subjects may not mention many ideas because they seem to be too intimate, crazy, abnormal, or banal. The experimenter is in a situation similar to Freud's, who first had to instruct his patients in the uncensored verbalizing of free associations. Also other effects already recognized from previous experimentation can influence verbalization. For example, some subjects view the instructions to elaborate aloud while reading as a type of creativity test. In other words, they attempt to report as much as possible and to be as original as they can (subjective task-orientation).

This latter criticism of the *thinking aloud* method relates to other assessment situations as well. The first two criticisms are more serious. The *thinking aloud* method is based on the assumption that ongoing processing can be expressed directly in speech with no disturbances and that as a result the verbal protocols offer at least a partial insight into the actual occurrences. The truth of this assumption can only be elucidated when an empirically supported theory of verbalization exists. Two approaches will now briefly be reviewed, the verbalization model from Ericsson and Simon (1979, 1980) and Chafe's model (1977, 1979, 1980).

Ericsson and Simon

In a series of articles, the authors investigate the validity of different forms of verbalization (Ericsson & Simon, 1978, 1979, 1980). They take as a basis a simple processing model as had been developed in the information processing paradigm of cognitive psychology (Lachman, Lachman, & Butterfield, 1979; Simon, 1979). In this model, three memories can be differentiated: the sensory register (SR), the short-term memory (STM), and the long-term memory (LTM). The SRs of the different sensory modalities kept for a short time the information input from the sensory organs. Their capacity is large, but storage duration limited. The LTM represents an extremely large network of interconnected concept nodes; both capacity and storage duration are limitless. The concept nodes can be activated either directly by sensory information from the SR (recognition) or by other nodes in the LTM (association). The information units from the SR and the LTM to which attention is being directed at the time are joined together in the STM or working memory. A central processor (CP) controls what is given attention. The STM is equipped only with a limited capacity; however, its information units can be kept in a state of readiness for a longer time through rehearsal and can eventually be transferred to the LTM. Should neither of these processes take place, the information units extinguish and/or are displaced by new ones (forgetting). According to Ericsson and Simon, this model represents the core of the theories and findings of information processing in a generalized form, which avoids all of the specialized and still unresolved problems. Thus, the model takes no position, for example, on the question whether the memories correspond to delimitable storage systems (multistore model, cf. Jüttner, 1979) or to a continuum of processing levels (levels of processing model, cf. Cermak & Craik, 1979). On the basis of this simple model, Ericsson and Simon produce a typology or taxonomy of types of verbalization in which the decisive dimensions are the time of the verbalization (on-line or retrospective) and the relation between the heeded and the verbalized information. We need not concern ourselves in any further detail with the taxonomy at this point, because only the verbalization method is of any interest for our purposes. Ericsson and Simon are of the opinion that thinking aloud represents a direct articulation of the information units and processes that are present at the time in the STM. For this, they recognize two articulation levels. On the first level, that which is present in the STM in verbal or phonemic code is directly verbalized. On the second level, the information must first be translated into the verbal code, as it is, for example, a visual image. At that level, intermediate recording processes operate between the information of the STM and its verbalization. In this case, it is to be expected that the processing time will be somewhat longer or that only a portion of the STM contents will be verbalized. In general, however, Ericsson and Simon are of the opinion that thinking aloud alters neither the structure nor the sequence of the cognitive processes; at most, a slight reduction in processing speed can be established. The Ericsson–Simon verbalization model is represented in Fig. 11.1. Here, the graphic conventions of the multistore model are used without taking all of its theoretical implications.

According to their findings, nonautomated processes that are operating in the STM can be registered with the thinking aloud method (in other words, processes which operate when attention is consciously being directed towards something). Thus, for example, intended inferences are mainly automated in the comprehension process whereas elaborative inferences as conscious activation of prior knowledge from the LTM should be accessible to verbalization as a matter of principle.

Chafe

Chafe (1980) uses three main constructs, *knowledge, consciousness,* and *self,* to develop a simple theory of thinking. *Knowledge* represents all of the information accessible from perception and memory. From this enormous store of knowledge, an executive or central control instance brings during thinking certain knowledge units into consciousness, a process which is normally described as *paying attention.* Chafe also calls the executive the *self,* in which needs and interests of the reader are organized into goals. *Consciousness* is the activation of certain knowledge units in the interest of the self. The consciousness has four basic properties:

1. It has a limited capacity, that is, only small information units are activated at one time; Chafe calls these *foci.*
2. An information unit of this type remains activated only for a limited duration.
3. The "stream of thought" does not flow continuously, rather it is a saltatory succession of foci.
4. The actual consciousness can be divided in each case into a focus and a *periphery.* The focus is maximally activated and conscious while a series of other knowledge units with a lower degree of consciousness lie ready in the periphery.

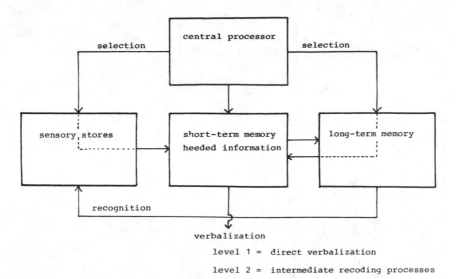

FIG. 11.1.   Processing model of Ericsson and Simon (1980).

This model explicitly relies on the findings of the evaluation of visual information through saccadic eye movements (cf., Just & Carpenter, 1976). According to Chafe, seeing and thinking use the same strategy of information processing. Just as a visual field can be successively scanned, so can an area of knowledge be scanned through the consciousness.

By *verbalization* Chafe means all cognitive processes that lead from nonverbal knowledge to verbal expression. In order to investigate these verbalization processes, he proceeded in the following empirical manner. He showed his subjects a short narrative film that they had to recall at different time intervals. By looking at a film a knowledge structure is built up. This structure may be analyzed in its various verbalizations in the recall protocols. Chafe assumes that speaking reflects the sequence of activated knowledge units or foci, respectively. As an empirical support for this assumption he points out the fact that spoken language may be subdivided into natural units by paralinguistic and syntactic cues. In the section on evaluation procedures there will be a detailed description of how verbalizations can be divided through the use of intonation contours, speech pauses, and syntactic criteria into information units that correspond to sentence segments with six words on the average. Each of these linguistic units corresponds to a focus of attention according to Chafe. The succession of foci portrays the scanning with which the knowledge is scrutinized. The contents of the foci of attention reflect the distribution of attention, which is controlled by the self. Because for every succeeding verbalization, a new scrutinization is carried out, differences arise in the various renarrations. Figure 11.2 serves to illustrate this theory.

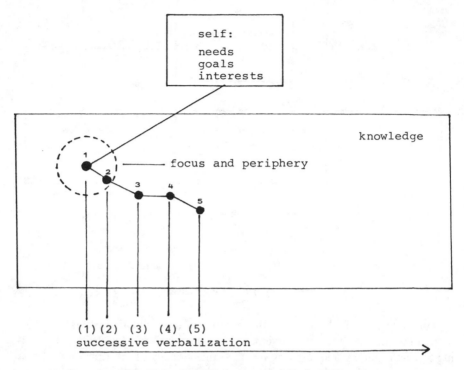

FIG. 11.2.   Verbalization model of Chafe (1980).

   A hierarchical organization of the underlying knowledge can be reconstructed from the linear organization of the foci during speech. To do this, several foci are combined together to form *centers of interest;* longer pauses and thematic changes serve as criteria. A center of interest corresponds to an activated schema. Thus, the foci that form the schema, represent a special description of the schema. The centers of interest can also be combined to form higher units in the hierarchy, which Chafe calls *episodes* in his narrative structures. The episodes together constitute the knowledge structure on which the verbalization was based. The horizontal and vertical organization of spoken language can be seen in Fig. 11.3. Also Chafe's verbalization theory implies that speaking does indeed portray thinking or the operating cognitive processes. Thus, thinking aloud would provide an excellent possibility for tracking elaborations during reading. Furthermore, Chafe offers a reliable and valid method of analysis for verbalizations, which is presented more completely later in this article.

Summary and Evaluation

When both of the reviewed approaches are compared, similarities become apparent. Both assume an executive that controls the distribution of attention during

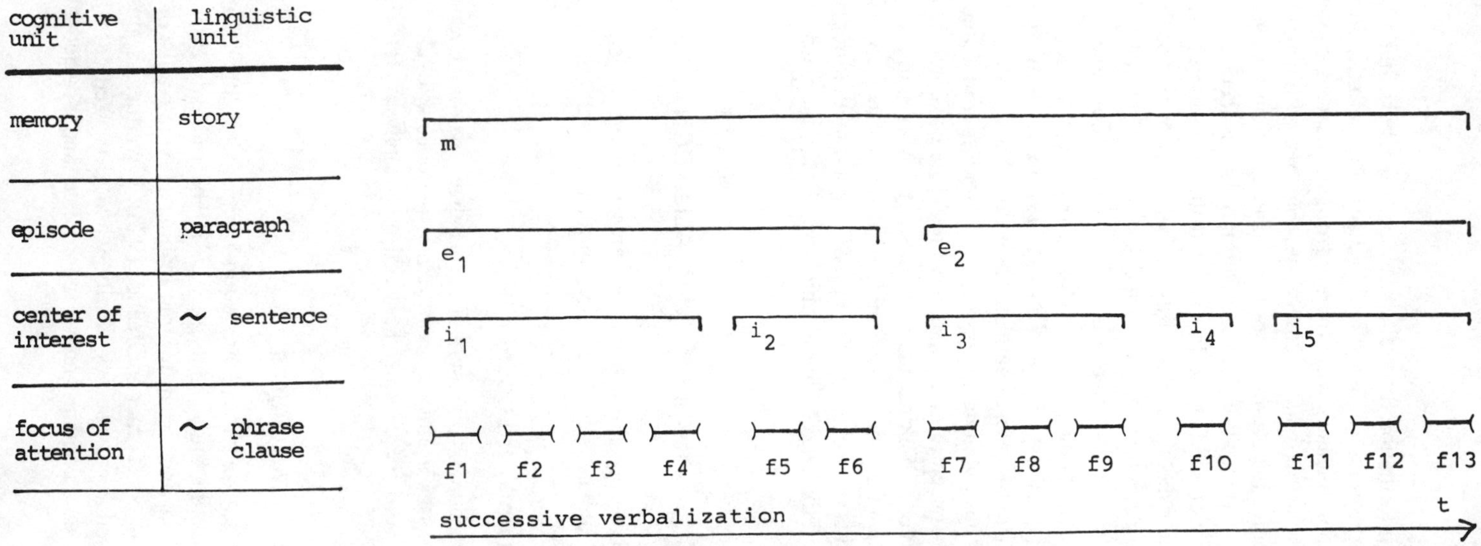

FIG. 11.3.   Hierarchical organization of Cognitive and Linguistic Units of Chafe (1980). f = focus, i = center of interest, e = episode, m = memory.

cognitive unit	linguistic unit
memory	story
episode	paragraph
center of interest	~ sentence
focus of attention	~ phrase clause

successive verbalization

the processing of information (central processor or the self). In both approaches, thinking aloud portrays the sequence of this distribution of attention. For Chafe, it is thought the consciousness was drawing from an ocean of knowledge. Ericsson and Simon assume particular memory mechanisms, within and between each of these, special information processes take place (recognition, association, selection, retrieval, verbalization, etc.). Although this conceptualization is more precise, it does not contradict the less refined theory proposed by Chafe. One advantage of Chafe's theory is suggesting foci of attention and centers of interest as units that have cognitive relevance and provide for a reliable analysis procedure. On the basis of both approaches, the thinking aloud method is suited to uncover ongoing nonautomated information processes.

Graesser (1981) and especially Waern (1979) argue along similar lines. A certain scepticism must be maintained when one deals with the collecting of elaborations. Self-observations and retrospective reports from subjects show that the concordance between thinking and speaking does not correspond to what is theoretically assumed. Thinking often *runs away* from speaking. In other words, more ideas arise than the time-consuming verbalization can accommodate. However, in spite of this qualification, the thinking aloud method registers more of text comprehension than the methods which try to gain the processes only from recall performances.

ANALYSIS OF VERBALIZATIONS

In this section, three possibilities will be presented for the analysis of spontaneously spoken language that are based on meaning units of different sizes.

Analysis Based on Word Count

The simplest procedure is to count the verbalized words. Every completely uttered word counts as a unit. A more expansive content evaluation could be imagined using word-frequency and word-type analyses (cf. Herrmann & Stäcker, 1969).

Analysis Based on Main Ideas

In text research, text and recall are often compared with one another using propositions as meaning units (Kintsch, 1974). There already exist rules, which have been worked out and tested, for transcribing a text into a list of propositions (Bovair & Kieras, 1981; Turner & Greene, 1978). Nevertheless, this is a lengthy and difficult procedure to use, especially when it is used for spontaneously spoken language that contains many incomplete and syntactically incorrect sentences.

A simpler, more easily manageable procedure consists of breaking the material down into so-called *main ideas*. To do this, the evaluator goes through the verbal protocol and marks those places where a new, self-contained idea appears. Every main idea is expressed in a statement. Due to everyday language competence, it is possible to classify main ideas as meaning units with a high degree of reliability (cf., Schnotz, Ballstaedt, & Mandl, 1981). It can be said that the propositions at the highest level of the hierarchy and those which are embedded in them correspond to main ideas for the most part. We will now give an example in German and in English from the material we investigated; in this case, the subjects were to elaborate on individual sentences from a text.

Example 1: Main Idea Analysis

Gelesener Satz

Die Heilpflanzenkunde oder Phytotherapie hat nach mehrtausendjähriger Tradition einen neuen Aufschwung genommen.

Transkript der Verbalisierung

Ich weiss nicht was Phytotherapie ist, ach so, ist Heilpflanzenkunde, ja. Ja die mehrtausendjährige Tradition verwirrt mich etwas, aber wenn man bisschen darüber nachdenkt, dann kann, ja dann komm' ich vielleicht drauf, dass viele Leute im Moment wieder so auf Heilpflanzen und Natur zurückkommen. Also dass sie nicht unbedingt mit, mit chemischen Mitteln irgendwas zu heilen versuchen, sondern halt mit natürlichen Mitteln und so.

Unterteilung in Hauptideen

1. Phytotherapie ist Heilpflanzenkunde.
2. Nach mehrtausendjähriger Tradition kommen die Leute wieder auf Heilpflanzen zurück.
3. Sie versuchen sich mit natürlichen, statt mit chemischen Mitteln zu heilen.

The sentence that was read

Herbal medicine, or phytotherapy, has received a new impetus after having a tradition of several thousand years.

Transcript of the verbalization

I don't know what "phytotherapy" is, oh, it's herbal medicine, yeah. Yeah, the tradition of several thousand years confuses me a little, but when you think about it a little, then you, yeah, then I can get the idea, maybe, that many people are going back to herbs and nature at the moment. That means that they don't really want to try to cure something with, with chemicals, instead with natural stuff and so on.

Division into main ideas

1. Phytotherapy is herbal medicine.
2. After a tradition of several thousand years, people are going back to herbs.
3. They attempt to cure themselves with natural means instead of with chemicals.

Foci of Attention Analysis

Transcription. To use Chafe's evaluation method (1980), the tape-recorded verbalizations are transcribed in a way that allows the paralinguistic aspects of the spoken language to be retained. To do this, the following symbols were used in the continuous text: (X) = pause X sec long; . . . . = short interruption; - - - - = lengthened vowel; . = falling intonation; , = rising intonation; ; = doubtful case.

Segmentation. On the basis of transcripts, the continuous texts are segmented into linguistic units, which each correspond to a focus of attention according to Chafe. The demarcation of the units occurs on the basis of three criteria: (1) rising or falling intonation; (2) speech pauses; (3) end of a syntactic sentential segment. Occasionally, all three criteria apply. According to Chafe, the most solid, and therefore most decisive criterion is the intonation contour. Normally, a rising intonation marks the end of a sentential segment; and falling intonation marks the end of a sentence. The speech pause can indicate various processes and cannot always be unambiguously interpreted as a result (Butterworth, 1975; Drommel, 1974; Rochester, 1973). Thus, for example, a speech pause can signify the search for a word in the lexicon and not the end of a linguistic unit or for a focus of attention. Even the ending of a sentential segment does not always provide a valid criterion, as the syntax of spoken language often deviates from normal. A speaker can even do without syntactic constructions to a great extent as long as a clear semantic interpretation remains possible (cf., Engelkamp, 1976). Two different examples, each in German and in English, will now be presented of the transcription and subdivision into linguistic units of material from the investigation, which is reported on later.

Example 2. Foci of Attention Analysis

Gelesener Satz

Die Heilpflanzenkunde oder Phytotherapie hat nach mehrtausendjähriger Tradition einen neuen Aufschwung genommen.

Transkript der Verbalisierung

Ich weiss nicht was Phytotherapie ist (1.5) ach so ist Heilpflanzenkunde ja. (5.3 (1.6) ähm (3.0)) Ja die mehrtausendjährige Tradition (0.6) verwirrt mich etwas, (3.2) aber we—nn ma—n bisschen länger darüber nachdenkt, (1.0) dann kann . . . ja dann komm ich vielleicht drauf dass (2.0 (1.0) ähm (0.9)) viele Leute im Moment (0.9) wieder so auf Heilpflanzen und Natur zurückkommen. (1.1) Also dass sie (0.7) nicht unbedingt mit (3.2 (1.3) ähm (1.6)) ja mit chemischen Mitteln irgendetwas zu heilen versuchen sondern halt mit (1.0) mit natürlichen Mitteln und so.

Unterteilung in foci:

(1) Ich weiss nicht was Phytotherapie ist; (2) ach so ist Heilpflanzenkunde ja; (3) ja die mehrtausendjährige Tradition verwirrt mich etwas; (4) aber wenn man bisschen länger darüber nachdenkt; (5) dann kann . . . ja dann komm ich vielleicht drauf dass; (6) viele Leute im Moment; (7) wieder so auf Heilpflanzen und Natur zurückkommen; (8) Also dass sie nicht unbedingt mit; (9) ja mit chemischen Mitteln irgendwas zu heilen versuchen sondern halt mit; (10) mit natürlichen Mitteln und so.

The sentence that was read

Herbal medicine, or phytotherapy, has received a new impetus after having a tradition of several thousand years.

Transcript of the verbalization

I don't know what "phytotherapy" is (1.5) oh it's herbal medicine yeah. (5.3 (1.6) uhm (3.0)). Yeah the tradition of several thousand years (0.6) confuses me a little, (3.2) but i—f y—ou think about it a little, (1.0) then you . . . yeah than I can get the idea maybe that (2.0 (1.0) uhm (0.9)) many people at the moment (0.9) are going back to herbs and nature. (1.1) That means that they (0.7) don't really want to (3.2 (1.3) uhm (1.6)) try to cure something with chemicals instead with (1.0) with natural stuff and so on.

Subdivision into foci:

(1) I don't know what "phytotherapy" is; (2) oh it's herbal medicine, yeah; (3) Yeah, the tradition of several thousand years confuses me a little; (4) but if you think about it a little; (5) then you . . . yeah then I can get the idea maybe that; (6) many people at the moment; (7) are going back to herbs and nature; (8) That means that they don't really want to; (9) yeah try to cure something with chemicals instead with; (10) with natural stuff and so on.

Example 3: Foci of Attention Analysis

Gelesener Satz

Durch die Entwicklung moderner Labormethoden wie Chromatographie, Isotopentechnik oder Photometrie kann die chemische Zusammensetzung einer Pflanze aufgeklärt werden.

Transkript der Verbalisierung

Chromatographie erinnert mich a—n, ä—h, (0.9) so ein Bild das man von Chromosomen machen kann, (1.0) so aufzeichnen die einzelnen Abschnitte die da drauf sind. (6.3) Ja es kann halt wahrscheinlich sinnvoll sein die chemischen Zusammensetzungen . . . zu erkennen, (1.0) und damit eben besser arbeiten zu können, (0.5) als man's einfach aus den Erfahrungen heraus weiss.

Unterteilung in foci:

(1) Chromatographie erinnert mich an; (2) äh so ein Bild was man von Chromosomen machen kann; (3) so aufzeichnen die einzelnen Abschnitte die da drauf sind; (4) Ja es kann halt wahrscheinlich sinnvoll sein die chemischen Zusammensetzungen . . . zu erkennen; (5) und damit eben besser arbeiten zu können; (6) als man's einfach aus den Erfahrungen heraus weiss;

Sentence that was read

Through the development of modern laboratory methods, such as chromatography, isotope techniques, or photometry, the chemical composition of a plant can be analyzed.

Transcript of the verbalization

Chromatography reminds me o—f, u—h (0.9) a picture like you can make of chromosomes, (1.0) to show each of the sections that are on them. (6.3) Yeah it can probably be worthwhile when the chemical composition . . . is known, (1.0) so that you can use it better, (0.5) than you know it just from the experience of using it.

Subdivision into foci:

(1) Chromatography reminds me of; (2) a picture like you can make of chromosomes; (3) to show each of the sections that are on them; (4) Yeah it can probably be worthwhile when the chemical composition . . . is known; (5) so that you can use it better; (6) than you know it just from the experience of using it.

Hierarchization.   In a further evaluative step, the foci can be combined to form centers of interest or even larger semantic units in the manner, which was illustrated previously (see Fig. 11.3). Two criteria can be used to demark the centers of interest: (1) long pauses; and (2) thematic change, which is often marked by a topic-marker.

Often both criteria are met. Nevertheless, it is not always easy to combine foci into a superordinate topic. It is occasionally difficult to determine if there really is a thematic change. When the subjects and the evaluator have divergent schemata, incorrect classifications can occur. In most cases, however, the evaluator who is a member of the same speech community as the subject can rely on her/his own comprehension processes. The foci of attention from Example 2 can be combined to form three centers of interest, which can each be given an identifying label: (1) + (2): definition herbal medicine; (3) – (7): tradition; and (8) – (10): natural versus chemical remedies.

Comparison of the Procedures

The word-count is certainly the simplest procedure to use for the quantitative evaluation of verbal protocols. Of course, all of the irrelevant verbal fillers and empty phrases, which are part of an individual's style, are included in the count. Thus, the total number of words can only be seen as a crude measurement. On the other hand, main idea analysis is oriented towards content units. The evaluator extricates the speaker's essential thoughts from the surface of the text. This is possible on the basis of everyday linguistic competence; however, it cannot be denied that the evaluator imposes an organization on the speech material in so doing. This is not the case in using Chafe's procedure; the spoken language is segmented on the basis of easily collected features, which are provided by the speaker. The evaluator does not alter the surface of the text while segmenting, so as not to destroy the order of the thoughts contained therein. On the basis of Chafe's theory and the empirical procedure, it is to be expected that the foci of attention do indeed correspond to functional units in the information process. Nevertheless, in organizing the foci into larger meaning units, such as centers of interest, a certain hermeneutic competence must be called upon. Through semantic hierarchical organization, prior knowledge activated to comprehend the text can be reconstructed in sections. In spite of the somewhat elaborate nature of this procedure, it should be allowed the opportunity to prove itself useful in as many issues being investigated in thinking, reading, and problem solving as possible.

INVESTIGATION

Issues to be Investigated

Question 1.   In the theoretical discussion, three procedures for the evaluation of verbal protocols were presented and discussed. Each makes use of a different content unit: foci according to Chafe, main ideas, and word-counts. It remains to be determined to what degree the three evaluation processes correspond with one another in quantitative respect.

Question 2.   A second complex of questions deals with the effect of elaborative processes on recall performances:

1. When two groups are given immediate recall as their task orientation, is the recall performance of the group also instructed to elaborate aloud better than that of the second group, which received no additional instructions?
2. In considering the investigation conducted by Mandl and Ballstaedt

(1982), it had been suggested as possible that elaborating during reading especially improves long-term retention as a result of the intensive text processing. Thus, in the investigation that is being reported on in this article, recall performances were unexpectedly collected again at a later time: Does a group that received instructions to elaborate exhibit better recall performances than a group which received no such instructions after a longer time-interval (one week)?

3. Is the difference between immediate and delayed recall less for the group instructed to elaborate than for the group that was not instructed to elaborate?

Question 3.   What relation exists between the number of verbalized content units and recall performance?

Method

Experimental Design and Procedure.   Two experimental groups were formed. Both groups received the text and the task orientation that they were to reproduce the contents of the text as completely as possible after reading it. Additionally, group 1 was instructed to elaborate aloud while reading. After every sentence, each of the subjects in group 1 was requested to say aloud all of the thoughts and ideas that were going through their heads. The subjects could determine when they wanted to go on to the next sentence. A demonstration tape of the elaboration situation was presented to the subjects in group 1. Immediately after the subjects had read the text, their interests and prior knowledge about the topic of the text were collected to serve as control variables by using a self-rating scale. No significant differences were found between the groups. After completing the questionnaire, each of the subjects from both groups gave a written reproduction (here labeled, recall 1). They were asked to return in one week for a second session. They received no information, however, that during the second session, they were to write a second reproduction of the same text (here labeled, recall 2). Table 11.1 summarizes the experimental procedure.

Subjects and Experimental Text.   Twenty male students (theology, education and law), 10 in each group, took part in the investigation. The text, which was

TABLE 11.1
Experimental Procedure

Group 1:	Task orientation; elaboration instruction	Reading + elaborating aloud	Rating: prior knowledge, interests	Immediate recall (t 1)	Recall after one week (t 2)
Group 2:	Task orientation; no elaboration instruction	Reading	Rating: prior knowledge, interests	Immediate recall (t 1)	Recall after one week (t 2)

specially written for this investigation, dealt with the topic of herbal medicine. It consisted of 15 sentences with a total of 240 words in the German version (see Appendix for an English translation). The sentences were syntactically simple. The text also had a simple content structure: After an exposition of the problem, first advantages then disadvantages of the use of herbs instead of chemical medications were discussed.

Evaluation Procedures.   The verbal protocols were analyzed with the three evaluation procedures discussed already: word-counts, main ideas, and foci of attention. In using Chafe's procedure, the foci were additionally combined to form centers of interest; furthermore, the quotient of the number of foci divided by the number of centers of interest was calculated. This figure is related to the average number of foci a subject verbalizes for each center of interest. Some subjects have only a few centers of interest, each of them having many foci (large quotient); other subjects have many centers of interest, with only a few foci for each (smaller quotient). (If every center of interest is represented by one focus, the quotient is 1.) Thus, this quotient represents a measure of copiousness, which might predict recall performance better than the raw number of content units. The analysis of the original text, as well as the analyses of both sets of recall protocols, resulted from the application of two procedures:

1. A first evaluation was carried out according to the main idea analysis procedure (see previous text). The original text consisted of 26 units when it was transformed into main ideas.
2. In a second analysis, each of the main ideas of the text and the recall protocols was weighed (one to five points) according to its importance or hierarchical position following Kintsch. Based on this evaluation, one would receive a maximum of 77 points for a complete reproduction of the original text.

Results

Question 1.   The calculation of the correspondence of the three evaluation procedures for elaborations—foci of attention, main ideas, and word-counts—with one another yielded significant correlations among all of the procedures as can be seen in Table 11.2. Thus, the three procedures do correspond with one another to a great extent in quantitative aspects.

Question 2.   In comparison to the group without instructions to elaborate, the group with instructions to elaborate achieved significantly higher immediate recall performances with respect to both the number of main ideas ($t = 2.19$, p $< .025$) and the value for weighted main ideas ($t = 2.37$, p $< .025$). A week later, this finding only persisted in the recall value for weighted main ideas ($t = 2.35$, p $< .025$). The assumption could not be substantiated that the absolute as well as relative difference between immediate and delayed recall would be small-

TABLE 11.2
Covariation of the Three
Evaluation Procedures for
Elaborations

Evaluation Procedures for Elaborations	Group 1 Task Orientation/ Elaboration
Word-count - main ideas	.98 (p < .001)
Word-count - foci	.99 (p < .001)
Main ideas - foci	.97 (p < .001)

er in comparison for the group with instructions to elaborate than for the group that did not receive those instructions. The results show an improved performance on the immediate recall when the sentences were explicitly elaborated on. This was less distinct in the recall written a week later. In particular, a better (more resistant) recall performance for the elaborating group could not be confirmed, as can be seen in Table 11.3.

Question 3.   The connections, which were calculated on the basis of polynomial equations, among the four elaboration measures—foci, quotient of foci divided by centers of interest, main ideas, and word-counts—produced no meaningful relations for either recall with neither of the evaluation procedures. Neither an inverse U-shaped nor a linear relation could be found.

DISCUSSION

It is surprising, first of all, to note from the findings the appreciable correspondence in quantitative respect among the three evaluation procedures. This means that word-counts represent a useful and economical measure to use for purely quantitative questions (e.g., effect of the number of elaborations on the learning performance). Word-counts are, however, hardly usable for qualitative questions (effect of certain types of elaborations on the learning performance) because they destroy the contextual connections.

On the other hand, the results confirm that elaborative information processes have a distinct influence on recall performance. Yet, it must be pointed out that elaborative information processes were certainly also utilized by the subjects in group 2, which received no elaboration instructions. Thus, the two groups do not differ in the presence of elaboration in group 1 and the lack of it in group 2, but rather, they differ in the extent and intentionality of elaboration. A greater long-term effect when elaboration was explicitly requested could not definitely be established.

TABLE 11.3
Elaborations, Recall Units, Prior Knowledge, and Interest Scores

	Group 1 Task Orientation/ Elaboration		Group 2 Task Orientation No Elaboration		t-Value (df = 18)
	Mean	Standard Deviation	Mean	Standard Deviation	
Elaborations: foci of attention	130.00	74.21			
Elaborations: main ideas	58.10	31.31			
Elaborations: word-count	1007.40	638.65			
Elaborations: centers of interest	31.30	11.45			
Elaborations: quotient foci / centers of interest	4.48	1.01			
Recall t1: main ideas	14.90	3.41	11.50	3.54	2.19[a]
Recall t2: main ideas	12.30	3.40	9.78	3.56	1.67 ns
Recall t1: weighted main ideas	43.30	10.33	33.05	8.93	2.37[a]
Recall t2: weighted main ideas	35.90	10.99	25.44	9.34	2.35[a]
Rate of forgetting: main ideas: absolute	2.60	1.71	1.72	1.89	1.09 ns
relative					.39 ns
Rate of forgetting: weighted main ideas: absolute	7.40	5.17	7.61	7.42	0.07 ns
relative					1.32 ns
Prior knowledge	2.10	0.74	2.40	0.70	0.9 ns
Interest	1.70	0.68	1.90	0.57	0.72 ns

[a] $p < .025$

The attempt to find a regular connection between the number of elaborations and recall performance was unsuccessful. No relation, which could be meaningfully interpreted, could be found with any of the three types of meaning units. Even the hopes which had been placed on Chafe's procedure could not be realized: A prediction of recall performance is not possible by using the number of foci, the number of centers of interest, or the quotient of foci divided by centers of interest. This negative finding should not be overrated, however. Extent and style of elaboration differ so much from individual to individual that every effect could be concealed through the small size of the sample. Thus, it would be worthwhile in future investigations not only to form larger experimental samples but also to form homogeneous groups based on certain relevant variables. For example, extreme groups could be formed of people who elaborate copiously or of people who elaborate sparingly.

In general, it seems doubtful whether learning success can be predicted with the number of elaborated content units. The findings previously mentioned from Bransford and his associates suggest that a qualitative estimation of the elaborative processing would be more promising. Here are a few suggestions on that topic. In order to get an insight into the successive construction of an elaborative network structure, this network could be reconstructed through single case analyses. Anderson (1980) has demonstrated this procedure in a preliminary fashion. Thus, it would be possible to obtain an estimation of the integrative value of each elaborative process through the number of nodes and the number and type of the connections. A second possibility would be an estimation of the material elaborated to single sentences with the help of a scale for the measurement of the cognitive complexity or of integratedness (Mandl & Huber, 1978; Schroder, Driver, & Streuffert, 1975). It is to be expected that a higher degree of integratedness of the elaborative network structure would cause a better learning performance. Finally, usable category systems for elaborative content units should be developed. For foci in narrative retellings, Chafe (1980) has proposed a category system based on a simple story schema. A reliable and valid category system is not so easy to produce for expository texts, however. Mandl and Ballstaedt (1982) use a system with the categories "context of personal experience," "imagery," "critical comments," "paraphrase," and "metastatements." They could prove no effect on recall performance with these categories, however. It will be necessary for future investigation to be concentrated on a qualitative analysis of elaborations.

REFERENCES

Anderson, J. R. *Cognitive psychology and its implications*. San Francisco, Ca: W. M. Freeman & Co., 1980.

Anderson, J. R., & Reder, L. M. An elaborative processing explanation of depth of processing. In

L. S. Cermak & F. I. M. Craik (Eds.), *Levels of processing in human memory.* Hillsdale, N.J.: Lawrence Erlbaum Associates, 1979.

Ballstaedt, S. -P., Mandl, H., Schnotz, W., & Tergan, S. -O. *Texte verstehen, Texte gestalten.* München: Urban & Schwarzenberg, 1981.

Bartlett, F. C. *Remembering. A study in experimental and social psychology.* Cambridge, Mass.: University Press, 1932.

Bovair, S., & Kieras, D. E. A guide to propositional analysis for research on technical prose. Technical Report No. 8, University of Arizona Department of Psychology, 1981.

Bransford, J. D. *Human cognition, understanding and remembering.* Belmont, Cal.: Wadsworth, 1979.

Bransford, J. D., Franks, J. J., Morris, C. D., & Stein, B. S. Some general constraints on learning and memory research. In L. S. Cermak & F. I. M. Craik (Eds.), *Levels of processing in human memory.* Hillsdale, N.J.: Lawrence Erlbaum Associates, 1979.

Bühler, K. Tatsachen und Probleme einer Psychologie der Denkvorgänge. *Archiv für Psychologie,* 1907, *9,* 297–305.

Butterworth, B. Hesitation and semantic planning in speech. *Journal of Psycholinguistic Research,* 1975, *4,* 75–87.

Chafe, W. L. Creativity in verbalization and its implications for the nature of stored knowledge. In R. O. Freedle (Ed.), *Discourse production and comprehension* (Vol. I, *Discourse processes: Advances in research and theory).* Norwood, N.J.: Ablex, 1977.

Chafe, W. L. The flow of thought and the flow of language. In T. Givon (Ed.), *Syntax and semantics* (Vol. 12, *Discourse and syntax).* New York: Academic Press, 1979.

Chafe, W. L. The development of consciousness in the production of a narrative. In W. L. Chafe (Ed.), *The pear stories. Cognitive, cultural, and linguistic aspects of narrative production.* (Vol. III, in R. O. Freedle (Ed.), *Advances in discourse processes).* Norwood, N.J.: Ablex, 1980.

Cermak, L. S., & Craik, F. I. M. (Eds.) *Levels of processing in human memory.* Hillsdale, N.J.: Lawrence Erlbaum Associates, 1979.

Drommel, R. Ein Überblick über die bisherigen Arbeiten zur Sprechpause. *Phonetica,* 1974, *30,* 221–238.

Duncker, K. *Zur Psychologie des produktiven Denkens.* Berlin: Springer, 1935.

Engelkamp, J. On the interrelations of syntax and semantics. *Psychological Research,* 1976, *39,* 87–98.

Ericsson, K. A., & Simon, H. A. *Retrospective verbal reports as data. CIP Working Paper No. 338,* Carnegie-Mellon University, Department of Psychology, 1978.

Ericsson, K. A., & Simon, H. A. *Thinking-aloud protocols as data: Effects of verbalization.* Carnegie-Mellon University, Department of Psychology, CIP Working Paper No. 397, 1979.

Ericsson, K. A., & Simon, H. A. Verbal reports as data. *Psychological Review,* 1980, *87,* 215–251.

Graesser, A. C. *Prose comprehension beyond the word.* New York/Heidelberg/Berlin: Springer, 1981.

Herbart, J. F. *Lehrbuch zur Psychologie.* Königsberg: Unzer, 1816.

Herrmann, T., & Stäcker, K. H. Sprachpsychologische Beiträge zur Sozialpsychologie. In C. F. Graumann (Ed.), *Handbuch der Psychologie,* Vol. 7, *Sozialpsychologie. Theorien und Methoden.* Göttingen: Hogrefe, 1969.

Huber, G. L., & Mandl, H. Verbalisationsmethoden zur Erfassung von Kognitionen im Handlungszusammenhang. In G. L. Huber & H. Mandl (Eds.), *Verbale Daten.* Weinheim: Beltz, 1982.

Just, M. A., & Carpenter, P. A. Eye fixations and cognitive processes. *Cognitive Psychology,* 1976, *8,* 441–480.

Jüttner, C. *Gedächtnis. Grundlagen der psychologischen Gedächtnisforschung.* München: Reinhardt, 1979.

Kintsch, W. *The representation of meaning in memory.* Hillsdale, N.J.: Lawrence Erlbaum Associates, 1974.

Lachman, R., Lachman, J. L., & Butterfield, E. C. *Cognitive psychology and information processing.* Hillsdale, N.J.: Lawrence Erlbaum Associates, 1979.

Mandl, H., & Ballstaedt, S. -P. Effects of elaboration on recall of texts. In A. Flammer & W. Kintsch (Eds.), *Discourse processing.* Amsterdam: North-Holland Publishing Company, 1982.

Mandl, H., & Huber, G. L. (Hg.), *Kognitive Komplexität. Bedeutung - Weiterentwicklung - Anwendung.* Göttingen: Hogrefe, 1978.

Mayer, R. E. Elaboration techniques that increase the meaningfulness of technical text: An experimental test of the learning strategy hypothesis. *Journal of Educational Psychology,* 1980, *72,* 770–784.

Nisbett, R. E., & Wilson, T. D. Telling more than we can know: Verbal reports on mental processes. *Psychological Review,* 1977, *84,* 231–259.

Reder, L. M. The role of elaboration in the comprehension and retention of prose: A critical review. *Review of Educational Research,* 1980, *50,* 5–53.

Rochester, S. R. The significance of pauses in spontaneous speech. *Journal of Psycholinguistic Research,* 1973, *2,* 51–81.

Schnotz, W., Ballstaedt, S.-P., & Mandl, H. Kognitive Prozesse beim Zusammenfassen von Lehrtexten. In H. Mandl (Ed.), *Zur Psychologie der Textverarbeitung. Ansätze, Befunde, Probleme.* München: Urban & Schwarzenberg, 1981.

Schroder, H. M., Driver, M. J., & Streuffert, S. *Menschliche Informations verarbeitung.* Weinheim: Beltz, 1975.

Simon, H. A. *Models of thought.* New Haven, Conn.: Yale University Press, 1979.

Stein, B. S., Morris, C. D., & Bransford, J. Constraints on effective elaboration. *Journal of Verbal Learning and Verbal Behavior,* 1978, *17,* 707–714.

Turner, A., & Greene, E. Construction and use of a propositional text base. JSAS *Catalog of Selected Documents in Psychology, 8,* 1978.

Waern, Y. Thinking aloud during reading. A descriptive model and its application. Report No. 546, University of Stockholm, Department of Psychology, April 1979.

Weidle, R., & Wagner, A. C. Die Methode des lauten Denkens. In G. L. Huber & H. Mandl (Eds.), *Verbale Daten.* Weinheim: Beltz, 1982.

Weinstein, C. E. Elaboration skills as a learning strategy. In H. F. O'Neil, Jr. (Ed.), *Learning strategies.* New York: Academic Press, 1978.

Weinstein, C. E., Underwood, V. L., Wicker, F. W., & Cubberly, W. E. Cognitive learning strategies: Verbal and imaginal elaboration. In H. F. O'Neil, Jr. & C. Spielberger (Eds.), *Cognitive and affective learning strategies.* New York: Academic Press, 1979.

APPENDIX

HERBAL MEDICINE

Herbal medicine, or phytotherapy, has received a new impetus after having a tradition of several thousand years. The recommendations, which derived from experience, of the old herbalists are being replaced by pharmacological findings. Through the development of modern laboratory methods, such as chromatography, isotope techniques, or photometry, the chemical composition of a plant can be explained. With these methods, the active ingredients or *drugs* can be ascertained, and their effects on an organism can be tested. Natural drugs have certain advantages over synthetic medications. Through the use of herbs, the patient is given natural combinations of essential and less important active ingredients, which complement one another for the most part. For example, camomile contains substances that work together to inhibit infection and to relax cramps. An additional advantage is that they produce significantly fewer side-effects than synthetic medications. Thus, herbs are suited for long-term treatment and for self-use for everyday indispositions, such as indigestion, nervousness, or sleep disturbances. A financial advantage can be noted in the economical agricultural and industrial production of these drugs. Herbs have one important disadvantage in comparison to synthetic medications. In their normal form as a tea or an extract, the effectiveness of the conventional herbal drugs is limited and is not capable of curing serious illnesses. Less than 10% of the plants thriving on the earth today have been investigated to determine their composition. However, new discoveries of active ingredients from plants are constantly being reported in technical journals. Perhaps, herbal medicine can become an equal competitor for synthetic medications.

12 Memory Interactions During Question Answering

Wendy G. Lehnert
University of Massachusetts

Scott P. Robertson
John B. Black
Yale University

THE UNIFICATION OF SENTENCE AND QUESTION ANALYSIS

In early natural language processing systems (e.g., Cullingford, 1978; Riesbeck & Schank, 1976; Schank, 1975; Wilensky, 1978) and psychological memory models (Anderson, 1976; Norman & Rumelhart, 1975), modular designs were used to separate processes of sentence analysis from processes of inference and memory construction. In these systems, an intermediate memory representation was produced for each sentence processed, and this *short-term* representation was then input to a memory module of some sort that sought to integrate the conceptual content of that sentence into large *long-term* episodic memory structures. More recent language processing systems have been exploring the advantages of integrated designs that allow processes of sentence analysis to interact with inference mechanisms and memory searches (DeJong, 1979; Dyer, 1981; Lebowitz, 1980; Lehnert, 1982; Lehnert, Dyer, Johnson, Yang, & Harley, 1983; Schank, Lebowitz, & Birnbaum, 1980). Sentences are normally understood within the larger context of a narrative or language interaction, and various contextual factors can facilitate syntactic analysis, polysemous word-sense recognition, and other low-level processing problems. Because many contextual factors are derived from information in memory, an integrated approach to sentence analysis has clear advantages over its modular *context-independent* counterpart.

355

Integrated analysis techniques become particularly interesting when they are applied to questions as well as declarative sentences. Most question answering systems have adopted a modular design that cleanly separates understanding the question from finding the answer (Lehnert, 1978; Winograd, 1972; Woods, 1978). But there are obvious difficulties with this modular approach that we can illustrate with some simple examples. First we look at how the conceptual representation of a text can affect the understanding of a question, and then turn to the issue of how the processing of a question can affect the representation of a text.

THE INTERACTION OF TEXT AND QUESTIONS

Text Representation Effects on the Understanding of Questions

When a story is read, symbolic structures are generated in memory to represent the conceptual content of that story. Any subsequent questions about the story are then interpreted in terms of that underlying context. In particular, potentially ambiguous questions are unconsciously interpreted in whatever manner makes it possible to answer the question. For example, suppose a subject reads the following story about two executives:

> John and Bill went to a restaurant to discuss a business deal. When the dinner was over, John left a very large tip and apologized to Bill for wasting his time.

Now consider the question, "Was the dinner a success?" This question can be reasonably interpreted two ways. From the perspective of a restaurant visit, the answer should be "yes." An inference about their dinner can be made on the basis of the large tip: Restaurant patrons do not normally leave generous tips unless the meal meets with their expectations. But at another level of comprehension "the dinner" is merely a social setting for the higher level goal of a business deal. For the dinner to be successful at this level, the business deal had to be negotiated satisfactorily. Because John apologized to Bill, we should infer that no agreement was reached, and the higher goal failed to be realized. The dinner did not go well at this level.

Question answering behavior in this case must be analyzed qualitatively rather than quantitatively. A positive response indicates that "the dinner" was interpreted very literally, and an inference about restaurants was successfully made. A negative response indicates that "the dinner" was interpreted as an instrumental event, and a probable inference about apologetic behavior was made. A response of "I don't know," suggests that neither inference was made. Possibly the best response would be "yes and no," indicating that the ambiguity of the question was perceived and all the relevant inferences were made. In any case, we are in a position to assess a subject's ability to make appropriate inferences and interpret events accordingly.

Ambiguities in questions can occur at many different levels. In addition to the potential ambiguities of single words, the entire focus or conceptual emphasis of a question may be ambiguous. For example, consider another story about John:

> John had just bought a new car. He was so happy with it that he drove it at every possible opportunity. So last night when he decided to go out for dinner, he drove to Leone's. When he got there he had to wait for a table . . .

If asked, "Why did John drive to Leone's?," subjects will naturally explain something about John liking his new car. The question has been interpreted to be asking about the act of driving. John could have walked to the restaurant or taken a cab—why did he drive? Now take a different context:

> John had a crush on Mary. But he was so shy that he was happy just to be in her proximity. So he was in the habit of following her around a lot. He knew that she ate at Leone's very often. So last night when he decided to out for dinner, he drove to Leone's. When he got there he had to wait for a table . . .

And reconsider the same question, "Why did John drive to Leone's?" Suddenly the focus of the question has shifted to the destination of John's trip. Why Leone's? Why not the corner diner?

The question is lexically invariant, but its conceptual interpretation changes as the context around it changes. We interpret the question in whatever way allows us to answer it. This means that our conceptual memory representation for the story text is being accessed and searched as we read the question. In this case a potential ambiguity of focus must be resolved by the internal memory representation (Lehnert, 1978).

Yet another problem for modular processors arises from conceptual ellipses in questions. For example, consider the following text:

> John closed up his office and went to an office party after work on Friday. While he was there, he overheard a conversation between two executives concerning a special account that John had been working on. From what they were saying, it became clear that John was not receiving credit for the time and energy he had devoted to the project. After hearing this, John felt extremely frustrated and in no mood to socialize. In an effort to get his mind off his troubles, John excused himself and went out to a movie. After the movie, he went out and got drunk.

Twenty-five subjects in an informal classroom experiment heard this text and then answered the question, "Why did John leave?" All 25 subjects answered the question by explaining that John was upset by a conversation he had overheard or that he was preoccupied. Although there were many conceptual distinctions across the answers, all answers addressed the cause of John's early departure from the party. When asked if the question was unclear or ambiguous, none of the subjects indicated any conscious confusion. Yet there is a glaring ambiguity in this question. Why did John leave *where?* The question could have been interpreted to be asking why John left his office or why John left the movie. Yet everyone immediately interprets this question to be asking about why John left the party. Intuitively this is perhaps natural because the bulk of the story describes why John left the party. But in order to favor any interpretation over another, the memory representation for the story must first be examined to arrive at a preferred interpretation of the question.

All these examples illustrate how an internal memory representation can affect the conceptual interpretation of questions in a top–down or predictive manner. In each of these cases, we appear to have a memory interaction that carries information from the story representation to the conceptual interpretation of a question. This predictive processing can be used to disambiguate multiple word senses, potentially ambiguous focus assignments, and conceptual ellipses or omissions in questions.

Predictive Text Processing and Memory Instantiation

An integrated approach to question analysis does not automatically solve all problems with word-sense ambiguity, question focus, and conceptual ellipsis, but an integrated framework permits a far more flexible environment for experimentation than modular designs can provide. Predictive processing techniques for text comprehension allow processes of sentence analysis to interact with processes of memory access in order to build a conceptual representation for the sentence. Very often the conceptual representation of a sentence is not an isolated structure, but an addition or refinement to an existing structure in episodic memory. The construction of an episodic memory representation for text is a cumulative result of individual sentence representations that ideally interact and combine to represent the larger text being processed. Graesser, Robertson, and Clark (in press) report that 59% of the potential inferences about a story statement that remain in a story representation (potential inferences were elicited by asking why questions about statements in a story) are generated by the interaction of the statement itself with previous material in the story. The comprehension process is, therefore, at least as much a process of integration as it is a process of construction. For example, consider a slight variation on an earlier text example:

> John and Bill went to a restaurant to discuss a business deal. When the meal was over, John left a very large tip and apologized to Bill for wasting his time. Bill thanked John for lunch, and they went their separate ways.

In the third sentence, a reference to ''lunch'' allows us to refine our previous memory representation for a meal at a restaurant. The meal might have been breakfast, lunch, or dinner—but no such further specification is explicit at the time a memory node is first created for a meal. (It is possible that a default inference might be made about the type of meal after the first sentence, but this would be either reinforced or overridden when the reference to "lunch" is made.) When the reference to lunch appears, readers have no difficulty integrating this new information into their memory representation for the story. It is accepted as a further specification on the aforementioned meal without conscious effort or consideration.

Now consider a slight variation of our story, followed by a question:

> John and Bill went to a restaurant to discuss a business deal. When the meal was over, John left a very large tip and apologized to Bill for wasting his time. Bill encouraged John to look for another investor, and they went their separate ways.

> Q: Why did John apologize to Bill after lunch?

In order to answer the question, episodic memory must be accessed to establish who John and Bill are, whether John apologized to Bill, and whether John apologized to Bill after lunch. The search processes that are needed to establish these connections are identical to the search processes that we need to access episodic memory during text comprehension. So it seems that we should use the same memory integration during question answering that we used at the time of story understanding. When we enlist the integrated processing techniques used during story understanding in order to understand the question, it is now possible for the reference to "lunch" in this question to be understood and integrated by the same mechanism that handled a reference to "lunch" when it appeared in the story text.

Question Processing Effects on the Representation of Text

One side-effect that arises when we unify the processing of text sentences with the processing of questions is the ability to alter a memory representation in the course of answering a question. This means that episodic memory can be receptive to further specifications presented in questions and possibly more dramatic alterations as well.

> John and Bill went to a restaurant to discuss a business deal. When lunch was over, John left a very large tip and apologized to Bill for wasting his time. Bill encouraged John to look for another investor, and they went their separate ways.

> Q: Why did John apologize to Bill after dinner?

If a reader does not notice the discrepancy between "lunch" in the story and "dinner" in the question, it is possible that the reference to a dinner will be integrated as an overriding specification for the meal. Because our computational model for integrated question answering can easily simulate such an override, we must now try to determine when human text comprehenders can be misled by false presuppositions in questions.

EXPERIMENTAL EVIDENCE FOR
QUESTION-ANSWERING EFFECTS ON MEMORY

Loftus Experiments

In a series of experiments designed to test the reliability of eyewitness testimony, Elizabeth Loftus has determined that people are frequently misled by questions that are not consistent with information in episodic memory (Loftus, 1975, 1979). In one experiment, subjects were shown a series of slides depicting successive stages of an automobile accident. In one slide a car approaches an intersection with a stop sign. After the slides were shown, subjects were asked some questions about what they had seen. Subject group A was asked, "Did another car pass the red car while it was stopped at the stop sign?" Group B was asked, "Did another car pass the red car while it was stopped at the yield sign?" Half of the subjects (in both groups, A and B) had been shown a slide with a stop sign, whereas the other half had seen a slide with a yield sign. A week later the subjects were tested for their memory of the slides. As many as 80% of the subjects given the false-presupposition question identified the sign in question incorrectly. This error rate is significantly worse than the error rate for subjects who received consistent questions, and it is also significant when compared to the error rate for subjects who received no questions after the initial viewing. There was no significant bias favoring memory for stop (yield) signs over memory for yield (stop) signs.

Although the Loftus experiments demonstrate that information in questions can be integrated into episodic memory structures, her experimental materials were visual (slides) rather than textual. Our first set of experiments were, therefore, designed to test whether memory modifications can be imposed on episodic structures created by narrative text as well. A preliminary experiment indicated that we could, in fact, duplicate the *Loftus effect* with textual materials. In the following we discuss a misleading question experiment, which addresses a number of questions that the Loftus experiments did not.

Memory Modification Issues

Our first concern is to determine the specific conditions under which memory modifications occur. Some misleading questions entail false presuppositions. When a glaring contradiction is encountered, we would not expect a memory alteration to occur. But which presuppositions are noticed and rejected by subjects? Which ones are accepted and result in memory modifications? Can we find any patterns that distinguish vulnerable memory items from invulnerable ones?

One prediction along these lines involves the relative stability of actions versus states in memory. An action or event concept represents a change of state generally brought about by the goal directed behavior of an actor. A state concept represents a descriptive, static property of an object, person, or location. It has been suggested that narrative representations are composed primarily of causally related actions and that states may not play as important a role. It may be that many states are not represented explicitly in memory at all because they are easily inferred at a later time from memory of actions. Many psychological studies have demonstrated that memory for actions is superior to memory for states (Black, 1980; Graesser, Higgenbotham, Robertson, & Smith, 1978; Graesser, Robertson, Lovelace, & Swinehart, 1980), and Seifert, Robertson, and Black (1982) have recently shown reading time evidence for the on-line generation of action inferences but not state inferences. In short, states seem to play a less central role in memory than actions. If this is true, then it should be much more difficult to modify memory about actions than states, and this is our first prediction.

Another issue concerns the scope of a memory modification. If an event is directly altered by a question, are the causally connected states resulting from that event also altered? Similarly, if a state is directly altered by a question, are causally-dependent events also altered? Any indirect memory modifications resulting from a misleading question would indicate that direct memory modifications force a *ripple effect* throughout the memory representation. How far can a modification ripple go? Are some paths in memory more susceptible to ripple effects than others?

As a final concern, we hoped to tease apart legitimate ripple effects from reconstructive memory retrieval. If a subject exhibits indirect memory modifications after answering a misleading question, how can we be certain that this is the result of a memory modification ripple, and not just a reconstruction based on the direct memory modification? Because there is evidence for reconstructive memory retrieval [Bartlett, 1932; Cofer, 1973, Lindsay & Norman, 1972; Norman, 1970; Spiro, Esposito, & Vandruska, 1978), we must try to separate the effects of modification ripples from reconstructive retrieval.

The results of the experiment that follows shed at least some light on all of these questions. Further experiments along these lines will contribute substantially to our understanding of memory retrieval and internal memory representations for narrative text.

Leading Question Effects on States, Actions, and Their Consequences

We designed an experiment to test the effects of misleading questions on different parts of a memory representation for narrative text. In the experiment subjects read a series of narratives and were then asked two sets of questions about each narrative. Some of the questions in the first set contained misleading presuppositions. Target questions in the second set (which followed a delay) tested whether these misleading questions altered memory for the narratives. We varied whether the initial questions were misleading about actions or states and tested for direct modifications of these two types of items. We also tested for indirect modifications on remote consequences of the direct modifications (i.e., for ripple effects).

Specifically, we gave 24 Yale undergraduate students 10 minutes to read five short narratives (with an average length of 491 words per narrative) and then asked them 12 questions about the content of each story. After answering these questions, the subjects spent 10 minutes on an unrelated task before answering another set of eight test questions about each story.

Each of the five narratives contained two *target items,* one state and one action. One of these narratives (entitled *The Lizard Photographer*) is given as an example in Appendix A. In this example, the state target item was ". . . the . . . lamps inside the den were too high." The action target item was ". . . the lens papers had gotten smeared with some mascara." In general, the target items were states or actions on which we attempted to mislead our subjects. In cases where the story mentioned one object and our questions referenced a different one (e.g., lipstick versus mascara or sunglasses versus an umbrella), we were careful to work both objects into the story so that both memory tokens would be present in the subjects' memories while only one was used in conjunction with the target item.

In the questions that subjects answered immediately after reading the narratives, we asked about each of the five pairs of target items. Thus, there was one *target question* about a state and one *target question* about an action for each story. There were two versions of each target question, one which was designed to mislead a subject and a second which was intended to be neutral. For example, if the story target item was "Shelly noticed that her lamps were too high." (state), a misleading version of the target question would be "Was it on the first or second day . . . that Shelly noticed her lamps were too low?" and a neutral version would be "Was it on the first or second day . . . that Shelly noticed her lamps were wrong?" Each subject received one misleading target question and one neutral target question per story. The neutral and misleading versions of the target questions for each story appear in Appendix B.

The other 10 questions per narrative were fillers designed to keep the subjects from being suspicious. The nontarget questions did not differ in any obvious ways from the target questions. Some examples of nontarget immediate questions were: "What was the name of Susan's lawyer?," "Where did Ed discover a fire?," and "Did the alarm go off too late or not at all?"

In the later questions answered after a 10 minute intervening task, there was a pair of *test questions* for each target item. A *direct test question* asked directly about the misled item. For the example about Shelly's lamps, the direct test question was "Were the lamps . . . too high or too low?" A *remote test ques-*

tion was asked about an inference that followed from the item. For the lamps example, the remote test question was "Did Shelly raise or lower the lamps . . .?" If the directly misled item was a state, then the remote inference queried was always an action that followed from it. If the directly misled item was an action, then the remote inference queried was always a state, either an enabling state or a consequence. Appendix B also gives the direct and remote test questions for each story. The four nontest questions for each story did not differ from the test questions in any obvious ways. Some examples of nontest questions from the later questions are: "On what day of the week did Susan have her accident?," and "Did John finance the jeep or pay for it right there?"

Equal numbers of subjects were assigned to each of the following conditions:

1. Action misled, direct query first.
2. Action misled, remote query first.
3. State misled, direct query first.
4. State misled, remote query first.

Subjects in conditions one and two were given the misleading version of the target questions about actions and the neutral version of the target questions about states, whereas subjects in conditions three and four were given the misleading version of the target questions about states and the neutral version of the target questions about actions. In conditions one and three, the direct test question appeared before the remote test question in the later question set, whereas in conditions two and four the remote test question appeared before the direct test question.

We varied the order of the test questions as a way of addressing the issue of whether apparent ripple effects were the result of true memory modification at the time a misleading question was answered or reconstruction of a consistent answer to a later question based on the answer to an earlier question. We reasoned that an apparent modification of remote items could occur at test time if a subject noticed that a later, unmodified remote item was inconsistent with an earlier modified direct item. If *reconstruction* at test time is responsible for modifications of remote items, then the degree of modification should be much greater when the remote items appear after the direct items than when they appear before the direct items. If we find that the order of direct and remote test items has no effect on the amount of remote item modification, then the reconstruction argument is weakened, and we will be able to argue more forcefully for a true modification of memory.

We measured memory modification in two ways: misleading difference scores (MD scores) and confusion difference scores (CD scores). The proportion of a subject's answers judged as misled across all of the misled items minus the proportion of answers judged as misled across all the neutral items yielded a subject's overall MD score. An answer was judged as misled if it was consistent with the presupposition of our misleading question for that item. The MD score provides a measure of how much subjects were misled when given a misleading question over and above any tendency to answer in the misled direction when given a neutral question. Higher MD scores indicate more misleading.

Similarly, the proportion of a subject's answers judged as confused across all of the misled items minus the proportion of answers judged as confused across all of the neutral items yielded a subject's overall CD score. Answers such as "I don't know" and blanks were judged as confused. It was assumed that a misled presupposition could well lead to a muddled or incomplete representation of the misled item, which would then prove to be inadequate for answering a question. A CD score measures the tendency for "I don't know" types of answers to become more prevalent when a subject was misled over and above the baseline for such answers when subjects received a neutral question.

MD scores and CD scores were computed separately for subjects' answers to the local test questions and the remote test questions. Sometimes, answers to our test questions did not address the issue we intended and thus proved to be indeterminate about whether an item was modified or not. Forty-two percent of the answers for the action item of story 5 (see Appendix B) were indeterminate in this way, so the results from that item are not included here.

Table 12.1a shows the mean MD scores for directly misled states and actions in both test question orders, and Table 12.1b shows the mean CD scores in the same conditions. The directly misled items had an overall mean MD score of .12 and an overall mean CD score of .08. Both of these values differ significantly from zero, $t(23)=2.77$, $p<.01$ and $t(23)=2.46$, $p<.05$ for Md scores and CD scores, respectively, indicating that our attempts to mislead subjects about what they had read succeeded. In both cases, the states were more easily modified (or confused) than the actions, although both main effects are marginal, $F(1,20) = 3.13$, $p<.10$ and $F(1,20)=3.02$, $p<.10$. It is clear that the action scores are at or

TABLE 12.1
Mean Misleading Difference Scores (MD-scores) and Confusion
Difference Scores (CD-scores) for Subjects' Answers to the Test
Questions about Direct States and Actions in Both Test Positions

Dependent Measure	Type of Direct Modification	Test Position		
		Direct First	Remote First	Mean
MD-scores	State	.30	.07	.19
	Action	.04	.05	.05
	Mean MD	.17	.06	.12
CD-scores	State	.09	.18	.14
	Action	.04	.01	.03
	Mean CD	.07	.09	.08

near zero, whereas the state scores show effects of the misleading questions. In fact, for both MD scores and CD scores the states alone differ from zero, $t(11)=3.46$, $p<.01$ and $t(11)=2.63$, $p<.05$, respectively, whereas the actions do not, both $t(11)<1.0$. Thus, states were more easily modified directly than actions and, in fact, on average the actions seemed to resist modification completely.

The position of the direct test question relative to the remote test question had no effect on either MD scores or CD scores for the directly misled items, $F(1,20)=1.97$,ns and $F(1,20)<1$,ns, respectively. Thus, a prior answer about a remote item did not affect judgment of the related direct item when it was asked about later. There were no interactions of the position and type of modification factors.

Table 12.2 gives the results for the remote items. Recall that the modified states are actually remote states related to directly modified actions, and the modified actions are actually remote actions related to directly modified states. When looking at the MD scores, there appears to be very little remote modification of states or actions, and there was no difference in the amount of modification between states and actions, $F(1,20)<1$, ns. The CD scores, however, tell a different story; remote actions proved to be more often confused than remote states, $F(1,20)=7.62$, $p<.05$, and the mean remote action CD score was significantly different from zero, $t(11)=2.17$, $p<.05$. From this data it can be argued that some rippling took place at least from the more easily modifiable states to their related actions. The rippling creates confusion about the remote action rather than changing it completely, but this is reasonable if we remember how difficult it is to directly change an action in memory. It is unreasonable to expect this measure to show strong ripple effects from the directly misled actions to their related states because the degree of misleading was initially so low for actions. We use more appropriate, conditional measures for this purpose.

TABLE 12.2
Mean Misleading Difference Scores (MD-scores) and Confusion
Difference Scores (CD-scores) for Subjects' Answers to the Test
Questions about Remote States and Actions in Both Test Positions

Dependent Measure	Type of Remote Modification	Test Position		
		Direct First	Remote First	Mean
MD-scores	State	.11	.04	.08
	Action	.05	.07	.06
	Mean MD	.08	.06	.07
CD-scores	State	−.09	−.06	−.08
	Action	.12	.18	.15
	Mean CD	.01	.06	.035

The relative positions of direct and remote test questions had no effect on either MD scores or CD scores for the remote items, both $F(1,20)<1$, ns. We interpret this lack of a test-position effect as indicating that any modifications evident in the remote actions were the result of memory modifications while answering the misleading questions rather than reconstructions when answering the final test questions. There were no interactions.

Hence, we have shown that memory for states can be directly modified by misleading questions and that the modification will ripple through the memory representation to cast doubt on memory for related actions. We were not able to modify memory for actions to the same degree and were therefore also unable to show a ripple to remote states using the above analysis. The relative stability of actions over states is consistent with other psychological evidence suggesting that actions are represented *more strongly* in memory than states (Black, 1980; Graesser, Higgenbotham, Robertson, & Smith, 1978; Graesser, Robertson, Lovelace, & Swinehart, 1980). It is also consistent with any *act-based* systems of representation, such as Schank's (1975) conceptual dependency theory.

A more democratic method for examining the ripple of modifications through memory is to examine the conditional probabilities of remote modifications (answers scored as misled) in cases where there were and were not direct modifications. Table 12.3a gives the conditional probabilities for direct states modified, and Table 12.3b gives them for the few observed cases of direct actions modified. These probabilities show that a direct state modification was more likely to lead to a remote action modification than not and that remote action modifica-

TABLE 12.3
The Proportions of Remote Items Modified
and Not Modified When Direct Items Were
Modified and Not Modified

Category of Direct Item	Category of Remote Item	
	Remote Action Modified	Remote Action Not Modified
Direct State Modified	.73	.27
Direct State Not Modified	0	1.00
Category of Direct Item	Remote State Modified	Remote State Not Modified
Direct Action Modified	.50	.50
Direct Action Not Modified	.02	.98

tions were never made in the absence of a direct state modification. Table 12.3b shows that for the few direct action modifications that did occur a remote state modification was just as likely to occur as not, but there was a strong tendency for remote state modifications never to occur without a direct action modification. Thus, the conditional analysis indicates that remote modifications depend almost entirely on the occurrence of direct modifications, especially for state–to–action ripples and more weakly for action–to–state ripples. It is interesting to note that, although it was more difficult to modify actions directly than states, ripple effects to actions were common. This result suggests that internal changes to the representation are being made along conceptual links to actions and not to states, which is consistent with a view of memory that is act based. This result deserves further attention in future research.

Examining the items in more detail, it was found that the direct states in stories 2 and 3 (see Appendix B) showed particularly strong modification effects. Both instances involve a location—in one case the location of a photographer's lamps and in the other case the location of instructions. Because the other states were of different types (environmental state, ownership, and physical appearance), we conjecture that location states are particularly susceptible to modification. Further research is planned concerning the vulnerability of different kinds of information in memory to modification by leading questions.

The distinction between actions and states should be considered a preliminary and rather coarse distinction, which reflects more fine-grained structural distinctions in memory. We hope to clarify further the structural differences between different kinds of states and actions and conduct more detailed experiments based on these models. Finding modification effects as easily as was done in this initial study creates optimism that further research will prove fruitful.

CONCLUSIONS

We have provided evidence from both artificial intelligence and cognitive psychology that language understanding involves highly integrated memory processes. In particular, the text comprehension system BORIS demonstrates that a new sentence is understood in terms of the context provided by previous sentences. It makes no difference if the new sentence happens to be a question asking about the story. An interesting implication of such integrated understanding mechanisms is the effect of question answering on the memories being queried. These results from artificial intelligence research provide us with a new perspective on what has been until now a serendipitous result in cognitive psychology—namely, that people's memories can be altered by misleading questions. This perspective says that such modifications are a natural side-effect of integrated language processing techniques.

Because modification of prior memories is a natural part of question answering, it is important to determine the specifics of such modifications. In particular, it is important to know what kinds of information in memory are most vulnerable to modification and how extensive is this modification. We have begun a line of research using psychology experiments to investigate these issues. An initial experiment of this kind provided evidence that stative information is more directly modifiable than event information and that events causally related to modified states are also modified.

These findings and others from subsequent experiments will be used to help guide the design of new computer models of how questions are processed. Formulating these models will, in turn, provide perspective on current findings and raise new issues for experimentation; just as the perspective of integrated language processing from artificial intelligence provided a new look at the misleading questions research in cognitive psychology. In this way we hope to establish a methodological framework in which the computer modeling of artificial intelligence and controlled experimentation of cognitive psychology are used to complement one another in an interdisciplinary research program.

ACKNOWLEDGMENTS

This work was supported in part by the National Science Foundation under contract IST7918463, and in part by a grant from the Alfred P. Sloan Foundation. We are indebted to Larry Hunter for his assistance in the design and execution of this experiment, and we want to thank Tom Trabasso for his comments on an earlier version of this chapter.

REFERENCES

Anderson, J. R. *Language, memory and thought.* Hillsdale, NJ: Lawrence Erlbaum Associates, 1976.

Bartlett, F. C. *Remembering: A study in experimental and social psychology.* New York: The MacMillan Co., 1932.

Black, J. B. *Memory for state and action information in narratives.* 21st Annual Meeting of the Psychonomic Society. St. Louis, Mo., 1980.

Cofer, C. N. Constructive processes in memory. *American Scientist,* 1973, *61,* 537–543.

Cullingford, R. *Script application: Computer understanding of newspaper stories.* Research Report #116, Department of Computer Sicence. Yale University, 1978.

DeJong, G. F. Prediction and substantiation: A new approach to natural language processing. *Cognitive Science,* 1979, *3,* 251–273.

Dyer, M. Integration, unification, reconstruction, modification: An eternal parsing braid. *Proceedings of the Seventh International Joint Conference on Artificial Intelligence,* Vancouver, British Columbia, August 1981.

Graesser, A. C., Higgenbotham, M. W., Robertson, S. P., & Smith, W. R. A natural inquiry into the National Enquirer: Self-induced versus task-induced reading comprehension. *Discourse Processes,* 1978, *1,* 355–372.

Graesser, A. C., Robertson, S. P., & Clark, L. F. A Q/A method of exploring on-line construction of prose representations. In J. Fine & R. O. Freedle (Eds.), *New directions in discourse processing*. Norwood, N.J.: Ablex, in press.

Graesser, A. C., Robertson, S. P., Lovelace, E. R., & Swinehart, D. M. Answers to why-questions expose the organization of story plot and predict recall of actions. *Journal of Verbal Learning and Verbal Behavior*, 1980, *19*, 110–119.

Lebowitz, M. *Generalization and memory in an integrated understanding system*. Research Report #186, Department of Computer Science. Yale University, 1980.

Lehnert, W. G. *The process of question answering*. Hillsdale, N.J.: Lawrence Erlbaum Associates, 1978.

Lehnert, W. G. Text processing effects and recall memory. *Cognition and Brain Theory*, 1982, *5*, 3–28.

Lehnert, W. G., Dyer, M., Johnson, P., Yang C., & Harley, S.   BORIS—An experiment in indepth understanding of narratives. *Artificial Intelligence*, 1983, *20*, 15–62.

Lindsay, P. H. & Norman, D. A. *Human information processing: An introduction to psychology*. New York: Academic Press, 1972.

Loftus, E. F. *Eyewitness testimony*. Cambridge, Ma: Harvard University Press, 1979.

Loftus, E. F. Leading questions and the eyewitness report. *Cognitive Psychology*, 1975, *7*, 560–572.

Norman, D. A. & Rumelhart, D. E. *Explorations in cognition*. San Francisco, Ca: Freeman, 1975.

Norman, D. A. *Remembrance of things past*. Technical Report 11, Department of Psychology. University of California, San Diego, 1970.

Riesbeck, C. & Schank, R. *Comprehension by computer: Expectation-based analysis of sentences in context*. Research Report #78, Department of Computer Science. Yale University, 1976.

Schank, R. C. *Conceptual information processing*. New York: North-Holland, 1975.

Schank, R. C., Lebowitz, M., & Birnbaum, L. An integrated understander. *American Journal of Computational Linguistics*, 1980, *6*, 13–30.

Seifert, C., Robertson, S. P., & Black, J. B. Pragmatic inference generation during comprehension. *Proceedings of the Fourth Annual Conference of the Cognitive Science Society*, Ann Arbor, Mi., August 1982.

Spiro, R. J., Esposito, J., & Vandruska, R. The representation of derivable information in memory: When what might have been left unsaid is said. *Proceedings of Theoretical Issues in Natural Language Processing-2*, Champaign-Urbana, Ill., 1978.

Wilensky, R. *Understanding goal-based stories*. Research Report #140, Department of Computer Science. Yale University, 1978.

Winograd, T. A. *Understanding natural language*. New York: Academic Press, 1972.

Woods, W. A. Semantics and quantification in natural language question answering. In *Advances in Computers, 17*, New York: Academic Press, 1978.

Appendix A

THE LIZARD PHOTOGRAPHER

Shelly was a photographer for Nature Magazine on one of her best assignments yet. She had traveled all the way to South America to photograph a little green lizard about the size of a cigarette. It took her six weeks to locate a suitable site and start setting up her equipment.

Shelly's intention was to photograph the lizard "where it lived," so to speak, which unfortunately for her was in small holes in tree trunks about 10 feet off the ground. This habit forced the photographer to build a platform next to the tree trunk that she could sit on when operating her equipment.

It took all of a day to prepare the equipment. First a small hole was bored into the tree trunk exposing the animal's den. Next, small lamps were installed, and then a special small-subject wide angle lens was pushed into the hole. The camera itself was installed on the outside where Shelly could look at her subject and shoot at will.

To complicate matters further, the small lizard came home only at night, which meant that Shelly had to set up her equipment during the day and hope that it was arranged properly for the night's shooting. If she tried to move anything while the lizard was in its den, it would be likely to frighten the lizard away. If this happened, she would probably never see it again.

The first den Shelly tried took three days before any good pictures were acquired. Before leaving for the jungle, she had apparently kept some makeup in with her camera equipment because *the lens papers had gotten smeared with some mascara*. She didn't notice the black smears on the pictures until after the first night's shooting. She decided to give up makeup altogether after this incident. Except for the time she used her lipstick to write numbers on some film envelopes she hardly ever used it anymore—and this was really the last straw.

The next night she noticed that the shadows were all wrong and that *the little lamps inside the den were too high.* She had to wait until the next day to lower them, however. Each modification like that took several hours, and the more the den was disturbed, the more unlikely her little green friend was to stay the next night. It was already a little unusual in there with lights and a big glass "picture window."

Finally, on the third night her pictures were a success. She was lucky enough to photograph a den with two parent lizards and five smaller offspring. She photographed them feeding, the young ones scuffling, and was even witness to an unexpected (and unwelcome) visit from another lizard. Over the next week, Shelly collected almost 350 pictures of this small group. This was only part of the work though. She intended to eavesdrop on at least three more lizard families before going home. Once home, she would have over 1000 photographs to look through and write about. If she was lucky, she would be able to return to South America within a year, perhaps to track and photograph her green friends' activities during the day.

Appendix B

EXAMPLE QUESTIONS AND ANSWERS

The target questions for each story are shown here along with their associated direct and remote test questions. Both the misleading and neutral versions of the target questions are shown. Neutral target questions are preceded by *Nt-targ*, misleading target questions are preceded by *Ml-targ*. The direct test questions are preceded by *Dr-test*, the remote test questions are indicated by *Rt-test*. "Correct" and "misled" answers to the remote test questions are also shown. Correct answers are preceded by *Cr-ans*, misled answers are preceded by *Ml-ans*.

STORY 1

Direct
State
___

Nt-targ: What was the name of the portly man who used the pen?
Ml-targ: What was the name of the portly man who owned the pen?

Dr-test: Who owned the pen at the beginning of the story?

Rt-test: Who said "thank you" at the beginning of the story, and for returning what?
Cr-ans: Mr. Haight.
Ml-ans: Mr. White. (Mr. White was described as portly)

Direct
Action

Nt-targ: What did Mr. Haight ask Susan after he adjusted the window?
Ml-targ: What did Mr. Haight ask Susan after he closed the window?

Dr-test: What was Mr. Haight doing to the window when he noticed the traffic jam outside his office?

Rt-test: Why did Mr. Haight fix the window?
Cr-ans: Susan was warm.
Ml-ans: Susan was cold.

STORY 2

Direct
State

Nt-targ: What did Ed do after he smothered the fire and took care of Fritz?
Ml-targ: What did Ed do after he smothered the fire and let Fritz out?

Dr-test: What did Ed do after he smothered the fire, before he answered the phone?

Rt-test: Was Fritz inside or outside when Ed discovered the fire?
Cr-ans: Outside.
Ml-ans: Inside.

Direct
Action

Nt-targ: What was Cynthia supposed to leave for Ed in the other room?
Ml-targ: What was Cynthia supposed to leave for Ed in the living room?

Dr-test: Where was Cynthia supposed to leave Johnny's feeding instructions?

Rt-test: What was Ed doing when it occurred to him that he was completely on his own?

Cr-ans: Getting the feeding instructions in the kitchen.
Ml-ans: Getting the feeding instructions in the living room.

STORY 3

**Direct
State**

Nt-targ: Was it on the first or second day of shooting that Shelly noticed her
            lamps were wrong?
Ml-targ: Was it on the first or second day of shooting that Shelly noticed her
            lamps were too low?

Dr-test: Were the lamps in the lizard den too high or too low?

Rt-test: Did Shelly raise or lower the lamps after the second night's shooting?
Cr-ans: She lowered them.
Ml-ans: She raised them.

**Direct
Action**

Nt-targ: What was Shelly's makeup smeared on?
Ml-targ: What was Shelly's makeup lipstick on?

Dr-test: What got smeared on the lens of Shelly's camera?

Rt-test: What color was the smear on Shelly's camera lens?
Cr-ans: Black.
Ml-ans: Red.

STORY 4

**Direct
State**

Nt-targ: Who told John that it seemed like his weight was changing and he
            needed exercise?
Ml-targ: Who told John that it seemed like he was losing weight and he needed
            exercise?

Dr-test: Why did John's boss think John needed exercise?

Rt-test: Did John have dessert at lunch?
Cr-ans: No.
Ml-ans: Yes.

Direct
Action

Nt-targ: What did Gary ask John to adjust on the highway, the radio or the tape deck?
Ml-targ: What did Gary ask John to turn up on the highway, the radio or the tape deck?

Dr-test: What did John do to the tape deck, turn it up or down?

Rt-test: Was the tape deck in the car too loud or too soft?
Cr-ans: Too loud.
Ml-ans: Too soft.

STORY 5

Direct
State

Nt-targ: Was Jack inside or outside when he noticed what kind of day it was?
Ml-targ: Was Jack inside or outside when he noticed it was a cloudy day?

Dr-test: What did Jack notice when he ran out to the car?

Rt-test: What did Jack rush back inside the house to get, his umbrella or his sunglasses?
Cr-ans: Sunglasses.
Ml-ans: Umbrella.

Direct
Action

Nt-targ: Where was Jack's car when he checked his hair?
Ml-targ: Where was Jack's car when he checked his hair in the rearview mirror?

Dr-test: What did Jack do about his hair just before he sprinted across the street to work?

Rt-test: Where was Jack when he checked his hair?
Cr-ans: Next to his car.
Ml-ans: In his car.

13 Development of Strategies in Text Processing

Marlene Scardamalia
York University

Carl Bereiter
Ontario Institute for Studies in Education

The two studies reported in this chapter sought to obtain information, primarily through the use of thinking-aloud protocols, on how young readers deal with text comprehension difficulties. There were two reasons for focusing on situations in which comprehension is problematic. The first is methodological. Fluent, easy reading is a fairly automatic process in which little of the mental activity is available for self-report (cf. Just & Carpenter, 1980; Perfetti & Lesgold, 1977; Woods, 1980). Consequently, text processing tasks are used that contain problems or impediments intended to bring normally covert processes into sufficiently deliberate use so that relevant kinds of self-report data may be obtained. The second reason—and the more significant reason in the context of the present volume—is an interest in educational applications.

When students try to comprehend and learn from written texts, they often work under the combined handicaps of having limited knowledge of the subject matter and limited familiarity with the genre they are reading. Thus they lack the benefits that Voss (Chapter 6) attributes to "high knowledge" in a content domain and the benefits that Stein and Trabasso (1982) attribute to having a well-developed discourse schema that organizes information for memory storage and serves to guide inferencing into relevant channels. If students are to be successful at learning in such situations—situations that are normal rather than exceptional in formal education—then they need powerful problem-solving strategies. Studying what strategies they do have available and how these compare to expert strategies would seem to be a vital first step in building a developmentally sound program of instruction (Case, 1978).

There is evidence that skilled readers have special strategies that they can bring to bear in cases where comprehension is difficult. Flower, Hayes, and

Swarts (1980) found that in trying to make sense of complex regulations, skilled readers constructed scenarios or narratives that permitted them to restructure the text content in a way they could better comprehend. Bird (1980) collected thinking-aloud protocols from adults reading a variety of texts. Among the strategies she found skillful readers using when they encountered comprehension difficulties were the following:

1. Ongoing summarization. It appeared that readers were consciously creating the macro-structure that normally, according to Kintsch and van Dijk's model (1978), is created automatically.

2. Strategic backtracking. Bird found that both more skilled and less skilled readers backed up and reread when they encountered difficulties, but skilled readers appeared to back up to where the information they needed was located, whereas less skilled readers tended to backtrack only to the beginning of the sentence in which they experienced difficulty.

3. Problem formulation. Skilled readers tended to formulate explicitly their difficulty as a problem, which they then tried to solve. Although this does not sound like a strategy in itself, it apparently has strategic value, in that it helps the reader bring general-purpose problem-solving procedures to bear on the comprehension difficulty.

4. Setting up "watchers." Rieger (1977) proposed that in story comprehension certain story elements activate "watchers" in the reader's mind, which remain active until a particular kind of required information is received. Olson, Mack, and Duffy (1981), as well as Bird (1980), found direct evidence of readers setting up such watchers, thus anticipating categories of information to appear in the text—reasons to support opinions, definitions to explain unfamiliar words, examples to illustrate general statements, etc.

In subsequent analysis of protocols from seventh- and eighth-grade students, Bird (1980) found some incidence of all these strategies. However, only 17 out of 46 subjects showed a single instance of problem formulation in the course of reading about 1500 words of expository material even though comprehension was only about 60%, as measured by factual and inferential test items following brief passages. Direct instruction with modeling boosted this incidence to approximately 2.5 problem formulations per student on a post-test with large increases also in the use of ongoing summarization and strategic backtracking. Comprehension test scores likewise showed significant increases.

These findings indicate that young readers do not make optimum use of strategies experts use for dealing with comprehension difficulties, but they do not show us: (1) to what extent the strategies are available but simply not called up; and (2) what strategies students do employ, that may be different from those observed in experts. Answering the first question requires experiments that try to maximize the likelihood that students will use the most powerful strategies they have available. Study 2 (this chapter) attempts to do this by means of a sentence arrangement task that poses a clear-cut problem of putting together meaning in text. Study 1 involves a more ordinary reading activity designed to bring out the strategies students normally employ. The texts contain difficulties, but students are not warned of them in advance.

STUDY 1

The purpose of this study was to obtain descriptive information on comprehension strategies used by students in the middle years of school in reading expository texts. Protocol data were obtained by having subjects "think aloud" while reading (Bird, 1980; Olson, Mack, & Duffy, 1981; Swaney, Janik, Bond, & Hayes, 1981). The procedure is similar to the one frequently used in studies of problem solving (Ericsson & Simon, 1980). Subjects read aloud expressing any thoughts as soon as they occur. Examples of the protocols thus obtained are shown in Table 13.1.

As the examples show—and as was also true of the protocols collected by Bird (1980), who studied readers in the same age range—reading protocols are not nearly so rich in detail as those obtained from slower-moving problem-solving activities. Consequently, one cannot expect to construct a complete strategy on the basis of a single subject's protocol, as is frequently done in other domains (Newell & Simon, 1972). Strategy descriptions must instead be constructed from fragmentary data obtained from a number of subjects.

The texts that students read were two paragraphs taken from a study by Markman (1979). These constitute the unitalicized portions of the protocols shown in Table 13.1. Each paragraph contains an item of information intended to be incongruous or logically inconsistent. In the Fish passage, the statement that fish at the bottom of the sea know their food by its color is incongruous with the preceding statement that there is absolutely no light there. In the Ice Cream passage, the statement that Baked Alaska is made by putting ice cream in a hot oven clashes with everyday knowledge about the propensity of ice cream to melt.

Markman (1979) used these passages in a study that indicated striking deficiencies in comprehension monitoring among children and early adolescents. Because Markman's research has stirred up considerable controversy and follow-up research (summarized in Brown, Bransford, Ferrara, & Campione, 1983), it must be made clear that the present study was not concerned with confirming, disconfirming, or explaining Markman's findings. The objective was to have subjects in the study read texts that presented obstacles to comprehension but not obstacles of an obvious kind (such as unfamiliar vocabulary) that would immediately alert them to the problematic nature of the task. Any of a variety of texts might have served the purpose, but Markman's paragraphs had a special advantage. Markman had found that students in the age range used in the present study

TABLE 13.1
Sample Reading Protocols

"Fish" Passage

Many different kinds of fish live in the ocean. Some fi . . . some fish have heads that make them look like alligators and some fish have heads that make them look like cats. Fish live in different parts of the ocean *um . . . What's happening there? Like where . . . where.* Some Fish live near the surface of the water. *um There's the answer.* Some fish live at the bottom of the oceans. *So I think those kind of fish are probably shrimp and lobster.* There's absolutely no light at the bottom of the ocean. *So the problem's cold.* Some fish that live at the bottom of the ocean know their food by its color. *What's its color got to do with it? Color, color doesn't mean anything . . . Yah that's all. Some of that stuff wasn't relevant. Like it doesn't . . . the color . . . what does color of the food . . . Doesn't matter to them. I don't think they can see very good. We did that last year. And a and a that's about it. And living at the bottom. That's . . . That was OK . . .*

"Ice Cream" Passage

Lots of different kinds of desserts can be made with ice cream. Some fancy restaurants serve a special dessert made out of ice cream called Baked Alaska . . . *I don't know what "Baked Alaska" . . . Never seen the word "Baked Alaska" . . . Looks like . . .* To make it . . . To make it they bake the ice cream . . . *If they bake ice cream it would melt . . .* As soon as it is finished baking they cut it into pieces with a knife and serve it right away. . . . *How could, how could they . . . cut ice cream? Oh, and when it's been in the oven heated, it would be just milk . . . Like water . . .* One of the things children like to eat everywhere is . . . in the world is ice cream. Some, some ice cream stores sell many different flavors of ice cream, but the most popular flavors are chocolate and vanilla . . . *Not to me . . . orange is.*

Note: Portions not italicized indicate reading aloud from text. Italicized portions indicate thinking-aloud statements. Texts are taken from Markman (1979). The ice cream passage was rearranged to avoid having the anomalous information come at the end in both passages.

detected the anomalous information when alerted to be on the watch for something wrong but tended to miss it if not alerted. Thus, the critical items of information in these paragraphs seemed to meet the twin requirements of (1) not being obvious; and (2) not being so esoteric or subtle as to lie entirely outside the grasp of the students. These requirements were intended to ensure that the texts provided some scope for the operation of text-processing strategies rather than depending entirely, for instance, on the availability of subject-matter knowledge.

Method

The study used 12 students from sixth grade and 12 students from tenth grade (approximate ages, 12 and 16 years) in Metropolitan Toronto schools serving middle-class populations. Each group received 45 minutes of preliminary training in thinking aloud while reading using methods devised by Bird (1980). The training conducted by Bird included demonstrations of the major types of reading behaviors and protocol statements she had identified in previous research, followed by supervised practice. On the following day, in individual sessions, students were tape-recorded as they read the two passages discussed previously. Students were told that the purpose of the study was to find out what goes on in people's minds when they read, and they were encouraged to read normally. They were not alerted to the possibility of there being anything unusual in the texts, and the Fish passage was always presented first, because prior testing had indicated its anomaly to be less frequently recognized than that in the Ice Cream passage. After reading a passage, subjects were encouraged to continue thinking aloud. It was thought that efforts to resolve a detected anomaly might surface at this time. Then subjects were asked to recall the passage orally as completely as possible and then to write a summary of it from memory.

Findings

Analysis of Protocol Statements.   Each protocol statement made during or immediately after reading was typed on a separate slip of paper and independently classified by two raters. Three-fourths of the statements were judged to be concerned with interpretation of the text and to be clear enough in reference to be classifiable. (Statements such as "That's weird," for instance, were eliminated because it could not be determined whether such a statement referred only to the immediately preceding item of text or to a larger unit.) The interpretive statements that remained were sorted into the following two categories:

1. *Detail interpretations.* These are protocol statements that interpret, paraphrase, or question particular items of text content without reference to other items or to more inclusive propositions. Typical items scored as detail interpretations are "Cats?" (referring to the statement that some fish look like cats) and "Why would they live at the bottom of the ocean?" Inferential statements were included in this category if they were judged to involve only a single item of text content related inferentially to the subject's world knowledge. A frequent inference of this type was that fish said to look like cats must be catfish.
2. *Macro-interpretations.* These are statements concerned with relating particular text elements to other elements or to the overall gist of the paragraph. For example, one student, on reading the statement about no light at the bottom of the ocean, remarked, "which means that these fish that live at the bottom of the ocean live in the dark." This statement adds little content to what has already been explicitly stated in the text, but it performs the important function of connecting the fact about no light to the fact that there are some species of fish that live at the bottom of the ocean and, consequently, live in darkness. Also included in this category were statements referring to the topic or intent of the discourse, such as, "So it's just sort of a summary of the fish and their existence."

These two categories have obvious similarities to the categories of micro-propositions and macro-propositions defined by van Dijk (1980). The difference is that the categories used here include not only statements of text content but also comments and questions related to it.

Table 13.2 presents data on the frequency of the two types of protocol statements in sixth and tenth grades based on averages of the two raters. The correlation between raters was .90 for detail interpretations and .81 for macro-interpretations. Detail interpretations are the more numerous at both grade levels with a nonsignificant tendency for the younger students to produce more of them. The older students, however, produced on the average almost four times as many macro-interpretations as the younger students.

Recognition of Anomalies.   All but two of the subjects explicitly recognized the anomaly in the Ice Cream passage (concerning baking ice cream in the oven) making a comment such as "It would melt." Of the two who did not make such a remark, one indicated a familiarity with Baked Alaska. We will later consider what may have made this item so easy to detect, but for the present performance on the Fish passage will be examined, which was considerably more variable. Eight of the 24 subjects made no comments at all related to the sentences about there being no light at the bottom of the ocean and about the fish finding their food by its color. For the other 16 subjects, all their comments related to these statements were extracted along with any statements from their recall protocols or abstracts that contained other than literal statements of the two points. Each subject was then rated on a 0- to 3-point scale, with scale points indexed as follows: 0 = no sign of recognition of the anomaly, 1 = vague indication of

TABLE 13.2
Reading Protocol Data

| | Grade | | | | | Group Recognition of Anomaly | | | | |
| | 6 (n = 12) | | 10 (n = 12) | | | Some (n = 9) | | None (n = 15) | | |
Variable	M	S.D.	M	S.D.	t	M	S.D.	M	S.D.	t
Detail Interpre-tations	4.42	2.18	3.75	3.23	<1	5.28	3.37	3.37	2.04	1.74
Macro-inter-pretations	.54	.78	1.96	1.78	2.52[b]	2.44	1.49	.53	1.04	2.73[a,b]
Anomaly Recognition Score	.54	2.08	1.00	1.30	<1	2.06	.68	0	0	—

[a]Tested against $H_o: \mu_1 - \mu_2 = 1$.
[b]$p < .05$

concern, 2 = raising the issue of vision in a relevant way but without clear recognition of the conflict between *no light* and *find food by its color,* and 3 = clear recognition of a conflict between the two statements. (The conflict did not have to be accurately formulated; most students who recognized the anomaly declared it would be difficult, rather than impossible, to see with no light.)

Mean scores on the scale of anomaly recognition are presented in Table 13.2. The mean score is higher for tenth-grade students, although this effect is not statistically significant, mean scores being small in relation to variance. Only nine subjects in all obtained nonzero scores on the scale of anomaly recognition, and of these only five (two sixth graders and three tenth graders) were credited with explicit recognition of the inconsistency. Table 13.2 presents a comparison of reading protocol data for the group of nine subjects with that for the remaining 15. The some-recognition group averaged 2.44 macro-interpretations each, compared to .53 for the no-recognition group. (Because a statement recognizing the Fish anomaly would itself be scored as a macro-interpretation, the difference between groups was tested against a null hypothesis of one point, rather than the customary null hypothesis of zero difference.) The some-recognition group also exceeded the no-recognition group in detail interpretations, although not to a statistically significant extent. When the number of detail interpretations is partialed out, there remains a significant correlation of .51 between macro-interpretations and anomaly score. Accordingly, it is concluded that although recognition of the Fish passage anomaly is not significantly associated with school grade, it is significantly associated with reading strategy. The favorable strategy is one that includes explicit attempts to formulate macro-propositions.

Clues to the Nature of Immature Strategies

The quantitative data reported in the preceding section characterize skilled readers in a way that is congruent with the Kintsch and van Dijk (1978) model of text comprehension. Because the validation of that model has rested on indirect evidence, it is gratifying to find in reading protocols direct indications of readers constructing macro-propositions. Unfortunately, however, the quantitative data leave us in the position of defining novice competence solely in terms of lacks. Younger students were found to engage in element-by-element interpretations of text details but so were older students. The difference was that in addition the older students engaged in higher-level interpretations relating details to one another or to the gist of the text. In this section a more holistic look at reading protocols is taken in an effort to see if it is possible to characterize younger readers in terms of what they do do rather than solely in terms of what they do not do.

First, to provide a basis for comparison, a look is taken at a reading protocol excerpt from one of the more sophisticated tenth-grade students. This excerpt shows the student coming to grips with the Fish passage anomaly:

There's absolutely no light at the bottom of the ocean, *which means that these fish that live at the bottom of the ocean live in the dark. They probably can't see much of anything—either that or they have very good vision.* And some fish live at the bottom of the ocean know their food by its color and how could they see the color of the food if it's dark unless they had really good vision?

In this protocol the reader actively formulates propositions that synthesize information contained in several text propositions and formulates tentative macro-propositions that are subsequently tested against text content.

The Ice Cream passage protocol shown in Table 13.1 is representative of the younger subjects, who show active interpretation of details but little or no interpretation at the macrolevel. These students appear to do the same kind of questioning and inferencing as the older students. The difference is in their exclusive focus on single details: What kind of fish look like alligators? What is baked Alaska? Are chocolate and vanilla really the most popular ice cream flavors?

Worth examining more closely is the response shown to the baked ice cream anomaly by the protocol in Table 13.1. Almost all subjects, as noted previously, registered some objection to the effect that ice cream would melt. In the protocol in question, the student is seen going on to question how the ice cream could later be sliced, because it would have been reduced to liquid. Seven of the 24 subjects raised such an objection, all but one of them being from the lower grade. Recognition of the slicing ice cream anomaly is unrelated to recognition scores for the Fish anomaly ($r = -.07$).

One could well argue that the chain of inference involved here is as sophisticated as that involved in recognizing the Fish passage anomaly. In the one case, *no light* implies *darkness* which contradicts *know food by its color.* In the other case, *bake ice cream* implies *melt* which contradicts *slice.* The difference, then, is not in the logical operations involved. The difference, we would argue, is in the kind of text processing that is required in order to set inferencing in motion. In the case of the Fish anomaly, inferencing must be applied to items of content that have no obvious relation to one another except for the fact that they follow one another in the text. In other words it is not a perceived conflict between factual statements that sets inferencing in motion in the case of the Fish anomaly. It is the effort to construct a coherent connection between the *no light* sentence and the *find food by its color* sentence that brings the factual discrepancy to light. In the case of the Ice Cream anomaly, on the other hand, the statement that ice cream is baked in an oven is immediately recognized as discordant with known facts. Once this discrepancy is noted, the further statement about slicing the ice cream is also recognizable as discordant with world knowledge. Thus, the important difference between the two anomalies from a text-processing point of view is that the Ice Cream anomaly will be recognized by someone who actively questions the plausibility of individual statements as they are encountered, but the

Fish anomaly will be recognized only by someone who is in addition trying to construct macro-propositions linking apparently disjoint statements.

As a first step toward characterizing immature comprehension strategies, then, it may be proposed that young readers appear to proceed through text by testing individual items of information against their world knowledge. If the item is seen as inconsistent or uninterpretable (if, for instance, it involves an unfamiliar key word), then inferential processes are set in motion, otherwise they are not. This conjecture is consistent with observations by Markman (1981) on younger children who were directed to search for anomalous information in texts. She found that they questioned the truth of individual claims but did not consider the relation of one claim to another.

Children who do nothing but interpret details one-at-a-time could never grasp the gist of a text, however. Summaries produced by the subjects in the present experiment all show at least some evidence of gist construction. The following examples give an idea of the range from most to least in the amount of synthesis of details into statements of gist:

1. There are many fish living in all parts of the ocean. Some have heads that look like other animals. It seems most fish have extremely good vision.
2. There are many kinds of fish. Some fish have heads like cats or alligator. Some fish live near surface of the water. There are many fish in parts of the ocean.

Example 1 consists of constructed statements that interpret sets of propositions included in the text, whereas example 2 consists of paraphrases of selected statements from the text. But the selection of statements in example 2 is clearly not random, two of the four statements being high-order ones. The performance of subjects in this study was consistent with that found by Brown and Day (1983), with the less mature students relying on deletion and selection and only the most mature making use of invented statements of gist.

Brown, Day, and Jones (in press) propose a strategy that they call "copy-delete" to account for the way fifth-grade students were found to summarize texts. The strategy consists of reading text elements sequentially, deciding for each element whether to include or delete it, and copying out any items selected for inclusion. The copy-delete strategy has an obvious parallel in the element-by-element interpretation of details that was suggested previously.

In the Kintsch and van Dijk (1978; van Dijk, 1980) model, text comprehension is conceived as cyclical, with deletion, selection, and construction of new propositions going on during each cycle, with previously selected details sometimes being deleted in later cycles and previously deleted details being called back for use in constructing revised macro-propositions, and so on. The reading protocols of the more mature readers that were examined in this study are congruent with such a cyclical model of text comprehension. Protocol data from the less mature readers, however, along with the observations of Markman (1981) and of Brown and co-workers, all point to the possibility of a different control structure for novice readers. Comprehension in immature readers shows signs of being more of a single-pass process with details being definitively matched to existing knowledge and assessed as important or unimportant, true or false, at the moment of first encounter. The interpretive rules that immature readers apply are perhaps no different from those applied by experts, but they tend to be applied in a once-and-for-all manner, and the order of their application is keyed to the order of elements in the text rather than to processing cycles.

Labeling a mature comprehension strategy as "cyclical" and the immature strategy as "single-pass" is, of course, an oversimplification. At a sufficiently detailed level of analysis, all comprehension probably involves cyclical retrieval of elements into short-term memory (Kintsch & van Dijk, 1978). At a more molar level of analysis even mature readers are found to proceed in a largely single-pass manner (Just & Carpenter, 1980). A comparison of mature and immature comprehension strategies must accordingly be made relative to a specified level of analysis. In the studies reported in this chapter, the level of analysis is the relatively molar level that is tapped by thinking-aloud protocols (Ericsson & Simon, 1980). At this level, marked differences do appear in the extent to which readers recall and reconsider previously processed units of text content.

In considering the possibility of qualitative changes in reading comprehension strategies, it is interesting to look for transitional cases—cases that might illustrate the breaking up of an immature strategy and the beginnings of a new one. Such a case seems to be represented in the Fish passage protocol in Table 13.1. It comes from a tenth-grade student who generated above-average amounts of both detail and macro-interpretations. Twice in the Fish passage protocol she indicates a concern about the relevance of particular items to the gist of the text ("What's happening there? Like where . . . where" and "What's its color got to do with it?"). Thus, the student does not simply judge items singly as important or unimportant but raises questions and looks for connections. On the other hand, she shows signs of interpreting details in isolation and in a once-and-for-all fashion. Fish living at the bottom of the sea are interpreted to be shrimp and lobster. The implication of no light at the bottom of the sea is determined to be coldness. Both of these are, of course, reasonable interpretations. It is their finality that stands in the way of successful gist construction. The student worries at some length about what to make of the subsequent sentence about fish knowing their food by its color but in the process does not consider alternative interpretations of the earlier sentences that might make sense in relation to the item about color. On matters of topical relevance, it appears, the student has learned to apply provisional operations that keep data available for further processing, whereas on matters of factual interpretation, she appears to apply prematurely strong macro-rules that eliminate data from further processing (cf. van Dijk, 1980, pp. 49–50).

STUDY 2

One way of getting more insight into text processes is to employ special tasks that render aspects of the process problematic that are not normally problematic. Such a strategem runs the risk, of course, of so altering the task that it no longer elicits the same cognitive behavior that one set out to investigate. In fact, it probably goes without saying that in any experimental task some unspecifiable amount of what one observes is task specific. Consequently, in the end one can only rely on findings that converge under principled interpretations. That is the basis on which we try to advance our understanding of text processing in the present study.

The experimental task is that of arranging a set of sentences to make a coherent text. In study 1 it remained unclear how, or to what extent the younger students were forming a coherent mental representation of the texts they read, in as much as their thinking-aloud statements were focused overwhelmingly on individual details. It is possible that their silence on matters of overall text meaning simply indicates that they encountered no problems in this respect. In sentence arrangement the task of producing a coherent representation is rendered salient and concrete. It was therefore hoped that this task would bring into the open whatever strategies young readers have available for dealing with problems of coherence and overall meaning.

Sentence arrangement also resembles the reading of difficult texts as follows:

1. Interpretation of individual sentences often requires a search through other sentences in order to discover referents or to establish the semantic context.

2. Initial hypotheses about meaning will often prove inadequate in the light of subsequent information. Ways in which students dealt with these problems in sentence arrangement were studied by investigating their behavior in reading the sentences, the extent to which they made provisional orderings and groupings, and the kinds of justifications they gave for sentence placements.

Method

The same 24 subjects of the previous study (12 in each of the sixth and tenth grades) served in the present study. They received the scrambled sentence tasks the day after completing work with the anomalous texts.

These subjects received, in a counter-balanced order, two sets of sentences to unscramble. One set, consisting of 10 sentences, formed the text of a narrative fairy tale (a summary of St. Exupery's *The Little Prince*). The other set, consisting of six sentences, formed an expository text about early travel to the East Indies for spices. The two texts are shown in Table 13.3. The sentences are shown in their original order with numbering added. Subjects saw the sentences on separate slips of paper randomly arranged. They were instructed to put sen-

TABLE 13.3
Sentences Used in Sentence Arrangement Task

"Prince" Passage

---

1. The little prince lived alone on a tiny planet.
2. The planet was so tiny, it was no bigger than a house.
3. There were three volcanoes on such a small planet.
4. The prince had a flower.
5. It was unlike any flower in the galaxy.
6. It was special because it could talk.
7. One day, something the flower said made the prince very unhappy.
8. It was this unhappiness that started the prince on his travels.
9. He met a magic fox on another planet.
10. The fox told him the secret to happiness.

"Spices" Passage

---

1. In ancient times and throughout the middle ages, all the spices known in Europe, such as pepper, cloves, mace, nutmeg and cinnamon, were obtained from India and the East Indies.
2. These were in great demand since Europeans, who were heavy meat eaters, had discovered that these substances would not only flavour, but help preserve meat.
3. At first the overland route was used, and spices were carried across the middle east to Europe by caravans.
4. When the Turks captured Constantinople in 1453, and extended their rule into the eastern lands of the Mediterranean, this route became too dangerous.
5. Fortunately, ships were soon improved enough that navigators could sail into unknown seas in search of a water route to the famous spice islands, the East Indies.
6. In fact, one of the aims of Columbus on his celebrated voyage was to find spices.

---

tences into the order they thought best. Subjects were tested in tape-recorded sessions where they were free to work on the tasks for as long as they wished. They were instructed to think aloud as they worked. Experimenters intervened freely to clarify statements and observable manipulations and were directed to elicit a justification of any sentence placement that a subject did not explain spontaneously. Experimenters recorded all sentence placements in a way that permitted subsequent coordination with protocol statements.

Findings

Sentence Manipulation Strategies.   Two statistical analyses were carried out on students' manipulations of the slips of paper on which sentences were written. The variable *linear placement* was defined as the number of moves in which a single sentence was added to an existing series minus the number of moves in which a sentence was either inserted or moved from its original placement. The mean linear placement score for the two texts was 2.38 at the sixth grade. For the tenth grade, it was −1.04 indicating a preponderance of moves involving insertions or reorderings. The difference between grades was significant at the .05 level (t(22) = 2.14). There was a substantial correlation between scores for the two texts (.80 in sixth grade, .70 in tenth grade) suggesting consistent individual differences in approaches to the task.

In the other analysis, subjects were classified according to whether or not they at any time in the experiment put sentences into clusters or subgroups prior to assigning them a place in the reconstructed text. Only three of the 12 subjects in sixth grade ever grouped sentences, whereas nine out of the 12 subjects in tenth grade did so (p < .025, Fisher's exact test).

These analyses indicate markedly different overt strategies predominating in the two grades with the younger students tending to add sentences one-at-a-time to an arrangement with little subsequent alteration to the linearly developed text, whereas the older students more often made use of preliminary groupings, insertions, and revisions.

Reading Strategies.   Linear placement of sentences could reflect a sophisticated or an unsophisticated approach to sentence arrangement depending on the intellectual processes involved in selecting the sentences to place. With a simple text involving few sentences, one could imagine an expert working the whole arrangement out mentally and then placing the slips one-by-one to display the order. Verbal protocol data were examined from two different perspectives to obtain information on intellectual processes. In this section, global reading strategies that students applied to the text sentences are examined. In the next section, the justifications students gave for the sentence placements they made are analyzed.

The protocol of each subject on each of the two sentence arrangement tasks was rated for the presence or absence of the following three types of reading activity: (1) surveying content—defined as reading ahead of the sentence being placed; (2) rereading and checking—defined as rereading more than the sentence just placed or making any statement indicating that a placement was temporary; and (3) summarizing content—defined as stating the gist of information contained in more than two sentences. Two raters independently scored one-fourth of the protocols. Agreement was obtained on 92% of the 36 judgments involved. Final scores were determined by consensus on the three strategy scores on which there was disagreement. The remaining protocols were scored by only one rater.

Surveying content was shown on at least one task by nine out of 12 sixth graders and 10 out of 12 tenth graders. Rereading and checking was shown by seven sixth graders and by all of the tenth graders—a difference significant at the .05 level by Fisher's exact test. The most pronounced difference between grades, however, was in the incidence of summarization. None of the sixth graders was rated as showing summarization on either task, whereas eight of the 12 tenth graders did so (p < .01, Fisher's exact test). Summarization was more often elicited by the expository than the narrative passage. The eight students who showed evidence of summarization all did so on the expository passage, but only four of them also did so on the narrative passage.

The relation between reading strategies and sentence placement strategies was tested by correlating the linear placement score described in the preceding section with the number of tasks (zero to two) on which each subject exhibited the various reading strategies. The resulting correlations are shown in Table 13.4. Use of each of the three strategies is negatively associated with linear placement of sentences, the correlations involving the rereading and checking and the summarization strategies both being significant beyond the .05 level. Table 13.4 also shows the correlations between reading strategy use and use of macro-interpretations, as assessed on these same subjects in study 1. Summarizing, the strategy most clearly related to macro-interpretation, correlates .60 with that variable indicating a significant degree of stability of reading strategy across the two quite different kinds of tasks.

Findings considered up to this point indicate a developmental trend toward handling sentence arrangement problems by means of tentative groupings and placements of sentences guided by rereading and checking and by summarizing portions of text already assembled. The approach taken by the more mature students appears, therefore, to parallel the process of gist construction posited by the Kintsch and van Dijk (1978) model. This parallel is reinforced by a significant correlation between use of summarization in sentence arrangement and the use of interpretations oriented toward macro-structure in ordinary reading. Younger students, on the other hand, tend to approach sentence arrangement in the same element-by-element fashion that has been hypothesized they use in normal reading, making seldom reconsidered judgments about the placement of sentences, much as they appear to make once-and-for-all judgments about the significance and meaning of statements as they encounter them serially in reading texts. How they make these placement decisions has not yet been made clear and is a question that will be pursued further in the next section. Results noted

TABLE 13.4
Correlations of Reading Strategy Use
with Other Strategy Variables

	Correlated Strategies	
Reading Strategy	*Linear Placement*	*Macro-interpretation*
Surveying content	−.29	.16
Rereading and checking	−.58[b]	.09
Summarizing	−.50[a]	.60[b]

[a]p < .05.
[b]p < .01.

thus far indicate that young students make about as much use as older ones do of surveys of content, reading ahead of the sentence under immediate consideration. What is attended to in such surveys could vary, however. Surveying content might involve looking for unifying themes or topics, or it could involve only the serial consideration of alternative sentences for the next placement. For indications of what students may be attending to in their examination of sentences, the explanations students offered when asked to justify sentence placements are discussed.

Justifications of Sentence Placements.   One subject from sixth grade and two subjects from tenth grade were eliminated from the following analyses because of experimenter failure to probe for justifications. Each statement by the remaining 21 students justifying a sentence placement was typed on a separate slip of paper and classified by two raters who were blind as to subject identity and grade. The total corpus consisted of 242 justifications, 133 from sixth grade and 109 from tenth grade. Six of these justifications were rejected by one or both raters as unclassifiable. The remaining sentences were sorted into the 13 categories shown in Table 13.5. Table 13.5 also presents mean frequencies for each grade and reliabilities, which were estimated by the Spearman–Brown prophecy formula applied to the correlation between frequencies assigned to each subject by the two raters.

The grouping of categories in Table 13.5 into five types is conceptual. Only in the case of the *Meaning Construction* group does the grouping prove to have an empirical basis as well.

Unexplained justifications are ones in which the call for justification produced a relevant response but one that did not actually say what it was about a sentence that justified its placement. One kind was *paraphrase* of the sentence in question (e.g., "It's about the route they were taking and it gets too dangerous," which paraphrases a portion of one sentence of the expository passage). Another was *default,* where the reason given for placing a sentence was that no better placement could be found. By far the largest number of unexplained justifications, however, were of the kind labeled *general effect,* which included statements that sentences "sounded good" and responses such as "Because this one says . . . ," followed by reading of the sentence, sometimes in context with or in contrast to another sentence but with no explanation. Not surprisingly, sixth-grade students exceeded tenth-grade students in all these categories, significantly so in the case of *paraphrase* and *general effect.*

Argument overlap is a term taken from Kintsch and van Dijk (1978), who propose that a fundamental process in comprehension is the construction of a text base composed of propositions that are cohesively linked by the overlap of arguments with terms in preceding propositions. Here we use the term to refer to justifications that rest solely on the match or mismatch of arguments without reference to predicates. Examples of *single topic* overlap justifications are "It's

TABLE 13.5
Mean Frequency of Types of Sentence Placement Justifications

Justification	Reliability	Grade	
		6 (n = 11)	10 (n = 10)
Unexplained			
Paraphrase	.67	.59	.10[a]
Default	.94	.55	.05
General effect	.98	4.41	1.65[a]
Argument overlap			
Single topic	.98	2.18	.40[b]
Multiple topic	.88	.18	.25
Text function			
Beginning/ending	.95	1.32	1.35
Implicit function	.74	.50	.35
Explicit function	.85	.32	2.70[c]
Meaning construction			
Elaborated topic	.66	.27	.75
Linking inference	.91	1.09	2.70[a]
Extrapolation	.97	.05	.35
Cohesion	.91	.23	.65

[a] $p < .05$, two-tailed, for difference between grades.
[b] $p < .01$.
[c] $p < .001$.

still talking about the spices'' and ''It tells you about Europe again.'' Any argument overlap justification that mentioned or implied more than one topic was classified as *multiple topic*—for instance, ''It's talking about a flower, then all of a sudden it's talking about the planet . . . It doesn't go well together.'' Sixth-grade students gave five times as many *single topic* argument overlap justifications as did tenth-grade students. With *multiple topic* justifications there is a slight trend in the other direction.

Text function justifications were statements that referred either to the structural role of a sentence in a text or to the kind of information it provides. *Beginning/ending* justifications were ones that asserted without further explanation that a certain sentence looked like an appropriate beginning or ending sentence. Such justifications averaged about one per subject at both grade levels. An example of *implicit function* justification is the statement, ''Why it's special,'' referring to the sentence, ''It was special because it could talk.'' It is inferred that this means the sentence explains the preceding sentence, which says the flower ''was unlike any flower in the galaxy.'' A justification that spelled this relationship out would be classified as an *explicit function* justification. The statistically most significant difference of any between the grades is in the incidence of *explicit function* justifications, which are almost an order of magnitude more frequent in the tenth grade than in the sixth grade. *Implicit function* justifications are less frequent and slightly favor the younger group.

Meaning construction includes types of justifications that seem to reflect an effort to construct a meaningful gist, superordinate to the particular sentences under consideration. *Elaborated topic* justifications referred to proposition arguments. They were distinguishable from *argument overlap* items in that they indicated some meaningful relationship between arguments. An example is, "That one is talking about land, and then it says ships were soon improved." *Linking inferences* offered some deductive reason for relating two sentences. For instance, one subject related the sentences "It was special because it could talk" and "One day something the flower said . . ." by inferring, "So we know it's the flower that could talk." *Extrapolation* involved inferences to sentences anticipated but not yet encountered. For instance, one student, after arranging sentences that established the prince as living on a tiny planet, said, "Now to find out what he's doing there, or what's there. Tenth-grade students exceeded sixth-grade students in all three types of justifications in this group, although the difference was significant only in the case of *linking inference*, which was the most frequent of the three types. This was the only homogeneous group of justification types in terms of intercorrelation (coefficient alpha = .66), and so combined scores for these justifications are used in some later analyses.

A final type of justification was justification on the basis of *cohesion*. Examples of this type are "It can't be the fox because it says 'it' instead of 'he'" and "This 'in fact' sounds like a followup." The few such justifications found at each grade level did not differ significantly in frequency.

Relation of Justifications to Other Variables.   Each subject's final arrangement of sentences for the two texts was rated for coherence by two raters on a 5-point scale. There was no difference between grades in the combined ratings (t(22) <1), but coherence ratings correlated significantly with the use of *meaning construction justifications (r = .54, p < .05). The only other variable that correlated significantly with coherence ratings was beginning/ending* justifications, which correlated negatively (r = −.60, p < .01). Evidently, judgments as to what looked like an appropriate beginning or ending sentence tended to be ill-founded. It is interesting that use of *explicit function* justifications did not correlate with coherence ratings (r = −.03). Although this type of justification was highly related to grade level, it appears not to have been carried out in such a way as to be effective for solving problems of coherence, whereas *meaning construction* was. Evidence of a direct connection between *linking inference* and coherence of the resulting sentence arrangements comes from separately correlating scores for the two texts. Amount of inference on the expository passage correlates significantly with coherence rating for the expository passage but not with coherence rating for the narrative passage. The reverse is true for amount of inference on the narrative passage.

The *linear placement* score, based on overt sentence manipulations, correlated .47 (p < .05) with use of *single topic* argument overlap justifications, which suggests that the kind of superficial analysis involved in argument overlap justifications is compatible with an overt strategy involving few modifications in sentence arrangement. The only other significant correlation involving *linear placement* was a negative one (−.50, p< .05) with use of *cohesion* as a justification. This may indicate a tendency for cohesion to be used as a criterion for altering arrangements originally made on some other basis.

The *macro-interpretation* score from study 1, which was previously shown to correlate with use of summarizing in the sentence arrangement task, also proved to correlate significantly with use of *meaning construction* verifications (r = .44, p < .05). Thus, again, we find macro-interpretation in ordinary reading to be correlated with its most obvious counterpart in sentence arrangement. Macro-interpretations did not correlate significantly with any other justification variables.

Summary of Quantitative Findings.   The approach of the more mature students to sentence arrangement was found to be characterized by tentative placements of sentences and use of preliminary groupings, rereading and checking, and summarization of text. Placement decisions were justified mainly on grounds of their explicit function in the text or on grounds of the meaning generated by a sentence string. If the word *placement* were replaced by the word *interpretation* one would have an approximate description of the ordinary reading behavior of the more mature students as observed in study 1. Indeed, the use of macro-interpretations in study 1 was significantly correlated with the use of meaning construction justifications in study 2. Thus, as far as more mature competence is concerned, study 2 serves mainly to reinforce study 1 and to provide some basis for confidence that the strategies revealed in sentence arrangement are the same strategies that are used in reading.

Unlike study 1, however, study 2 reveals distinctive characteristics in the approach of the less mature students as well. The less mature students were characterized by a linear placement of sentences, with little revision, by little rereading and checking and a complete absence of summarization, and by sentence placement justifications that were either unexplained or explained in terms of overlap between arguments. The unexplained justifications mainly consisted of appeals to the general effect of a string of sentences.

These characteristics seem to add up to a strategy that makes it possible to deal with a sentence arrangement task without having to construct the overall meaning of the text. The behavior of the younger subjects in sentence arrangement is consistent with that attributed to them in study 1: element-by-element interpretations that are not analyzed further in the light of subsequent information. But does their behavior in sentence arrangement tell us anything about how they manage to comprehend text with such a limited processing strategy? That question will be considered by a more detailed examination of selected protocols.

Ways of Reconstructing Texts

In reading through the protocols of both the most sophisticated and the least sophisticated students, the orderliness and apparent ease with which they go about their dramatically different treatments of the sentence arrangement problem becomes obvious. One of the most sophisticated students, after selecting a likely beginning sentence for the Spices passage, begins his deliberations by formulating an overview:

> So that, you know, it looks like it's going to be something about spices. So it gives the time period—in ancient times and throughout the middle ages—and it gives the subject, all the spices known in Europe.

Thus oriented to the topic, he proceeds to select sentences on the basis of inferences about the meaning of the text aided by summary statements that consolidate what he has established up to that point. For example:

> So—so now we know that they [spices] are in great demand, so we have to have some way of getting them there. . . . So I guess it's that the overland route was used. That's at first, so we know that's the first one. . . .

Were it not known that this was a sentence arrangement protocol, one might suppose it was the protocol of someone carrying out a very careful reading of an intact text. What the sentence arrangement task seems to do in a case such as this is to produce an overt display of the macro-operations that are presumed to go on covertly in normal text comprehension (cf. Kintsch & van Dijk, 1978). For sophisticated students, then, sentence arrangement appears to consist of constructing a mental representation of text meaning and is accomplished by the processes normally employed in comprehension.

A quite different sort of orderliness is displayed in the protocols of less sophisticated students. The following, for instance, is the complete set of comments of one student assembling the Spices passage minus references to the physical placement of slips of paper:

> . . . because it sort of starts "in ancient times."
> . . . because it just seems to carry it on.
> . . . It's the only one that sounds right.
> . . . because it's talking about. . .
> . . . It's still talking about the route.
> . . . It's the only one left and it sounds okay.

Here there is no apparent effort to grasp the meaning of the text. Argument overlap and general effect are the main criteria applied. Nevertheless, this student produced a reasonable sentence arrangement, one that received a rating of 4 on a 5-point scale of coherence.

Two questions are raised by protocols of this kind:

1. Is the behavior displayed here unique to the sentence arrangement task or does it, as appears to be the case with the more sophisticated students, reflect more general ways of processing text?
2. How is it possible to construct coherent text by means of the kinds of operations displayed?

Studies of children's writing have identified both argument overlap and general effect as playing central roles in children's composing processes. In a study of coherence in children's texts, McCutchen and Perfetti (1982) found that most of the connections in the texts of second graders were on the basis of reference (argument overlap), whereas by the eighth grade, students were beginning to make use of complex syntactic connections. They observed:

> A simple count of repeated words, or argument overlap (Kintsch & van Dijk, 1978), would overestimate the degree to which coherent texts are produced by young writers.

The same would be true in sentence arrangement. Use of argument overlap justifications did not correlate significantly with rated coherence of the resulting arrangements ($r = .29$ for the narrative passage, .19 for the expository passage).

In a study of revision abilities, Bartlett (1982) found that elementary school students could recognize that something was wrong in passages where there were failures of cohesion (as in faulty reference), but they could not locate the source of the trouble. Their appeal, instead was to the general effect or sound of the language.

Thus there is evidence from other areas of text processing that children make use of argument overlap and general effect in cases where more mature people would make use of meaning-based inferences and connections. In sentence arrangement, children appear quick to recognize overlapping arguments even when they are not based on exact repetition of words. This apparently well-practiced skill suggests that the micro-operations that Kintsch and van Dijk (1978) specify for creating a cohesive set of propositions extracted from text are part of children's repertoires. In addition to connecting one sentence to another, however, children show signs of identifying the repeated arguments that indicate the topic of a text segment. This is clearly a kind of macro-operation, although it is one that can be carried out without reference to text meaning.

Children's appeals to *general effect* are difficult to interpret, because it is not clear to what extent the vagueness resides in the child's comprehension of text and to what extent it resides in the child's expression. Notions such as *flow* and *sound* are common in expert discussions of text and point to the fact that mature language users often have global impressions of the appropriateness or inappropriateness of a text sequence without a statable explanation. Such global impressions of coherence together with a recognition of topical connections could provide a workable basis for comprehension monitoring in children. Such a basis would often permit superficial or incorrect comprehension as indicated in children's response to anomalous texts, but it would probably serve for most kinds of easy reading. Thus, it is not unreasonable to suppose that the processes that immature students display in sentence arrangement are processes that serve them in normal reading and writing as well, enabling them to achieve a degree of coherence through limited processing of text meaning.

The two approaches to sentence arrangement illustrated previously seem worlds apart. In an effort to gain insight into what is involved in changing from one approach to the other, as with study 1, an examinination of what appears to be a transitional case is made. It is perhaps worth noting that the two selections of transitional cases were carried out independently by different ones of the two authors, but the same student turned out to be chosen in both cases. In study 1 this student was observed to be carrying out sophisticated interpretations of individual statements and to be showing concerns about relevance but to be hampered in making sense of the text by the persistence of a strategy of element-by-element interpretation. In sentence arrangement she again makes sophisticated inferences but is unable to integrate these inferences into a coherent interpretation of the text.

In tackling the Spice passage, this student first infers a sequential relationship between the sentence that begins "When the Turks captured Constantinople in 1453 . . ." and the sentence about Columbus by drawing on world knowledge that associates Columbus with the year 1497. Later she establishes a meaning-based connection between the sentence referring to caravans and the sentence about ships being improved: "The caravans, see, at first—makes you think, like, that was at first, then ships came along." A number of other connections are established on the basis of logical inference or discourse structure knowledge.

Where this student runs into trouble is in trying to combine all these separate insights into a basis for ordering the complete set of sentences. In attending to one relationship she loses track of another; for instance, the 1453–1497 connection later disappears without comment. She attempts an overall ordering on the basis of temporal cues, but there are not enough of those. She ends up placing some sentences on the basis of argument overlap (spices), one on the basis of its being "like a beginning statement," and then subjecting the whole to rereading to test for how it sounds.

This student appeared to have the elements of a sophisticated text processing strategy but to lack the higher-level executive procedures that could make these elements work effectively in producing a coherent text representation. Unlike the more successful student whose protocol was examined previously, she attempted no overview of what the text was about. Although she reread sentence sequences to see how they sounded, she did not generate summary statements that might have enabled her to see where the text was heading or to spot out-of-place sentences. Unlike the other two protocols cited, this student's protocol does not convey an impression of orderliness and ease. Confusion and struggle are evident. It seems that she was trying to handle meaning-construction processes like those of the more mature student but with an executive structure more like that of the younger student.

Individual cases can, of course, only illustrate, not prove points. The point this transitional case illustrates is that progress toward mature text processing involves not only acquiring particular macro-rules but also developing an executive structure within which those rules can be applied effectively and without overloading or disrupting the cognitive system.

GENERAL DISCUSSION

Although the two studies reported in this chapter used unconventional tasks, their intent was to yield information about normal text processing—in particular, about how immature readers deal with difficult texts. Let us be clear about what is and is not being assumed when we try to generalize from experimental tasks like sentence arrangement to everyday activities of reading and studying from texts. We do not assume that the calibre of performance, however measured, is the same. Experimental conditions might degrade performance to a less mature level, or they might, on the other hand, provide motivation and aids to the structuring of cognitive behavior that enable students to perform above their normal levels (cf. Bransford, 1981). It is assumed, however, that the cognitive strategies students use in experimental tasks must have had a life outside the experimental situation. They may be adapted to experimental task demands, but they could not have been created *de novo* for the experiment. This assumption receives empirical support from the cross-task correlations observed in the two studies, which were run on the same subjects, as well as from the general conformity of the behavior of more mature subjects to that expected from existing knowledge of the comprehension process. Accordingly, although findings from these studies cannot be taken as normative measures of the competence of 12-year-olds and 16-year-olds, they can be taken as indicative of developmental changes in the strategies students have available for dealing with text processing difficulties.

The characterization of the more sophisticated text-processing strategies that emerges from these studies contains no surprises. The sophisticated student approaches both ordinary reading and sentence arrangement tasks as tasks that call for the construction of a coherent gist or message. In ordinary reading, inferential processes are brought into play not only when there is an inconsistency between text statements and world knowledge but also when there is a difficulty in making a coherent propositional connection between textually linked statements. Sentence arrangement differs from ordinary reading for these students primarily in that establishing coherence is problematic throughout and thus requires more of what they do normally. This characterization, as noted several times previously, is virtually a gloss on the Kintsch and van Dijk (1978) model of text comprehension, its only novelty arising from the fact that it is drawn from quite different kinds of data.

It is easy to characterize younger students by the absence of features of mature competence. Data from the present studies support the notion that the kind of competence represented in the Kintsch and van Dijk model is not inherent in the human information-processing system but is an acquisition. In both studies, younger students showed significantly lesser amounts of the kind of activity associated with construction of macro-propositions—less summarizing, less re-reading and checking, less questioning of intersentence connections, less production of linking inferences.

These characterizations have relevance to instructional design, supporting efforts like those reported by Brown, Palincsar, & Armbruster (Chapter 8) to teach expert-like strategies of text processing. It has been intended, however, in carrying out the reported studies to go beyond identifying what students lack and to obtain insight into the strategies immature students actually use. This is a much more speculative venture than identifying what students lack, but the studies have provided a basis for at least the beginnings of such a venture.

A starting premise, which has support from other research, is that young students have the capacity to make the same kinds of inferences as older ones (cf. Trabasso, Stein, & Johnson, 1981). In study 1 such inferencing was sparked by conflicts between text statements and world knowledge and not by problems of text coherence. The protocol statements of younger students in study 1—heavy on detail interpretations, light on macro-interpretations—and the linear placement strategy they exhibited on sentence arrangement tasks in study 2 suggest a model of text processing that proceeds element by element, relying to a large extent on text characteristics that can be extracted without deep analysis—on the sharing of arguments among propositions and on a general impression of flow that may result both from surface cohesiveness and local coherence (McCutchen & Perfetti, 1982).

The mental representation of a fully comprehended text, as described by van Dijk (1980) for instance, consists of hierarchically arranged propositions. At the top of the hierarchy are topics—propositions that indicate what the text is about. At a lower level are propositions that summarize major substantive points in the text. Much of the activity of comprehension, according to Kintsch and van Dijk's model, goes into the construction of these macro-propositions. At a still lower level are propositions capturing the detailed content of the text. An immature processing strategy of the kind described would be capable of generating high-level propositions of the "what it's about" variety, because these could be derived from the analysis of argument overlap that has been evidenced in young readers. But such a processing strategy would not generate macro-propositions of the "what it says" variety. Hence the absence of invented summary statements in the summaries of young readers studied by Brown and Day (1983).

The resulting mental representation of text, then, would consist of high-level nodes representing topics, directly connected to low-level nodes representing details of content. Missing would be the intermediate level of macro-propositions that distill the substance of the text. Such a *topic-plus-detail* mental representation is obviously deficient from the standpoint of meaningful learning from text. Most of the knowledge worth carrying away from an instructional text is captured in macro-propositions of the "what it says" type. Higher-level "what it's about" propositions encode information mainly about the text itself rather than about the world and consequently are of limited long-term value; also, propositions representing single details have obvious inadequacies as knowledge.

Although the structure of this hypothesized strategy is but crudely sketched in these remarks, and although much of what has been said is speculative, collateral evidence makes it seem likely that some kind of strategy based on element-by-element interpretation and a shallow structure of mental representations underlies immature text processing. The previously cited *copy-delete* strategy identified by Brown, Day, and Jones (in press) seems to be the same kind of strategy applied to summarization that is applied to ordinary reading and to sentence arrangement. In research on composition a variety of evidence has been amassed, pointing to the existence of a similar strategy labeled "knowledge telling" (Scardamalia & Bereiter, in press b). It consists of generating text content serially under constraints of topic and discourse schema—essentially the same process displayed in the more immature approaches to sentence arrangement in study 2. There is, thus, a certain convergence of results from varied data sources. Progress toward a more general and definitive description of immature text processing strategies will likely depend on such convergence rather than on exploiting particular experimental paradigms.

PROSPECTS FOR DEVELOPMENTALLY BASED
INSTRUCTION IN TEXT-PROCESSING STRATEGIES

There have recently begun to appear a number of reports of successful attempts to teach expert-like text-processing strategies to young or unskilled readers (Bird, 1980; Brown, Palincsar, & Armbruster, Chapter 8; Day, 1980; Hannigan, Shelton, Franks, & Bransford, 1980). The strategy differences identified in the present studies lend support to this kind of endeavor; but there are also indications that a more developmentally based approach may be needed.

By direct teaching of expert strategies, Day (1980) was able to get students to increase their use of summarization rules involving selection, deletion, and superordination but encountered much less success in getting them to invent summary statements. Similarly, Bird (1980) was able to promote several expert-like strategies but did not produce significant gains in use of the most abstract principle, that of setting up *watchers* for required text elements. In both cases, trouble arose at the point of trying to teach a rule that could not be applied within an element-by-element processing strategy as hypothesized. Comparable difficulties have occurred in writing instruction with efforts to get students to advance beyond the *knowledge-telling* strategy referred to in the preceding section. Refinements that can be accommodated within the structure of the knowledge-telling strategy are readily adopted by students, but the strategy itself proves resistent to change (Scardamalia & Bereiter, in press b).

It would seem, then, that in addition to teaching particular rules and procedures, there may be a need to help students modify the executive structure that controls text processing. At present the most promising approaches appear to be ones that involve temporary external supports to aid in sustaining the more complex executive procedure—and the design of such supports depends on a detailed model of the student's existing procedure so that an appropriate next step in development can be introduced (Case, 1978; Scardamalia & Bereiter, in press-a).

A miniature example of such an external support system is provided in a study by Paris, Scardamalia, & Bereiter (1982). Students in the sixth and tenth grades were given disconnected pairs of sentences and told to compose paragraphs that incorporated the two sentences in a sensible (i.e., logically coherent) way. The task might be construed formally as that of inventing a macro-structure onto which the given sentences could be mapped as micro-structure. The initial approaches of students in both grades was much in line with the topic-plus-detail structure of text representation referred to in the preceding section. Generally, they identified a topic common to the two sentences and then composed a paragraph on the topic incorporating the sentences as details. However, the sentence pairs were chosen so that such a strategy almost never resulted in a coherent paragraph. For instance, one pair of sentences was:

There are books written on every subject you can think of.
      and
Comic books are a waste of time.

Merely producing a paragraph on the topic *books* is not likely to achieve an adequate integration of these sentences. A subsuming proposition is needed, such as, "It is important to be selective about what you read."

Modeling of appropriate solutions to such problems did not have any effect nor did modeling the process of thinking out a solution. Evidence of learning began to appear only when students were taught a procedure that gave them an external structure for the necessary mental operations—a procedure that involved underlining similar and contrasting terms in the paired sentences and checking tentative solutions against all the underlined terms. Even at that, the only clear cases of catching onto the strategy occurred among students in tenth grade.

Brown, Bransford, Ferrara, & Campione (1983) have discussed the copy-delete strategy of summarization and the knowledge-telling strategy of composition as examples of immature strategies that tend, because they work moderately well and demand less mental effort than more sophisticated strategies, to persist beyond the age when they might be outgrown. Because strategies for learning from text are mainly acquired and applied in school, it may be important for educational planning to examine the conditions of schooling that sustain or thwart various cognitive strategies. Elsewhere (Bereiter & Scardamalia, in press), 11 common school practices have been itemized that would tend to support the knowledge-telling strategy. Is it possible also that there are school conditions that support persistence of immature comprehension strategies?

A likely candidate is the pervasive school practice of question-and-answer as the instructional technique for testing and practicing learning from text (cf. Bellack, Kliebard, Hyman, & Smith, 1966). While a reading strategy that leads to a topic-plus-detail representation of text may not be an effective way for independently acquiring world knowledge, it may be an effective way of preparing for school tests and lessons. Such a way of organizing information is effective for retrieving details given either a topic or a related detail. It may also be an efficient way of preparing for thought questions, because it avoids commitment to high-level propositions that might prove inappropriate to the questions. From this standpoint, the immature strategy may be seen as a strategy of incomplete text processing, which depends on class discussions or other school learning activities to complete the processing of text details into macro-propositions that will be incorporated into world knowledge.

Data reported in this chapter show indications of substantial development toward more mature reading strategies occurring between sixth and tenth grades, but they also suggest that development is not universal. One-third of the tenth graders made no overt use of summarization in sentence arrangement. Only one student showed consistent efforts at gist construction in all the experimental tasks. How prevalent different kinds of reading strategies are, and to what extent immature strategies persist in older students and adults, are important questions that cannot be answered on the basis of present evidence.

ACKNOWLEDGMENTS

Research reported in this chapter was supported by grants from the Alfred P. Sloan Foundation and the Social Sciences and Humanities Research Council of Canada. The authors are indebted to Jud Burtis for consultation and assistance in data analysis, particularly for his help in developing protocol analysis categories. We also wish to thank Walter Kintsch and the editors of this volume for comments on an earlier draft and to acknowledge the valuable contributions of Clare Brett and Suzanne Hidi to conduct of the research.

REFERENCES

Bartlett, E. J. Learning to revise: Some component processes. In M. Nystrand (Ed.), *What writers know: The language, process, and structure of written discourse.* New York: Academic Press, 1982, 345–363.

Bellack, A., Kliebard, H. M., Hyman, R. T., & Smith, F. L., Jr. *The language of the classroom.* New York: Teachers College Press, 1966.

Bereiter, C., & Scardamalia, M. Cognitive coping strategies and the problem of "inert knowledge." In S. S. Chipman, J. W. Segal, & R. Glaser (Eds.), *Thinking and learning skills: Current research and open questions* (Vol. 2). Hillsdale, N.J.: Lawrence Erlbaum Associates, in press.

Bird, M. *Reading comprehension strategies: A direct teaching approach.* Unpublished doctoral dissertation, The Ontario Institute for Studies in Education, 1980.

Bransford, J. D. Social-cultural prerequisites for cognitive research. In J. Harvey (Ed.), *Cognition, social behavior, and the environment.* Hillsdale, N.J.: Lawrence Erlbaum Associates, 1981.

Brown, A. L., Bransford, J. D., Ferrara, R. A., & Campione, J. C. Learning, remembering, and understanding. In J. H. Flavell & E. M. Markman (Eds.), *Carmichael's manual of child psychology* (Vol. 3). New York: Wiley, 1983.

Brown, A. L., & Day, J. D. Macrorules for summarizing texts: The development of expertise. *Journal of Verbal Learning and Verbal Behavior,* 1983, *22* (1), 1–14.

Brown, A. L., Day, J. D., & Jones, R. S. The development of plans for summarizing texts. *Child Development,* in press.

Case, R. A. A developmentally based theory and technology of instruction. *Review of Educational Research,* 1978, *48*(3), 439–463.

Day, J. D. *Training summarization skills: A comparison of teaching methods.* Unpublished doctoral dissertation, University of Illinois, 1980.

Ericsson, K. A., & Simon, H. A. Verbal reports as data. *Psychological Review,* 1980, *87,* 215–251.

Flower, L. S., Hayes, J. R., & Swarts, H. Revising functional documents: The scenario principle. (Document Design Project Technical Report No. 10). Pittsburgh, Pa.: Carnegie–Mellon University, 1980.

Hannigan, J. L., Shelton, T. S., Franks, J. J., & Bransford, J. D. The role of episodic and semantic effects in the identification of sentences masked by white noise. *Memory and Cognition,* 1980, *8,* 278–284.

Just, M. A., & Carpenter, P. A. A theory of reading: From eye fixations to comprehension. *Psychological Review,* 1980, *87,* 329–354.

Kintsch, W., & van Dijk, T. A. Toward a model of text comprehension and production. *Psychological Review,* 1978, *85*(5), 363–394.

Markman, E. M. Comprehension monitoring. In W. P. Dixon (Ed.), *Children's oral communication skills.* New York: Acadmic Press, 1981, 61–84.

Markman, E. M. Realizing that you don't understand: Elementary school children's awareness of inconsistencies. *Child Development,* 1979, *50,* 643–655.

McCutchen, D., & Perfetti, C. A. Coherence and connectedness in the development of discourse production. *Text,* 1982, *2,* 113–139.

Newell, A., & Simon, H. A. *Human problem solving.* Englewood Cliffs, N.J.: Prentice-Hall, 1972.

Olson, G. M., Mack, R. L., & Duffy, S. A. Cognitive aspects of genre. *Poetics,* 1981, *10,* 283–315.

Paris, P., Scardamalia, M., & Bereiter, C. *Synthesis through analysis: Facilitating theme development in children's writing.* Paper presented at American Educational Research Association, New York, March 1982.

Perfetti, C. A., & Lesgold, A. M. Discourse comprehension and sources of individual differences. In M. Just & P. Carpenter (Eds.), *Cognitive processes in comprehension.* Hillsdale, N.J.: Lawrence Erlbaum Associates, 1977.

Rieger, C. Spontaneous computation in cogntive models. *Cognitive Science,* 1977, *1,* 315–354.

Scardamalia, M., & Bereiter, C. Fostering the development of self-regulation in children's knowledge processing. In S. S. Chipman, J. W. Segal, & R. Glaser (Eds.), *Thinking and learning skills: Current research and open questions* (Vol. 2). Hillsdale, N.J.: Lawrence Erlbaum Associates, in press. (a)

Scardamalia, M., & Bereiter, C. Written composition. In Wittrock, M. (Ed.), *Handbook of research on teaching,* 3rd ed, in press. (b)

Stein, N. L., & Trabasso, T. What's in a story: An approach to comprehension and instruction. In R. Glaser (Ed.), *Advances in instructional psychology.* Hillsdale, N.J.: Lawrence Erlbaum Associates, 1982.

Swaney, J. H., Janik, C. J., Bond, S. J., & Hayes, J. R. *Editing for comprehension: Improving the process through reading protocols* (Document Design Project Technical Report No. 14). Pittsburgh, Pa.: Carnegie-Mellon University, June 1981.

Trabasso, T., Stein, N. L., & Johnson, L. R. Children's knowledge of events: A causal analysis of story structure. In G. Bower (Ed.), *The psychology of learning and motivation: Advances in research and theory* (Vol. 15). New York: Academic Press, 1981.

van Dijk, T. A. *Macrostructures: An interdisciplinary study of global structures in discourse, interaction, and cognition.* Hillsdale, N.J.: Lawrence Erlbaum Associates, 1980.

Woods, W. A. Multiple theory formation in speech and reading. In R. J. Spiro, B. C. Bruce, & W. F. Brewer (Eds.), *Theoretical issues in reading comprehension.* Hillsdale, N.J.: Lawrence Erlbaum Associates, 1980.

14 Information-Processing Demand of Text Composition

Carl Bereiter
The Ontario Institute for Studies in Education

Marlene Scardamalia
York University

Investigators into the psychology of text composition frequently remark that the information-processing demands of the activity appear to be very high. DeBeaugrande (1981) refers to "the impression that can be obtained from large stores of empirical evidence, namely: that *discourse production routinely operates near the threshold of OVERLOADING* [p. 2]." We agree, certainly, that this is the impression supported by the bulk of empirical observations. On the other hand, in experimental research on written composition we have repeatedly come upon observations that give a somewhat different impression. The purpose in this chapter is to subject the hypothesis of high information-processing load to critical scrutiny in the light of evidence and theory. How heavy is the processing load in text composition, and what are the implications of processing load for the development of competence in composition?

A degree of definiteness about processing load is important for theoretical progress. It isn't enough simply to acknowledge that there is a processing load and that difficulties in performance may arise from it. At the very least we need some way of judging whether a theory is realistic or whether it runs afoul of human limitations.

More definite knowledge about processing load is also important for instructional planning (cf. Case, in press-a). As shown in a companion paper (Scardamalia & Bereiter, this volume), language processing—both comprehension and composition—can be handled by a variety of strategies differing in complexity. In designing instruction for language-processing skills accordingly, a major decision is the level of complexity of strategy to teach. Should one press for a complex strategy that will involve students in coordinating more variables than they do already, or should one aim for a simplified strategy that will reduce an already too complex task to one that is within their processing capacity? The fact that educators usually make such choices intuitively and without conscious attention to the issue of processing load does not make the choice any less crucial. A wrong choice could lead to promoting strategies that students are incapable of applying or that impede rather than aid skill development.

These theoretical and practical concerns form the motivation for this chapter. Empirically, the focus is on text composition. The most general points apply equally to text comprehension, however, and in the final section some specific speculations are offered about the processing load of text comprehension.

THE INADEQUACY OF INFORMAL EVIDENCE

There seem to be three main bases—all of an informal or suggestive nature—for belief in the high processing demands of discourse production. The first is the quality of speech output, which Chomsky (1967) described as consisting to a substantial degree of "false starts, disconnected phrases, and other deviations from idealized competence [p. 441]." These characteristics, together with the misfirings that show up as systematic speech errors (Fromkin, 1971), suggest a language production system that is barely coping. They do not, however, necessarily point to an inherent overload problem in text composition. In the first place, these phenomena suggest that overload is associated with the need to keep up with the pace of social speech. In writing or dictation, where pauses are unrestricted and normally take up ⅔ of the time (Gould, 1980), the processing-load difficulties associated with rate should not occur. Although according to Hotopf (1980), "slips of the pen" occur, these do not necessarily reflect processing load (Hotopf, 1980). Omitted function words, for instance, may indicate automatization of the transcribing process (Scardamalia, Bereiter, & Goelman, 1982). People will make errors in lengthy arithmetic calculations as well, yet the standard arithmetic algorithms are well-designed to minimize processing load. Clearly, if we are to infer processing load from pause and error data, we must come equipped with sufficiently sophisticated theory and techniques to sort out competing hypotheses.

A second basis is direct experience of processing load. People who approach writing seriously generally agree that it is very taxing mental work, and they will report experiencing difficulty in keeping cognitive control over all the content and constraints. We do not doubt the validity of such subjective reports. Even children give what appear to be accurate reports on variations in their mental effort (Osherson, 1975). We must, however, distinguish between isolated moments of peak processing demand and a continuously high processing load. While driving an automobile one occasionally experiences moments of high processing demand—for instance, driving on an expressway and simultaneously trying to recall the directions given by a friend, to comprehend a rapidly passing series of road signs, and to cross from the inner lane to the outer lane through heavy traffic. Yet automobile driving is the standard case of a low-processing-load complex activity, one that typically leaves mental resources free for other activities. What writers experience as the high processing load of text composition may be only occasional, though memorable, instances when a particularly complex problem had to be solved. On the other hand, occasional overloads in composition could be critical, if they mean the failure of efforts to achieve overall syntheses or optimum solutions to problems and a consequent down-sliding to more simplistic strategies. To sort this issue out, we need to examine the composition process in ways that will permit us to evaluate the processing load of critical moves.

The third basis is simply the list of things that must be taken into account in composition, ranging across the whole spectrum from fine points of style to deep matters of truth and authenticity in content. Contemporary views about the architecture of the text-production system almost universally recognize the inter-dependence of decisions made across this spectrum. This interdependence implies that in executing a particular subprocess the products of other subprocesses must be mentally available, which in turn implies a big task for working memory. This argument is a particularly compelling one because it seems to follow directly from well-accepted assumptions about the composition process. The trouble with the argument is that if carried far enough it can easily lead to the conclusion that text composition is impossible (cf. Elbow, 1973)—that the processing load is not only high but far too high for a cognitive system that tends to break down when asked to multiply three-digit numbers mentally. (This task is comparable, because products of previous operations must be stored mentally while other operations are being executed.) But language processing is generally like that; it seems to demand more intellectual resources than it is plausible to believe are available, especially in the very young. If Chomsky's innateness and modularity hypotheses, which are partly motivated by these considerations, are correct (Chomsky, 1980), then it may simply be that we are a great deal smarter in language than we are in other things and that, consequently, ordinary param-eters of processing load do not apply. Before we can accept the *laundry list* argument for high processing load in composition, therefore, we need to deter-mine whether language performance behaves the way other kinds of performance do with regard to the quantitative aspect of processing demand.

The preceding reflections serve mainly as cautions against a facile treatment of the processing-load problem. No arguments were actually brought against the hypothesis that composition entails a severe information-processing load. Let us turn, therefore, to experiences that have led us to raise questions about the hypothesis.

When we first began experimental research on writing in 1976, one of the few things we were confident about was the high processing load of composition. We were so confident of this assumption, in fact, that it formed the basis of what was intended to be one of our major research approaches. It was reasoned that if writers are working at or near their information-processing capacity limits, then it should be relatively easy to degrade their performance or possibly break it down entirely by putting additional burdens on working memory. Therefore, it seemed, a useful experimental methodology could be built around testing to see what kinds of interventions disrupt writing performance and in what ways they disrupt it—a sort of Luria without Lesions approach to mapping the cognitive system. The methodology was also expected to be illuminating with respect to the developmental psychology of writing. Children fairly new to literacy might be expected to have fragile systems of production that would be vulnerable to interventions to which more mature writers would have means of accommodating.

The first ventures centered around the use of *blind* writing, a method suggested by Britton, Burgess, Martin, McLeod, and Rosen (1975). The subject writes with an inkless pen—carbon paper or some other device being used to obtain a record of the composition[1] This intervention seemed promising because it left the composing process largely unmolested but added an additional burden on short-term memory because of the need to carry information in memory that would normally be available from the visible text. After eight pilot studies, the procedure was abandoned. With subjects ranging in age from 10 years to adult and with a variety of easy to difficult writing tasks, significant disruption of writing performance was never produced.[2] There were a few interesting hints of style variables that might depend on visual monitoring, but they are not germane to the processing-load issue, and furthermore they were observed only in the most skilled writers. Children, on the other hand, seemed to be unbothered by blind writing and sometimes even found it facilitating. It is possible, in fact, that blind writing had the opposite effect for children to that intended: By giving them less to worry about at the graphical level it may actually have reduced processing load.

But children's writing performance seemed to be invulnerable to other sorts of interference as well. Doing mental arithmetic between sentences had no measurable effect. In one experiment (Scardamalia & Bracewell, 1979) children were required after each sentence to compose a pair of alternative next sentences and then to choose one. This forced divergent production led to compositions that may have been somewhat below par in coherence, but doubling the sentence production burden did not produce anything resembling a breakdown in performance[3]

---

[1]Much of this research was done by R. J. Bracewell.

[2]J. Gould was also doing research on blind writing at about the same time using adults composing business letters. He reported the same finding of no measurable effect (Gould, 1978). Both Gould's studies and ours involved short compositions. Naturally, if composition goes on long enough, a point will be reached where inability to review the previous text will cause problems, but these would be problems of long-term storage and retrieval and relevant to a different set of issues from those being considered here.

[3]The *whole* burden of composing was not doubled, of course. Doubling would be achieved by having people compose distinct essays in parallel, a task we have never tried but that might be worth

In a dozen or more other studies, children have shown themselves invulnerable to or even to thrive on different kinds of interruptions and additional tasks (Bereiter & Scardamalia, 1982). In one instance, however, an unequivocal decrement in performance was observed. That instance is instructive as to the amount of additional processing burden that must be imposed on children before they begin to show evidence of overload.

What appears to have been an information-processing overload occurred when 14-year-old students for the first time composed opinion essays on a computer, using an interactive program that led them after each sentence through a branching sequence of questions designed to induce means–end planning of the next sentence (Woodruff, Bereiter, & Scardamalia, 1981–82). The decrement did not occur if students had one prior experience of composing on the computer without the questioning program. Thus a significant degrading of performance apparently required the combination of: (1) a novel production mode—composing on a computer[4] and (2) a highly intrusive intervention that presented students with taxing questions and suggestions at each sentence juncture. Neither factor alone produced a measurable decrement.

It appears, then, that writers can experience a disruption of performance because of information-processing overload, given a sufficient concentration of novel demands to contend with. But it also appears that during normal composition, writers—including young and not particularly proficient ones—are not operating near the threshold of overload.

The reasons cited for doubting the high processing load of writing are, of course, as informal and impressionistic as the reasons for believing in it. On the basis of informal evidence, then, it is possible to believe almost anything one wishes about the processing load of writing. Before drawing on more formal evidence we must state more definitely what is meant by information-processing load.

INFORMATION-PROCESSING DEMAND AND COMPLEXITY

Information-processing demand and information-processing capacity are manifestly quantitative concepts, and unless they can be quantified at some level, they are of little value. Psychologists have for the most part confined themselves to quantifying these concepts at the ordinal level—for example, task A has a greater processing demand than task B. Although even this level of quantifica-

---

exploring. But the burden in certain phases of the composing process should have been greatly increased, and this should have led to breakdown if the processing load during those phases was already near capacity.

[4]The students had used computers before and were familiar with screen editing functions, but their experience had been mainly with games and with computer-assisted mathematics instruction so that they had little if any experience with the computer as a mode of producing written language.

tion is a challenge when it comes to text composition, it will help clarify concepts if we direct our attention first to tasks in which a high level of quantification has been achieved.

In the ensuing discussion we equate information-processing demand with load on working memory. Information-processing demand, accordingly, depends on the amount of information—task constraints, data, etc.,—that must be held in immediate memory while carrying out a mental operation[5] This processing load will, of course, vary from moment to moment in the course of executing a task. When we speak of the processing demand of a *task,* we refer to the working memory load imposed by the most demanding step in task execution.

For a variety of mental tasks it has been found profitable to quantify information-processing demand up to the level of an absolute scale—that is, to quantify it in terms of countable units of information (Bereiter & Scardamalia, 1979; Case, 1974; Pascual-Leone, 1970; Pascual-Leone & Smith, 1969; Scardamalia, 1973, 1975, 1977). Tasks that have lent themselves best to this kind of quantification have been ones that involve a set of more or less equivalent elements that can be varied in number without altering the structure of the task. The most familiar task of this kind is backward digit span, where processing load may be increased by increasing the number of digits that must be repeated in reverse order. Other tasks having similar properties are: (1) generating all possible combinations of stimulus features, where load is increased by increasing the number of stimulus dimensions (Scardamalia, 1977); and (2) Raven's Progressive Matrices, where for a given matrix type the processing demand increases with the number of dimensions that must be taken into account (Bereiter & Scardamalia, 1979).

On tasks of this kind, people tend to have an absolute level of performance that is constant across tasks. Thus, for instance, the person who can reverse four digits but not five tends also to be able to produce combinations of four stimulus dimensions but not five (Scardamalia, 1977), whereas the person who can reverse five digits can also produce combinations of five dimensions and so on. The appearance of such constancy across tasks, noted first by Miller (1956), supports the notion that a person can hold a fixed number of *chunks* of information available for immediate use and that, correspondingly, the information-processing demand of a task can be specified by the number of such chunks that must be kept simultaneously available in order to execute the task (Bachelder & Denny, 1977a, 1977b; Case, 1974; Pascual-Leone & Goodman, 1979).

Most mental tasks of ordinary life do not lend themselves to straight-forward manipulation of information-processing demand. Usually, the elements that must be handled in working memory are not equivalent, and adding or removing one

---

[5]There are other aspects of information-processing load, most notably time pressure. We will not consider time pressure here, however, because it is not normally a factor in text comprehension or production. Furthermore, where time is a factor people probably respond to it by changing strategy rather than by carrying out the same process under greater load (Just & Carpenter, this volume).

changes the nature of the task. Furthermore, it is often not obvious what will constitute a chunk. In writing, for example, taking account of audience when one has not previously done so is not simply a matter of adding an element to the composition task. A substantial overhaul of strategy may be required, such that writing becomes a differently structured process altogether (Bereiter & Scardamalia, in press). Furthermore, the *audience* may constitute not just one chunk of information in the mind of the writer but rather a set of procedures—a subtask, as it were—having its own possibly high or possibly low information-processing demand. Whether *taking account of the audience* is a task element that accounts for one unit of information-processing demand, or no units, or several units is an issue for analysis and research, not something that can be assumed by rule.

Difficulties of the sort just noted have made some psychologists skeptical about the value of quantitive theories of information-processing capacity and demand (Flavell, 1978; Shatz, 1978). In science, however, one never expects to be able to measure a variable in every situation where it is theoretically invoked. Other kinds of evidence are normally relied on to provide assurance that principles established in situations where measurement is possible apply in other situations where measurement is not possible. (Consider, for instance, the generalizations made from genes that happen for largely fortuitious reasons to be identifiable to the much larger number of genes that are not yet identifiable.)

The fact is that quite a bit of progress has been made, largely by Case and his co-workers, in analyzing and verifying the processing demand of tasks composed of nonequivalent elements—tasks, in other words, where adding a new element changes the structure of the task (Case, in press-b; Case & Khanna, in press; Gold, 1978; Liu, 1981). It appears that adding a new loop to a processing strategy does typically amount to adding one unit to information-processing demand, just as adding another stimulus feature does to a combinatorial- or matrix-reasoning task.

As for the problem of determining what constitutes a *chunk,* this appears to be a fatal difficulty only for those who expect that there should be an objective way of doing it. For the special cases mentioned earlier—backward digit span, for instance—it happens that the chunks normally correspond to objective elements or dimensions. But this should not deter us from recognizing that in these cases as in all others, the chunk is a *subjective* unit—it is what the subject treats as a unit, not what the experimenter decides to treat as a unit. Identifying such units, given that they may be neither observable nor reportable, is a difficult task but not an unfamiliar task. Indeed, identifying subjective elements of cognition— representations, rules, etc.—may be properly regarded as a constitutive task of modern cognitive psychology, so that if one is not wrestling with problems of identifying subjective elements one is probably not doing cognitive psychology.

A current best guess at the information-processing capacity of normal adults is five chunks (Case, Kurland, & Goldberg, in press; Simon, 1974). This may be thought of as the number of chunks a person can hold in working memory while executing some attention-demanding operation. Higher estimates of capacity, such as that of Pascual-Leone (1970), include capacity required by the operations themselves. We will stick with the lower estimate here, because in the ensuing discussion of processing load in language, we shall consider only items, such as task constraints, that must be held in memory and operated on rather than taking account also of the kinds of operations that must be performed on them.

An important additional consideration has to do with the lower performance of children on processing capacity tasks. Although there is considerable uncertainty about the cause of this lower performance, it has been observed on a large range of working memory tasks. On tasks where the adult capacity is four or five units, that of 7-year-olds is two units, and of 9-year-olds, three units. (Reviews in Case, 1974, 1978, in press-b). Indeed, the empirical basis for across-task generality of processing capacity is a good deal more solid for children than it is for adults. That is, there is more evidence that a seven-year-old will be able to handle two chunks of information and no more than two across a variety of tasks than there is evidence that adolescents and adults will handle five.

If, therefore, we are to infer from well-analyzed tasks to language-processing tasks, it would appear that any language task that required the speaker to hold more than five chunks of information in working memory would create an overload and that language tasks that an adult might handle may nevertheless be substantially beyond the capacity of school children. These statements, of course, tell us nothing until we are able to describe language tasks in terms of information-processing load. How complex is a language task that requires holding five chunks of information in working memory? Is it something on the order of composing a sonnet or is it something on the order of carrying on small talk? In order to answer such questions, we must look for evidence, equivocal as it might be, that bears more directly on the subjective units and task demands of language processing.

Information-Processing Load in Language Tasks

The preceding section has already suggested some of the obstacles to determining the information-processing demand of language tasks. Tasks that lend themselves to such determination are ones in which the strategy for task execution can be clearly specified or experimentally controlled and in which the subjective elements to be processed correspond to denumerable objective features of the task. These ideal conditions are perhaps never met by real tasks, but language tasks do not come close.

The difficulty of specifying executive strategies is exacerbated by the ill-structured nature of language tasks. Thus, on a typical composition task, each writer is pursuing a significantly different goal. The processing load for one writer may be greater than it is for another simply because the first writer has undertaken a more demanding task. The difficulty of specifying subjective units or chunks is complicated by the multilevel nature of text processing. As the Hayes and Flower (1980) protocols show, writers continually switch between levels of planning and language generation, and it seems obvious that each switch involves switching to chunks of a different grain. Similarly in text comprehension, readers must switch attention between micro- and macro-propositions (Kintsch & van Dijk, 1978) as well as the surface language units out of which micro-propositions are extracted. Finally, in natural language processing, what constitutes a chunk is likely to vary enormously depending on the person's knowledge. Whether a phrase like *barometric pressure*, for instance, will be stored as one chunk or two will depend, among other things, on whether the reader understands barometric pressure as a unitary concept or understands it as some kind of pressure (one chunk) associated with a barometer (another chunk).

These kinds of difficulties beset any effort to achieve a detailed understanding of language processes. They are not unique to the investigation of information-processing load. In order to get some leverage on these difficulties, we shall examine a variety of studies in which language tasks have been engineered or controlled so as to reduce some of the uncertainties about strategies and chunking.

There has been quite a bit of research devoted to finding the basic unit of language planning (Reviews in Fodor, Bever, & Garrett, 1974; McNeill, 1979). One safe conclusion from such research is that people do process language in packets as would be expected from general expectations of chunking as a principle in information processing. As Smith (1979) has argued, however, attempts to discover subjective units that correspond precisely to units defined in grammatical theories have failed and are probably destined to keep failing. This is because the considerations that determine what grammarians will treat as a unit have no reference to the performance limitations that constrain what real speakers and listeners will be able to process as single units.

Introspection suggests that anything from a single letter or phoneme up to the topic of a whole composition may at times engage the attention of a language user and thus function as a subjective unit. However, there is evidence that a few basic kinds of units may constitute the main ones that most people use for most of their language processing.

One of these is a phrasal unit influenced by both syntactical and length constraints. The unit tends to run about six words in length but has some syntactic integrity, being either a whole clause or the beginning or end of one. Such a unit has been identified by actual pauses in speech (Chafe, 1981), by having people mark spots in written text where they would expect to pause (Johnson, 1965), by a probe-latency technique (Case & Kurland, 1980), by click location studies (Fodor, Bever, & Garrett, 1974), and by writers' reports of language already mentally formed in advance of transcribing it (Bereiter, Fine, & Gartshore, 1979). Case and Kurland (1980) tested short-term recall of sentences consisting of varying numbers of these phrasal units. Subjects tended to be able to recall the same number of phrasal units as they could recall of isolated words. This suggests, accordingly, that the unit in question may commonly constitute a chunk in determining the working memory load of some aspects of language processing.

In our research on text production and recall, we see a unit of larger size, which we call a *gist unit*. Frequently it corresponds to a sentence but sometimes more and sometimes less. What is more important, however, is that it is a unit of content and not a unit of language; accordingly, the same gist unit might appear in text in any of a variety of linguistic embodiments, differing in form and magnitude. Evidence for these units appears most clearly when subjects talk about problems of text arrangement or when they are recalling their own texts. In a recent experiment, not yet reported, students were questioned a month after all of them had written essays on the same topic. Among other things they were asked to identify sentences as their own or not and to state whether or not some additional sentence had occurred between two presented sentences from their old texts. Finally they had to arrange in order sentences from their own text and sentences from another child's. Their discourse on these tasks consisted mainly of sentences like these:

I might have said *x*, but I would never say *y*.

I think I remember I said *x*, then I said *y*.

Something goes between *x* and *y*, but I can't remember what it is.

In all these sentences, *x* and *y* were briefly labeled items of content such as "we have a right to" or "kids would choose the wrong things." These had no fixed linguistic rendering but might be referred to differently at different times. Finally, after the subjects had done 20 or 30 minutes of work reexamining and making judgments about their original texts, they were asked to recall the texts verbatim. What generally came back was recall of gist units with virtually no verbatim recall. This suggests that for the kinds of text processing these students were carrying out units of meaning were processed, but there was virtually no processing of phrasal units of the kind discussed previously.

Several studies using gist units indicate that these units also function as chunks in the processing load sense. This occurs when the task involves manipulating meanings rather than surface language. McDonald (1980), testing children of ages 6 and 8, used tasks in which the processing load inherent in the inferences drawn from statements. Children heard and repeated back series of sentences like the following:

The desk is in front of the window.

The paper is under the doll.

The doll is little.

The doll is on top of the desk.

Treating each of these statements as a chunk, McDonald classified possible inferences according to the number of chunks that had to be integrated to generate them. In the example, a two-chunk inference is *The doll is in front of the window*. A three-chunk inference is *The paper is in front of the window*. McDonald found that the level of inference children could correctly evaluate corresponded to their estimated working memory capacity.

Two supplementary findings of McDonald's study are of most direct application to language processing. One is that if the filler item, *The doll is little*, was replaced by a topically irrelevant filler item like *The book is beside the chair*, the apparent processing demand of the inferential tasks was increased by one unit. It would appear that with the first kind of filler item, which gives descriptive information about some previously mentioned topic, the new information is immediately chunked with the topic and so does not survive as a separate chunk. An unconnected item of information, on the other hand, is retained in working memory, waiting for other information to be attached to and thus usurps memory resources needed for the making of inferences.

This result is not surprising and was in fact predicted. The difficulty of the irrelevant filler items is not unlike that of multiple clause embeddings, which are widely recognized as placing a high processing demand on the comprehender. But the parametric implications are interesting. Suppose each embedding or other bit of dangling information adds one unit to processing load during the time that the information remains unattached. Given a processing capacity of only about four units, an incidental variation in processing load of one or two chunks is a large variation. People can obviously handle a considerable amount of such additional processing load without a breakdown in comprehension. This suggests that either the processing load of language comprehension is normally well within processing capacity or that people's processing capacities are frequently exceeded but that what happens in overload is not a dramatic breakdown in comprehension but rather a loss of deeper-level inferences—in other words, a shift to a more simple-minded interpretation of what is said. McDonald's findings are only suggestive on this latter point, but the suggestion makes sense both for language comprehension and production.

The suggestion that deeper inferences are what gets lost under overload may seem to conflict with the well-accepted notion that high-level ideas are the most securely retained in text comprehension (cf. Meyer, Chapter 1 of this volume). The two notions are not in competition, however. The inference *the paper is in front of the window* is not high-level in a text-structure sense; it is a deeper inference than *the doll is in front of the window* because it requires the integration of more chunks of information. Deep inferences will often not be main ideas. On the contrary, they may be hidden assumptions, subtle inconsistencies, or remote implications not even known to the author.

McDonald's other germane finding was that when children were asked to compose inferences instead of evaluating them, the highest level inference they produced was one level lower than the highest level they could evaluate correctly. The implication is that composition adds one unit of processing load at some point where it interferes with inferencing. Possibly this finding is only applicable to the young ages studied. If inferences are drawn and then put into words, it is not obvious how processing load associated with expression could degrade inferences. But the practice of thinking before writing does not seem to be well established at the local level until about the age of 10 (Scardamalia, Bereiter & Goelman, 1982).

On the other hand, McDonald's finding of composition usurping processing capacity from conceptual operations is consistent with observations of Scardamalia (1982) on children older than 10. Analyzing brief opinion essays, Scardamalia estimated the number of chunks of content information that needed to be integrated in order to achieve the most complex point made in each essay. This number ranged from one to four, the expected range according to recent theorizing (Case, in press-b). However, the typical number was two, which suggests that for most of the writers not all of their processing capacity was available for operations on content.

Some striking findings on the relation between information-processing capacity and ability to handle content constraints are emerging from thesis research in progress by Jacqueline Tetroe. Tetroe had subjects compose stories that would culminate in designated sentences. The ending sentences were designed to vary in the number of constraints they imposed on the plot of the story. An example of a three-constraint ending is:

> That's how Melissa came to be at the laundromat with a million dollars in her laundry bag.

A five-constraint version of the same theme is:

> That's how Melissa came to be at the wrong laundromat with a million dollars in her laundry bag and a trail of angry people behind her.

(Tasks were counterbalanced so that subjects did not write twice on the same theme.) The information-processing capacity of subjects was independently estimated by memory span tests. Each subject wrote four stories, with the number of constraints ranging from one less than the subject's estimated capacity to two more than the subject's estimated capacity. Figure 14.1 shows the average percentage of constraints met by subjects of different capacity levels on tasks with different numbers of constraints. Graphs for the three capacity levels all show a decline in performance as the number of constraints exceeds measured capacity. The point at which the decline occurs is one constraint higher for each additional unit of capacity. When in Fig. 14.1(b), where the graphs are displaced horizontally to conform with hypothetical capacity, it is seen that the graphs for the three capacity levels are rendered virtually identical. This shows that the differences between groups are essentially entirely accounted for by the differences in estimated processing capacity. (Artifacts due to item idiosyncracies are effectively

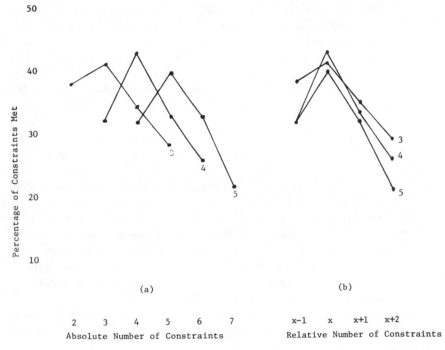

Fig. 14.1. Percentage of ending sentence constraints met by subjects at three information capacity levels as a function of (a) absolute number of plot constraints imposed by ending sentence and (b) number of constraints relative to capacity level (x).

ruled out as an explanation for these profile similarities: The items on which level three subjects scored lowest are the same items on which level-five subjects scored highest.)

As described so far, these results provide strong support for the conformity of text composition to previously established parameters of information-processing demand and capacity. They show the same extraordinary symmetry found by Scardamalia (1973, 1975, 1977) on highly engineered combinatorial and controls–of–variables tasks. But on the logic and span tasks that have previously been used in studying processing capacity, performance is generally near perfect on tasks that are below capacity. On Tetroe's composition tasks, top performance averaged only about 40%.

Postponing the question of what psychological factors could account for this attenuated performance, we may first ask how the performance displayed in Fig. 14.1 could be accounted for formally. It will not do to hypothesize additional factors that add a constant amount to processing load. This would be inconsistent with the fact that performance drops off precisely where it was predicted to. It seems more promising to look for some independent factor that adds a large random element to performance. A physical model of such a situation would be the following: Imagine the task of throwing a ball through a very large frame. The frame is so large that it is almost impossible to miss. However, as the frame is moved increasingly far away, a distance is reached that begins to exceed the distance a person can throw. At that point, balls will start failing to go through the frame because they fall short. This phenomenon corresponds to exceeding a person's information capacity. The drop-off in performance will occur at different distances for different people, reflecting individual differences in the distance people can throw a ball. This would produce differential drop-off curves like those shown in Fig. 14.1(a). But suppose that the frame is covered with a grating such that a ball thrown at the grating has a 40% probability of passing through. This added factor should yield performance graphs that have both the same shape and the same level as those in Fig. 14.1(b).

Speculation on what this *grating* factor might be must await further analysis by Tetroe of her data.[6] For purposes of the present discussion, however, the main point is that it does not appear on formal grounds that such a grating factor would call for an alteration of ideas about processing load in composition. Tetroe's findings support the view that even in a fairly high level of the composing process and plot construction, processing load can be counted in subjective units, the same as in other mental tasks, and that people's capacities to handle processing load in composition are equivalent to their capacities as demonstrated on other tasks.

We have so far considered two kinds of units that figure in text processing—a phrasal unit that appears to be a common subjective unit in processing surface language and a gist unit that serves as a chunk in processing text content both in comprehension and production. With respect to both kinds of units, the available evidence indicates that information-processing load and capacity for language tasks is in the same scale as that for other kinds of intellectual performance and reveals the same age norms for functional capacity.

Several cautions must be entertained, however, before we may rest easy with the conclusion that language performance may be treated the same as other kinds of intellectual performance. These cautions are as follows:

1. What about other subjective elements involved in language, besides the two that have been considered?
2. What about the multilevel nature of language processing, which may require that the several types of units be processed in parallel?
3. What about the modularity hypothesis (Chomsky, 1980), which raises the

---

[6]Although the "grating" metaphor suggests a random factor, it should be noted that this does not suggest a random strategy on the part of the subject.

possibility that the language-processing system may have a different set of parameters and possibly a different structure from the general cognitive system?

That there are other subjective units and that the ones discussed are only a kind of average (in the sense of qualitative descriptions of the *average* person), we have already acknowledged. DeBeaugrande's model (Chapter 5 of this volume) posits a unit larger than what we call the gist unit, a unit he calls the "idea." This is a complex unit in which both content and rhetorical strategy are condensed. Such a unit may well figure in the composing process of expert writers, but we have not found evidence of its use by average student writers. There may, on the other hand, be units that novice writers use but experts don't, the experts having developed some more efficient encoding of the relevant information. Any attempt at an exhaustive categorization of the elements involved in text processing is bound to describe only an idealized average. Consequently, the only way we have of testing quantitative theoretical notions in language processing is to see whether, in cases where a meaningful average value can be calculated, the value corresponds to theoretical expectations. This seems to have been accomplished in the research reviewed here. This leaves untouched vast areas of performance in which it is not meaningful to predict or compute average values, but there is not much to gain by agonizing over this fact.

The question of parallel processing is an important one that present knowledge doesn't allow us to deal with. May not the person who is manipulating four gist units in working memory be at the same time retaining four phrasal units and some other kinds of units as well that must either enter into the same linguistic decision or be held in readiness for the next step? This is certainly a possibility, although Kintsch and van Dijk (1978) offer a theory that allows multilevel text processing to go on with only a single working memory of fixed capacity. At present the best we can say is that whether or not a language task will exceed processing capacity appears to be a question that can be answered satisfactorily by considering separately the different levels of processing that might be involved. Whether this implies separate working memories, time-sharing, or something architecturally more esoteric can be passed over in the present discussion.

Much of the evidence we have brought forward showing that language performance is like other performance in respect to processing demand could be disputed by an upholder of the modularity hypothesis. The argument could be that if you give people memory tasks or problem-solving tasks that only incidentally involve linguistic material, then it is to be expected that they will handle these tasks not with the language faculty but by use of the general-purpose cognitive mechanisms normally employed for memory and problem-solving tasks. Thus it is not surprising that the same performance parameters emerge as with other mental tasks, but this tells us nothing about the architecture or capabilities of the language faculty.

Some observations do involve normal language behavior, however. Scardamalia's (1982) observations of processing loads in the one-to-four chunk range were based both on a laboratory-type sentence construction task and normal school writing assignments. Kintsch & van Dijk (1978) obtained results compatible with a working memory capacity of similar size using a normal summarization task. It may be objected, of course, that in both cases the investigators knew they were looking for something in this range and would no doubt have found some way to reinterpret results that suggested, say, a working memory capacity in the range of 10 to 40 chunks!

Available evidence on processing load, we are forced to conclude, has nothing to say one way or the other about the hypothesis of a separate language faculty—but the reverse is also true. In other words, there does not appear to be either any empirical or theoretical reason to suspect that the constraints working memory capacity puts on language performance are of any different kind or degree from the constraints they put on other kinds of intellectual performance.

The reader may well have been prepared to believe this without much argument. We hope, however, to have made it clear that the issue is far from settled.

Minimum Requirements of Text Processing

In text composition, the mental activity that goes into developing the content of the composition is typically regarded as part of the composition process. This being the case, there is obviously no limit to how high the information-processing load of composition can be—except, of course, for limits inherent in the capacity of the writer. The information-processing load of composition is at least as high as the load imposed by the most complex content problem the writer wrestles with in the course of composing.

If, therefore, we are to talk about the information-processing burden of writing in any sense that is not dependent on options of the writer, we must talk about some minimal processing load, sufficient for composition that just gets by— whatever that might mean. In this section we shall offer some provisional suggestions about what ''just getting by'' might mean in terms of composition and its information-processing demands.

The speculations that follow rest on the assumption that there are certain priorities in discourse processing and that when people are faced with overload dangers they will sacrifice performance on low-priority criteria in order to maintain performance at an acceptable level on high-priority criteria. (The human body is full of such back–up mechanisms to preserve vital functions when there is a threatened shortage of some essential resource, such as oxygen. We do not suggest, however, that there is anything innate about the back–up strategies we are talking about.)

In discourse production there seem to be two high and sometimes competing priorities: to produce sufficient language to fill the perceived social void and to maintain local coherence. The void-filling requirement includes such things as the need to forestall extended silences in conversation, the need to write a letter of sufficient length to substantiate one's regard for the receiver, and the need in a school composition to meet the teacher's expectation of effort as it is reflected in quantity. The local coherence requirement is the minimum requirement for upholding the presumption of competence. People whose utterances do not follow in any discernible way from their predecessors are judged to be distracted, drunk, senile, schizophrenic, or otherwise incapacitated.

We do not, of course, mean to imply that void-filling and local coherence are the central purposes of discourse production. It is simply that they are critical functions that, if they fail, result in the failure of most other functions as well. Consequently, the processing demand involved in meeting these top-priority requirements may be thought of as the basic processing demand of composition.

On the basis of our efforts to infer information-processing complexity from children's compositions (Bereiter & Scardamalia, 1978; Scardamalia, 1982), we hypothesize that the minimal processing demand of sustained, locally coherent text composition is, for most genres, two chunks. This demand is critical at the point where a gist unit has been expressed, and a next gist unit must be selected. At that point it seems necessary to have available in working memory at least one chunked representation of the intention for the whole text (which may amount to nothing more than memory for the topic) and another chunk representing the preceding utterance. If the first is absent, discourse will tend to wander away from the topic in an associative chain. If the second is missing, any of several things may happen:

1. A loss of local coherence, resulting in a series of content items each related to the topic but not to each other.
2. Perseveration, repeating past items or starting the discourse over from the beginning (common in inebriates).
3. Termination of the discourse (common in children who experience having exhausted their ideas on the topic).

An apparent exception to the two-chunk requirement is narrative composition. This is an inference based on reports that children as young as 5 or 6 can produce sustained and coherent narratives (Stein & Trabasso, 1982; Mennig-Peterson & McCabe, 1977). Because children of this age are found in other kinds of mental activities to have a working memory capacity to store only one chunk while carrying out another operation (Case, 1974), it should follow that it must somehow be possible to meet the minimal demands of narrative discourse with only this much processing capacity.

Exactly how it is possible to generate a well-formed narrative while holding only one chunk of information at a time in working memory is not clear. No doubt it depends on having a highly efficient discourse schema for narrative

(Stein & Trabasso, 1982). In the case of personal experience narratives, the structure of information in memory may ensure a schematic structuring of items recalled. It may then be necessary only to retain in short-term storage a trace of the previous item expressed in order to activate an appropriate next item. In fictional narrative the dynamics must be somewhat different but perhaps not fundamentally so. It may be that the memory schema for a story episode is so strong that as the child thinks of story ideas they are promptly encoded into long-term memory in a story framework. Accordingly, telling an impromptu invented narrative would be similar to recalling a narrative and would demand only enough working memory capacity to ensure orderly recall. In trying to explain the coherence of narrative in young children, we should also not ignore the power of the schema in the mind of the listener. People may be so efficient at story comprehension that they are able to form a coherent macro-structure out of much more disconnected material than they are able to comprehend in other genres.

Texts that meet the requirements of sustained local coherence may be thought of as the textual equivalent of small talk, which has similar requirements (Schank, 1977). Small talk, too, probably takes up one or two chunks of working memory capacity, depending on whether the speaker is relating an anecdote or dispensing facts and opinions. This would explain why small talk is often boring to generate as well as to listen to; it takes up only a portion of available mental capacity yet interferes with using the spare capacity for anything else. We have the impression that school writing assignments are often boring to students for the same reason. Far from straining the limits of information-processing capacity, perfunctory execution of school assignments may be too far below limits to sustain motivation.

As soon as the writer aspires to something beyond minimally adequate text, however, the processing demands of composition can mount rapidly. These additional processing demands may arise from the addition of rhetorical constraints (the composition must be interesting, convincing, original, etc.) or through deeper processing of content, as in critical analysis, synthesis of ideas, or solution of problems discovered in the content. For reasons that we have given previously, not much can be said quantitatively about the highly variable demands of these activities. What does seem safe to surmise, however, is that it is very easy for processing demand to exceed the overload level.

A parallel argument to the one developed here for text composition could be developed for text comprehension. There is no upper limit to processing demand in text comprehension because the demand will be at least as high as the processing load for understanding the most complex ideas presented in text. We may, however, think of a minimal processing load required for "just getting by." In the case of text comprehension, "just getting by" would be a subjective matter. It would mean avoiding the experience of "I don't get it" "This doesn't make any sense," or "This is all beyond me." It would appear that the minimum requirements for staving off these experiences of incomprehension are parallel to the requirements for sustaining minimal performance in text composition. They are local coherence—perceiving the present language unit as semantically linked to a predecessor—and global intentionality—having some sense of why the present idea is being expressed.

We would not be surprised to find that the processing load for a minimal level of comprehension is the same as it is for composition, two chunks. (We have not studied text comprehension enough to make any stronger statement than that.) The two chunks might, again, be similar to those required for composition: one chunk representing the perceived topic and purpose of the text, another representing the preceding gist unit. A lot of what we call *cursory* reading might go on at this minimal level of processing load, with a jump up to a higher load occurring when some item of particular interest is encountered. A processing load less than two could result in the familiar experience of reading along for a paragraph or more and then realizing that one was not paying attention and was comprehending nothing. This might result either from losing hold of intentionality while coninuing to track local coherence or from the reverse.

The text comprehension model of Kintsch and van Dijk (1978) could in this light be regarded as model of minimal two-chunk comprehension.[7] Similarly, the knowledge-telling strategy previously described by us (Bereiter & Scardamalia, in press) may be regarded as a model of minimal two-chunk composition. Models of minimal performance have an important part to play in the development of text processing theory, we believe. They allow us to see whether we can account for performance at all within recognized limitations of the cognitive system. If we cannot, then it is likely that our more glorified models, describing expert performance, are mere metaphors—aids to discourse about discourse but not theories in any serious sense.

Although our examination of processing demands in text composition leaves many loopholes and loose ends, we believe that it has arrived at some conclusions. We find that, in spite of formidable obstacles, empirical observations can be made on the information-processing load of language tasks. Language tasks, according to these observations, appear to conform to the same principles as other mental tasks with respect to the size and nature of information-processing capacity and demand. Whereas the processing demand of text processing can run very high, its minimum demand takes up half or less of adult information-processing capacity. It thus appears that under normal circumstances people should have a substantial amount of spare information-processing capacity to allocate to higher-level goals of text processing.

This conclusion has an important bearing on instruction. The prevailing belief

---

[7]Kintsch and van Dijk (1978), treating working memory capacity as a free parameter in their model, found that any capacity between one and four chunks would provide an adequate fit to adult data.

in the high processing load of composition has led to the assumption that novice writers will profit from being guided toward load-reducing strategies (cf. Flower & Hayes, 1980). Although such strategies are undoubtedly an asset to all writers it may be that where novices most need help is in learning profitable ways to put unused processing capacity to work. Research by Bird (1980) and by Brown (this volume) in teaching reading comprehension strategies points to a similar conclusion

ACKNOWLEDGMENT

Preparation of this chapter was aided by a research grant from the Alfred P. Sloan Foundation.

REFERENCES

Bachelder, B. L., & Denny, M. R. A theory of intelligence: I. Span and the complexity of stimulus control. *Intelligence,* 1977, , 127–150. (a)

Bachelder, B. L., & Denny, M. R. A theory of intelligence: II. The role of span in a variety of intellectual tasks. *Intelligence,* 1977, *1,* 237–256. (b)

Beaugrande, R. de.*Modelling the operations of the writing process.* Paper presented at American Educational Research Association, Los Angeles, April 1981.

Bereiter, C., Fine, J., & Gartshore, S. *An exploratory study of micro-planning in writing.* Paper presented at the annual meeting of the American Educational Research Association, San Francisco, 1979.

Bereiter, C., & Scardamalia, M. *Cognitive demands of writing as related to discourse type.* Paper presented at the annual meeting of the American Educational Research Association, Toronto, Ontario, 1978.

Bereiter, C., & Scardamalia, M. Pascual-Leone's *M* construct as a link between cognitive-developmental and psychometric concepts of intelligence. *Intelligence,* 1979, *3,* 41–63.

Bereiter, C., & Scardamalia, M. From conversation to composition: The role of instruction in a developmental process. In R. Glaser (Ed.), *Advances in instructional psychology* (Vol. 2). Hillsdale, N.J.: Lawrence Erlbaum Associates, 1982.

Bereiter, C., & Scardamalia, M. Cognitive coping strategies and the problem of "inert knowledge." In S. S. Chipman, J. W. Segal, & R. Glaser (Eds.), *Thinking and learning skills: Current research and open questions* (Vol. 2). Hillsdale, N.J.: Lawrence Erlbaum Associates, in press.

Bird, M. *Reading comprehension strategies: A direct teaching approach.* Unpublished doctoral dissertation, The Ontario Institute for Studies in Education, 1980.

Britton, J., Burgess, T., Martin, N., McLeod, A., & Rosen, H. *The development of writing abilities (11-18).* London: Macmillan Education Ltd., 1975.

Case, R. Structures and strictures: Some functional limitations on the course of cognitive growth. *Cognitive Psychology,* 1974, *6,* 544–573.

Case, R. Piaget and beyond: Toward a developmentally based theory and technology of instruction. In R. Glaser (Ed.), *Advances in instructional psychology* (Vol. 1). Hillsdale, N.J.: Lawrence Erlbaum Associates, 1978.

Case, R. A developmentally based approach to the problem of instructional design. In S. S. Chipman, J. W. Segal, & R. Glaser (Eds.), *Thinking and learning skills: current research and open questions* (Vol. 2). Hillsdale, N.J., Lawrence Erlbaum Associates, in press (a)

Case, R. *Intellectual development: A systematic reinterpretation.* New York: Academic Press, in press (b)

Case, R., & Khanna, F. The missing links: Stages in children's progression from sensorimotor to logical thought. In K. W. Fischer (Ed.), *New Directions for Child Development.* San Francisco: Josey-Bass, in press.

Case, R., & Kurland, D. M. A new measure for determining children's subjective organization of speech. *Journal of Experimental Child Psychology,* 1980, *30,* 206–222.

Case, R., Kurland, D. M., & Goldberg, J. Operational efficiency and the growth of short term memory span. *Journal of Experimental Child Psychology,* in press.

Chafe, W. L. *Linguistic differences produced by differences between speaking and writing.* Paper presented at Conference on the Nature and Consequences of Literacy, St. Marys, Ontario, October, 1981.

Chomsky, N. The formal nature of language. In E. H. Lenneberg (Ed.), *Biological foundations of language.* New York: Wiley, 1967.

Chomsky, N. *Rules and representations.* New York: Columbia University Press, 1980.

Elbow, P. *Writing without teachers.* London: Oxford University Press, 1973.

Flavell, J. H. Comments. In R. S. Siegler (Ed.), *Children's thinking: What develops?* Hillsdale, N.J.: Lawrence Erlbaum Associates, 1978.

Flower, L. S., & Hayes, J. R. The dynamics of composing: Making plans and juggling constraints. In L. W. Gregg & E. R. Steinberg (Eds.), *Cognitive processes in writing.* Hillsdale, N.J.: Lawrence Erlbaum Associates, 1980.

Fodor, J. A., Bever, T. G., & Garrett, M. F. *The psychology of language: An introduction to psycholinguistics and generative grammar.* New York: McGraw-Hill, 1974.

Fromkin, V. The non-anomalous nature of anomalous utterances. *Language,* 1971, *47,* 27–52.

Gold, A. P. *Cumulative learning versus cognitive development: A comparison of two different theoretical bases for planning remedial instruction in arithmetic.* Unpublished doctoral dissertation, University of California, Berkeley, 1978.

Gould, J. D. An experimental study of writing, dictating, and speaking. In J. Requin (Ed.), *Attention and performance VII.* Hillsdale, N.J.: Lawrence Erlbaum Associates, 1978.

Gould, J. D. Experiments on composing letters: Some facts, some myths, and some observations. In L. W. Gregg & E. R. Steinberg (Eds.), *Cognitive processes in writing.* Hillsdale, N.J.: Lawrence Erlbaum Associates, 1980.

Hayes, J. R., & Flower, L. Identifying the organization of writing processes. In L. W. Gregg & E. R. Steinberg (Eds.), *Cognitive processes in writing.* Hillsdale, N.J.: Lawrence Erlbaum Associates, 1980.

Hotopf, N. Slips of the pen. In U. Frith (Ed.), *Cognitive processes in spelling.* London: Academic Press, 1980.

Johnson, N. F. The psychological reality of phrase structure rules. *Journal of Verbal Learning and Verbal Behavior,* 1965, *4,* 469–475.

Kintsch, W., & van Dijk, T. A. Toward a model of text comprehension and production. *Psychological Review,* 1978, *85*(5), 363–394.

Liu, P. A. *An investigation of the relationship between qualitative and quantitative advances in the cognitive development of preschool children.* Unpublished doctoral dissertation, University of Toronto, 1981.

McDonald, J. D. *Memory capacity and inferential abilities in 5- and 7-year-old children.* Unpublished master's thesis, York University, 1980.

McNeill, D. *The conceptual basis of language.* Hillsdale, N.J.: Lawrence Erlbaum Associates, 1979.

Mennig-Peterson, C., & McCabe, A. *Structure of children's narratives*. Paper presented at the biennial meeting of the Society for Research in Child Development, New Orleans, March 1977.

Miller, G. A. The magical number seven, plus or minus two: Some limits on our capacity for processing information. *Psychological Review*, 1956, *63*, 81–97.

Osherson, D. N. *Logical abilities in children* (Vol. 3). N.J.: Lawrence Erlbaum Associates, 1975.

Pascual-Leone, J. A mathematical model for the transition rule in Piaget's developmental stages. *Acta Psychologica*, 1970, *63*, 301–345.

Pascual-Leone, J., & Goodman, D. Intelligence and experience: A neopiagetian approach. *Instructional Science*, 1979, *8*, 301–367.

Pascual-Leone, J., & Smith, J. The encoding and decoding of symbols by children: A new experimental paradigm and neo-piagetian model. *Journal of Experimental Child Psychology*, 1969, *8*, 328–355.

Scardamalia, M. *Mental processing aspects of two formal operational tasks: A developmental investigation of a quantitative neopiagetian model*. Unpublished doctoral dissertation, The Ontario Institute for Studies in Education, 1973.

Scardamalia, M. Two formal operational tasks: A quantitative neopiagetian and task analysis model for investigating sources of task difficulty. In G. I. Lubin, J. F. Magary, & M. K. Poulsen (Eds.), *Piagetian theory and the helping professions*. Los Angeles: University of Southern California Publications Dept., 1975.

Scardamalia, M. Information processing capacity and the problem of horizontal decalage: A demonstration using combinatorial reasoning tasks. *Child Development*, 1977, *48*, 28–37.

Scardamalia, M. How children cope with the cognitive demands of writing. In C. H. Frederiksen & J. F. Dominic (Eds.), *Writing: The nature, development and teaching of written communication*. Vol. 2, Hillsdale, N.J.: Lawrence Erlbaum Associates, 1982.

Scardamalia, M., Bereiter, C., & Goelman, H. The role of production factors in writing ability. In M. Nystrand (Ed.), *What writers know: The language, process, and structure of written discourse*. New York: Academic Press, 1982.

Scardamalia, M., & Bracewell, R. J. *Local planning in children's writing*. Paper presented at the annual meeting of the American Educational Research Association, San Francisco, 1979.

Schank, R. C. Rules and topics in conversation. *Cognitive Science*, 1977, *1*, 421–441.

Shatz, M. The relationship between cognitive processes and the development of communication skills. In B. Keasey (Ed.), *Nebraska Symposium on Motivation*. Lincoln, Neb.: University of Nebraska Press, 1978.

Simon, H. A. How big is a chunk? *Science*, 1974, *183*, 482–488.

Smith, N. V. Syntax for psychologists. In J. M. Morton and J. C. Marshall (Eds.), *Psycholinguistics Series* (Vol. 2). London: Paul Elek, 1979.

Stein, N. L., & Trabasso, T. What's in a story: An approach to comprehension and instruction. In R. Glaser (Ed.), *Advances in instructional psychology* Vol. 2. Hillsdale, N.J.: Lawrence Erlbaum Associates, 1982.

Woodruff, E., Bereiter, C., & Scardamalia, M. On the road to computer assisted compositions. *Journal of Educational Technology Systems*, *10*(2), 1981–82.

15

Comprehending and Learning: Implications for a Cognitive Theory of Instruction

Lauren B. Resnick
University of Pittsburgh

The task in this concluding section is to consider the implications of the present chapters for instruction. Let us begin by considering what is meant by the word "instruction." The chapters in this book press us toward a definition that is different from the one that has guided scientific thinking about education for many decades. Together they stress a theme that has become central in cognitive science: People *construct* rather than receive knowledge. Knowing something, whether a body of interrelated concepts or a performance skill, is a result of mental activity by an individual. This activity uses external information, and is thus responsive to what an individual may be told or shown. But the person does not simply "store" this information as received. Instead the person transforms it, links it to knowledge already held, and uses it to build a coherent interpretation of the world and its events. If knowledge is constructed rather than recorded as received, it does not make sense to think of instruction as directly conveying knowledge or skill. Rather, we must think of instruction as setting in motion learners' natural processes of knowledge construction and providing external information that is likely to be used productively.

If instruction is a matter of activating and nourishing processes of knowledge construction, then to arrive at a prescription for instruction it is important to know what these processes of knowledge construction are. This means that we cannot construct a scientific theory of instruction by passing directly from statements of knowledge or skill objectives to prescriptions for intervention. We are forced, instead, to seek a theory of instruction that has three major elements: (1) a theory of expertise that describes the kind of skilled performance or elaborated knowledge structure we hope to evoke in the learner; (2) a theory of acquisition that describes the processes of knowledge and skill construction that people use

431

in the course of acquiring a new competence; and (3) a theory of intervention that prescribes the actions to be taken by an instructor in order to activate the learner's acquisition processes and to provide appropriate external information.

Up to now, cognitive psychology has concerned itself almost exclusively with the first of these three components. For much of its history, cognitive psychologists have been engaged in what may be termed "cognitive task analysis." In this work, the fundamental concern is to describe the mental processes that are involved in performing various kinds of tasks during a given state of competence. Although younger and older people, or novices and experts in a domain, are occasionally contrasted, transitions between states of competence are largely ignored. As a result, we do not presently have a well-developed theory of acquisition, although there has been considerable progress made in describing the nature of cognitive processes used on a variety of complex tasks. In instructional terms, we have moved forward on the agenda of building a theory of expertise in various domains relevant to instruction, but we have not as yet begun to build the theory of acquisition that is needed for a cognitive theory of instruction.

The chapters in this volume reflect the just described state of cognitive science and instructional theory. Most of the chapters report cognitive analyses of tasks in the broad domain of language comprehension and production (e.g., understanding, composing, and answering questions about texts). In the first section of this chapter, I examine each contribution as a statement of a theory of expertise in language processing. From this examination, I attempt to draw an enriched description of goals and objectives of instruction in the domain of text processing. It is also possible to treat several chapters as contributing to an emerging theory of cognitive acquisition. That is what I do in the second section of this chapter. Finally, a few chapters directly explore the effects of instructional interventions in reading or writing. These provide a basis for examining the implications of emerging theories of expertise and acquisition for instructional prescriptions. I discuss these in the third section of the chapter.

THE NATURE OF EXPERTISE IN TEXT PROCESSING

Common Processes in Diverse Tasks

Taken together, the chapters in this volume highlight the fact that skilled language comprehenders seem to call upon very similar processes regardless of the particular task in which they are engaged. Whereas most of the chapters focus on written text comprehension, some are on question answering or on composing texts. In addition, several different kinds of text processing tasks are studied, and a variety of different kinds of texts are the object of attention. Despite this variety, a striking impression emerges that similar processes are involved.

Lehnert, Robertson, and Black are explicit about this. Their account of question answering makes it clear that in order to even interpret a question, people attempt to relate it to prior knowledge of the context to which the question refers. This prior knowledge may have been gleaned from immediately preceding reading or conversation, or it may exist in the form of general schemata that are used to interpret specific events. In either case, the kinds of knowledge called upon and the kinds of processes involved in using it are much like those described in the formal text comprehension models of Just and Carpenter as well as in the story comprehension theories outlined by Voss and by Stein and Policastro, and in the structure seeking theories of expert text processing developed by Meyer and by Scardamalia and Bereiter. What is more, Brown, Palincsar, and Armbruster suggest that the skilled comprehender of a text is one who is able to pose appropriate questions about it. And it is processes of accessing and coordinating knowledge so as to produce text that is coherent at several levels of analysis that create the information processing demand in text composition that is the subject of Bereiter and Scardamalia's chapter. Given all of these commonalities, it seems more fruitful to try to understand the various kinds of language comprehension and production observed as variations built out of a set of common processes and knowledge than as separate and independent capabilities.

The Role of Prior Knowledge

A central theme in many of the analyses presented is the pervasive and powerful role of prior knowledge in text comprehension and text production. For reading, for answering questions, and for composing texts, schemata are activated and then "instantiated" in accordance with the specific situation represented by the text. In each case, the relevant schemata are presumed to be already available for activation. Lack of appropriate schemata, or failure for some reason to access relevant schemata, is a source of difficulty and even a direct cause of failure to understand or to produce sensible text.

Three broad classes of prior knowledge are explored in the papers in this volume. The first is domain-specific knowledge—that is, knowledge about the topic discussed in the text. Voss and Schnotz each develop examples of the ways in which differences in the amount of domain-specific prior knowledge affect the ways in which the text is processed and understood. Lehnert, Robertson, and Black show how such knowledge may be used in answering questions. In the Just and Carpenter model, a process of schema instantiation involving domain specific knowledge is necessary for building a coherent representation of a text's topic.

The second class of knowledge is general world knowledge—that is, knowledge of social relationships and causal structures that are common to many specific situations and domains. The role of knowledge about physical and psychological causality in comprehension is a central theme of Trabasso, Secco, and van den Broek's chapter, and the role of knowledge about goals, plans, actions, and outcomes as well as personal and social conflict concerns Stein and Policastro and Voss.

The third class is knowledge of rhetorical structures that constrain the form of written communication. Structural knowledge of this kind is a central theme in Stein and Policastro's chapter on the story concept. Scardamalia and Bereiter discuss how rhetorical structure knowledge may help children develop a more sophisticated strategy for interacting with texts. Meyer suggests that knowledge of conventions for organizing and signalling the organization of texts may be part of what distinguishes expert from less-skilled adult readers.

A question raised by several authors is the extent and nature of the interaction between general world knowledge and knowledge of rhetorical structures, especially stories. Trabasso, Secco, and van den Broek find that events are important and are recalled for two reasons: (1) they lie on a causal chain and therefore have several causal connections, and (2) they serve functions as categorized content. Both of these aspects were contained in the original formulations of story grammars. Stein and Policastro's discussion of the many competing definitions of stories, and their distinction between minimally acceptable stories and "non-stories," suggest that certain kinds of world knowledge are systematically embedded in the story structure, which serves as a "guide" to readers and listeners to search a text for particular kinds of social relationships.

Some suggestions for instructional objectives in reading and writing skills emerge from these analyses of the role of prior knowledge in text understanding. First, improvement in reading skill probably depends to a large degree on enlargement of domain-specific and general world knowledge. We need to think of reading instruction as including, or as being closely linked to, instruction in specific domains of knowledge rather than as a separate and largely content-free "skill." If a learner is helped to build an appropriate body of knowledge in some domain, he or she is also helped to become a more skilled reader. The objectives of reading instruction are thus broadened to include specific knowledge about the domains in which people are likely to read. Even more instructional power is likely to accrue from efforts to teach general world knowledge, such as causal inferences and social-personal relationships and expectations. Such knowledge may provide a useful interpretive structure in a wide range of situations.

A second suggestion is that rhetorical structural knowledge itself become an objective of instruction. This suggestion is explicit in several chapters. Stein and Policastro, for example, suggest that both children and teachers would benefit from more explicit knowledge of good story content and structures. Scardamalia and Bereiter suggest that their greater mastery of story schemata, as opposed to other rhetorical structures, makes it easier for children to write stories than other types of texts. Bereiter and Scardamalia's analysis implies that well-established knowledge of various rhetorical conventions and formats helps in reducing the processing demands of composing and inducing more sophisticated texts. Meyer's contrast of adults with different levels of reading skill suggests that one way of helping people become expert would be to help them acquire knowledge about how various conventional rhetorical markers signal the structure of textual arguments.

In suggesting that certain common rhetorical forms become the direct objects of instruction, it is important to note that we are reviving an older instructional agenda rather than proposing a completely new one. Rhetoric was, after all, a standard part of the school curriculum not very long ago, and remains a part— although not occupying a privileged place—in some countries today. This means that many useful instructional models probably already exist, and that we will do well, as we adopt this new set of objectives, not to overlook the analytic and instructional efforts of the past.

The Role of Strategies

We turn now to the processes involved in using and coordinating prior knowledge with information in the text. Two classes of processes have been discussed in certain chapters. The first class involves processes in skilled reading that occur automatically and without conscious awareness. These are the processes of inference and linkage construction that are at the heart of building a coherent representation of a text. Examples of such constructions are found in Just and Carpenter, Stein and Policastro, and Trabasso, Secco, and van den Broek. Just and Carpenter's model involves a concatenation of local interpretation processes that are largely automatic and may not be open to direct inspection in humans. The latter assumption is not necessarily shared by the models of Trabasso et al. and by Stein and Policastro. These investigators imply that both deliberate and unconscious inferencing is necessary for production and comprehension of a text.

The second class of processes includes those that are more open to manipulation by the reader. Many authors in this volume have called these processes "strategies" for interacting with text. Strategies have a heuristic and flexible character. The adoption of a strategy is influenced both by variations in the reader's purpose and by the features of a text. Strategies also allow the possibility of conscious control and are potential objectives for instruction—a set of procedures that can be taught to learners as a way of improving general reading performance.

Strategies for Subordination and Hierarchization.   Several chapters in this volume suggest that one of the hallmarks of the expert reader is the ability to recognize or construct hierarchies of knowledge in which successive "layers" of subordination create a logically coherent elaboration of a topic. Bereiter and Scardamalia, Ballstaedt and Mandl, Meyer, Schnotz, and Voss develop such arguments in contrasting groups of expert (knowledgeable) and non-expert (less knowledgeable) readers. For example, Meyer's expert subjects were better able to discriminate levels of importance of the ideas presented in the text, were more likely to focus their attention on high-importance material while reading, and showed evidence of looking for logical connective relationships rather than simply amassing details in memory. They were also more able than the non-experts to make good use of rhetorical devices that signaled which material in the text was most central to the author's argument. Similar findings are reported by Voss and Schnotz.

Scardamalia and Bereiter describe similar contrasts between younger and older readers. Younger readers tend to use a strategy in which details are emphasized in such a way that the hierarchical structure of the text is not apparent to them. Little discrimination of the relative importance among the details occurs and analysis of how specific pieces of information may support (or contradict) one another is not given by the children. A similar lack of attention to subordination structures is also noted for tasks such as scrambled sentences and writing compositions.

Generally, then, more highly skilled people tend to recognize or construct hierarchical knowledge structures as they read. They are also more likely to produce hierarchical knowledge structures when they write. This suggests another set of instructional objectives: The promotion of knowledge about the nature of various subordination relationships and of skill in using these relationships.

Self-monitoring and Questioning Strategies.   Several authors propose a facilitating role for strategies by which readers monitor understanding and deliberately use their knowledge to help them understand and remember text. Two chapters report studies that assess the validity of this general proposal. Ballstaedt and Mandl's request for elaborations from readers, for example, is based on a hypothesis that when readers add their own knowledge to the information in the text, they are likely to better remember the material in the text. The hypothesis was confirmed in their study only for short-term recall; in a delayed test, the differences between subjects who elaborated aloud and those who did not had disappeared. Ballstaedt and Mandl attribute their lack of long-term effects for elaboration to subjects' in the non-elaboration group engaging in covert elaboration. But why, then, did the elaboration-aloud subjects do better in the short run?

Another possibility is that the elaboration strategy is good for studying or deliberately learning about a topic. A person who is trying to gain information from a text attempts to go beyond the text itself to a coordinated body of knowledge about the domain in question. Elaborations, especially those that establish relations between what the student already knew and what the text says, are likely to contribute to learning. Two distinct processes may be confounded if studying is equated with understanding a text. When one studies a text for purposes of learning about a domain, one is not interested in establishing or retaining a memory of the text itself or the author's particular intention. One is interested in using the information in the text as part of a more general effort to construct a mental representation of a knowledge domain. For this purpose, it makes sense to add the text information to what one already knows and then to forget about the text *per se*. Ballstaedt and Mandl's criterion measure—recall of the text itself—may not have discriminated actual differences in learning the domain.

Brown, Palincsar, and Armbruster suggest that strategies for assessing one's state of understanding and figuring out what the author meant to say are likely to improve comprehension. Posing and attempting to answer questions is a way of meeting the goals of monitoring and finding out the author's intent. They report successful studies of direct training in question-generating strategies. Brown et al. were interested in a general skill of understanding texts rather than in comprehension of a particular text. Their criteria for success were that the strategies learned must be durable, must be applied to texts other than those on which they were trained, and that application of the strategies must improve comprehension. These criteria raise questions about the relationship between the kind of deliberate strategies taught and automated reading skill.

It is not at all clear that skilled readers regularly use the kinds of deliberate strategies taught by Brown et al. The chapters by Just and Carpenter, and by Lehnert et al., for example, present a picture of skilled performance in which processes of coherence building are largely automatic and are relatively local. Lehnert et al. find limited "ripple effects" as the result of questions. And the "immediacy" principle in Just and Carpenter's system means that the system works mainly on local coherence problems. These expert systems stay very close to the texts they are given and only rarely reorganize an already developed representation or interpretation. Nothing like posing questions about a text occurs. How can instruction that focuses on overt, self-conscious procedures for interpreting texts, and seeks to alert readers to general logical relationships rather than allowing them to attend only to local connections, improve a process that in its skilled form proceeds automatically and largely locally? The answer must lie in the fact that self-questioning strategies evoke processes of inference and interpretation that eventually evolve into the automated performances of skilled readers. This suggests, however, that metacognitive strategies may be less an aspect of reading *expertise* than of the *acquisition* of reading skill, a point to which I return in the next section.

ELEMENTS OF A COGNITIVE THEORY OF ACQUISITION

Learning, like comprehending, involves the construction of new knowledge. It is possible, therefore, to examine what is known about comprehension for elements of a theory of acquisition.

Learning As Coherence Building

Virtually all of the models of reading comprehension, formal and informal, discussed in this volume characterize reading as a process of coherence-building. That is, they describe text comprehension as resulting from a linking of new information to representations already in place or a formation of new connections between established knowledge elements. This coherence-building can be very local and immediate, a process of linking propositions in the text successively as they appear. The suggestion here for learning is that learning, too, proceeds in part by efforts to link each new piece of information to at least one other piece of information. This kind of very local coherence building is apparent in many well-studied learning tasks—for example, in memorization through the creation of mnemonics. We know that strategies of this kind enhance learning when there is a minimum of meaningful structure available. However, we are less accustomed to looking for local coherence-building efforts of this kind in the context of "meaningful" learning of organized domains of knowledge. Nevertheless, there may be more of a role for local linking processes in complex learning than has generally been assumed. Substantial amounts of new knowledge construction may proceed in small increments, without dramatic moments of "insight" or "restructuring."

Learning As Schema Instantiation and Schema Construction

A central way in which new information is interpreted and thereby appropriated by the reader is by instantiation of already established schemata. Specific events become interpretable when they provide the information needed to "fill slots" in schemata. Schema activation and instantiation are also aspects of learning. One learns about situations by interpreting them in terms of already held schemata. At the same time, the process of successive reinstantiation of schemata with new specifics enriches the schemata themselves and extends their range of applicability. Close consideration of the ways in which schema activation and instantiation works in various models of comprehension can, then, provide an important set of hypotheses about the processes of learning.

But how are the schemata called upon in learning established in the first place? If schema instantiation mechanisms, and the limited schema modification that accompanies instantiation, were the only mechanisms available for learning, we could not account for the range of people's knowledge or for their capacity for acquiring new ideas. The chapters in this volume have had little to say about the process of new schema building. Beyond a shared recognition of the importance of schema construction in learning, we have virtual theoretical silence. This remark is not intended as a criticism of the authors, but rather as a comment on the current state of cognitive theory. The chapters in this volume are by no means alone in their silence on the issue of schema construction, indeed of the construction of declarative knowledge more generally. Piaget gave us the label accommodation to refer to this aspect of cognitive acquisition, contrasting it with assimilation (schema instantiation) in his general model of equilibration. More recently, David Rumelhart and Donald Norman have proposed that learning proceeds through three interacting processes rather than two: accretion, tuning, and restructuring. Accretion is essentially what I have called schema instantiation. Tuning and restructuring are mechanisms for the creation of new schemata, in the first case by gradual modification of existing structures, in the second by the building of brand new structures. This distinction between gradual modification of old schemata and all-in-one creation of new ones is a useful enrichment of our thinking about schema acquisition. But it is an invitation to build a theory, not an already developed theory of schema acquisition. Like Piaget, Rumelhart and Norman label the kind of learning involved, but make only general suggestions about what the actual processes of tuning and restructuring may be. Recent efforts to build formal cognitive theories of acquisition do not illuminate the question much either. These focus largely on the automation of cognitive skills and on detailed accounts of how local knowledge linkages take place. They do not really address the problem of the acquisition of new schemata. The chapters in the present volume, then, serve to highlight what is surely one of the most important current challenges for a cognitive theory of learning.

Acquiring Processing Skill

We turn next to the question of how skilled processes or procedures are learned. This is a better developed area of cognitive learning theory than is schema acquisition. The focus in most work up to now has been on how procedures become automated, and on how smooth performance is built in the course of practice. The procedural focus in the present volume, by contrast, is on conscious strategies for interacting with texts and not on automated performance. As already noted, several chapters are concerned with how people gain conscious control over their reading or writing processes. Yet implicit in this interest is a concern for the effects of strategic self-control on the automatic processes of skilled reading or writing. There are, then, two questions raised about the acquisition of processing skill. First, how are deliberate strategies acquired? Second, how do these strategies affect the acquisition of the automatic processes of skilled readers?

Acquiring Self-management Strategies.   Brown, Palincsar, and Armbruster propose that deliberate processing strategies are acquired in the course of social interaction. At the beginning, another person, usually a parent or a teacher, monitors the child's state of knowledge, posing questions or prompting the child to pose them, and directing a search for information related to the question at hand. As these "management" functions are taken over by the child, he or she becomes increasingly able to function independently. Strategic skills, then, are learned through a process of externally guided practice coupled with successive internalization of the monitoring, prompting, and evaluation aspects of the performance. A similar view is expressed by Scardamalia and Bereiter. The internalization of control theory provides a plausible account of how people learn more fruitfully to use processes already available in their repertoires. However, it does not account for how one acquires the repertoire of processes. For example, internalization alone can be expected to produce more question asking, but not necessarily to improve the quality of the questions posed. Brown et al. propose that *modeling* of high quality question asking and inferencing is the mechanism by which new repertoires are built. But they do not ask the next logical question: How does the modeling work? How do people learn from watching models perform? The modeling mechanism, then, has the same status as does accommodation, restructuring, or tuning for schema acquisition. It invites but does not provide a cognitive theory of learning.

From Self-management to Automaticity.   Giving oneself directions, posing questions for oneself, and engaging in deliberate self-management strategies eventually enhance skilled performance. As we have seen, however, these activities may not themselves be implicated in skilled performance. Instead they may function as "pump primers" for setting in motion processes that will eventually function independently. Not all strategies that are useful in acquisition need be incorporated into skilled performance. I once had a piano teacher who taught me to make my playing romantic and emotional by telling me stories that evoked various emotions (loneliness, joy, despair, etc.). She asked me to play the music "so as to illustrate the events and emotions involved." As time went on, I gradually took over the storytelling as well as the piano playing role, and eventually overt storytelling was dropped. The instruction worked. I became, at least for a while, a young pianist very much in the romantic mode—a fact that was noted with varying degrees of approbation by my later music teachers. Through a process of internalization, I learned a strategy for controlling and managing the style of my piano playing. In this case it is absolutely clear that the strategy I learned, storytelling, was not itself a part of the skilled performance. I did not directly describe to myself, and therefore come to control, the actions of my fingers. My skill as a piano player nevertheless improved to a certain degree under the control of the storytelling strategy. How? That remains a mystery, a question perhaps to be answered by future research on motor skill acquisition. However, it is, I submit, no more a mystery than how Brown et al.'s subjects managed to become somewhat better comprehenders even in situations where they did not apparently consciously utilize the specific strategies they had been taught. We must be careful to distinguish between reading skill itself and the strategies that help in acquiring that skill.

THE QUESTION OF INTERVENTION

Campione and Armbruster describe two goals of intervention research: (1) modifying the learning *materials* in order to make learning easier; and (2) modifying the learners' *processes* in order to enable them to learn from less than optimal texts. The issue of materials is raised here primarily as a question of text design, most directly in the chapter by Schnotz, but also in commentaries of Meyer, Stein and Policastro, and Trabasso, Secco, and van den Broek. The processes question is raised by Brown, Palincsar, and Armbruster, Fischer and Mandl, Scardamalia and Bereiter, and Ballstaedt and Mandl, each of whom describe efforts to evoke or teach text-processing strategies. These strategy teaching efforts raise the question of what we mean by "direct instruction" when learning is assumed to be the result of individual mental constructions by the learner.

Text Design: Implications of Cognitive Theory

One of the ways in which instructors can help people to learn is to provide them with texts that are optimally designed to highlight the most important information. There is a long history of concern for the design of teaching materials— especially textbooks—and an appreciable body of research on how to make texts more efficient tools for learning. As de Beaugrande points out, however, most past research on text design has not been based on an adequate theory of how people process texts, thereby limiting its utility. Consider the history of research on "adjunct aids" in texts—in-text questions, headings, and the like. Investigators have sought to compare the effectiveness of different kinds of adjuncts, different placements in the text, and a host of other variables; but they have been able to provide few strong and generalizable rules for when and how to use such aids. A similar point can be made by looking at the history of research on "readability." De Beaugrande documents the extent to which the question of text difficulty has been addressed independently of a theory of how people read and the difficulties that this can produce. An effort to apply theories of text processing to text design is very much needed.

Schnotz's research on optimal text organization is a welcome step in this direction. He compared two different text organizations. However, he predicted that people with different levels of prior knowledge would process the texts differently so as to benefit differently from the organizational features of the two kinds of texts. Although Schnotz's processing theory is informal, his findings demonstrate the complex interaction that a processing-based theory of text design would anticipate. Schnotz's work represents an approach to questions of text design that is explicitly concerned with adapting texts to known characteristics of people's knowledge states.

Direct Instruction—A New Meaning?

Brown et al.'s chapter indicates the possibility of directly teaching strategies and procedures that traditionally have been left up to learners to discover on their own. The authors suggest that principles of direct instruction that have proven effective for teaching limited bodies of knowledge and relatively algorithmic performances can also be applied to more heuristic kinds of skills. In the past, direct instruction has been limited to closed and predetermined bodies of knowledge and skill that could be practiced in a standard form and performed unvaryingly. Strategic and heuristic learning—the very things that distinguish between expert and novice performers in a domain—were left for people to acquire more or less on their own, or from informal commentary and criticism.

The suggestion that we directly teach heuristic skills and strategies turns out to be less simple than it seems. In particular, proposals for direct teaching of strategies raise the question of just how direct we really mean to be. As we have seen, the strategies taught are often not the ones actually used by experts. Furthermore, the strategy training methods may work only insofar as learners already have important elements of the strategies available. Strategy instruction, then, does not really work very "directly." That is, it does not directly communicate a skilled form of performance. Yet *deliberate,* if not very direct, instruction does seem to improve performance. How? Let us consider two possibilities.

One thing that instruction may do is to simply help individuals find what they already know that is relevant to the task at hand. The knowledge that is "cued" by instruction may be either procedural or declarative. Strategy teaching procedures show how procedural elements, such as the asking of questions, can be effectively called into play in the service of understanding or remembering a text. This can be done by various direct suggestions of an instructor. Questions posed by an instructor can also serve as "pointers" to declarative knowledge. In an instructional interaction that is conversational and individual, the instructor's questions and prompts can lead the student to new understanding of a domain without adding any new external "facts." In such cases, the instructor has a certain skill or body of knowledge in mind that he hopes the student will acquire. He carefully arranges patterns of interaction and/or practice that are intended to evoke that skill or knowledge. In this sense, the instruction described is "direct"—that is, intentional and instructor-led. But in another significant respect, the instruction is very indirect, for it basically only prompts the students to find and use knowledge that they already had. Nothing is directly given to the student.

A second thing that instruction may do is set the learner up to discover expert forms of knowledge. If knowledge construction is a pervasive aspect of learning, then we cannot insist on instructional intervention plans that present knowledge directly in its expert form. Instead, we may often want to teach a simplified version of expert knowledge that learners themselves will be able to transform into a more sophisticated skill or knowledge representation. For example, Scardamalia and Bereiter asked children to use two particular sentences as part of a story they were to compose. This posed a problem for the children, as the sentences that were given were not obviously related to one another. What eventually helped the children was a set of rather mechanical procedures: finding common words, locating synonyms, underlining phrases, and the like. These are not procedures that experts routinely use as they write. The apparent effectiveness of the teaching probably derives from the fact that the easily demonstrable procedures that were taught evoked certain processes of word meaning instantiation and semantic interpretation that could eventually proceed independently, without the support of underlining and synonym-finding algorithms. The instructors in this experiment had a clear instructional goal in mind and deliberately constructed exercises intended to promote it. In this sense their work was entirely in the spirit of direct instruction. Yet they did *not* directly teach the processes involved in creating stories. Instead, they set the children up to discover those processes.

These examples force us to a broadened definition of direct instruction, one that is in keeping with the constructive character of learning. Direct instruction is any deliberate attempt to intervene in learning so that the outcome of the learner's processes will be a particular form of knowledge or skill. Psychologists or educators interested in direct instruction should look for forms of explanation or demonstration, and forms of practice, that set in motion the learning processes which lead to expert performance. They should not seek to engage novice learners directly in performances of experts.

Author Index

Numbers in *italics* denote pages with complete bibliographic information.

Subject Index